The Conflagration of Community

The Conflagration of Community: Fiction before and after Auschwitz

J. Hillis Miller

The University of Chicago Press :: Chicago and London

J. Hillis Miller is Distinguished Research Professor of Comparative Literature and English at the University of California, Irvine. He is the author of many books and articles on literature and literary theory, most recently of *For Derrida*.

The University of Chicago Press, Chicago 60637
The University of Chicago Press, Ltd., London

Printed in the United States of America

20 19 18 17 16 15 14 13 12 11   1 2 3 4 5

ISBN-13: 978-0-226-52721-5 (cloth)
ISBN-13: 978-0-226-52722-2 (paper)
ISBN-10: 0-226-52721-2 (cloth)
ISBN-10: 0-226-52722-0 (paper)

Library of Congress Cataloging-in-Publication Data

Miller, J. Hillis (Joseph Hillis), 1928–
The conflagration of community : fiction before and after Auschwitz / J. Hillis Miller.
p. cm.
Includes index.
ISBN-13: 978-0-226-52721-5 (cloth : alk. paper)
ISBN-10: 0-226-52721-2 (cloth : alk. paper)
ISBN-13: 978-0-226-52722-2 (pbk. : alk. paper)
ISBN-10: 0-226-52722-0 (pbk. : alk. paper) 1. Holocaust, Jewish (1939–1945), in literature. 2. Kafka, Franz, 1883–1924—Criticism and interpretation. I. Title.
PN56.H55M55 2011
809.3'93584053l8—dc22

2010052464

♾ This paper meets the requirements of ANSI/NISO Z39.48-1992 (Permanence of Paper).

For Jakob Lothe

Old Friend and Prime Instigator

Contents

Preface

Nach Auschwitz noch ein Gedicht zu schreiben ist barbarisch.
(After Auschwitz to write even a single poem is barbaric.)
Theodor Adorno

Critics have teased Adorno's famous dictum this way and that. Adorno later modified his statement by saying that "perennial suffering has as much right to expression as the tortured have to scream. . . . Hence it may have been wrong to say that no poem could be written after Auschwitz." Comparing poetry to the screams of the tortured is a little odd, to say the least, though it can be made to make sense. Nevertheless, it hardly does justice, for example, to the complexity of poetry by Paul Celan, a survivor. Adorno does not say, "To write poetry after Auschwitz is barbaric." He says, "To write even one poem [*noch ein Gedicht*], is barbaric." Or Adorno's sentence phrase might be translated, "Writing even one more poem after Auschwitz is barbaric." It is barbaric now to sit down in cold or hot blood, facing the famous blank sheet of paper or a blank computer screen, and write a poem, that is, anything that has the nature of poetry, long or short. Adorno's stress is on the concrete act of setting pen to paper or fingers to keyboard and composing a poem. After Auschwitz, doing that is barbaric.

Adorno might have meant, among other things, I suppose, that everybody's business, after Auschwitz, is to focus all his or her energies on making sure Auschwitz does not happen again. It is barbaric not to do that. Writing poetry is of no help in this work. In these dire times, we do not have time for aesthetic activities, activities detached from politics. These are the times after Auschwitz, when the impossible has turned out to be possible. Auschwitz was a decisive turning point in history. It was the moment when the German-speaking region of Europe, the region that produced some of Western culture's highest achievements—Beethoven, Kant, Hegel, the Jena school, not to speak of Marx, Rilke, Thomas Mann, Wittgenstein, Heidegger, and Kafka—could murder six million Jews in a technologically and bureaucratically enhanced monstrous genocide.

The context of Adorno's statement is what we have learned to call "aesthetic ideology." This ideology includes the assumption that poetry, as the highest form of verbal art, is primarily concerned with the "sinnliche Scheinen der Idee," as Hegel put it, the "sensible shining forth of the idea." "Idea" is here Hegel's name for what Heidegger was to call "Being." Poetry is a revelation of the transcendent, of Being with a capital B. Heidegger expressed this by way of his commitment to the Greek term *aletheia*. He understood this word to name a bringing back of Being from forgetting: *lethe* plus the privative *a*. *Aletheia* was Heidegger's name for what poetry does. Poetry is an act of unveiling, of remembering what has been forgotten: *Sein*, Being.[1] Or Adorno may have been thinking of a poem as the expression of subjective feelings. Or he may have thought of a poem as a self-enclosed beautiful object, an organic unity made of words. A poem is something analogous to a flower or a beautiful human body, as two prominent metaphors in this tradition put it.

A famous sentence in Mallarmé's "Crise de vers" ("Crisis of Verse") expresses these assumptions in a different, distinctively Mallarméan, idiom, this time in terms of poetic speaking rather than writing: "Je dis: une fleur! et, hors de l'oubli où ma voix relègue aucun contour, en tant que quelque chose d'autre que les calices sus, musicalement se lève, idée même et suave, l'absente de tous bouquets" (I say, a flower! and, outside the forgetting to which my voice relegates every contour, as something other than the known calyxes, musically there rises, suave idea itself, the something absent from all bouquets [my trans.]).[2] None of these three versions of aesthetic ideology, Adorno implies, justifies giving the writing of poems an active role in life after Auschwitz. Poetry is not concerned with making something happen in the social and political realms, for example, making sure Auschwitz does not happen again. The latter is our real business. We do not have time for anything else.

Adorno's word "barbaric" merits attention. Why did he use just this word, rather than, for example, "immoral" or "irresponsible"? A barbarian is someone who is outside the bounds of civil society. The Greeks, scholars say, called those not Greek "barbarians" because their language sounded, to the Greeks, as if they were saying "bar bar bar bar," that is, uttering nonsense sounds, not good Greek. Poetry, in these bad days, Adorno suggests, is nonsense syllables, full of sound and fury, signifying nothing: "bar bar bar bar," with no purchase on reality. "Bar bar bar bar" is something like the babble brought about by Jehovah's confusion of tongues at the Tower of Babel. This barbaric blabbering made each workman unable to understand his fellows.

Putting this famous aphorism back in its context as the fourth sentence from the end of a complex essay entitled "Cultural Criticism and Society" would be a long business. Not to speak of putting it in the larger context of the volume in which the essay appears, *Prisms*, or in the context of all Adorno's writing. That is not my business here, but a word may be said. Somewhat surprisingly, the context is not the barbarity of writing poetry now, but Adorno's argument that cultural criticism (*Kulturkritik*) is now impossible because society as a whole is so corrupt and empty that cultural critique instantly becomes complicit in what it would criticize. It becomes co-opted by the object it attempts to dominate. The "traditional transcendent critique of ideology is obsolete," says Adorno.[3] Such critique is impossible in these bad days after Auschwitz. Adorno's essay is strikingly relevant to our social situation today in the West and to the academic project of cultural studies, or even to my rather different project in this book, committed as it is to rhetorical reading as well as to cultural criticism. Reading Adorno's essay gives me pause, however. Here is the immediate context of the phrase in question:

> Even the most extreme consciousness of doom threatens to degenerate into idle chatter. Cultural criticism finds itself faced with the final stage of the dialectic of culture and barbarism. To write poetry after Auschwitz is barbaric. And this corrodes even the knowledge of why it has become impossible to write poetry today. Absolute reification, which presupposed intellectual progress as one of its elements, is now preparing to absorb the mind entirely. Critical intelligence cannot be equal to this challenge as long as it confines itself to self-satisfied contemplation. (34)

Presumably, though he does not say so, Adorno used "writing a poem" as a synecdoche for writing what we call literary works in general, for example, a novel or a play, that is, writing anything fictive. Literature in our culture is a use of words that is in a peculiar way nonreferential, though it may use real place-names or even present fictional versions of historical personages.

Since Adorno announced his stern prohibition, many writers, including many Holocaust survivors, for example, Paul Celan or Imre Kertész, have defied Adorno's injunction. They have written poems or other works of literature. If doing that remains still suspect, how much more suspect it may be to spend one's time "analyzing" literary works, even those that are part of what is called "Holocaust literature." That is nevertheless what I am doing in this book.

How can I justify doing that? Where did Adorno go wrong in his stern prohibition? One answer is that he did not recognize the way literature may be a valid testimony to Auschwitz, however problematic that testimony may be. Literature can be a bearing witness that contributes essentially to keeping us from forgetting those more than six million dead. It may therefore lead us to act on that remembering. Testifying through literature is something quite different from those screams of the tortured that Adorno, as an afterthought, allowed poems after Auschwitz to express. Moreover, though Celan was right, in a famous verse, to say that no one bears witness for the witness,[4] nevertheless, my readings can testify to my response to these particular works. Such readings may perhaps work toward what Jacques Derrida calls "the democracy to come."

As scholars of the Holocaust have argued, the Nazi genocide was exceptional for at least two reasons. Christopher Browning, for example, writes: "I believe that the Holocaust was a watershed event in human history—the most extreme case of genocide that has yet occurred. What distinguishes it from other genocides are two factors: first the totality and scope of intent—that is, the goal of killing every last Jew, man, woman, child, throughout the reach of the Nazi empire; and second, the means employed—namely, the harnessing of the administrative and technological capacities of a modern nation state and western scientific culture."[5]

Though I agree that Auschwitz was exceptional in these two ways, almost unimaginably so (since a total exception resists categorizing and therefore forbids rational understanding or "imagining"), nevertheless, literature about Auschwitz is echoed by literature about somewhat analogous events. Analogies, please remember, are not identities, but juxtaposition of "somewhat analogous events" may help to understand both sides of the analogy. This book constructs a Benjaminian constellation, a configuration or a mosaic juxtaposing (1) Jean-Luc Nancy's reflections on community after Auschwitz, which he calls "the conflagration of community"; (2) three novels by Franz Kafka that foreshadow Auschwitz; (3) four novels about the Holocaust written by authors at varying degrees of distance from it: Thomas Keneally's *Schindler's List*, Ian McEwan's *Black Dogs*, Art Spiegelman's *Maus*, and Imre Kertész's *Fatelessness*; (4) *Beloved*, Toni Morrison's great novel about the feature of American history that most resonates with Auschwitz: slavery and the situation of the many millions of African-American descendants of slaves (hence my subtitle, "Fiction Before and After Auschwitz"); (5) the chilling resemblance between what happened in Germany and adjacent countries in the years leading up to the Nazi takeover and what has happened recently in the United States and abroad as a result of its actions. I am thinking, among other things, of the occupation of Iraq, the resulting death of six hundred thousand or more Iraqis (some say the number is now over one million) and the displacement of six million others, the condoning of torture and illegal electronic surveillance here and abroad, and the gradual erosion of our civil liberties, such as the right to habeas corpus. A larger proportion of the United States population is in jail than in any other highly industrialized country in the world. Guantánamo Bay is not Auschwitz, but it is not absolutely different from the Nazi "work camps" either. Our perilous situation has certainly been facilitated by "the administrative and technological capacities of a modern nation state and western scientific culture." These have been enormously augmented since Auschwitz. President Barack Obama is doing much to reverse this drift toward fascism, but the corruptions of our democratic ideals have penetrated deeply into our national culture and are proving hard to eradicate. If we are withdrawing from Iraq, we have escalated the war in Afghanastan.

No readings are wholly disinterested or objective. They are oriented by certain questions. If the question of what it means to speak of "the conflagration of community" in the twentieth century is one of my chief concerns, another is the question of what it means to think of the novels I discuss as acts of testimony. I also keep returning to the question of speech acts' efficacy in communities in conflagration. Finally, I have continually before me the question of what resonance there may be between, on the one hand, the difficulty of imagining, understanding, or even in remembering Auschwitz, a difficulty so often a theme in historical (and fictional) records of the Holocaust, and, on the other hand, the exasperating resistance to clear, conclusive interpretation manifested by the novels I discuss, from Kafka through Kertész to Morrison.

An enormous, and to some degree contentious, literature about the

Holocaust exists: historical works, psychoanalytic studies, memoirs, taped testimonies, films, poems, and novels written both by survivors and by those who were not in the camps, critical books about those novels and poems, books that attempt to survey from some definite perspective this enormous literature. The topic is important enough and difficult enough to have generated controversy and conflicting perspectives. Robert Eaglestone's brilliant *The Holocaust and the Postmodern* makes a wide-ranging assessment of this literature for the purpose of demonstrating that what is called "post-modern" is decisively influenced by the Shoah.[6] He includes, for example, admirable chapters about the relation of Emmanuel Levinas's work and that of Derrida to the Holocaust, as well as a chapter about several fictions written by Holocaust survivors, though he only mentions Kertész briefly several times in passing, *Fatelessness* only once.

My project has a different focus from Eaglestone's. I want to relate several novels explicitly about the Holocaust to fictions that were written before and after Auschwitz and to explore the resonances among these in the light of recent theoretical work about the effects of the Holocaust on the possibility of community. Kafka, I claim, foreshadows Auschwitz, Kertész's *Fatelessness* echoes Kafka, and Morrison's *Beloved* is a post-Auschwitz novel that also has Kafkaesque features. My primary focus remains on reading as best I can the novels I have chosen, in the light of the questions about testimony I have named. The resonances among the five elements in my constellation that I seek to detect, as a *Stimmung* or vibration testifying to analogies, can only be generated if something specific, a close reading, with citations analyzed, is, in each case, set down side by side with readings of the other texts similarly interrogated.

Some remarks here and there in different chapters of this book refer to the circumstances that led me to take up the works being discussed. I do not think of this book as a "memoir," but it does register a significant turn in my work. This turn, of course, has its personal and professional history, as my dedication of the book to Jakob Lothe and the other acknowledgments indicate. The new turns in my recent work include an interest in the question of community, a return to Kafka after many years, an attempt to come to terms with the Holocaust and with Holocaust literature, and an attempt, by way of Toni Morrison's *Beloved*, also to come to terms with the history of slavery in the United States. Such "coming to terms" is not at all easy, perhaps not ever wholly possible. Whenever I fly these days by way of the Cincinnati airport, which is actually across the Ohio River in Kentucky, I think how that river once, not all that long ago, formed the border between a free state and a slave state. That re-memory (Morrison's word) makes me think again of that river's role in *Beloved*, and of my own relation to slavery by way of my Virginia forebears. Another personal association is the way my recent visit to Buchenwald was a major event for me, as I report in more detail in chapter 6. All the works I discuss in this book are matters of urgent personal concern for me, not just objects of impersonal academic analysis. That concern is also registered in the references now and then to disturbing features of recent American history: Abu Ghraib, Guantánamo Bay, the extraordinary rendition of our captives to secret CIA prisons around the world, illegal surveillance of United States citizens, and so on. Even under Barack Obama's presidency these practices have to some degree persisted. It is still as true as ever that those who do not study history are condemned to repeat it. The works of fiction discussed in this book are a way of studying history.

I have consulted a number of photographs, all obtained originally from online websites. Amazing collections of such photographs are obtainable in a few mouse clicks through Google: many photographs of Kafka and his family; photographs of Auschwitz, including a sample from the recently discovered Karl Hoecker album, and a moving series that documents Auschwitz victims from their arrival by train, through the *Selektion*, and up to just a few minutes before they were to be gassed, still in ignorance of their imminent fate; a large set of photographs of lynchings in the United States, many originally circulated as postcards; photographs of torture at Abu Ghraib. These photographs are a form of testimony. They might also be thought of as embodiments of Sethe's claim, in Morrison's *Beloved*, that nothing ever dies, that once something has happened it goes on happening. Kafka's life, Auschwitz, lynchings in America, Abu Ghraib go on repeating themselves, over and over, interminably, in those photographs stored in cyberspace, from which anyone with a computer connected to the Internet may retrieve them. It has proved impractical to include these photographs in this book, but I have included URLs for those most important for my thinking and writing. Anyone who has an Internet connection may look them up and see how photographs bear witness. I urge all my readers to do so.

Sedgwick, Maine
January 27, 2010
Deer Isle, Maine
May 11, 2010

Acknowledgments

Parts of several chapters of this book have been previously published or will be published. All are much shorter versions of the chapters in which the material appears here. All have been substantially revised, expanded, and reoriented to fit the overall argument of this book. I am grateful to all those who published this material and who have granted permission for its reuse. I am also grateful to those friends and colleagues who asked me to write on these topics.

Several pages on Wallace Stevens's "The Auroras of Autumn" and part of the material on community in chapter 1 have appeared in shorter and different form in three places: "The Indigene and the Cybersurfer," in a special issue of *Ariel*, "Globalization and Indigenous Cultures," edited by Wang Fengzhen and Shaobo Xie, vol. 34, no. 1 (January 2003): 31–52; "The Indigene and the Cybersurfer," a Chinese translation of this essay by Jin Huimin, in a collection of Chinese translations of selected essays by me entitled *The Indigene and the Cybersurfer* (Changchun: Jilin People's Press, 2004), 3–27; "Stevens in Connecticut (and Denmark)," in *Wallace Stevens across the Atlantic*, edited by Bart Eeckhout and Edward Ragg (Houndmills: Palgrave Macmillan, 2008), 23–40; pp. 30–34 are reproduced in revised form with permission of Palgrave Macmillan. "The Indigene and the Cybersurfer" was also presented as a seminar at Dartmouth College in 2003 and as a lecture in 2004 at Zhengzhou University in the Peoples Republic of China.

An earlier, shorter version of chapter 3 appeared in a German translation by Charlotte Oldani and Beatrice Sandberg as "Geglückte und mißlungene Sprechakte in Kafkas *Der Proceß*," in *Franz Kafka: Zur ethischen und ästhetischen Rechtfertigung*, edited by Beatrice Sandberg and Jakob Lothe (Freiburg im Breisgau: Rombach Verlag, 2002), 233–46. Rombach holds the copyright of the German translation of my original essay. This essay was presented as a lecture (in English) at a conference on Kafka held at the University of Bergen May 12–14, 2000. I thank Jakob Lothe and Beatrice Sandberg for inviting me to participate in this conference.

An earlier and much shorter version of chapter 4 was presented in Oslo at a conference on Kafka arranged by a research group on narrative theory and analysis sponsored by the Centre for Advanced Study, Oslo, and located in the building of the Norwegian Academy of Science and Letters. I thank Willy Østreng, then director of the Centre for Advanced Study, and his administrative colleagues for many courtesies during my several visits there. Jakob Lothe led this research group. I thank him and his colleagues in the research group, Susan Suleiman and James Phelan, for inviting me to write this essay and for their helpful comments about it. I thank also the other members of the research group, from whom I learned much and from whom I received many kindnesses: Daphna Erdinast-Vulcan, Anniken Greve, Jeremy Hawthorn, Beatrice Sandberg, Anette Storeide, and Anne Thelle. The essay on which chapter 4 is based has appeared with the title "The Sense of an Un-Ending: The Resistance to Narrative Closure in Kafka's *Das Schloss*," in a volume entitled *Franz Kafka: Narrative, Rhetoric, and Reading*, edited by Jakob Lothe, Beatrice Sandberg, and Ronald Speirs (Columbus: Ohio State University Press, 2011).

An earlier, much shorter, and differently organized version of chapter 6 was presented in Berlin at a conference held June 28–30, 2007, and sponsored by the research group named in the previous paragraph and at the invitation of Jakob Lothe, Susan Suleiman, and James Phelan. I thank them for their comments on the first version of my essay. It will appear in early 2012 under the title "Imre Kertész's *Fatelessness:* Fiction as Testimony" in a volume to be published by Ohio State University Press entitled *After Testimony: The Ethics and Aesthetics of Holocaust Narrative*, edited by Jakob Lothe, Susan Suleiman, and James Phelan.

Chapter 7 is a much longer, much revised and reoriented, version of an essay entitled "Boundaries in *Beloved.*" This was published in a special issue, "Cinema without Borders," edited by Jeffrey R. Di Leo and Allyson Nadia Field, of *Symplokē: A Journal for the Intermingling of Literary, Cultural and Theoretical Scholarship*, vol. 15, nos. 1–2 (2007): 24–39. This essay was presented at a conference organized by Professor Geoffrey Hill at the University of New Hampshire, May 30–April 1, 2006, entitled "Border Crossings and Boundary Definitions." It had also been presented earlier as a lecture at the Future of American Studies Institute at Dartmouth College in June of 2005, and subsequently at the University of Cardiff, on July 26, 2006. I am grateful to Geoffrey Hill, to Donald Pease, and to Ian Buchanan for these opportunities to try out my ideas on responsive audiences.

Some of the material that was eventually revised for this book was also presented as seminars at Dartmouth College in the fall of 2003 and as Critical Theory Emphasis Mini-Seminars at the University of California, Irvine, in various years beginning in 2005. I thank Donald Pease, Lawrence D. Kritzman, and others for inviting me to lecture at Dartmouth at various times and for many kindnesses to me there. I thank C. Namwali Serpell for brilliant and challenging comments on my paper on *Beloved* when I presented it at Dartmouth. Later I sent her my paper and she commented on it. She sent me in return a draft of her admirable dissertation chapter on *Beloved.* Our interchange altered the way I read the novel. I also thank past dean of humanities at Irvine, Karen Lawrence, and the present dean, Vicki Ruiz, as well as the past director of the Critical Theory Emphasis, Steven Mailloux, the present director, Rei Terada, and the coordinator of the CTE, Susan Showler, for inviting me to give miniseminars at Irvine and for many courtesies to me in arranging them. I am grateful also to the two anonymous readers of the manuscript of this book for the University of Chicago Press. Not only did their approval reassure me, but productive suggestions by one of the readers have also led to some brief additions here and there throughout.

Finally, I thank with all my heart Jakob Lothe, professor in the Department of Literature, Area Studies and European Languages at the University of Oslo. The dedication of this book testifies to my great friendship for him over many years as well as to my admiration for his work. I first met Jakob in 1998 at a game preserve in South Africa. We were on an excursion from a conference at North-West University in Potchefstroom on Conrad's *Heart of Darkness*. We have been good friends ever since. He is an extraordinary scholar and person. Without his encouragement, in the ways these acknowledgments specify, I would never have had the courage to turn to Holocaust literature or back again to Kafka, and this book would never have been written. I would not, for example, have written the first versions of this book's Kafka and Holocaust-novel chapters had the obligation to do so not been a feature of my participation in conferences and a research group at the Norwegian Academy of Sciences in Oslo, led by Lothe, that had these works as their foci. I am grateful to Lothe and to my other colleagues in Oslo, especially James Phelan and Susan Suleiman, for encouragement and canny criticism. The privilege of meeting Imre Kertész at a Berlin meeting of our research group and hearing his answers to our questions was especially precious to me.

Part One | Theories of Community

1 Nancy contra Stevens

Le témoignage le plus important et le plus pénible du monde moderne, celui qui rassemble peut-être tous les autres témoignages que cette époque se trouve chargée d'assumer, en vertu d'on ne sait quel décret ou de quelle nécessité (car nous témoignons aussi de l'épuisement de la pensée de l'Histoire), est le témoignage de la dissolution, de la dislocation ou de la conflagration de la communauté. **Jean-Luc Nancy, *La communauté désoeuvrée***[1]

(The gravest and most painful testimony of the modern world, the one that possibly gathers together all other testimonies which this epoch finds itself charged with assuming, by virtue of who knows what decree or necessity [for we bear witness also to the exhaustion of thinking by way of History], is the testimony of the dissolution, the dislocation, or the conflagration of community.)
Jean-Luc Nancy, *The Inoperative Community*[2]

We were as Danes in Denmark all day long
And knew each other well, hale-hearted landsmen,
For whom the outlandish was another day

Of the week, queerer than Sunday. We thought alike
And that made brothers of us in a home
In which we fed on being brothers, fed

And fattened as on a decorous honeycomb.
This drama that we live—We lay sticky with sleep.
Wallace Stevens, "The Auroras of Autumn"[3]

This chapter builds on recent theoretical investigations of community to establish a set of tentative hypotheses for my investigations of community's conflagration in fiction before and after Auschwitz. The chapter juxtaposes, or causes to "compear," two quite different models of community. "Compear" is "a legal term that is used to designate appearing before a judge together with another person."[4] The word will come up again later in this chapter as part of a translation of Jean-Luc Nancy's word *comparution*. My setting side by side, as if haled before a tribunal, of two concepts of community will provide a somewhat uneasy foundation for my investigation of community or the lack of it in some novels written before and after the Holocaust.

My initial citation is the first sentence from one of many recent philosophical or theoretical works that have reflected on what is meant by the word "community" and on what has happened to community in modern times.[5] What Nancy says is peculiar in several ways. For one thing, he starkly opposes giving testimony and clear knowledge, such as historians are supposed to supply. Witnessing is a speech act, a performative enunciation, while "la pensée de l'Histoire" (thinking by way of History) leads to constative statements. These are statements of facts that are verifiable as true or false. We can bear witness to what has happened to community in modern times—its dissolution, dislocation, or conflagration. We cannot know it or understand it. We have to accept the burden of testifying to the conflagration of community, but we must do that by virtue of some unknown decree or necessity. Someone or something has decreed our painful obligation to bear witness to the end of community, but who or what has done that is unknown. Even the decree itself is unknown, though it obliges us implacably. We are obligated by a decree whose exact formulation and whose source of authority we cannot know.

That is exceedingly strange, if you think of it. What does it mean to be coerced by a decree or law whose wording we cannot know? Ignorance of the law is no excuse, but, still, it is unpleasant, to say the least, to be subject to a decree of which we must remain ignorant. It is a little like Joseph K.'s experience, in Kafka's *The Trial*, of being arrested one fine day even though he has not done anything wrong. Playing a little on the word "trial," one could even translate Nancy's assertion that we are "chargée d'assumer" (charged with assuming) this painful testimony by saying such bearing witness is a trial we must endure, even though we are not aware of having done anything wrong. This bearing witness, Nancy assures us, is so important and so painful (*penible*) that it seems as if it possibly involves all the other responsibilities of witnessing to which we in the modern world are subject.

A further peculiarity of Nancy's sentence is that it contradicts itself. It exemplifies the thinking by way of history that, at the same moment, it says is exhausted. The passage implies that once community existed, but now, in the modern world, community has been dissolved, dislocated, or conflagrated. Something had to be there initially to suffer those transformations. That is a historical proposition if there ever was one. It is a statement capable of being true or false. Nancy's book as a whole, moreover, contradicts this historical proposition. It does so by expressing, as is characteristic of Western philosophical thinking, its definition of an "inoperative community" as a universal human condition. Nancy's propositions, his way of stating his assertions implies, are true in all places, in all cultures, and at all times.

La communauté désoeuvrée as a whole deconstructs, if I may dare to use that word, its strikingly apodictic first sentence. A thesis/antithesis with no possible sublation, a suspended or hovering self-canceling, bears witness to the way any thought of the dissolution of community depends on the traditional idea of community it would put in question. In a reciprocal way, the traditional concept of community, as expressed, for example, in Stevens's poem, contains already its apparent opposite. You cannot have one concept of community without the other, as both Nancy and Stevens show, almost in spite of themselves.

A final peculiarity of Nancy's sentence, in its relation to the title of his book, might be expressed in two ways. (1) The terms Nancy so carefully chooses to name what has happened to community in the modern world by no means say the same thing. Each is a little strange. (2) Nancy seems to have gone out of his way to avoid using the word given worldwide currency by his friend Jacques Derrida: "deconstruction." The English translation gives *La communauté désoeuvrée* as *The Inoperative Community*, presumably because "unworked," the literal meaning of *désoeuvrée*, is not an ordinary English word. But "unworked," neologism or not, would much better catch the force of what Nancy wants to say in the title and in the book itself. "Inoperative" suggests a passive condition. Modern communities just do not work. They are like an inoperative piece of machinery, in need of repair. *Désoeuvrée*, "unworked," on the other hand, though it is used in French to describe an apparatus that is out of order, puts the stress on the process by means of which some forces or other have actively worked to dismantle community. It has not just passively happened.

"The Deconstruction of Community," in its double antithetical meaning as a simultaneous doing and undoing, constructing and taking apart, would be a good English translation of Nancy's title. Even that translation, however, would not catch the resonances of "work" in *désoeuvrée*, with its allusions to the Marxist or Sartrean notions of collective, communal work that has constructed communities. Marx and Sartre are important explicit references for Nancy's thinking in this book. These references embed the book in the time and place when and where it was written.

Désoeuvrée suggests that any human community has been constructed by collective human work. That work has put together roads, buildings, houses, machines of all kinds (including communication machines), institutions, laws, and conventions of family life to make a whole that we call a "community." Counterwork has been required in modern times to dismantle or deconstruct those material and immaterial elements of community. Having first been "worked," they now have had to be "unworked," as George W. Bush and his colleagues went far toward "unworking" or "deconstructing" the United States Constitution and the other laws and institutions that have held our national community together for over two hundred years as a fragile democracy—government of the people, by the people, and for the people.

Nancy's words, "dissolution," "dislocation," and "conflagration," are three not quite compatible terms for the unworking of community. Each implies a different model for what has happened.

"Dissolution" implies a disintegration of something once whole, as a dictator will "dissolve parliament" when he does not like the laws elected representatives are promulgating.

"Dislocation" implies that modern communities have been set outside or beside themselves, displaced. It is hard to grasp what Nancy may have had in mind when he used this word. Perhaps he meant a breaking of the ligatures that have held communities together as living, quasi-organic wholes, as when we say: "He dislocated his shoulder." The dislocation of community is the disarticulation of the bonds, the joints, which have held its members together.

"Conflagration" is the most striking word in the series. It suggests that the whole community has not only been dissolved, its parts disarticulated from one another. It has also been consumed, burned up. The more or less explicit allusion is to the Holocaust, which means of course "sacrificial burning," and to those crematoria at Auschwitz and Buchenwald. The Nazis did not simply work to make inoperative the Jewish communities within their *Reich* by dislocating through deportation millions of Jews, or by dissolving the family and community bonds that held together the inhabitants of the ghettos. They destroyed those communities altogether by murdering more than six million Jews in the gas chambers and then cremating their bodies, in an unspeakable conflagration.

Stevens's Model of Community

My second citation is from a poem by Wallace Stevens written in 1947. This was just the time when the Holocaust, as a turning point in Western history, was being assimilated into the American consciousness, insofar as that happened at all. "The Auroras of Autumn," as its title suggests, is a poem in which an autumnal conflagration of community is signaled by an uncanny display of northern lights.

The passage by Stevens I have cited movingly chants what it is like to live in a sequestered indigenous community. Stevens is an American poet who has expressed as well as any of our great writers a sense of homeland places, whether it is Hartford, Connecticut, where Stevens lived, or Pennsylvania Dutch country, where Stevens was born, or Florida, where he vacationed, or even Tennessee, as in "Anecdote of the Jar": "I placed a jar in Tennessee" (*CP*, 76). One thinks of all the American place-names in Stevens's poetry, for example, the magical line "The wood-doves are singing along the Perkiomen" ("Thinking of a Relation Between the Images of Metaphors," in *CP*, 356), or of "The Idea of Order at Key West" (*CP*, 128–30), or of a mention of "the thin men of Haddam," in "Thirteen Ways of Looking at a Blackbird" (*CP*, 93), or of the line "Damariscotta da da doo" ("Variations on a Summer Day," in *CP*, 235). "Perkiomen" is the name of a small river in Stevens's native Pennsylvania. Haddam is the name of a small town in Connecticut. Damariscotta is the name of a coastal village in Maine. It is a Native American name meaning "river of little fish." The list could be extended. Stevens's early poem "Sunday Morning" (*CP*, 66–70) celebrates the particularities of the United States landscape as determining the life that is lived there. Many others of Stevens' poems do the same, as in the line "The natives of the rain are rainy men" ("The Comedian as the Letter C," in *CP*, 37).

Just what are the salient features of an indigenous community, according to Stevens? I say "indigenous *community*" because Stevens stresses that it is an experience shared by a "we": "We were as Danes in Denmark all day long." This assumption that the indigene lives in a community of other indigenes like himself or herself is one main feature of Stevens's indigene ideology. To be an indigene is to be part of a collectivity and to have collective experience. An indigenous community, moreover, is located in a place, a milieu, an environment, an ecosystem. This milieu is cut off from the outside world, the "outlandish," the "queer," one might almost say the uncanny, in the sense implied by the German word *unheimlich*, literally "unhomelike," "unhomey." Indigenes are "hale-hearted landsmen." They belong to the land, to its rocks, rivers, trees, soil, birds, fish, animals, and to ways of living on the land. They would feel uprooted if they moved elsewhere. The indigene feels at home in his place, as Danes feel at home in Denmark, or as bees are at home in their honeycomb.

To be an indigene is to be innocent, childlike, almost as if asleep while awake. This innocence is like that of Adam and Eve before the Fall. The indigenes know not good and evil. They do not suffer the "enigma of the guilty dream" that persecutes fallen men and women, for example, the terrifying (but perhaps secretly attractive) Oedipal male dream of having killed one's father and slept with one's mother. "Enigma" refers perhaps to the Sphynx's riddle that Oedipus solved, but also to the Delphic oracle's prediction to Oedipus that he is destined to slay his father and sleep with his mother. Indigenes lack self-consciousness, as though they were sleepwalkers. They are "sticky with sleep." "Sticky" here is associated with the decorous honeycomb on which the indigenes feed. Their at-home-ness makes their milieu a kind of sleep-inducing narcotic, as eating the honey they have made puts bees to sleep.

Not only are the indigenes not aware of themselves, with the painful self-awareness and habit of guilty introspection that is supposed to characterize Western peoples. The indigenes are also not aware of their environment, in the sense of holding it at arm's length and analyzing it. They take their milieu for granted as something that has always been there and always will be, eternally, as Denmark is for the Danes, according to Stevens. The resistance to the evidence of global warming may be generated in part by this mythical assumption that our environment is unchangeable, endlessly renewable. Why does Stevens choose Danes as exemplary of an indigenous community? I suppose because they live in a small country, have a relatively homogenous culture, and speak a "minority" language that cuts them off from others. That fits most people's idea of an indigenous community.

To mention language leads me to note that language plays a crucial role in Stevens's description. An indigenous community is created not just through shared ways of living, building, and farming on a particular homeland soil. It is also created out of language, by way of language, a particular language that belongs to that place. One radical effect of the global hegemony of Western cultural capital is to endanger, if not extinguish, so-called minority languages everywhere. The indigenous peoples who inhabited the state of Maine, where I live in the United States, had dwelled here for as much as twelve thousand years before the white man came. By "here" I mean right here, within a mile of where I am writing this. On a nearby shore there is a large shell midden going back at least seven thousand years. We eradicated most of the indigenes and their cultures in a couple of centuries. Only a few still speak the "native languages" of the Penobscots or the Micmacs. Their goal is often to run gambling casinos, hardly consonant with maintaining their "native culture." To shift to the other coast, a dozen indigenous languages often disappear forever in California in a single year, as the last "native speaker" of each one of them dies. Apparently languages cannot be resuscitated when no one is left who has learned the language as a baby. Learning a language from a recording or from a grammar book does not bring a dead language back to life.

Thinking of the vanishing of indigenous languages makes the language theme in Stevens's lines all the more poignant. He sees an indigenous community as generated by language, in an act of maternal and artistic creation that mimes the creation of the world, in *Genesis*, out of the primordial darkness: "As if the innocent mother sang in the dark / Of the room and on an accordion, half-heard, / Created the time and place in which we breathed . . . / And of each other thought." Why "on an accordion"? I suppose because it is a "folk instrument." An accordion is suitable for creating the togetherness of a folk. Perhaps also it is because overtones of consonant togetherness in the word "accord" are buried in the word "accordion." The members of an indigenous community are in accord. They are "of one accord." In an assertion that recalls Heidegger's argument in "Bauen Wohnen Denken" ("Building Dwelling Thinking") and in his essays on Hölderlin's poems, Stevens asserts that the time and place of an indigenous community are not there to begin with and then occupied by a given people.[6] A native language creates the homeland that gives a people breathing room, a place to breathe, and therefore also a place where they can speak to one another.

Stevens's sentence just analyzed ends with the phrase "And of each other thought." The language that creates the time and place of an indigenous community is also the medium in which the "natives" or "autochthons" think of one another. Each indigene can penetrate the minds of his or her fellows because they all speak the same language, the same "idiom," that is, a dialect peculiar to a specific group.

Indigenes speak in the "idiom of the work," that is, I take it, an idiom special to the work the innocent mother plays on the accordion. I hear also an overtone of "work" as the collective creation of an indigenous community through language and through the physical transformation of the environment. This would be akin to the Marxist notion of work or to Heidegger's notion of "Bauen," building.

The mother's accordion work is also in "the idiom of an innocent earth." The earth is innocent because it too has not yet fallen with Adam and Eve's fall. The language spoken by indigenes is, as they are, born of the earth, and remains rooted in it. Language, for Stevens here, is the embodiment of thought. Each native knows what his or her fellow is thinking because, as we say, "they speak the same language." The result is that we "knew each other well," because, in Stevens's sexist formulation, "we thought alike / And that made brothers of us in a home / In which we fed on being brothers." I shall return to this exclusion of women in the invocation of "brotherhood," blood brotherhood. This at-home-ness, finally, means that the place and the community dwelling within it are sacred. These happy autochthons "lie down like children in this holiness" (*CP*, 418).

Wonderful! Hooray! Or, as Stevens puts this exuberance a few lines later in "The Auroras of Autumn": "A happy people in a happy world— / Buffo! A ball, an opera, a bar" (*CP*, 420). Only two problems shadow this celebration. One is that the indigenous community is a myth. It always a matter of something that hypothetically once existed and no longer exists. "We *were* as Danes in Denmark," but we no longer are. As Stevens puts this:

> There may always be a time of innocence.
> There is never a place. Or if there is no time,
> If it is not a thing of time, nor of place,
>
> Existing in the idea of it, alone,
> In the sense against calamity, it is not
> Less real.
> (CP, 418)

An indigenous community is real enough, but it has the reality of something that exists only in the idea of it, before time, and outside all place.

The other menace that shadows this idea is that even the mythical innocent community was always darkened by the terror of invasion. It exists as "the sense against calamity," but that calamity is always imminent. That calamity appears suddenly as a stark fear or terror just a few lines beyond the long passage I have been discussing:

> Shall we be found hanging in the trees next spring?
> Of what disaster is this the imminence:
> Bare limbs, bare trees and a wind as sharp as salt?
> (CP, 419)

The poem, after all, is called "The Auroras of Autumn." Its chief figure is terrifying autumnal displays of aurora borealis, or northern lights, as they presage winter and figure the conflagration of community. Simply to name all the features of an indigenous community, even in a lyric poem so celebratory of its idea as this one is, is to destroy it by bringing it self-consciously into the light. To name it is to call up its specular mirror image: the terror of its destruction. This obverse is generated out of its security, as a sense of disaster's imminence. "A happy people in a happy world" sounds, and is, too good to be true. To imagine having it is to be terrified of losing it. The imagination of being at home, in a homeland, or *Heimat*, instantly raises the fearful ghost of the *unheimlich*, the uncanny, the terrorist at the door or probably already secretly resident somewhere inside the homeland.

Jennifer Bajorek, in a brilliant essay entitled "The Offices of Homeland Security; or, Hölderlin's Terrorism," has shown the way the rhetoric of the George W. Bush administration, in a genuinely sinister way, echoed the mystified appeal of fascist states, for example, the Nazi one.[7] Both appeal to the notion of a "homeland" mingling *Blut und Erd*, that is, racial purity and being "rooted in one dear particular place," to borrow a phrase from Yeats.[8] Our Department of Homeland Security presupposes that we are a homogeneous homeland, an indigenous people whose security and racial purity are endangered by terrorists from the outside, racially and ethnically strangers, not to speak of our twelve million "illegal immigrants" or all our African-American citizens, including the present president of the United States, Barack Obama. The terrorists are probably also already inside, we are led to fear, *unheimlich* presences within the homeland. It is easy to see what is fraudulent about this use of "homeland" and "security."

I do not deny the "terrorist threat." Lots of people hate the United States and plan terrorist attacks on it. Nevertheless, the United States is not and never was a "homeland" in the sense the word implies. Relatively few United States citizens stay in the place they were born. We are nomads, even if we were born here. I was born in the state of Virginia, as were my parents and grandparents, descendants of Pennsylvania Dutch migrants into Virginia, but my family left Virginia when I was a few months old, and I have never been resident there since. The Pennsylvania Dutch were Germans (*Deutsch*). Some were descended from British-conscripted Hessian soldiers who surrendered during our War of Revolution. Some of the Hessians after the war joined the many Germans already in Pennsylvania. The latter were refugees from religious persecution and the threat of conscription, especially in different parts of not-yet-unified Germany. The Germans among my maternal ancestors were presumably from the latter group. One direct ancestor on the Miller side, however, was a Hessian soldier. He named his son, born in 1786, George Washington Miller, presumably to show his patriotism. Many Pennsylvania Dutch, such as my ancestors, moved down into Virginia to become farmers there. The ones in my family were Baptists or Presbyterians, not Amish. I have lived all over the United States, as many of our citizens have. Huge numbers of our citizens, moreover, are immigrants, many quite recent immigrants, twelve million of them illegal immigrants Almost all of us are descended from immigrants who occupied an alien land. Only the tiny number of Native Americans can truly call themselves indigenes, "first people." Their ancestors too were once newcomers, travelers from Asia who crossed by the Bering land bridge just after the last ice age.

The United States is made up of an enormous diversity of different races and ethnic groups speaking many different languages. The Department of Homeland Security in its surveillance activities has made many citizens or residents of the United States markedly less secure. We are certainly far less able to maintain the privacy of our homes or of our e-mail or of information about the books we read. Analogously, the invasion of Afghanistan and Iraq in the name of national security has arguably made our "homeland" far less secure. It has done this by multiplying many times over the terrorist threat and by leading a country like North Korea or Iran to conclude that its only possible safety lies in developing deterrent nuclear weapons as fast as possible. To be "secure," as Bajorek observes, means to be "without care." As I have shown, the myth of the indigenous community generates the terror of losing it. It generates the insecurity it would protect us against.

Bajorek's paper, in a subtle, balanced, and careful analysis, shows that Heidegger's claim that Hölderlin accepts the notions of homeland security and of an indigenous German community is a mystified misreading. Hölderlin, rather, in his poems about rivers and valleys and mountains, for example, "Heimkunft/An die Verwandten" ("Homecoming/To the Related Ones"), read in admirable detail by Bajorek, presents the homeland as the place of lack of ground, of *Abgrund*. The German-speaking homeland is a place of unhealed fissures and unfathomable abysses, rather than a place where an indigenous community in the sense I have identified it, with Stevens's help, could dwell. "If for Hölderlin home, if and insofar as it is a place," says Bajorek, "can only be a place to which one returns, and more precisely to which one is *always* returning, this is not only because the home that man makes on this earth is not a dwelling place ('*Wohnen ist nicht das Innehaben eine Wohnung*' ['To dwell is not the occupation of a dwelling.']). It is because, for Hölderlin, 'being-there' is always a 'being-elsewhere' and first takes place by way of a departure."[9]

An Alternative Model of Community

Stevens eloquently dramatizes, but also puts in question, the ordinary commonsensical idea of human togetherness that most people have in mind, explicitly or implicitly, when they speak of community. Jean-Luc Nancy has articulated another less intuitive model of community, one inextricably entwined with the first. One resists taking Nancy's model seriously, since it is hard to think and has disastrous consequences for the first model. The second model of community "unworks" the first.

A common notion of a human community, as I have said, sees it as the construction of a group living and working together. They have made the community over time. It is the product of their combined and cooperative work, as well as the result of a social contract they have explicitly or implicitly signed. Their collective work has constituted their community, sometimes on the basis of an explicit "constitution." The communities of my university departments, if they are communities, are governed by departmental "constitutions." The community of American citizens is based on the United States Constitution, our founding document. Under George W. Bush's presidency our governance under the Constitution was deeply endangered by the executive and judiciary branches of the federal government.

The commonly accepted model of community sees the individuals within it as preexisting subjectivities. These subjectivities have bound together with other subjectivities for the common good. Their mode of communication with one another can be called "intersubjectivity." This communication is an interchange between subjectivities. Such an interchange presupposes that the other is like me. Our common language makes it possible for me, in spite of my individuality, to communicate to my neighbor what I am thinking and feeling, what I am. I can, so I assume, also understand through language and other signs what the other person is thinking and feeling, what he or she is. As Stevens says, in the passage already cited, we "knew each other well, hale-hearted landsmen." These cohabiting subjectivities have made together a language, houses, roads, farms, industries, laws, institutions, religious beliefs, customs, mythical or religious stories about their origin and destiny that are told communally or written down in some sacred book to be recited to the group. Christian church services, for example, include each week readings from the Old and New Testaments that are synecdoches for a recital of the whole Bible. The entire Bible used to be read aloud in the church over the course of several years. The Bible is the sacred Book that binds a Christian community together.

Literature within such a community is the imitation, or reflection, or representation of community, the construction of cunningly verisimilar miniature models of community. *Bleak House* allows you to carry the whole of Dickens's London in your pocket. Literature is to be valued for its truth of correspondence to a community already there, for its constative value, not for any performative function it may have in constituting communities. Valid language, for example, the language of literature, is primarily and fundamentally literal, not, except as embellishment, figurative, just as the conceptual terms describing this model of community are to be taken literally, *à la lettre*. The primary figure employed is the figure of synecdoche. This figure allows a few examples to stand for the whole, as Gridley, the Man from Shropshire, in *Bleak House*, stands for the whole class of those whose lives have been destroyed by the Court of Chancery.

Though the individuals living together in such a community no doubt think of themselves as mortal, and though one of their community places is the cemetery, nevertheless, mortality does not essentially define community life. The community's constant renewal from generation to generation gives it a kind of collective immortality, just as the living together of individuals in a community tends to project a hypothetical sempiternal "community consciousness" or "collective consciousness." Each individual participates in, is bathed or encompassed in, this collective consciousness, as a fish swims in water, or as Danes all know Danish. Death tends to be covered over, suppressed, almost forgotten, as is notoriously the case within many American communities, if they can be called that, today.

It is possible (though it would be an error) to see Victorian novels, for example, George Eliot's novels, or Charles Dickens's, or Anthony Trollope's, as straightforwardly based on such a conception of community and as reflecting or imitating actually existing communities of the sort I have been characterizing. An example of such fictive communities is the Barsetshire community in Trollope's Barset novels. The omniscient or telepathic narrators in such novels are the expression of the collective consciousness of the community I mentioned above. Victorian multiplotted novels are, according to this view, "models of community." They are cunning miniature replicas of communities that, it is often assumed, actually existed historically. Their object of representation is not one individual life story but a whole community. The existence of such communities, in reality and in fictive simulacra, so this (false or only partially true) story about Victorian novels goes, ensures the execution of felicitous performatives. In Trollope's novels, as in Victorian fiction generally, the most important speech acts or writing acts are the marriages of young women and the passing on from generation to generation, by gifts, wills, and marriage settlements, of money, property, and rank. Most often, in Victorian novels, these two themes are combined. The heroine's marriage redistributes property, money, rank, and carries it on to the next generation.

Another model of community has been articulated in recent years. This has been done in different but more or less consonant ways by many theorists, among them those mentioned in note 5: Georges Bataille, Giorgio Agamben, Alphonso Lingis, and Jean-Luc Nancy. A widely influential book by Benedict Anderson, *Imagined Communities*, is, on the whole, no more than a subtle, postmodern version of the first model of community, the one whose features I have already sketched. I shall describe the second model primarily on the basis of Nancy's *The Inoperative Community*.[10]

Nancy sees persons not as individualities but as "singularities." He sees people, that is, as agents each fundamentally different from all the others. Each singularity harbors a secret alterity that can by no means be communicated to any other singularity. These singularities are essentially marked by their finitude and by their mortality. Each is from moment to moment, from the beginning, defined by the fact that it will die. Here is Nancy's expression of this, in a passage that is cited in part by Blanchot, in *La communauté inavouable*. Blanchot says it is the fundamental affirmation in Nancy's *La communauté désoeuvrée*:

> That which is not a subject opens up onto a community whose conception, in turn, exceeds the resources of a metaphysics of the subject. Community does not weave a superior, immortal, or transmortal life between subjects (no more than it is itself woven of the inferior bonds of a consubstantiality of blood or of an association of needs), but it is constitutively, to the extent that it is a matter of a "constitution" here, calibrated on the death of those whom we call, perhaps wrongly, its "members" (inasmuch as it is not a question of an organism). But it does not make a work of this calibration. Community no more makes a work out of death than it is itself a work. The death upon which community

> is calibrated does not *operate* the dead being's passage into some communal intimacy, nor does community, for its part, *operate* the transfiguration of its dead into some substance or subject—be these homeland, native soil or blood, nation, a delivered or fulfilled humanity, absolute phalanstery [this word means "a community of the followers of Charles Fourier," from *phalanx* ("any close-knit or compact body of people") plus *monastère*, monastery.], family, or mystical body. Community is calibrated on death as on that of which it is precisely impossible to *make a work* (other than a work of death, as soon as one tries to make a work of it). Community occurs in order to acknowledge this impossibility, or more exactly—for there is neither function nor finality here—the impossibility of making a work out of death is inscribed and acknowledged as "community."
>
> Community is revealed in the death of others; hence it is always revealed to others. Community is what takes place always through others and for others. It is not the space of the *egos*—subjects and substances that are at bottom immortal—but of the *I*'s, who are always *others* (or else are nothing). If community is revealed in the death of others, it is because death itself is the true community of *I*'s that are not *egos*. It is not a communion that fuses the *egos* into an *Ego* or a higher *We*. It is the community of *others*. The genuine community of mortal beings, or death as community, establishes their impossible communion. Community therefore occupiers a singular place: it assumes the impossibility of its own immanence, the impossibility of a communitarian being in the form of a subject. In a certain sense community acknowledges and inscribes—this is its peculiar gesture—the impossibility of community. (*IC*, 14–15)

The reader will see that Nancy's model of community puts in question, point by point, all the features of Stevens's indigenous community, the community of those who live together like Danes in Denmark. Each singularity, in Nancy's model of community, is not a self-enclosed subjectivity, such as the first model assumes. Each singularity is exposed, at its limit, to a limitless or abyssal outside that it shares with the other singularities, from the beginning, by way of their common mortality. Their community is defined by the imminence of death. This death we experience not in our own deaths, since they cannot be "experienced," but in the death of another, the death of our friend, our neighbor, our relative. The language defining this other model of community is, necessarily, figurative, catachrestic, since no literal language exists for it. Even conceptual words are used "anasemically" by Nancy, that is, against the grain of their dictionary meanings. They are also used with an implicit or explicit play on their metaphorical roots. Examples of such words in Nancy's book are *singularité* itself, or *désoeuvrée*, or *partagé*, or *comparution*, or *limite*, or *exposition*, or *interruption*, or even *littérature*, as in Nancy's phrase "literary communism." Blanchot's complex use of the word *désastre* in *L'écriture du désastre* is another example. I give the words in the original French, because their nuances are not easily translated.

The first model of community is easy to understand because it is the one most of "us" take for granted. Nancy's model is more difficult to understand or to think. Moreover, as I have said, one resists thinking it or taking it seriously because it is devastating, a disaster, for the other model. Nancy's systematic dismantling of that other model's assumptions confirms that. No subjectivities, no intersubjective communication, no social "bonds," no collective consciousness, exist in Nancy's "unworked community." This set of negations is perhaps what leads Jacques Derrida to say of Nancy's theory of community: "Why call it a community? Just to conform to what certain of our friends have attempted to do, to Blanchot's 'unavowable' community or Nancy's 'inoperative' [*désoeuvrée*] one? I have no qualms about these communities; my only question is, why call them communities?"[11]

Nancy carries on his thinking about community by permutation of certain recurrent key terms. These words are incorporated again and again in new formulations. These attempt once more to say what cannot be said. They keep trying to say what is, strictly speaking, unsayable. The last sentence of *The Inoperative Community* in the original French form, avers just this. (The original version has just the first three chapters of the five chapters in the English version.) "Here I must interrupt myself: it is up to you to allow to be said what no one, no subject, can say, and what exposes us in common" (*IC*, 81).

This essential "impossibility of saying" determines several features of Nancy's style. First, the key words he uses are twisted away from their normal or casual use. They are suspended from everyday discourse. They are, as it were, held out in the open, dangling, unattached, since they tend to detach themselves through their iteration in different syntactic combinations with other key words. The reader notices them as separate, somewhat enigmatic locutions. A second stylistic feature is outright contradiction, unsaying in the same sentence what has just been said, as in "allow to be said what no one, no subject, can say." Well, if no subject can say it, who or what can be imagined to say it? A third feature is an odd sort of implicit spatialization of the story Nancy tells. The figures of limit, sharing/shearing (*partage*), articulation, suspension, exposition, and so on, are all implicitly spatial. These words invite the reader to think again what Nancy is thinking in terms of a certain weird space, in which the topographical terms are withdrawn as soon as they are proffered. The limit, for example, is not an edge, border, or frontier, since there is nothing that can be confronted beyond it. It is like the cosmologists' finite but unbounded universe. You confront a limit, a boundary, but you cannot get out of your enclosure because no beyond exists, no transcendent outside. "*Partagé*," to give another example, is a double antithetical word meaning both shared and sheared. It is a spatial or topographical word, but you cannot easily map something that is both shared and sheared, "*partagé*." Nancy has written a whole book, *Le partage des voix*,[12] exploiting the contradictory nuances of the French word *partage*.

A final feature of Nancy's style (which is to say, of his "thought") is that the model of community he proposes is explicitly the negation (though that is not quite the right word) of the community model that most people have in mind when one asks, "What is a community?" The two models are not antithetical or negations of one another, in the Hegelian sense of a determinate negation allowing for dialectical sublation. Each presupposes the other, is entangled with the other, is generated by the other as soon as you try to express it alone, for example, in a novel or in a theoretical treatise, such as Nancy's or such as these paragraphs you are now reading, or such as the lines from Stevens I read earlier. The "ideological" model presupposes preexisting, self-enclosed "individuals," "subjectivities," "selves," "persons." These egos are finite, no doubt, mortal, no doubt, but totalizing, oriented toward totality, and in that sense immortal. These individuals then encounter other individuals and subsequently establish, by intersubjective communication leading to a compact or contract, a society, a community made up of shared stories (myths of origin and end), a language, institutions, laws, customs, family structures with rules for marriage and inheritance, gender roles, and so on, all organically composed and all the combined work of individuals living together. A group of people living and working together establishes an immanent close-knit community, geographically located, closed in on itself, autochthonous, indigenous. Language is a tool that "works," or makes, or produces, the interchanges of community.

Nancy says we now know no such community ever existed, though the first sentence of *The Inoperative Community* reaffirms this familiar historical myth. This myth or ideologeme presumes such communities once existed and that modernity is characterized by their dissolution: "The gravest and most painful testimony of the modern world," says Nancy in the passage already cited in the introduction, "the one that possibly gathers together all other testimonies which this epoch finds itself charged with assuming, by virtue of who knows what decree or necessity (for we bear witness also to the exhaustion of thinking by way of history), is the testimony of the dissolution, the dislocation, or the conflagration of community" (*IC*, 1). The commonly presumed model is always already unworked, *désoeuvré*, by the alternative model. That model is a negation, if not in the dialectical sense allowing some synthesizing *aufhebung*, or sublation, then at least in the sense that it says no to the other one. It defines itself point by point as opposed to the "first" model. In place of individuals with self-enclosed subjectivities Nancy puts singularities that are aboriginally *partagés*, shared, sheared, open to an abyssal outside called death, sharing in it willy-nilly. Singularities are extroverted, exposed to other singularities at the limit point where everything vanishes. Language in such a community becomes literature, "writing" in the Blanchotian or Derridean sense, not sacred myth. Literature becomes the enactment of the performative unworking of community.

Here is a key example of Nancy's mode of expressing both what the "unworked," or "inoperative," community is like and also the way it differs from traditional notions of social bonds and of intersubjective communication. A long citation is necessary. The passage is by no means all that easy to understand. I give it in the English translation, though with French words or phrases along the way where the nuance of the French is important:

> Communication consists before all else in this sharing and in this compearance [*comparution*] of finitude: that is, in the dislocation and in the interpellation that reveal themselves to be constitutive of being-in-common—precisely inasmuch as being-in-common is not a common being. The finite-being exists first of all according to a division of sites, according to an extension—*partes extra partes*—such that each singularity is extended (in the sense that Freud says: "The psyche is extended"). It is not enclosed in a form—although its whole being touches against its singular limit—but it is what it is, singular being (singularity of being), only through its extension, through the areality that above all extroverts it in its very being—whatever the degree or

> the desire of its "egoism"—and that makes it exist only *by exposing it to an outside*. This outside is in its turn nothing other than the exposition of another areality, of another singularity—the same other. This exposure, or this exposition-sharing, gives rise, from the outset, to a mutual interpellation of singularities prior to any address in language (though it gives to this latter its first condition of possibility). Finitude compears, that is to say it is exposed: such is the essence of community.
>
> Under these conditions, communication is not a bond. The metaphor of the "social bond" unhappily superimposes upon "subjects" (that is to say, objects) a hypothetical reality (that of the "bond") upon which some have attempted to confer a dubious "intersubjective" nature that would have the virtue of attaching these objects to one another. This would be the economic link or the bond of recognition. But compearance is of a more originary order than that of the bond. It does not set itself up, it does not establish itself, it does not emerge among already given subjects (objects). It consists of the appearance of the *between* as such: you *and* I (between us)—a formula in which the *and* does not imply juxtaposition, but exposition. What is expressed in compearance is the following, and we must learn to read it in all its possible combinations: "you (are/and/is) (entirely other than) I" [*toi (e[s]t) (tout autre que) moi*]. Or again, more simply, "*you shares me*" [*toi partage moi*].
>
> Only in this communication are singular beings given—without a bond *and* without communion, equally distant from any notion of connection or joining from the outside and from any notion of a common or fusional interiority. Communication is the constitutive fact of an exposition to the outside that defines singularity. In its being, in its very being, singularity is exposed to the outside. By virtue of this position or this primordial structure, it is at once detached, distinguished, and communitarian. Community is the presentation of the detachment (or retrenchment) of this distinction that is not individuation, but finitude compearing. (*IC*, 29)

"Compearing," as I said at the outset of this chapter, means "appearing together," a variant of "appearance." *Comparution*, in French, means "an action of *comparaître*." *Comparaître* means to present oneself by order, for example, the order of a court, so the judge can adjudicate between conflicting accounts. The assumption that being with, or "finitude compearing," is a fundamental feature of human existence is the basic presupposition of Nancy's other big book about community, *Being Singular Plural*.[13] Nancy argues tirelessly in this book that the "with" of "being with" goes all the way to the bottom, so to speak, both of each individual ego and of Being in general. We cannot help but share our existence with others. For Nancy, "being" is always already simultaneously divided and unified by the togetherness of a plural being with. We are each both singular and plural at once, as in Nancy's punning title, *Being Singular Plural*, where *Being* (*Être*) is both a noun and a verb. Here is one example of Nancy's way of expressing this complex assumption:

> That Being is being-with, absolutely, this is what we must think. The *with* is the most basic feature of Being, the mark [*trait*] of the singular plurality of the origin or origins in it. . . . What is proper to community, then, is given to us in the following way: it has no other resource to appropriate except the "with" that constitutes it, the *cum* of "community," its interiority without an interior, and nevertheless perhaps it too, after its fashion, *interior intimo suo* [(has) its own intimate interior]. As a result, this *cum* is the *cum* of co-appearance, wherein we do nothing but appear together with one another, co-appearing before no other authority [*l'instance*] than this "with" itself, the meaning of which seems to us instantly to dissolve into insignificance, into exteriority, into the inorganic, empirical, and randomly contingent [*aléatoire*] inconsistency of the pure and simple "with." (*BSP*, 61–62, 63, trans. altered; *ESP*, 83–84, 85)

If "myth," for Nancy, is the linguistic expression of those living together according to the first model of community, "literature" names the contestation of that by one expression or another, however implicit, of the second model of community. This gives literature (which includes, for Nancy, philosophy, theory, and criticism, as well as literature proper in the sense of novels, poems, and plays) an explicitly political function, as he asserts at the end of "Le communisme littéraire," the third and final part of *La communauté désoeuvrée* in its original French version:

> It is because there is community—unworked [*désoeuvrée*] always, and resisting at the heart of every collectivity and in the heart of every individual—and because myth is interrupted—suspended always, and divided by its own enunciation—that there

> exists the exigency of "literary communism." And this means: thinking, the practice of a sharing of voices [*un partage des voix*] and of an articulation according to which there is no singularity but that exposed in common, and no community but that offered to the limit of singularities.
>
> This does not determine any particular mode of sociality, and it does not found a politics—if a politics can ever be "founded." But it defines at least a limit, at which all politics stop and begin. The communication that takes place on this limit, and that, in truth, constitutes it, demands that way of destining ourselves in common that we call a politics, that way of opening community to itself, rather than to a destiny or to a future. "Literary communism" indicates at least the following: that community, in its infinite resistance to everything that would bring it to completion (in every sense of the word "*achever*"—which can also mean "finish off"), signifies an irrepressible political exigency, and that this exigency in its turn demands something of "literature," the inscription of our infinite resistance.
>
> It defines neither *a* politics, nor *a* writing, for it refers, on the contrary, to that which resists any definition or program, be these political, aesthetic, or philosophical. But it cannot be accommodated within every "politics" or within every "writing." It signals a bias in favor of the "literary communist" resistance that precedes us rather than our inventing it—that precedes us from the depths of community. A politics that does not want to know anything about this is a mythology, or an economy. A literature that does not say anything about it is a mere diversion, or a lie. (*IC*, 80–81; *CD*, 197–98)

The reader will see that Nancy's model of an inoperative community is based on a strange contradictory spatial model in which singularities are at one and the same time enclosed within unbreachable "limits" and at the same time exposed, across or through those limits, to all the other singularities, in a preoriginary "with" or "being with." This being with is always already there, as a fundamental feature of every singularity, but it is also an infinite abyss, the place where each singularity joins all the others.

One more question must be asked and an answer posited. If the first kind of community ensures the felicitous uttering of performatives—promises, marriage oaths, contracts, wills, and the like—what about speech acts in the second kind of community? No solid ground for doing things with words is offered by the community joining a "set, a group of 'exposed' singularities that are wholly other to one another." This joining takes place by way of the impossibility of community. None of the conditions for felicitous speech acts laid out by J. L. Austin in *How to Do Things with Words* is met within an "unworked community." The members are not enclosed selves or egos capable of taking responsibility for what they say and enduring through time so that promises made yesterday may be kept today. No social contract or constitution making possible the establishment of functioning laws and institutions exists. No transparent "intersubjective" communication, no social bond, can be counted on to certify for me the sincerity of speech acts uttered by another person.

Such a community is *inavouable*, unavowable, in the double sense that Blanchot means the word in *La communauté inavouable* (*The Unavowable Community*). An unworked community remains secret, unable to be publicly avowed. Blanchot's example is the secret community Georges Bataille and his associates established. This was a community committed to the clandestine sacrifice of one or another of its members by beheading (hence the name Acéphale). Such a community is certainly something one would want to keep secret, though one might note that the early secret communities of Christians performed a ritual sacrifice, commemorating Christ's crucifixion, in the communion service. This ceremony was modeled on the sacrifices, sometimes actually bloody, in ancient Near Eastern mystery cults. United States solidarity is held together today, it might be argued, by the sacrificial enactment, over and over again, of the "death penality."

Such an unworked community is "unavowable" in another way, however. It does not provide solid ground for any avowals or speech acts. This does not mean that speech acts do not occur within unworked communities, or that they may not be efficacious. What it does mean, however, is that such speech acts are not endorsed by any public laws and institutions. They work by a resolution to go on being true to them that is continuously self-generated and self-sustained. Such speech acts are a kind of lifting oneself by one's own bootstraps over that abyss to which Nancy and Blanchot give the name "death."

Matthew Arnold expresses something like this form of unavowable vow in the contradictory last stanza of "Dover Beach." Arnold's formulation is Blanchotian in its positing of a love between singularities that is without grounds in love as a universal, Love with a capital L. Nor does it have grounds in any of the other universals, certitude, peace, joy, light, and so on, that would seem necessary prerequisites for felicitous vows of fidelity exchanged between lovers. Arnold's speaker exhorts his beloved to join him in what Blanchot might have called an *amour sans amour*. This would be the only love possible in an unworked community:

> Ah, love, let us be true
> To one another! for the world, which seems
> To lie before us like a land of dreams,
> So various, so beautiful, so new,
> Hath really neither joy, nor love, nor light,
> Nor certitude, nor peace, nor help for pain.[14]

One word cognate with "community," "communion," leads Nancy's reflection to remarks on Christian communion and on Freud's theories of the primal horde. Here a challenge to Nancy by Jacques Derrida will help me to refine further the two notions of community I am juxtaposing. Derrida's target is not Nancy's *La communauté désoeuvrée* but his *L'experience de la liberté*. The members of a community of the first kind are in communion with one another by way of what they share. What they share, according to Freud, is that the have killed the father and have shared/sheared his body and eaten it. This makes them "brothers" and *semblables*. Baudelaire hails the "hypocrite lecteur" (hypocritical reader) of *Fleurs du mal* as "mon semblable,—mon frère."[15] All the members of the primal horde are the same. They share a guilt, the murder of the father. They are all like one another, hence transparent to one another, like the brothers in Stevens's poem. The culture of Stevens's brothers, you will remember, is generated by the mother's song on the accordion. The French revolutionary motto, "liberty, equality, fraternity," links freedom to fraternity. That freedom needed to be asserted in a violent act against monarchal sovereignty. The French revolutionaries shared the guilt of killing the king. Modern English democracy has the beheading of King Charles on its conscience. The Alhambra in Granada, Spain, was the scene of the killing of the primal father in reverse. The sultan had thirty-six princes, his sons, beheaded. The Fountain of the Lions ran with their blood.

A fraternal community is united in its opposition to those who are not *semblables*, who are different, who do not take communion, who do not repeat Christ's words to his disciples, a brotherhood if there ever was one: "This do in remembrance of me." Such a community is a community of intolerance, often of unspeakable cruelty to those outside the community, as was the Christian community that expelled Arabs and Jews from Spain. Such a community depends for its solidarity on exclusion. You are either with us or against us, and if you are against us you are "evildoers," as George W. Bush called Iraq, North Korea, Somalia, and so on, in the end every nation but the United States, and then only a small group there, the rest being sympathizers, "focus groups," peaceniks, communists, subversives, friends of terrorism—in short, evildoers. This happens by an implacable and frightening suicidal logic that is built into democracy defined as a brotherhood of *semblables*. Ultimately only Bush and his cronies would be left, and then they would begin bumping one another off. This did indeed happen, as one or another of them "fell on his sword" by resigning and disappearing from public view, even while Bush still ruled. Where is Donald Rumsfeld now? Or John Ashcroft? The Teapartyers today (2011) are held together, if you can call it that, by the same perverse logic.

Where are the women in this paradigm, the sisters, mothers, wives, lovers? Are they *semblables*? Maurice Blanchot thinks they are rather members of a different sort of community, as did Marguerite Duras. In "The Community of Lovers," in *The Unavowable Community*, Blanchot proposes, on the basis of a reading of Marguerite Duras's *récit The Malady of Death*, and with reference to Emmanuel Levinas and to the story of Tristan and Isolde, another version of the "unavowable community" he has delineated in the first part of his book. This one is the impossible "community of two" made up of lovers:

> And let us also remember that even the reciprocity of the love relationship, as Tristan and Isolde's story represents it, the paradigm of shared love, excludes simple mutuality as well as a unity where the Other would blend with the same. And this brings us back to the foreboding that passion eludes possibility, eluding, for those caught by it, their own powers, their own decision and even their "desire," in that it is strangeness itself, having consideration neither for what they can do nor for what they want, but luring them into a strangeness where they become estranged from themselves, into an intimacy which also estranges them from each other. And thus, eternally separated, as if death was in them, between them? Not separated, not divided: inaccessible and, in the inaccessible, in an infinite relationship.[16]

Jacques Derrida, in *Voyous*, is closer to Blanchot than to Nancy's notion of a brotherhood of free men. Against Nancy, and with a covert allusion to Levinas, Derrida poses a (non)community of dissimilars, of non-*semblables*. This (non)community is made up of neighbors who are defined by their absolute difference from one another: "Pure ethics, if there is any, begins with the respectable dignity of the other as the absolute *unlike* [*à la dignité respectable de l'autre comme absolu* dissemblable], recognized as nonrecognizable, indeed as unrecognizable [*reconnu comme non reconnaissable, voire comme méconnaissable*] beyond all knowledge, all cognition and all recognition: far from being the beginning of pure ethics, the neighbor as like or as resembling, as looking like [*comme semblable ou resssemblant*], spells the end or the ruin of such an ethics, if there is any."[17]

Derrida is even more explicit in his disagreement with Nancy in a forceful passage in his last seminars, and in a direct reference to Nancy's theory of community in one of the interviews in *A Taste for the Secret*, already cited. "Why call it a community?" asks Derrida in the interview. In the seminar Derrida says, in his most intransigent expression of his sense that each I is isolated, enisled like Robinson Crusoe before he encountered Friday:

> Between my world, the "my world," what I call "my world," and there is no other for me, every other world making up part of it, between my world and every other world, there is initially the space and the time of an infinite difference, of an interruption incommensurable with all the attempts at passage, of bridge, of isthmus, of communication, of translation, of trope, and of transfer that the desire for a world and the sickness of the world [*mal du monde*], the being in sickness of the world [*l'être en mal de monde*] will attempt to pose, to impose, to propose, to stabilize. There is no world, there are only islands.[18]

Suppose one were to take seriously Nancy's notion of a community of singularities, or, in Lingis's phrase, a community of those who have nothing in common. How would this lead one to think differently from the way Fengzhen Wang and Shabao Xie do in a recent essay the effects of globalization? Wang and Xie argue that globalization is destroying local cultures everywhere, transforming indigenes into cybersurfers.[19] One might respond that Wang and Xie are using Western concepts of local communities. Nancy's conception of community and the tradition to which it belongs, as well as Wallace Stevens's contrary model, are both as much Western inventions as are any other products of cultural capitalism, as is Derrida's repudiation of togetherness as something primordially given. Nancy's community of singularities is Western through and through. Nevertheless, it is, like other such products, asserted by Nancy with apodictic universality. It is not just Western men and women who are singularities exposed to others at the limit, according to him, but all men and women everywhere at all times. Nevertheless, Nancy's ideas are a Western product, perhaps even a product of the resources of the French language. I do not see any way out of this aporia. Any idea of community will be idiomatic, the product of a given language, but will tend to express itself as universal. Nevertheless, it would be plausible to argue that each community should have its own singular idea of community, appropriate only for that community alone. In that case, the whole issue of *Ariel* devoted to thinking in English about globalization and about the destruction of indigenous cultures would be a form of the thing it would resist.

The second thing to say if we take Nancy's model of community seriously, is that it disqualifies, to some degree at least, Wang and Xie's opposition between the happy indigene and the cybersurfer, penetrated through and through by global capitalism, corrupted by it, deprived of his or her specificity and made the same as everyone else. Wang and Xie put it this way: "Multinational capital with its hegemonic ideology and technology seems to be globally erasing difference, imposing sameness and standardization on consciousness, feeling, imagination, motivation, desire, and taste."[20] According to Nancy's model of community, the singularity of the indigene is not touched by the interpellations of indigeneous culture. Nor is the singularity of the cybersurfer touched by leveling American popular culture. Beneath these superficial cultural garments both indigene and cybersurfer remain wholly other to each other, though exposed to the others, even though they may be either living together as indigenes or, on the contrary, communicating, via e-mail, online chats, texting, or "tweets," as cybersurfers. To put this in Heideggerian terms, the loneliness of *Dasein*, fundamentally characterized by its "Sein zum Tode" (Being toward death), remains intact beneath the alienating superficialities of *das Man*, the "they," and even beneath the most dramatic technological, political, and social changes. It is as true as ever now that each man or woman dies his or her own death.

Nevertheless, it is plausible to argue that dwelling within the uniqueness of a so-called indigenous culture, that is, a local way of living untouched by globalization, if such a thing anywhere remains these days, is a better way to live the otherness of singularities in their exposure to one another than the global homogenizing culture that is rapidly becoming the most widely experienced way to be human today. Diversity of cultures, languages, idioms, it can be argued, is a good in itself, just as is a diversity of plant and animal species. Moreover, certain local cultures, it may be, are closer to recognizing the imminence of death in their religious and cultural expressions than is Western popular culture's bland avoidance of death through its banal spectacular presentation of death in cinema and television. Global capitalism has to be resisted by each local culture as best it can. One way, as Nancy suggests, is through what he calls "communist literature," that is, literature, including philosophy and critical theory, as well as poems, novels, cinema, and television shows, that does not avoid confrontation with singularity, even though it cannot be confronted. Blanchot's *récits* might be models of such literature. Perhaps little of that kind of literature exists any longer, though Kafka, Kertész, and Morrison are examples of its persistence, as my readings will attempt to show.

The leveling effects of global cultural capitalism are enormously powerful, but small-scale local ways exist to resist those forces in the name of the idiomatic and the singular. Though Western critical theory and literature are concomitants of global cultural capitalism, they can be used to support resistance to global leveling, just as the telecommunications products of capitalism can be mobilized against some aspects of it, as in the use of the Internet in Barack Obama's campaign for president in the United States in the summer and fall of 2008. It is a matter of strategic deployment, not necessarily of passive submission to an inevitable juggernaut. Or rather, the resistance to global capitalism is a matter of certain anomalous speech acts performed within "indigenous communities" now seen as gatherings of singularities. These speech acts perform local transformations of the global situation that might just possibly help maintain local communities of singularities. Somewhat paradoxically, another Western product, its secular literary writings, for instance, Wallace Stevens's poems or Victorian novels, or the novels discussed in this book, often assert the unknowable singularity of fictive or poetic personae, for example, in the crucial decisions they are shown making. Demonstrating that persuasively for some novels written before and after Auschwitz by Franz Kafka, Imre Kertész, Toni Morrison, and others is one goal of this book.

I do not think much is gained by vilifying new telecommunication technologies as a cause of the conflagration of community. Cinema, television, cell phones, computers, and the Internet are, as media, to some degree neutral, in spite of the way their existence radically transforms any "indigenous" culture that begins to use them. In spite of the differences between network TV and cable TV, versions of the same television technology are used to broadcast the PBS *News Hour* and to broadcast Fox so-called News. The Internet stores and distributes with indifference and equanimity both the rantings of Holocaust deniers and horrible photographs of a *Selektion* at Auschwitz. *Selektion* names the division by the SS men of the Jews when they first got off the train at Auschwitz. They were separated into two lines: those (women, children, weaker men) who were to be gassed and cremated immediately and those who were to be sent to the work camps. Even so, the media that transmit these "contents" change what is formatted for transmission. Blogging technology is indifferent to what is posted on the blogs. The cultural force of these devices depends on the uses that are made of them, even though they have in themselves, as media, enormous force in transforming the ways we think and feel, along with our relations to others, as I have argued in *The Medium Is the Maker*.[21]

New telecommunication devices, for example, the iPhone, can be used to reinforce and preserve local languages and local ways of life, however difficult it may be to do that. An essay several years ago in *Scientific American*, "Demystifying the Digital Divide,"[22] distinguished sharply between projects that simply set up computers in "underdeveloped countries," in which case they are likely to be used primarily to play computer games, thereby destroying the local culture, and those projects, like one in an impoverished region of southern India, that use computer installations to help support and maintain an indigenous culture. I would add that the new medium, nevertheless, transforms any culture that uses it, as print book culture transformed medieval manuscript culture in the West. In the few years since that *Scientific American* article was published, computers, cell phones, iPhones, iPods, and Blackberries have become far more widely distributed around the world, just as the distinction between "developed" and "underdeveloped" countries is fading. One sees as many people using cell phones on the streets of Beijing as in New York or Frankfurt. An enormous recent scholarly literature, following pioneer work by Katherine Hayles, Donna Haraway, and Derrida, analyzes the nature and effects of new digital media in their "intermediation" with print media.[23] The consensus is that an extremely rapid "critical climate change" is occurring by way of new media that is effecting even what it means to be human or "posthuman." Some of this work pays attention to the question of what one might mean by an online "community," a computer-game-playing community, or a Facebook or Twitter community, that is, communities generated by new teletechnologies. That, however, is a question for another book.

Nevertheless, it important to remember that it is a fundamental feature of our present-day relation to the Shoah that it is mediated to such a large degree by new digital communication technologies, for example, online photographs of a *Selektion* or the Wikipedia entries "Auschwitz" and "Buchenwald." The Shoah was made possible by the technologies, including communication technologies, of its day. Much of what we know and feel now about the Shoah comes by way of our current tele-technologies: films like Claude Lanzmann's *Shoah*, surviving photographs, and electronic recordings of testimony by survivors. Art Spiegelman's *Maus* is available on a DVD, as is the film of Kertész's *Fatelessness*, Such artifactualities, it may be, generate communities of survivors of the survivors, though, as my chapter on Kertész will argue, by way of another essay by Jean-Luc Nancy, "Forbidden Representation," representing the Shoah in any medium is extremely problematic. Even a visit, for example, to Buchenwald, such as I made in November 2009 with an extremely knowledgeable guide for our group, does not tell you much. Buchenwald is now so clean, so neat, so sweet smelling, even the surviving crematorium. It is now almost, but not quite, a tourist attraction, even though horrors took place there on a grand scale. The visitor can come and go as he or she pleases, which was not the case for the hundreds of thousands imprisoned there, around fifty-six thousand of whom died in the camp, or during the evacuation transports.[24]

A Third Paradigm for Communities

I turn now, in concluding this chapter, to a brief account of another model of community, or rather of communities. This other model exists in several forms. It is, moreover, exemplified, as I shall suggest in later chapters, in different ways by the novels read in this book. I have spoken so far, following both Stevens and Nancy, as if a community of any kind must be thought of as a sequestered group of people all related or, perhaps, nonrelated to one another in various ways. This third model thinks of a given society as made rather of a group of overlapping and interrelated communities, no one of which exists in total isolation from the others. One should, if following this paradigm, always speak of "communities," not of a "community." Any modern social group, such as a nation, this model would claim, is made up of a large number of interwoven institutions, bureaucracies, agencies, and what Michel Foucault calls *dispositifs* (apparatuses). For Foucault, *dispositif* is a name for the machinelike working of the whole social-legal-governmental-financial-bureaucratic assemblage in a given society at a given time. A willing worker for such an apparatus is called, in Sovietese, an "apparatchik." This apparatus, said Foucault, is "a thoroughly heterogeneous set consisting of discourses, institutions, architectural forms, regulatory decisions, laws, administrative measures, scientific statements, philosophical, moral, and philanthropic propositions—in short, the said as much as the unsaid. Such are the elements of the apparatus."[25] Kafka's "office writings," the bureaucratic documents he produced as a high-ranking lawyer in Prague in the Workman's Accident Insurance Institute for the Czech lands of the Austro-Hungarian Empire are a splendid example of such "discourses."[26] The concepts of heterogeneity, of lateral as well as vertical proliferation, and of the machinal, as opposed to the organic, are essential to mappings of this third model of communities.

Today Foucault might have added to his litany of wielders of power the media, including the Internet. Each element in the heterogeneous assemblage he calls an "apparatus" is determined by the use it makes of the information technologies available at a given time. Sociologists have studied the dependence of old-fashioned bureacracies on offices crammed with paper that secretaries type or write and that are circulated from office to office, up, down, and transversely among the proliferating hierarchies. Kafka's novels especially dramatize such bureaucracies, though the other novels I read in this book also exemplify them. The Holocaust was perpetrated by means of efficient, ramifying German governmental bureaucracies with the cooperation of bureaucracies, including police bureaucracies, within conquered countries like Hungary. The complex interrelation of these agencies was calculated to make it difficult for the left hand to know what the right hand was doing, or writing. Slavery in the United States, my topic in part 4 of this book, was also generated and controlled by a complex apparatus of interconnected institutions, businesses, laws, and customs. This went from the purchase by slave traders of captured Africans in Africa to their transportation in the slave trade by way of the notorious Middle Passage, to their resale in the United States, to their frequent reselling at auction in the United States, to the regulations and customs governing (sometimes) their treatment on plantations, to the slaves' establishment of fragile families, churches, and communities on the plantations, to such pre–Civil War legal institutions as the Fugitive Slave Law, to their emancipation followed by the subsequent century of southern Jim Crow laws, segregation, widespread lynchings, and so on. Slavery would have been impossible without this complicated legal, social, and commercial apparatus, all using the media of the day, such as posters to advertise slave auctions or the widespread circulation in the south of postcards with photographs of lynchings.

To turn to the present day: the recent collapse of the global financial system has depended on immensely complex use of computers and the Internet. Louis Althusser includes the media among ISAs, ideological state apparatuses, in his famous essay on ideology's interpellations.[27] It is a distinguishing feature, as I have said, of a given example of such an all-embracing social apparatus that it operates on its own, robotlike. What it brings about is "Nobody's Fault," to cite the title Dickens first presciently intended for *Little Dorrit*, with its Kafka-like presentation of the English Circumlocution Office. The latter is the model of an efficient bureaucracy of many layers receding to invisibility that just goes on and on, like the Energizer bunny, doing its intended work of procrastination. This is parallel to the legal system in Kafka's *Der Proceß* (*The Trial*), or, in a different form, to the bureaucracy binding the village to the Castle, while at the same time separating them, in Kafka's *Das Schloß* (*The Castle*).

Three other modes of this alternative paradigm, each substantially different from the others, may be briefly described, to bring this preliminary chapter to an end. Each would merit a lengthy exposition.

Stanley Fish's idea of "interpretive communities," as developed especially in *Is There a Text in This Class?*, presupposes that the university and those societies within which universities operate are made up of distinct groups of people who take certain interpretive assumptions for granted as objective and universal, though the groups are incompatible with one another, and though no solid foundation for such assumptions exists.[28] One group reads, for example, Milton's poems in one way, while another interpretive community reads Milton quite differently, though both assume, incorrectly, that the Milton they see is *there*, objectively. Similarly, Tea Partyers and progressive Democrats today interpret our present situation in the United States in strikingly opposed ways, though to each it seems that their ideological vision is objective truth.

I have already referred to Derrida's putting in question of Nancy's idea of the inoperative community. Derrida tends rather to think of each person's possible participation in a multitude of partially overlapping communities or institutions, as in the humanities communities in the university he addresses in *L'université sans condition* (*The University without Condition*).[29] In a striking passage in *A Taste for the Secret*, a passage that I have discussed in more detail in the chapter "Derrida Enisled" in my *For Derrida*,[30] Derrida affirms his unwillingness to belong to any of these intermeshed communities. "I am not one of the family," says Derrida, echoing André Gide. He then goes on to list the various communities to which he refuses to belong. Derrida sees society as a complex structure made up of multiple proliferating communities, side by side, overlapping, or one inside others:

> Let me get back to my saying "I am not one of the family." Clearly, I was playing on a formula that has multiple registers of resonance. I'm not one of the family means, in general, "I do not define myself on the basis of my belonging to the family," or to civil society, or to the state; I do not define myself on the basis of elementary forms of kinship. But it also means, more figuratively, that I am not part of any group, that I do not identify myself with a linguistic community, a national community, a political party, or with any group or clique whatsoever, with any philosophical or literary school. "I am not one of the family" means: do not consider me "one of you," "don't count me in," I want to keep my freedom, always: this, for me, is the condition not only for being singular and other, but also for entering into relation with the singularity and alterity of others. When someone is one of the family, not only does he lose himself in the herd [*gregge*, in the Italian version, as in the English word "gregarious"], but he loses the others as well; the others become simply places, family functions, or places or functions in the organic totality that constitutes a group, school, nation, or community of subjects speaking the same language.[31]

Derrida experiences himself as being besieged on all sides by exhortations, interpellations, calls, demands, addresses, beseechings, invocations, convocations, hailings, that he say "Yes!" and accept his belonging to this or that one of the superimposed communities large and small with which he is surrounded. He must say a resolute "No!" to all if he is to maintain his own integrity along with the possibility of genuine ethical relations to others. It is the 4most extreme and intransigent refusal of community I know. Nevertheless, Derrida was, whatever he said about refusing to belong, himself the center of a complex global set of interlocking communities. He had manifold belongings to institutions and groups all over the world, to the universities that hired him to teach or to lecture, to a network of translators and publishing houses, to archives, to sponsors of colloquiums and conferences on his work, to filmmakers, to friends.

My final example of the model of overlapping heterogeneous communities is Gilles Deleuze and Félix Guattari's concept of the social and linguistic rhizome. It is worked out in the most detail in "Introduction: Rhizome" at the beginning of *A Thousand Plateaus*.[32] Though Deleuze and Guattari's model is complex, subtle, and, as is usual with them, exuberantly creative, the bottom line is a rejection of any subject/object paradigm and a resistance either to a unitary model like Stevens's and Nancy's or to a hierarchical concept modeled on a tree's root, trunk, and dividing branches, as in a genealogical tree or as in the genetic tree that anthropologists use to trace our ancestry back to the apes. In place of those, Deleuze and Guattari put as mapping the rhizomatic plant that proliferates laterally, producing new plants growing up from underground or on the surface at a distance from the original plant:

> The world has become chaos, but the book remains the image of the world: radicle-chaosmos rather than root-cosmos. . . . A system of this kind could be called a rhizome. A rhizome as subterranean stem is absolutely different from roots and radicles. Bulbs and tubers are rhizomes. Plants with roots or radicles may be rhizomorphic in other respects altogether: the question is whether plant life in its specificity is not entirely rhizomatic. Even some animals are, in their pack form. Rats are rhizomes. Burrows are too, in all of their functions of shelter, supply, movement, evasion, and breakout. The rhizome itself assumes very diverse forms, from ramified surface extension in all directions to concretion into bulbs and tubers. When rats swarm over each other. The rhizome includes the best and the worst: potato and couchgrass, or the weed. Animal and plant, couchgrass is crabgrass. (*TP*, 6–7)

All this botanical detail sets up the paradigm Deleuze and Guattari want to use as a means of mapping social structures, including especially multiple languages as essential features of those structures:

> A rhizome ceaselessly establishes connections between semiotic chains, organizations of power, and circumstances relative to the arts, sciences, and social struggles. A semiotic chain is like a tuber agglomerating very diverse acts, not only linguistic, but also perceptive, mimetic, gestural and cognitive: there is no language in itself, nor are there any linguistic universals, only a throng of dialects, patois, slangs, and specialized languages. There is no ideal speaker-listener, any more than there is a homogeneous linguistic community. Language is, in Weinreich's words, "an essentially heterogeneous reality."[33] There is no mother tongue, only a power takeover by a dominant language within a political multiplicity. Language stabilizes around a parish, a bishopric, a capital. It forms a bulb. It evolves by subterranean stems and flows, along river valleys or train tracks: it spreads like a patch of oil. (*TP*, 7)

Deleuze and Guattari attempt to sidestep the organic implications of the rhizome as model by speaking of heterogeneity and of the machinal proliferation of rhizomatic structures. They speak of "the *abstract machine* that connects a language to the semantic and pragmatic contents of statements, to collective assemblages of enunciation, to a whole micropolitics of the social field" (*TP*, 7). I think it is difficult, however, to get away completely, if one uses the word "rhizome" at all, even in a somewhat twisted or "anasemic" way, from the fact that a rhizome is an organic copy of its parent plant. Nevertheless, Deleuze and Guattari use the rhizome model brilliantly in many provocative ways. Among them is the way the rhizome presides from the first page on over their way of reading Kafka in *Kafka: Toward a Minor Literature*.[34] Kafka's work, they say in the first sentence of this book, is "a rhizome, a burrow" (3). They go on immediately to exemplify this claim with three examples, the Castle in *The Castle*, the hotel in *Amerika*, and the burrow in "The Burrow":

> How can we enter into Kafka's work? This work is a rhizome, a burrow. The castle has multiple entrances whose rules of usage and whose locations aren't very well known. The hotel in *Amerika* has innumerable main doors and side doors that innumerable guards watch over; it even has entrances and exits without doors. Yet it might seem that the burrow in the story of that name has only one entrance; the most the animal can do is dream of a second entrance that would serve only for surveillance. But this is a trap arranged by the animal and by Kafka himself; the whole description of the burrow functions to trick the enemy. . . . Only the principle of multiple entrances prevents the introduction of the enemy, the Signifier and those attempts to interpret a work that is actually only open to experimentation. (*K*, 3)

I conclude this chapter by noting that Deleuze and Guattari's model is spatial. It thinks of Kafka's works as each generating in the reader the vision of an imaginary and extremely peculiar space, like that of the burrow in "Der Bau" ("The Burrow"), so elaborately described by the animal that has made it and that lives in it. I shall keep this rhizomatic spatial model in mind, along with the other models of community explored in this chapter, in my readings of Kafka's three novels and in subsequent chapters too. The spatial paradigms I derive from my novels, however, are somewhat different, as you will see.

Part Two | Franz Kafka: Premonitions of Auschwitz

2 Foreshadowings of Auschwitz in Kafka's Writings

Each epoch dreams the one to follow. **Jules Michelet, *"Avenir! Avenir!"*[1]**

Kafka and the Shoah

In this chapter, under the aegis of Michelet's dictum, I inflect, by anticipation, my readings of Kafka's *The Trial* and *The Castle* toward the question of the way Kafka's work foreshadows Auschwitz. It might seem perverse to relate Kafka's work to the Shoah. After all, he died in 1924, long before the Final Solution was contemplated. None of his works dramatizes genocide. Nevertheless, Kafka's work can, in numerous ways, be read in the afterlight of the "conflagration." The more one follows out these analogies, the more plausible it is to see fiction before Auschwitz, at least in Kafka's case, as a premonition of fiction after Auschwitz. My interest in this chapter is in the way Kafka's work preprograms the form fiction about Auschwitz took, as well as in its uncanny anticipations of what the Shoah would be like.

As Russell Samolsky has shown in a forthcoming book on "marked bodies and the violence of the text," a long tradition, going back to Walter Benjamin, Theodor Adorno, Bertolt Brecht, and, more recently, George Steiner associates Kafka's writing with the Shoah.[2] In Kafka's conversations with his friend Gustav Janouch, he is reported to have said that his inability to finish his writings and his desire to destroy them was a fear that they might be prophetic or might have the force to bring about on a large scale the individual sufferings and catastrophes they dramatize. In an exchange cited by Samolsky, when Janouch suggested to Kafka that "perhaps your writing is . . . only a mirror of tomorrow," Kafka covered his eyes, swayed back and forth, and replied, "You are right. You are certainly right. Probably that's why I cannot finish anything. I am afraid of the truth. But can one do otherwise? . . . One must be silent if one can't give any help. . . . For that reason all my scribbling is to be destroyed."[3] Whether or not you believe Kafka actually said this while swaying back and forth with his eyes covered depends on the credence you give to Janouch's report. We have only his word for it.

Kafka not only wanted his writings destroyed, as we know from other sources, but, it appears, did burn some of them. This was a way of keeping them from having their magic performative effect. Samolsky brilliantly reads this fear in the light of Derrida's use of autoimmunity as a figure for the way a text may exceed its author's intentions and operate on its own, in a machinal, prosthetic, ecotechnical way. The author cannot keep the text from creating its own future. Destroying it only buys into the self-destructive logic of automimmunity. What Kafka foresaw was a wholesale destruction of the Jewish people, in fulfillment of the dark anticipations of an Old Testatment prophet like Amos or of certain features of the Kabbalah. Kafka even dared to describe his own work as something that "might easily have developed into a new secret doctrine, a Kabbalah."[4]

Already in 1938 Benjamin was reading Kafka's work as a prefiguring of the Holocaust that had not yet come but that Benjamin too anticipated and that led to his suicide on the Spanish border. In "Some Reflections on Kafka," sent in a letter to Gershom Scholem and cited by Samolsky, Benjamin said that "Kafka's world . . . is the exact complement of his era which is preparing to do away with the inhabitants of this planet on a considerable scale. The experience which corresponds to that of Kafka, the private individual, will probably not become accessible to the masses until such time as they are being done away with."[5] Benjamin here argues, as I do in this chapter, that the experiences that Kafka's ascribes to unique individuals, the protagonists of his novels and stories, will become the collective experience of masses of persecuted people. The experiences of those luckless, or, to borrow Kertész's word, "fateless," individuals, K., Josef K., and Karl Rossmann, obscurely foreshadow the catastrophe of the Shoah. The singular will become the quasi-universal for the millions of Jews who are exterminated or who barely survive in the camps. This chapter explores how that is the case for *Amerika* (*The*

Man Who Disappeared). Kafka himself, in a remark to Janouch, also cited by Samolsky, made a similar dark prophecy as they stood looking at the old synagogue in Prague: "The synagogue already lies below ground level. But men will go further. They will try to grind the synagogue into dust by destroying the Jews themselves."[6] At least Janouch says Kafka said that.

Walter Benjamin and Werner Hamacher, as well as Deleuze and Guattari, have in different ways seen Kafka's work as deliberately blocking interpretation so as to delay a verdict or judgment. The reader, as Kafka sees her or him, is in the position of the trial system. "His texts," says Hamacher, "are made so as to avoid their interpretation."[7] He cites Benjamin's expression of this: "Kafka had a rare capacity for creating parables for himself. Yet his parables are never exhausted by what is explainable; on the contrary, he took all conceivable precautions against the interpretation of his writings."[8] Hamacher takes from Benjamin's "Franz Kafka" essay the notion that this "precaution against interpretation" takes the form of a "cloudy spot" at the center of Kafka's writings, especially the parables (Benjamin, 802). A traditional parable, such as the parables of Jesus in the New Testament, has an identifiable doctrinal meaning. The parable of the sower is explicitly said to be about the Kingdom of Heaven and how to get there. Kafka's parables have as their meaning their failure to mean any identifiable teaching, doctrine, or moral. Kafka's writings, like Scheherazade's storytelling, defer identification of their meaning as a way of postponing a judgment that may be identified with the judgment and execution of Joseph K. in the final chapter of *The Trial* (Hamacher, 298–300; Benjamin, 807).

In Kafka's writing, says Hamacher, "a shift [is made] to the literary form of a virtually endless postponement that no longer serves as an introduction to a teaching, a doctrine, a moral, or a law [hence the "cloudy spot" at the center of Kafka's parables], but has the task of deferring what is coming" (Hamacher, 299). Benjamin puts it this way: "In the stories which Kafka left us, narrative art regains the significance it had in the mouth of Scheherazade: its ability to postpone the future. In *Der Proceß* this deferral is the hope of the accused man only if the proceedings do not gradually turn into the judgment" (Benjamin, 807). What "was coming," this present chapter argues, was the Shoah, which Kafka obscurely, or perhaps not so obscurely, foresaw. As long as his novels remained unfinished, and as long as his stories and parables had a "cloudy spot" resisting clear-seeing interpretation, then the catastrophe would remain still "to come." Best of all would be to have those writings destroyed so they would not aid the coming of what was coming.

The biographical connections of Franz Kafka with the Shoah are well known. All Kafka's three sisters perished in the Holocaust, including his favorite sister, Ottilie (Ottla). Ottla often appears as a benign presence in Kafka's letters and diaries. She cared for him during part of his fatal illness.[9]

Other Kafka family members also died in the Shoah, as did his beloved Milena, to whom he wrote a wonderful series of letters. Kafka himself would almost certainly have met the same fate had he lived long enough. The Nazis perhaps confiscated and destroyed twenty notebooks and some letters that Kafka had left in Berlin in the apartment of his final girlfriend, Dora Diamant, when he went back with her to Czechoslovakia to die. Other authorities say Kafka burned these notebooks himself. Many of Kafka's works were published after his death through his friend Max Brod's efforts, but were included by the Nazis in 1935 in the notorious "Lists of Harmful and Undesirable Literature."

Kafka lived in Prague, in the twilight of the Austro-Hungarian Empire. As a Jew and insurance-man bureaucrat trained in the law, he experienced at first hand Czech anti-Semitism, as well as a sinister proliferation of bureaucratic institutions, both private and governmental, with their burgeoning technological apparatuses. Large-scale bureaucratization was, according to scholars like Christopher Browning, a necessary condition of the Nazi genocide. The German name of the government-supported insurance agency that Kafka worked for conjures images of such a bureaucracy. It was called *Arbeiter-Unfall-Versicherungs-Anstalt für das Königreich Böhmen* (Worker's Accident Insurance Institute for the Kingdom of Bohemia). Prague was at that point part of "the Kingdom of Bohemia." As for tele-technico-communications, the reader will remember the role of the telephone in *The Castle*, *The Trial*, and *The Man Who Disappeared* (*Amerika*). The plight of the first two novels' heroes depends on their relations to an immense, incomprehensible governmental and legal bureaucracy, with its components linked by written and transmitted documents and by telephone messages. The necessary bureaucratic, governmental, technological, and scientific conditions for the deportations and mass murders, events that occurred less than twenty years after Kafka's death, were already in place in Kafka's Prague and in his nightmarelike dramatizations of those conditions in his novels.

Kafka and Holocaust Literature

Kafka's way of writing anticipates, for example, Imre Kertész's way of writing in two fundamental ways. Kertész's novel about Auschwitz, *Fatelessness*, is the central subject of this book's third part.

Kafka, like Kertész, writes about the most horrible events in an ironic mode of black comedy. Kertész's *Fatelessness*, as I shall show, is an ironic work through and through. In the work of both Kafka and Kertész, the irony arises in part from the discrepancy between what the narrator knows and what the bewildered and innocent protagonist knows. In *Fatelessness* these two perspectives are embodied in the first-person hero-narrator, that is, in the discrepancy between what he knew then and what he knows now. As for black comedy, we are told that when Kafka read his first successful short story, "The Judgment," aloud to his friends, they laughed until the tears ran down their faces. In "The Judgment," the reader will remember, the father condemns the son to death by drowning. The son obediently goes out and drowns himself.

In a powerful moment of Orwellian or Chaplinesque comedy in *Fatelessness*, the hero-narrator imagines how the Final Solution was invented at the famous Wahnsee Conference. In an extended irony, the hero, Gyuri, says the carefully planned procedures of the bathhouses, gas chambers, and crematoria "all somehow aroused in me a sense of certain jokes, a kind of student prank."[10] Gyuri goes on to imagine the German officials thinking up one by one the gas chambers, the bathhouses, the soap, the flower beds outside, the soccer field, the soothing music, and so on, and congratulating one another for their inventiveness: "After all, people would have had to meet to discuss this, to put their heads together so to say, even if they were not exactly students but mature adults, quite possibly—indeed, in all likelihood—gentlemen in imposing suits, decorations on their chests, cigars in their mouths, presumably all in high command, who were not to be disturbed right then—that is how I imagined it" (Kertész, 111). This is chillingly close to what must actually have happened at the meeting in which the "final solution" was worked out in detail: "Some of the ideas may have provoked more prolonged discussion and amendment, whereas others would have been immediately hailed with delight, the men jumping up (I don't know why, but I insisted on their jumping up) and slapping one another's palms—this was all too readily imagined, at least as far as I was concerned. By dint of many zealous hands and much to-ing and fro-ing, the commanders' fantasy then becomes reality, and as I had witnessed, there was no room for any doubt about the stunt's success" (Kertész, 111–12).

I shall return in chapter 4 to Kertész's irony and to this passage as an example of it. This passage arouses, in me at least, the suspicion that Bush, Cheney, Rumsfeld, and their advisers in the military and in intelligence must have had similar meetings to invent Abu Ghraib, Guantánamo Bay, and the practice of "extraordinary rendition" to prisons in Egypt, Poland, and who knows where else, where prisoners were interrogated and tortured. Both Auschwitz and Abu Ghraib/Guantánamo Bay were triumphs of technological and bureaucratic inventiveness, like some monstrous student prank. The difference, of course, is that we have only "accidentally" killed or driven to suicide our prisoners, whereas the Nazis deliberately murdered millions of Jews at Auschwitz and other camps. Our interrogations, however, have as one goal, in addition to gathering intelligence, eventually imposing capital punishment, after our victims have been tortured into "confessing."[11]

A second feature of Kafka's work that foreshadows such Holocaust fictions as *Fatelessness* is the attention in these works to what might be called inconsequential detail. Such details are seen with the close-up vividness that they have in dreams and nightmares. The narrative notation of such details interrupts and defers the forward flow of the narrative toward some as yet unspecified goal. The details are inconsequential both in the sense of being trivial and in the sense of being disconnected from anything that comes before or after. Such images loom large in the spatiotemporal field of attention. They stop forward movement, perhaps for good. The intermediary becomes the blocking agent. These precisely noted details seem as if they must have some meaning or relevance, but what that might be is never specified, nor can it be inferred from the context. These details are just things that happen to be there, to be seen, heard, or felt in microscopic minutiae. They are detours or interruptions that inhibit progress toward any goal, perhaps indefinitely.

One salient example in Kafka's work is the episode of Karl Rossmann's encounter, in *Amerika*,[12] with a student in an adjacent balcony. Rossmann has gone out on the balcony of the apartment where he is imprisoned by Delamarche to see if he can identify what sort of head wound he has received in a scuffle with his captors. He soon forgets what he has come there to do and becomes fascinated by watching the student at work: "He looked silently across as the man read his book, turned the pages, occasionally looked something up in another book which he always took down with lightning speed [*mit Blitzesschnelle*], and several times jotting something down in a notebook, bending surprisingly low over it as he did."[13] Eventually Karl returns to the apartment and lies down to sleep, but is awakened by Brunelda, "who, evidently plagued by troubling dreams, tossed and turned on her bed" (die scheinbar von schweren Träumen geplagt sich auf ihrem Lager wälzte) (183e; 273g). That is the end of the chapter. Though Karl Rossmann's discussions with the student about his job search and about his imprisonment by Delamarche have some bearing on the plot, nothing is ever done to incorporate the student's reading habits into the novel's action or plot. The account of the student's behavior does not get anywhere. It just hangs there in the air, like a bridge abutment jutting out into empty space. It is inconsequential, a detour from the straight path. This detour might be interminable, a deliberate deferral by Kafka to keep from getting to "what is coming."

The last chapter of *The Man Who Disappeared*, called "The Nature Theater of Oklahoma" in Brod's invented title, though not in Kafka's manuscript, begins with Karl somehow freed from his captivity and, now in the open street, looking at a poster announcing that "at the racecourse in Clayton, today from 6 a.m. till midnight, personnel is being hired for the Theatre in Oklahoma! The Great Theatre of Oklahoma is calling you! It's calling you today only! If you miss this opportunity, there will never be another! Anyone thinking of his future, your place is with us! All welcome! Anyone who wants to be an artist [*Künstler*], step forward! We are the theatre that has a place for everyone, everyone in his place! . . . Accursed be anyone who doesn't believe us! Clayton here we come!" (202e; 295g). No way is given to get to this episode from the end of the previous fragmentary chapter, in which Karl takes Brunelda through the streets to a new dwelling place. The manuscript of that chapter ends with a word that appears to be the beginning of an incomplete sentence: "Sie" (She). The next and last chapter begins with abruptly and with discontinuous specificity, as though everything previously narrated had been utterly forgotten. This final chapter of *Der Verschollene* will be my main focus in this essay, since it most explicitly dreams the Shoah to come, as I shall show. It is perhaps worth noting at this point that that last sentence invoking a curse on those who do not believe, with its echo of the final verses of the Book of Revelation, is more than a little ominous. Moreover, the cliché about a place for everyone and everyone in his place chillingly fore-dreams not the famous "Arbeit macht frei" at the gateway to Auschwitz but the less famous, but no less horrifyingly ironic, inscription in elegant art nouveau iron letters at the gateway to Buchenwald, "Jedem das Seine," "to each his own," or, figuratively, "Everyone gets what he deserves."[14]

Another such moment in Kafka's writings is the close attention the man from the country, in "Before the Law," pays to the beard of the gatekeeper, to his nose, to his fur coat, to the fleas on the collar of that coat. The protagonist's fate depends on getting through the gate, but he pauses to look closely at things that seem to have nothing at all to do with getting on with it. These things seem impediments to the way: "The Law should be accessible to anyone at any time [*jedem und immer zugänglich sein*], he thinks, but as he now examines the doorkeeper in his fur coat more closely, his large, sharply pointed nose [*sein große Spitznase*], his long, thin, black tartar's beard, he decides he would prefer to wait until he receives permission to enter [*die Erlaubnis zum Eintritt bekommt*]. . . . He curses his unhappy fate [*Er verflucht den unglücklichen Zufall*], loudly during the first years, later, as he grows older, merely grumbling to himself. He turns childish, and since he has come to know even the fleas on the doorkeeper's collar over his years of study, he asks the fleas too to help him change the doorkeeper's mind [*bitte er auch die Flöhe ihm zu helfen und den Türhüter umzustimmen*]."[15]

This situation of endless postponement, or movement in place, through close attention, such as "realistic fiction" demands, to what is intermediary between me and my goal, is admirably expressed by juxtaposing two of Kafka's "Reflections on Sin, Pain, Hope, and the True Way":

> The road is endless, there is nothing that can be subtracted from it or added to it, and yet everyone insists on applying his own childish yardstick [*Elle*]. "Yes, you will have to go the length of that yardstick as well; it will not be forgiven you."[16]

> There is a goal, but no way; what we call the way is only wavering.[17]

I shall return to this structure of indefinite postponement in Kafka's narratives in my discussions of *The Trial* and *The Castle*. What corresponds, in Kertész's *Fatelessness*, as in other Holocaust narratives, to Kafka's attention to inconsequential detail, is the protagonists' acute noticing of what is to be seen as they are unwittingly taken, for example, to Auschwitz and to almost certain death in the gas chambers. Kertesz's Gyuri has an exceedingly sharp eye for what the warders in the camps look like, along with an ability to describe these with extreme accuracy and economy, often with the use of grotesque metaphors. Here is Gyuri's description of the prisoner and the soldier who usher the new work camp recruits, free men as they assume, into the bathhouses. This occurs just after Gyuri has unwittingly escaped the gas chambers by lying about his age and by being judged by the doctor at the *Selektion* fit for work:

> Here too a prisoner was again of assistance, an exceedingly fastidious convict, I could not help noticing. He too wore a striped outfit like other prisoners, that was true, but it had padded

> shoulders and was tapered at the waist, tailored and pressed, I would even say, in almost conspicuous conformity with the highest fashion, and just like us, free persons, he had a full head of carefully combed, darkly glossy hair. In greeting us, he stood at the opposite end of the room, and to his right, seated behind a small desk, was a soldier. The latter was very squat, of jovial appearance, and exceedingly fat, his belly beginning at his neck, his chin rippling in a circle over his collar, and no more than funny slits for eyes in his crumpled, hairless, sallow features; he put me a little in mind of those so-called dwarfs whom they had been looking for at the station [who would all have been gassed if any had come forward, as were twins, or the disabled, or Gypsies, most of them]. Nevertheless, he had an imposing cap on his head, a gleaming, evidently brand-new attaché case on the desk, and next to it what I had to admit was a beautifully crafted lash, braided from white leather, that was obviously his personal property. (Kertész, 90–91)

Gyuri "cannot help noticing," and that helps him survive by postponing his death. The similarity between Kafka's notations of inconsequential details and Kertész's notations is evident, as is the nightmare vividness generated by both. In each case, the reader suspects, the details may be signs. They may have significance. They are signs, however, that neither the protagonists nor the reader can fathom. Uncomprehending attention to them, attention generated just because they are incomprehensible (why does the doorkeeper have fleas in his collar? why does the soldier have a braided whip?), defers the horrifying understanding that will come later, at the moment of the protagonist's death or near death.

A third way Kafka's work anticipates both Holocaust fiction and Morrison's *Beloved* (the subject of this book's fourth part) is the resistance of these works to certain interpretation. This is exemplified, for example, in Joseph K.'s inconclusive argument with the priest about the meaning of the parable, "Before the Law," or in Gyuri's inability to make sense out of the way he has survived when so many others have been pitilessly killed, or in the difficulty in deciding whether Sethe, in Morrison's *Beloved*, has done the right thing when she cuts her beloved baby daughter's throat with a handsaw. A conspicuous problem with Auschwitz is that it is to a considerable degree inexplicable. How could something so awful have ever come to happen? It just does not make sense. Surely human beings, particularly citizens of a "civilized" country, could not be brought to commit evil on such a monstrous scale, even if bureaucratization and modern technologies came to make evil, in Hannah Arendt's term, borrowed from Karl Jaspers, "banal."[18]

The facts about the Holocaust have been identified in horrifying detail: the way the victims were sequestered in ghettos and then sent without foreknowledge of their fates by train to the death camps, with promise of work and benign treatment, the process of the *Selektion*, the construction of the baths, the gas chambers, the formula for Zyklon B and who manufactured it,[19] the crematoria, what it was like for those who were not gassed immediately, and so on, even including those flower beds Gyuri mentions. The sequence of events from the victims' arrival by train in Auschwitz through the *Selektion* up to the moment of their murder, as women, children, and unfit men wait unwittingly for their turn at the gas chambers was meticulously photographed.[20]

What is most horrible about these photos is that the victims still did not know what was going to happen to them in a few minutes. Like Karl Rossmann in the Oklahoma Theater fragment from *Der Verschollene*, they still believed they were entering a safe haven, a "family camp" where they would be fed, clothed, housed, educated, and given work commensurate with their training and abilities.

All this we know, but it still seems impossible that this could have happened and on such an immense scale: six million men, women, children murdered! How could that have gone on from day to day, month to month, and year to year, with bureaucratic and technological efficiency? Kertész's *Fatelessness* and my other Holocaust novels by no means explain Auschwitz. They just bear witness that it did indeed occur.

Kafka's work, notoriously, already presents similar resistances to conclusive interpretation. The fascinated reader, especially a teacher or critic, feels that he or she has an obligation to provide some explanation. That is what we are trained to do. Our collective failure is revealed in the wild discrepancies among the explanations proposed by Kafka's best and most careful readers. Some critics have proposed a biographical explanation, for example, by referring to Kafka's bad relations to his father or to the failures, for the most part, of his relations to the various women in his life. Some critics have proposed a more strictly psychoanalytic explanation, whether Freudian or Lacanian. Many critics, for example, Thomas Mann or Max Brod, have proposed a religious reading. They claim that Kafka's work is really about the search for salvation in a world in which God is distant or inaccessible. The Castle stands for unattainable grace. Other critics have related Kafka's work more narrowly to Judaism, to the Talmud, and to Kabbalah. Some critics have proposed a sociological or political interpretation. They claim that Kafka's work is to be explained by the way it reflects conditions in Prague during Kafka's lifetime and Kafka's situation as a bureaucrat and Jew in that milieu. I have already employed that explanation, for example, in my reference in the previous chapter to Kafka's *Office Writings*. Some critics, Maurice Blanchot most brilliantly, have claimed that Kafka's work is an investigation into what creative writing can do, an extreme exploration of the nature of literature. Literature's fate, the example of Kafka is said to demonstrate, is to be doomed to fail in what it attempts to do, that is, it fails to reach some transcendent goal. Many critics have tried to mix these various modes in different ways, even though they are, strictly speaking, incompatible, irreconcilable with one another. *Il faut choisir*. Even my claim that the meaning of Kafka's works is "undecidable" has its contexts and its preconceptions, though I shall, of course, try to make my way of reading as irresistibly plausible as I can. Nevertheless, any reading, in the sense of critical assessment, mine included, stops reading, in the sense of puzzling over the words, by proffering an interpretation. It passes judgment, and that is just what Kafka was aiming to make impossible with his writings.

The situation of the reader confronting Kafka's works, I am suggesting, is already like that of someone confronting the facts about Auschwitz. They just do not make sense, just as the facts about American slavery are fully ascertainable, but just do not make sense. How could we have enslaved so many African-Americans and treated them and their descendants so inhumanly, including those "Sixty Million and more" slaves who died, many on the way to America, to whom Morrison dedicates *Beloved*? Morrison perhaps emphasized this number because it is just ten times the number of Jews the Nazis are estimated to have killed. This not making sense is also represented in the best Auschwitz novels, such as *Fatelessness*, as I shall try to show for the latter.

The distinction between cognitive understanding and performative bearing witness is crucial in attempts to speak about this failure to comprehend. This failure is not to be assimilated to some negative theology. It is a human and this-worldly historical event. The name "conflagration of community" is as good a name as any for this predicament, since community togetherness, it may be argued, is a necessary condition for rational and communicable understanding. No community, no collective making sense of history, as Jean-Luc Nancy asserts. One feature of the conflagration of community, he says, in a passage already discussed in chapter 1, is that "we bear witness also to the exhaustion of thinking by way of History" (car nous témoignons aussi de l'épuisement de la pensée de l'Histoire).[21]

Kafka's Work as Prefiguration of Auschwitz

Another distinctive feature of Kafka's novels, as opposed to many of his other writings, may be read as an additional indication that they anticipate Auschwitz. This is the unfinished state of their manuscripts. Neither *Amerika*, nor *The Trial*, nor *The Castle* was ever finished. We have inherited, thanks to Max Brod's decision not to follow Kafka's strict order to burn them unread, finished chapters and fragments for all three novels but, in the cases of *Amerika* and *The Castle*, no ending, and, in the case of *The Trial*, an ending accompanied by indications of an indefinite number of intervening unwritten chapters that would have come before the end and would perhaps have endlessly deferred that end.

Why is that? Did Kafka just get bored with the work in each case? Did his attention get diverted to other writings? Did he just feel that they were failures? Did his mortal illness keep him from going further? Was there some loss of inspiration? None of these explanations seems plausible, since Kafka was able to finish many masterly short stories, parables, paradoxes, and aphorisms during the time he was not finishing the three great novels, even though those shorter works, it may be argued, are failures in the sense that they do not reveal a specifiable meaning. Their meaning is that they fail to mean.[22] Kafka went on writing almost up to his death. His life, as he said, was writing and nothing but writing: "All I am is literature, and I am not able or willing to be anything else."[23]

I claim that the explanation for the novels' unfinished state is that they fulfill Michelet's aphorism that says each epoch dreams the one to follow. Kafka's novels are uncanny premonitions of Auschwitz. They are ominous, foreboding, dreamlike anticipations of conditions for Jews under the Nazi regime, first in the ghettos, and then as they went from the trains to the *Selektion* and then, for those in the wrong line, straight to the gas chambers.

Kafka resisted finishing his novels, I assert, because the protagonist of each was going toward a monstrously unjust death. This death would happen by way of the remorseless workings of an incomprehensible bureaucracy and of a smoothly working technological apparatus. Iraqis who have done nothing wrong except to be in the wrong place at the wrong time during a "sweep," or to have been falsely accused by some informer, found themselves under the Bush regime indefinitely incarcerated, interrogated, and tortured at Abu Ghraib, Guantánamo Bay, or in some secret prison abroad. They were deprived of habeas corpus and of the right to a speedy and fair trial before a jury of their peers. They were deprived of the right to confront and challenge their accusers. That injustice has by no means even yet (2011) been rectified under Barack Obama's presidency. Such unfortunates probably feel much as Joseph K. may be imagined to have felt at the opening of *The Trial*: "Someone must have slandered Josef K., for one morning, without having done anything wrong, he was arrested" (Jemand mußte Josef K. verleumdet haben, denn ohne daß er etwas Böses getan hätte, wurde er eines Morgens verhaftet).[24]

A full reading, one by one, of the ways each of Kafka's works foreshadow Auschwitz would be possible, but it would a long business. I have already suggested some of the directions such an investigation would take, and now add several more.

Why do so many texts by Kafka express human life in terms of animal life? Among these are "The Burrow," "A Report to an Academy," "The New Lawyer," "The Metamorphosis," "The Worry of the Father of the Family," "Jackals and Arabs," "A Crossbreed," "Josefine, the Singer or The Mouse People," and "Researches of a Dog."[25] These stories are not modernized Aesopian fables. They are literal expressions of the way human life, or perhaps better, "bare life," can, in certain conditions, only be expressed as some form of animal life. These stories are not large-scale allegories or metaphors writ large—that is, not "Gregor Samsa's life is like that of a cockroach." If that were the case the reader could change the metaphor back from its vehicle to its literal tenor. Such stories are, rather, extended versions of what rhetoricians call "catachreses." They are expressions of something that has no literal name and therefore can be expressed in no other way than the one Kafka uses. An exemplary catachresis is "face of a mountain." No other way exists to name this feature of mountains, though it is not literally a face. The phrase is both literal and figurative at once, in an impossible/possible locution. Gregor Samsa is a cockroach. The reader becomes the animal making his burrow. The Nazis called the Jews "vermin" as a literal designation, not as a cruel figure of speech. As vermin they must be exterminated. Art Spiegelman in *Maus* has brilliantly made this metamorphosis visible. I shall discuss *Maus* in chapter 5.

The small-scale versions of such strange metamorphoses are those hidden multilingual puns that punctuate Kafka's works, for example, the obscure puns in many of his works on Kafka's family name and the Czech word for "jackdaw," *kavka*.[26] Kafka's father used a jackdaw as the logo for his family business as a retailer of men's and women's fancy goods and accessories. Another example is the name, so full of Slavic and other linguistic overtones, of the exceedingly strange animal-robot-machine that causes the father of the family so much worry: Odradek.[27]

Odradek adds another item to the continuum that goes from human to animal to machine. This chain makes a single agglomeration mixing human, animal, and machine, within which we more and more exist today. This is an all-inclusive realm of the "ecotechnical," to borrow a word from Jean-Luc Nancy.[28]

The Babelian features of Kafka's work will be evident especially to those who know German, Czech, and Yiddish, the three languages in which Kafka was at home. To be at home in several languages is to be a crossbreed, like the kitten-lamb in Kafka's troubling and infinitely moving little story "The Crossbreed," and so to be at home in no language. Kafka and his protagonists, human or animal, or human-animal, are always outsiders, crossbreeds. They are outside even themselves. Exemplary of this is Karl Rossmann, who, in *Amerika*, tells the recruiting officials that his name is Negro. A "Negro" in the United States is often treated as if he or she were an American, but not an American, a kitten-lamb, a crossbreed, some strange kind of animal.

The name Karl chooses for himself also foreshadows, it may be, what was to be his fate when he arrives at the Theater of Oklahoma. According to Michael Hofmann in his introduction to his translation of *Der Verschollene* (*The Man Who Disappeared*), Kafka had in "one of his sourcebooks" "a photograph labeled 'Idyll in Oklahoma' of a lynched black man surrounded by happy white faces" (xie).[29]

Kafka's choice of Oklahoma as the place of the theater toward which Karl Rossmann is journeying by train at the end of the last fragment of *Der Verschollene* may have had the sinister significance of connecting it to that photograph he possessed of a lynching in Oklahoma. Hofmann also notes, as I do, the way that train ride anticipates the *Judentransporte* to Auschwitz (xie). I shall return to this association, which I thought, naively, I might have been the first to make. Hofmann only mentions the analogy in passing, however, without following it out in detail, as I do below.

The situation of being a crossbreed, someone caught within the babble of different tongues, anticipates not only the way the Nazis treated Jews as vermin to be slaughtered. The figure of the crossbreed also figures the added pain in the camps of being among Jews from all over Europe. The prisoners, often, spoke languages that made them incomprehensible to one another. A memorial at Buchenwald gives the long list of countries from which the prisoners came, some of them, of course, not Jews, but political prisoners, Gypsies, homosexuals, and others. Kertész has his hero testify to the pain of this form of being an outsider. Ironically, Gyuri learns a new and paradoxical way to feel what it is like to be a Jew when his Yiddish-speaking fellow-inmates refuse to treat him as a Jew: "'*Di bisht nisht kai yid, d'bisht a shaygets.*' ('You're not a Jew, you're a Gentile kid.') . . . That day I learned that the discomfiture, the skin-crawling awkwardness which at times took hold between us was already familiar to me from back home, as if there had been something not quite right about me, as if I did not quite measure up to the proper ideal, in short as if I were somehow Jewish—a rather odd feeling to have after all, I reckoned, in the midst of Jews, in a concentration camp" (Kertész, 139–40). In a diary entry for January 8, 1914, Kafka wrote: "What have I in common with Jews? I have hardly anything in common with myself and should stand very quietly in a corner, content that I can breathe."[30]

Modes of Kafka's Writings: Inner Spaces

A panoramic view of Kafka's writings, with special attention, for the moment, to the shorter works and to their relation to death, shows them falling into three groups.

In some of Kafka'writings the unjust death Kafka feared and foresaw actually occurs as the climax of the story. Such texts include not only the last chapter of *The Trial*, Josef K.'s execution, which was to have been reached after an indeterminable number of unwritten or fragmentary intervening chapters, but also such works as "The Judgment," "The Starvation Artist," "The Metamorphosis," and "In the Penal Colony." In these the protagonist actually dies at the end.

In other equally characteristic and perhaps even more disturbing works, Kafka invents a situation that is, to use his own words, not death but an interminable process of dying, or, in some cases, a haunting situation of interminable imminence in relation to some infinitely threatening distant goal. "The Burrow" is one such work, as are "The Hunter Gracchus," "Building the Great Wall of China," "The Great Wall and the Tower of Babel," and "An Imperial Message." "The Burrow" breaks off unfinished in the middle of a sentence, with burrowing animal still unsure whether the other animal has heard it or not.

> Later, when I undertook experimental excavations, it might have heard me, though my style of digging makes very little noise; but if it had heard me, then I, too, would have noticed some sign of it; it would at least have had to stop work often to listen, but everything remained unchanged, the . . . (*Selected Stories*, 189)

The imperial message in "Building the Great Wall of China" will never reach its destination. The new Tower of Babel will never get built because the foundation can never be secure enough. "The Hunter Gracchus" ends with what are, for me, among Kafka's most chilling words, words that make your hair stand on end. Gracchus, you will remember, has died, but something has gone wrong with his journey to the afterworld. I cite both the translation and the German original, since the German is even more unsettling, particularly the last sentence as well as the sentence about moving up and down, left and right, on that infinitely wide stairway:

> "My death barge went off course, a wrong turn of the tiller, the momentary inattentiveness of the boatman, a distraction by my beautiful homeland, I don't know what it was. . . . I am always on the grand staircase . . . that leads up to it ["it" refers to what Kafka calls the hereafter (*das Jenseits*)]. On this infinitely wide and open stairway I drift, now toward the top, now toward the bottom, now to the right, now to the left, always in motion. . . . I am here, that's all I know, that's all I can do. My barge has no tiller, it is driven by the wind that blows in the nethermost regions of death." (*Selected Stories*, 111, 112)

> "Mein Todeskahn verfehlte die Fahrt, eine falsche Drehung des Steuers, ein Augenblick der Unaufmerksamkeit des Führers, eine Ablenkung durch meine wunderschöne Heimat, ich weiß nicht was es war. . . . Ich bin . . . immer auf der großen Treppe die hinaufführt. Auf dieser unendlich weiten Freitreppe treibe ich mich herum, bald oben bald unten, bald rechts bald links, immer in Bewegung. . . . Ich bin hier, mehr weiß ich nicht, mehr kann ich nicht tun. Mein Kahn ist ohne Steuer, er fährt mit dem Wind der in den untersten Regionen des Todes bläst."[31]

A third category of Kafka's writings is those parables, aphorisms, reflections, or twisted proverbs that so stick in the mind, two of which I have already cited. Their chief characteristic is to create out of words a little machine, a brief formulation turned back on itself like a hedghog, in impenetrable self-enclosure. Each such formulation creates an endless feedback loop, a miniature infinity or double bind of an interminable circling that both creates *jouissance*, the joyful miniature explosion of seeing the point of a joke, and at the same time distressingly baffles mastery by dialectical reason. These little linguistic bombs often juxtapose incompatible proverbs or received ideas to produce an implosion defying either saying yes or saying no: "One must not cheat anybody, not even the world of its triumph."[32] Well, of course, you say, it is wrong to cheat anybody, and it sounds reasonable to give the world a triumphant last say, but when you put these two ideas together something both funny and scandalous emerges, something that sticks in the mind as an obstacle to further thinking. Here is one more, out of so many: "Don't despair, not even over the fact that you don't despair" (*Diaries*, 224).

These three forms of Kafka's writing are, each in a different way, impossible attempts simultaneously to write death and to hold off death by writing, to keep death from happening. They ward off confrontation with the disaster that Kafka nevertheless obscurely foresaw.

The three great incomplete novels are large-scale assemblages of words that combine in different mixtures all three of these essential Kafkaesque relations to death. My readings of *The Trial* and *The Castle* will demonstrate some of these mixtures, as does my reading below of the last two fragments of *The Man Who Disappeared*. I end this section, however, by observing that each of Kafka's writings generates in the reader the sense of a specific imaginary inner space or of imaginary spaces, mises-en-scène within which the events take place. In the novels and stories, those sequences culminate, most often, but not always, in the protagonists' encounters with some person or other, often unexpectedly met. The protagonist then holds a conversation with that person, sometimes a virtually interminable one. These encounters are often reached by solitary movement through a characteristically Kafkaesque space of streets, corridors, stairways, doorways, basements, attics. Odradek, the strange little machine-animal-person in "Die Sorge des Hausvaters" ("The Worry of the Father of the Family") haunts stairways, hallways, landings, the attic, and the basement in the family house. He tells the *Hausvater* that he has "no permanent residence [*unbestimmter Wohnsitz*]."[33]

These inner spaces Kafka describes are real enough for the protagonists, but they have a hallucinatory, ominous, dreamlike quality that contributes as much as the always slightly wacky, off-base, or foreboding dialogue to the atmosphere that readers think of as distinctively Kafkaesque. That atmosphere might be defined as the reader's feeling that something very bad is always just about to happen, or has always already happened, even though the protagonist may not know it, though he (it is always a he) suspects. Josef K.'s condemnation and execution is a foregone conclusion, though he has done nothing wrong. The relation of this foreboding to the way Kafka's works are premonitions of Auschwitz is evident. My claim is that what used to be called "setting" is an important generator or objective correlative of this feeling of ominous imminence in Kafka's work. The protagonists' experiences of getting lost could even be called a Kafkaesque phenomenological cogito, in the sense George Poulet appropriates that Cartesian term in *Études sur le temps humain* (*Studies in Human Time*), and in other works.[34] Not "I think, therefore I am," but "I am lost, therefore I am, and everything in my life follows from that inaugural event."

I shall in the course of my readings of Kafka's three novels identify different versions of this important recurrent mise-en-scène: the protagonist's solitary, anxious hurrying through a labyrinthine interior that leads finally to a door which, when it opens, lead the hero to a surprising encounter with a stranger. I have briefly discussed, in chapter 1, Deleuze and Guattari's claim that Kafka's works are rhizomatic. A paradigm for this is "The Burrow." To say Kafka's works are rhizomorphic is true enough. To assert this, however, is implicitly to claim the power of a sovereign panoramic mapping that Kafka's works rarely explicitly provide, though the reader may impute or infer such a spread-out spatial design to the work's inner space. The concept of "inner space," by the way, is extremely problematic. The words on the page generate an interior space within the imagination of the reader, probably a somewhat different one for every reader. Just where does that inner space exist? What is it made of? How would one verify it or transmit it to another person? Most often, however, in the leitmotif in Kafka I am identifying, no sovereign panoramic mapping is given. The protagonist and the reader, rather, are lost in a bewildering labyrinth of corridors that do not seem to be leading anywhere until suddenly a door is opened and someone is met face to face. Here are two examples of this in *The Man Who Disappeared*.

In "The Stoker," the first written section of *The Man Who Disappeared*, Karl Rossmann reaches New York by ship and is about to disembark, with his sutitcase on his shoulder. Suddenly he remembers that he has forgotten his umbrella (an event Freud would have had no trouble interpreting). He leaves his suitcase with a friend and goes back into the ship to retrieve the missing object. That is when his troubles begin:

> [Karl] took a quick look around for his subsequent orientation, and hurried off. Below deck, he found to his annoyance that a passage that would have considerably shortened the way for him was for the first time barred, probably something to do with the fact that all the passengers were disembarking, and so he was forced instead to make his way through numerous little rooms, along continually curving passages and down tiny flights

> of stairs, one after the other, and then through an empty room with an abandoned desk in it until, eventually, only ever having gone this way once or twice previously, and then in the company of others, he found that he was totally and utterly lost [*ganz und gar verirrt*]. Not knowing what to do, not seeing anyone, and hearing only the scraping of thousands of human feet overhead and the last, faraway wheezings of the engine, which had already been turned off, he began without thinking to knock at the little door to which he had come in his wanderings. "It's open," came a voice from within, and Karl felt real relief as he opened the door. (3–4e; 9–10g)

This opening door leads to Karl's talk with the stoker, which leads to their confrontation with the captain, which leads to Karl's meeting in the captain's cabin with his Uncle Jakob, a senator, to the quasi-miraculous recovery of his suitcase and umbrella, and so to all his adventures in America. Those adventures, I am claiming, all happen under the aegis of this initial experience of getting lost. Getting lost in this particular way is a recurrent primal, inaugurative scene in Kafka's novels.

Versions of this experience recur here and there throughout *The Man Who Disappeared*, as in Kafka's other two incomplete novels. Such scenes are a leitmotif the careful reader comes to expect. The reader thinks, "Here comes another one," as does the listener to a Wagner opera when a leitmotiv recurs. I shall identify examples, each different from the others in form and function, from *The Trial* and *The Castle* in my chapters on those novels, and, in later chapters, from my Holocaust novels. I adduce now just one more case from *The Man Who Disappeared.* Karl visits Mr. Pollunder at his country house outside New York. It is an enormous unfinished labyrinthine mansion, with a cold draft blowing through its corridors from areas still under construction. After an interminable formal dinner, Pollunder's daughter Klara leads Karl to his room, though she invites him to hers. Note that Klara is a feminine anagram of Karl. In his bedroom she bests him in a strange wrestling match that is also, to Karl's half-aware horror, an aggressive sexual overture. " 'Why is she sighing like that,' thought Karl, 'it can't be hurting her, I'm not pressing at all,' and he didn't let go" (46e). After expertly grappling with him, Klara lays Karl out on a sofa and nearly chokes him to death. When Klara finally goes to her own room, Karl escapes into the corridor, where he promptly gets lost trying to find his way out of the house. Eventually he encounters an old retainer with a lantern. That fortunate meeting initiates the climatic conversation that is a feature of this recurrent mise-en-scène. The scene of Karl's wandering goes on for several pages. Here are excerpts:

> In the passageway Karl found that he had to contend with a draught—naturally he had turned left, away from Klara's door—that was quite weak, but still well capable of extinguishing the candle, so that Karl had to shield the flame with his hand, and also to stop at intervals to allow the guttering light to recover. He made slow progress, and the way back seemed to be twice as long. Karl passed great stretches of wall that had no doors at all, so that one couldn't imagine what lay behind them. Then it was one door after another, he tried several of them, but they were all locked, and the rooms evidently unoccupied. It was an extraordinary waste of space. . . . Suddenly the wall on one side of the corridor came to an end, and was replaced by an ice-cold marble balustrade. Karl put the candle down on it and carefully leaned forward. Empty darkness blew towards him. If this was the entrance hall of the house—by the light of the candle he saw what seemed to be a bit of vaulted ceiling—why hadn't they come in through it? What was this large and lofty room for? It was like standing in the gallery of a church up here. . . . The balustrade did not go on for very long, and soon Karl was swallowed up by the enclosed corridor again. Suddenly it made a sharp turn and Karl walked smack into a wall. . . . As the corridor seemed never ending, without a window anywhere and no sign of movement either high or low, it occurred to Karl that he was going round in a circle, he hoped to come upon the open door of his room soon, but neither that nor the balustrade returned. . . . He was just about to halloo loudly down the corridor in both directions, when he saw, from where he had come, a small light coming ever nearer [*ein kleines sich näherndes Licht*]. (48e, 50e; 77–78g, 79g)

The Man Who Disappeared Disappears

I end this chapter by turning to what, somewhat paradoxically, is the most explicit premonition of Auschwitz in all Kafka's writings. This is the last-written section of the work by him that most overtly dreams the epoch of the Shoah and World War II that was about to follow post–World War I Europe. Auschwitz was hovering already like a looming light coming ever nearer. Kafka's genius is to have foreseen this catastrophe, to have written endless texts that are obscure premonitions of what it would be like, while at the same time resisting with all his might, though unsuccessfully, his foreboding.

The text I have in mind is the two final fragments of *Amerika*, or *The Man Who Disappeared*, or *Missing* (*Der Verschollene*). The final fragments are joined and called, in the old Edwin Muir translation, "The Nature Theater of Oklahoma," though the word "nature" is Brod's invention, and Kafka did not give the fragments any titles at all.

Choosing these fragments seems paradoxical, because critics since Max Brod have seen *Amerika* as Kafka's comic novel, a novel, as Kafka himself said, modeled on Dickens. Hartmut Binder, in his *Kafka-Commentar*, however, takes a quite different view, one closer to my own reading.[35] "*Amerika* is unique in being Kafka's only novel in a comic vein," says the back cover of the old New Directions paperback edition of the now-outdated Muir translation.[36] Whoever wrote that must have had a somewhat odd idea of the "comic vein." I find the Brunelda segments, for example, nightmarish, not comic at all, or only grotesquely comic in their misogynist presentations of a distasteful female body and male enslavement to it. Brunelda is "la belle dame sans merci" grown old and excessively fat. Read for yourself and see. *The Trial* and *The Castle* have their comic sides too, after all, as does even "The Judgment," but none of these works strike me as primarily comic, except perhaps in the grim way Chaplin's *Modern Times* is comic. Max Brod, Kafka's close friend, but not an entirely trustworthy reader of Kafka, encourages this mistake in what he says in the "Afterword" to his original edition. "He worked at it with unending delight," says Brod, "mostly in the evenings and late into the night; the pages show amazingly few corrections and deletions. Kafka knew quite well, and discussed the fact, that this novel was more optimistic and 'lighter' in mood than any of his other writings" (*Amerika*, Muir trans., 298).

Critics have also, no doubt, been misled by what Brod claimed Kafka told him about the planned conclusion of *Amerika*, namely, that it would be a "happy ending," just as Brod claimed Kafka told him *The Castle* was to end with K. on his deathbed getting permission to stay and work in the village at the foot of the Castle mount, though as what we would these days call a "guest worker." This is the privilege proposed, though not yet granted, for our twelve million illegal immigrants in the United States: "He was not to relax in his struggle, but was to die worn out by it. Round his death-bed the villagers were to assemble, and from the Castle itself the word was to come that though K.'s legal claim to live in the village was not valid, yet, taking certain auxiliary circumstances into account, he was to be permitted to live and work there."[37] Not much of a happy ending there. In the death of the hero this side of his goal, it echoes the ending of Kafka's "Before the Law." Here is what Brod says about the planned ending of *Amerika*:

> Kafka broke off his work on this novel with unexpected suddenness. It remained unfinished. From what he told me I know that the incomplete chapter about the Nature Theater of Oklahoma (a chapter the beginning of which particularly delighted Kafka, so that he used to read it aloud with great effect) was intended to be the concluding chapter of the work and should end on a note of reconciliation. In enigmatic language Kafka used to hint smilingly, that within this "almost limitless" theater his young hero was going to find again a profession, a stand-by, his freedom, even his old home and his parents, as if by some celestial witchery. (*Amerika,* Muir trans., 299)

"Celestial witchery" indeed! I suspect that Kafka did say these things to Brod about these two novels, but that he said them to protect his friend from the darker truths of the goals toward which both novels were bound. Kafka, it may be, thought, correctly, that Brod was not capable of facing the truth about Kafka's writings, though his command to Brod to destroy all his manuscripts ought to have tipped Brod off. Brod consistently sentimentalizes Kafka's writings. He gives them a happier, more positive glow than they actually have, as in a remark about "the way," apropos of what Brod says Kafka told him about his planned ending for *The Castle*. Brod's formulation, comparing *The Castle* to Goethe's *Faust*, is certainly not congruent with the aphorism I have cited from Kafka about the absence of a way, about our condemnation to eternal "wavering":

> Certainly K. is a Faust in deliberately modest, even needy trappings, and with the essential modification that he is driven on not by a longing for the final goals of humanity, but by a need for the most primitive requisites of life, the need to be rooted in a home and a calling, and to become a member of a community. At the first glance this difference seems very great, but becomes considerably less so when one recognizes that for Kafka those primitive goals have religious significance, and are simply the right life, the right way (*Tao*). (*The Castle*, Muir trans., 330)

Who can blame Brod for softening things? The endpoints toward which Karl Rossmann and K. are rushing are almost intolerable to confront. If I am right, that would explain why Kafka broke off the writing of *Amerika* with "unexpected suddenness," and why *The Castle* manuscript ends in the middle of a sentence about a peripheral character, Gerstäcker's mother: "It was difficult to understand her, but what she said."[38] *The Castle* ends with a wavering, a wandering off the track. In an earlier important episode, K. falls asleep just as Bürgel, secretary to a Castle official, is promising K. access to the Castle itself. Kafka flinched from finishing *The Castle*. His pen dropped from his hand, "with unexpected suddenness."

Just how does the final fragment of the several about the Theater of Oklahoma uncannily anticipate Auschwitz? In the blank space between the previous fragment, called "Brunelda's Departure" (which describes Karl pushing Brunelda in a handcart through the streets to a new apartment), and the Theater of Oklahoma fragments, Karl Rossman has somehow escaped from his servitude to Brunelda, Delamarche, and Robinson.[39] Now in the open street, he reads the placard, already cited, announcing that on that day alone the Theater of Oklahoma is offering jobs, with a place for everyone (202e). Karl focuses on the sentence "All welcome!" He repeats it over and over to himself like a mantra. Karl, like so many in the United States today, has been trying unsuccessfully ever since he came to America to find a steady job, a secure place in American society. When he takes the train to the racecourse at Clayton to apply, as the placard invites people to do, he finds a strange scene, one of Kafka's most dreamlike visions. It is a prophetic dream, I am arguing, of the epoch to come. This dreamlike vision is accompanied by exceedingly odd conversations between Karl and the people he finds there. Young women in white robes with costume wings stand on high pillars and blow trumpets. (I kid you not!) One is Karl's friend Fanny, from whom he gets some information about the theater—for example, that its officials travel all over the country hiring people. A young man and his wife, the latter pushing a baby carriage, seem to be the chief applicants so far, though a crowd of boys is also present. Many more applicants arrive later. Behind the trumpet blowers, in the racecourse proper, officials are lining up applicants, selecting them, and interviewing them at different tables for different kinds of jobs, none of them acting jobs, strangely enough, if it is really a theater. The top official, who presides over Karl's final interrogation, wears "a broad white silk sash that said: 'Leader of the 10th Promotional Team [*Werbetruppe*] of the Theater of Oklahoma' " (211e; 308g).

Karl is distracted from answering the questions he is posed by a second high official through his fascination with the slender tapping fingers of the "Leader of the 10th Promotional Team": "These delicate and yet sinewy fingers, long and in rapid motion, occasionally distracted Karl, in spite of the fact that the other gentleman was really sufficiently taxing on his own" (Diese zarten und doch kräftigen, langen und schnell bewegten Finger lenkten zeitweilig Karls Aufmerksamkeit auf such trotzdem ihn der andere Herr genug in Anspruch nahm) (211e; 308g). This is another good example of the distracting attention to apparently meaningless detail. Those fingers are somehow sinister and menacing, like the fingers of an SS officer holding a whip while supervising a death camp, as in those unbearable photographs of a *Selektion* I have mentioned. Karl gives his name as Negro. This was "his nickname [*Rufname*] on his last jobs" (210e; 306g). Karl designates himself not with a proper name, but with a category, a general name, not a unique personal name. The official is scandalized: "His name is not Negro" (210e; 307g), he says, but Karl is nevertheless hired under that name.

Significantly, for my purposes, Karl applies to himself the name of the lowest stratum in American society, the group name that most closely approximates the term "Jew" as used in Europe in the years leading up to the Shoah. I say this is significant for my purposes in part because it makes an anticipatory link from Kafka to Morrison's *Beloved*, the topic of the third part of this book. As Jews were in Europe, so were blacks in America. I have mentioned earlier Kafka's possession of the photograph of a lynched black man surrounded by smiling white spectators labeled "Idyll in Oklahoma," a phrase close to "Theater of Oklahoma."

A telephone is in place on the master recruiter's desk for sending information from one selection table to another. The name and trade of each applicant who is hired is hoisted by some kind of whirring machine to a bulletin board. These details exemplify what I said earlier about bureaucracy and technology as prerequisites for the Shoah. Karl is hired, in spite of his total lack of preparation and his lack of identity papers, apparently just because he says he wants to be an engineer, or perhaps just because he looks strong and fit for work, just as Kertrész's Gyuri is saved at the *Selektion* in Auschwitz for perhaps similar reasons. In Kafka's scene, the phrase "Negro, Technical Worker [*Negro, technischer Arbeiter*]" appears eventually on the announcement board (213e; 311g).

Karl soon finds himself with many others on a train bound for the Theater of Oklahoma. This happens after all the recruits are fed a big meal at a long table with a white tablecloth and then immediately herded at a run from the racecourse to the train station, including the man and his wife with their baby in a perambulator, just as Jews were made to run through the streets to the trains for Auschwitz. A final fragment describes a two-day train journey to the theater in Oklahoma across what Kafka seems to have imagined American landscape was like, though it recalls to me more train rides over the Alps in Europe.

The term "nature theater" in Max Brod's title should give the reader pause. "Nature theater" does not make sense. It is an absurd oxymoron. A theater is always the place of artifice, of make-believe, of shows. There is nothing natural about a theater. A "nature theater" could only be a place that tries to camouflage the theatrical as if it were natural. Brod's invented title falsifies the fragment, which says nothing about "nature" in Oklahoma. Why "theater"? I suggest it is another sinister foreshadowing of the Shoah. None of the applicants to the Theater of Oklahoma are hired as actors, but as "technical workers," "lift boys," or "businessmen," and so on, but they are all unwittingly actors in a farcical but deadly scam. Karl ought to have been tipped off by the one picture of the Theater of Oklahoma that makes it to his end of the table at the big feast before the train ride. It shows in detail the theater where Abraham Lincoln was assassinated. Scholars of the mass exterminations at Auschwitz have emphasized the careful "dramaturgy" with which the SS choreographed the process, partly in order to lull the victims into thinking they were actors in a benignly preprogrammed sequence that would lead them to what they had been promised: a resettlement where each person would have a home, a place, and work suitable to his or her qualifications. Jean-Luc Nancy, in the essay referred to earlier, "Forbidden Representation," comments on this theatrical aspect of the Nazi atrocities: "The entire organization of the camp works toward this representation of the self [that is, in Nancy's analysis, discussed in chapter 6, the self of the SS men] to others and to oneself: the entire dramaturgy of the arrival on the ramp, the selection, the roll calls, the uniforms and the speeches, the slogans on the gates, 'work is liberty' [*Arbeit macht frei*] or 'to each his due' [*Jedem das Seine*], etc." ("FR," 42).[40]

The last fragment, only two paragraphs long, concludes with one of Kafka's most haunting images of a perhaps insignificant detail seen with hallucinatory vividness: the waterfalls Karl sees through the train window. It is a detail, moreover, that expresses continuous unfinished and interminable movement, so important a structural feature of Kafka's work generally, as in the ending of "The Hunter Gracchus," cited earlier, or in the "ending" of the unfinished story "The Burrow." Here is the last paragraph of all. I give both the English and German, since the precision and detail of the German original is important and not easily translated:

> On the first day they traveled over a high mountain range. Blue-black formations of rock approached the train in sharp wedges, they [Karl and his friend Giacomo] leaned out of the window and tried in vain to see their peaks, narrow dark cloven valleys opened, with a finger they traced the direction in which they disappeared, broad mountain streams came rushing like great waves on their hilly courses, and, pushing thousands of little foaming wavelets ahead of them, they plunged under the bridges over which the train passed, so close that the chill breath of them made the face shudder. (218e, trans. altered)

> Am ersten Tag fuhren sie durch ein hohes Gebirge. Bläulich-schwarze Steinmassen giengen in spitzen Keilen bis an den Zug heran, man beugte sich aus dem Fenster und suchte vergebens ihre Gipfel, dunkle schmale zerrissene Täler öffneten sich, man beschrieb mit dem Finger die Richtung, in der sie sich verloren, breite Bergströme kamen eilend als große Wellen auf dem hügeligen Untergrund und in sich tausend kleine Schaumwellen treibend, sie stürzten sich unter die Brücken über die der Zug fuhr und sie waren so nah daß der Hauch ihrer Kühle das Gesicht erschauern machte. (318g)[41]

That's it, the last words Kafka wrote of this magical novel: "so close that the chill breath of them made the face shudder" (so nah daß der Hauch ihrer Kühle das Gesicht erschauern machte). I claim these last unfinished fragments of *Amerika*, or *The Man Who Disappeared*, are an chillingly accurate foreshadowing of the process by which Jews—men, women, and children—were rounded up in the ghettos, lulled with promises of good work, generous treatment, and a safe haven, hurried through the streets to the train station, and then taken by train to Auschwitz, many of them to be gassed immediately, the rest, for the most part, to be killed by inches through starvation and hard labor. Only a few, such as Kertész's hero and Kertész himself, or Elie Wiesel, or Primo Levi, miraculously survived to tell their stories, whether in memoirs or in fictional transpositions. Kafka's account matches amazingly, for example, the account Kertész gives in *Fatelessness* of how Gyuri came to find himself in Auschwitz, and the ironically and sinisterly named "Theater of Oklahoma" even has resonances, as I have said, with the theatrical aspect of the trip to the camps and of the exterminations there, including the infamous *Arbeit macht frei* over the gateway to Auschwitz.

It is as though Kafka were indeed dreaming the epoch to come, in fulfillment of Michelet's aphorism, when he wrote that last chapter of *The Man Who Disappeared*, and when he wrote his other work too. Though of course I do not believe in telepathic foreshadowings, any more than did Freud and Derrida, so they claimed, nevertheless it almost seems as though Kafka must have had some occult telepathic premonition of what the genocide would be like, though he got the details sometimes a little garbled, for example, by putting the *Selektion* before the train ride rather than in the camp itself, where it happened just before many new arrivals were gassed.[42]

Are these final fragments of *Der Verschollene* and the other premonitions of Auschwitz I have identified in Kafka's work no more than fortuitous analogies? After all, Max Brod assures the reader that Kafka told him *The Man Who Disappeared* was to have a happy ending. Karl Rossmann was to have got back everything he had lost. I have given the reasons why I much doubt that this was to have been the case. I have noted that Michael Hofmann in his introduction to his new translation discreetly agrees with my darker reading of the novel (ix–xi), and supports it with references to Harmut Binder's *Kafka-Kommentar* as offering another version of this darker reading.

The first chapter of *Der Verschollene*, "The Stoker," is the only part of *The Man Who Disappeared* published during Kafka's lifetime. It opens with Karl Rossmann's view of the Statue of Liberty holding aloft not a torch, but a sword. This odd mistake might give the reader pause. That sword may be a foreboding of something that may happen to Karl Rossmann in the Land of the Free. As Karl looks at the statue from the liner that is bringing him to America, "he suddenly saw the Statue of Liberty, which had already been in view for some time, as though in an intenser sunlight. The sword in her hand seemed only just to have been raised aloft, and the unchained winds blew about her form" (3e). "A sudden burst of sunshine seemed to illumine the Statue of Liberty, so that he saw it in a new light, although he had sighted it long before. The arm with its sword rose up as if newly stretched aloft, and round the figure blew the free winds of heaven" (*Amerika*, Muir trans., 3).[43]

The winds are free. They have liberty. The statue's sword, however, seems to promise something quite different from freedom for those who immigrate to the United States. Kafka's phrasing seems based on a distinction between the free winds of nature and a social order that is governed by violence. America lives by the sword. Against Brod's promise of a happy ending for *Missing*, I set this decisive entry in Kafka's diaries for September 29, 1915: "Rossmann and K., the innocent and the guilty, both executed without distinction in the end, the guilty one with a gentler hand, more pushed aside than struck down" *(Diaries*, 343–44).[44] So much for Brod's happy ending! I claim that the "unexpected suddenness" with which Kafka broke off writing *Der Verschollene* may well have been a resistance to writing out the "execution" that awaited Karl Rossmann when he arrived at the Theater of Oklahoma, just as the gas chambers awaited those many millions who took the train ride to Auschwitz under the impression that they were on the way to a happy family settlement with work for everyone. Kafka, I suggest, may have feared that his words, once written, would performatively, on their own, mechanically, bring about some version of what they name. That refraining, in the event, failed to keep Auschwitz from happening.

At the end of *The Trial*, Josef K.'s last word and last thought, after his executioners stab him to death, expresses a wish to have the "verdict" (a speech act and a murder at the same time) survive after his death:

> Where was the judge he'd never seen? Where was the high court he'd never reached? He raised his hands and spread out his fingers.
>
> But the hands of one man were right at K.'s throat, while the other thrust the knife into his heart and turned it there twice. With failing sight K. saw how the men drew near his face, leaning cheek-to-cheek to observe the verdict [*die Entscheidung*]. "Like a dog!" he said; it seemed as though the shame was to outlive him. ["*Wie ein Hund!*" *sagte er, es war, als sollte die Scham ihn überleben.*] (*T*, 231; *P*, 312)

The shame outlives him only through the words on the page. Brod disobeyed Kafka by not destroying those words. In an analogous way, the six million Jews murdered in the camps can only be remembered by way of some testimony or other. Can one distinguish among foreseeing Auschwitz, foretelling it, performatively helping to bring it about, and bearing witness to it proleptically, before the fact? I would like to be able to make such distinctions, but I am not sure it is possible. Later chapters of this book will pursue this investigation.

3 The Breakdown of Community and the Disabling of Speech Acts in Kafka's *The Trial*

In memory of Tinka, a cat

Man muß das Geständnis machen. Machen Sie doch bei nächster Gelegenheit das Geständnis. Erst dann ist die Möglichkeit zu entschlüpfen gegeben, erst dann.
Leni's advice to Josef K., ***in Franz Kafka, Der Proceß***[1]

All you can do is confess. Confess the first chance you get. That's the only chance you have to escape, the only one. **Franz Kafka,** ***The Trial***[2]

There is a goal, but no way; what we call the way is only wavering.
Franz Kafka, "Reflections on Sin, Pain, Hope, and the True Way"[3]

The Contemporaneity of The Trial

What is the role of this chapter in the overall argument of this book?[4] The center of this book is the question of whether or not the Holocaust can be testified to by way of fictional works. Also essential is my claim that literary work can be seen in retrospect to have had a prophetic ability to foreshadow events to come. We read, or ought to read, old works, at least some of them, in terms of the way "each epoch dreams the one to follow." As I have argued in the second chapter here, Kafka's work can be seen as a premonition of Auschwitz. It also foreshadows features of our detainees' present-day situation in Guantánamo Bay and elsewhere. In just what way can *Der Proceß* be seen as "apocalyptic" in the etymological sense of unveiling a then-hidden future? As I shall show in my account, two features of *Der Proceß* are especially salient in this regard.

One is its resistance to coherent, totalizing, hermeneutic interpretation. Shosana Felman argues, in her now classic essay on Claude Lanzmann's *Shoah*, that this great film, made as it is of a metonymic series of videoed testimonies by victims, perpetrators, and bystanders of the Shoah, resists totalizing understanding. It does not hang together as a whole. This, Felman claims, says something fundamental about the Shoah. It forbids comprehensive comprehension. "The occurrence [of the Shoah]," says Felman, "is conveyed precisely by this fragmentation of the testimonies, which enact the fragmentation of the witnessing. The film is a gathering of the fragments of the witnessing. But the collection of the fragments does not yield, even after ten hours of the movie, any possible totality or any possible totalization: the gathering of testimonial incommensurates does not amount either to a generalizable theoretical statement or a narrative monologic sum."[5]

The reader of *Der Proceß* is in a situation similar to that of the viewer of Lanzmann's *Shoah*. The novel is incomplete and, one can argue, in principle was impossible to complete. Its unfinished state is not an accident. *Der Proceß* is made up of a series of chapters, some of them literally fragments. The series seems only somewhat arbitrarily ordered in the printed text. What we have stops short before a potentially infinite number of unwritten chapters that would have been inserted before the final chapter and then skips over to the final chapter, which describes Josef K.'s execution. The chapters are most often given titles that are names of characters or their professions, if flogging is a profession ("Frau Grubach," "Fräulein Bürstner," "The Student," "The Flogger," "The Uncle," "Leni," "Lawyer," "Manufacturer," "Painter," "Block," and so on). These characters serve as intermediaries whom Josef K. confronts and through whom he attempts to reach the court, identify the crime for which he has been arrested, and get on with the legal work of exonerating himself.

A single encompassing witness, the imperturbable, even-toned, faintly ironic narrator, speaks or writes all the chapters of *The Trial*. Kafka's third-person narrator is in this like Lanzmann as omnipresent effaced filmmaker, narrator, and interrogator in the interviews that make up his film. The various persons Josef K. encounters play roles similar to those of the witnesses Lanzmann interviews in *Shoah*. The chapters of *Der Proceß* accumulate uncertainty rather than adding up to growing comprehension. *Der Proceß* tells the story of a process (*Proceß* is the German word for a legal trial) that does not proceed. It just turns in place, until that leap over a potentially infinite gap to the execution at the end. *Der Proceß* narrates the "trial," in the sense of unrelieved suffering, that leads Josef K. not to a fair trial according to accepted institutional procedures of law and order, but to an execution that, in a monstrous absurdity, precedes the verdict. The reader remains as much in the dark at the end as Josef K. himself, as little able to make totalizing sense of what he has endured.

The other salient way in which *Der Proceß* anticipates the Shoah (and the situation of our "detainees" today) is Josef K.'s life experience of a horribly unjust social structure. It is a society lacking a viable legal system and lacking any community solidarity that would validate speech acts, legal ones and otherwise. What happens to Josef K. is entirely irregular and horrifyingly unjust when measured against any conceivable just legal system. In that it is like the experience of slaves in the pre–Civil War United States. It is also like the experience of African-Americans in the United States even after emancipation. They suffered lynching, voting disenfranchisement, and every conceivable kind of discrimination. Nor has this entirely stopped even today. Far from it. Josef K.'s experience is also like that of Jews under Hitler. They were herded into ghettos, shipped to concentration camps, and then murdered "like dogs," to borrow Josef K.'s expression at the moment of his death. Josef K.'s experience is also analogous to that of our detainees from the wars in Iraq and Afghanistan. They have been arrested often only because they happened to be in the wrong place at the wrong time. They have been imprisoned indefinitely without habeas corpus, without access to a speedy and fair trial, without the right to confront their accusers. They have been tortured into making often false confessions, refused release, and driven to suicidal despair. Something not altogether different, I am sorry to say, seems to operate today in the People's Republic of China, at least in some trials. The parents of an American "ecoterrorist," Justin Franchi Solondz, wanted in the United States, who hid out in the mountains of Yunnan Province in China until he was arrested there for manufacturing drugs, were not permitted to see their son's indictment until after his trial and conviction. He was sentenced to three years in prison.[6] This parallels Josef K.'s inability to learn what crime he is accused of committing, though the young man in China may have seen his indictment. But why not let the parents know it?

The United States, even under President Obama, is not all that much better. The existence even today of a Special Operations "Black Jail" at the Bagram Air Base in Afghanistan, along with another at the Balad

Air Base in Iraq, was not long ago reported (November 2009). Afghans who have been released testify that they have been held incommunicado for weeks at a time in windowless concrete cells lit by a single light bulb glowing twenty-four hours a day. They see no one except during the twice-daily interrogations. Their families do not know where they are, or whether they are alive or dead. No civilians, including International Red Cross officials, are allowed access to them. Most are eventually released without charge. There are no plans to close these jails, but the Obama administration did in August, 2009, restrict the time that detainees could be held in these jails to two weeks, whereas earlier some detainees were held for months.[7] I do not know the situation there now (2011).

An op-ed piece by Bob Herbert in the *New York Times* for June 30, 2009, "How Long Is Long Enough?" gives details about one detainee in the Afghanistan War, Mohammed Jawad. Afghan forces seized Jawad in Kabul in 2002 when he was twelve, fourteen, or sixteen—at any rate, as a teenager. His exact age was uncertain. He was then turned over to the Americans. He was accused of having thrown a grenade that seriously injured two American soldiers and a third person. He was tortured both at the Bagram prison in Afghanistan and later on in Guantánamo Bay. A confession was forced from him. After enough torture almost anyone will admit to almost anything. The evidence against Jawad has been discredited. He has tried to commit suicide by butting his head against the wall. The U.S Army officer assigned to prosecute him removed himself from the case, and a later prosecutor found out details about his torture. And yet he still remained in custody at least until June, 2009, although he was released and returned to Afghanistan in August, 2009.[8]

The suspension of law and order, especially for Jews, under Nazi rule has been described in detail by many survivor testimonies. These include many accounts of the knock on the door by the Gestapo, the arrest and "disappearance" of some or all of the family, the confiscation of their possessions and of their apartment or house. Elegant apartments in a Jewish section of Berlin became, for example, dwellings for high Nazi officials after their owners had been deported and killed in the camps. Each of these experiences of illicit arrest and eventual murder was unique, but one fictionalized example appears early in Imre Kertész's *Fatelessness*, discussed in detail in chapter 6 of this book. Gyuri, the teenage first-person narrator of this novel, is arrested one fine day, soon after his father has been sent to a labor camp in Austria, Mauthausen, where he eventually dies. Gyuri, with his usual understated irony, describes his arrest as "a slightly odd experience."[9] He is on the bus that takes him to work every day. The bus is stopped. All the Jewish passengers are asked to get off. The Hungarian police detain them and then eventually turn them over to the German occupiers of Hungary. This is the beginning of Gyuri's journey to Auschwitz, Buchenwald, and Zeitz. About five hundred and fifty thousand Hungarian Jews had some version of this "Kafkaesque" experience. Only a few thousand, such as Kertész himself, survived their deportation.[10] The experience of each one was something like Josef K.'s experience, with the crucial difference that Josef K.'s arrest, prolonged interrogation, and execution are presented as to some degree unique, whereas the six million Jews who died in the Shoah all experienced something like Josef K.'s trial.

I have used the cliché "Kafkaesque." It is possible that Kertész's way of describing Gyuri's arrest was influenced by his reading of Kafka. That, however, does not detract from its specificity in relation to what may have happened to Kertész himself when he was as a teenage Jew arrested and deported from Budapest to the camps. In any case, both Josef K.'s experiences and Gyuri's are described in exquisite detail, with ironic objectivity. Both share with Joseph Conrad a conviction, as Conrad puts it, apropos of Lord Jim's feeling during his trial, that "only a meticulous precision of statement would bring out the true horror behind the appalling face of things."[11]

No one of these situations—that of an American slave, that of Josef K. after his arrest, that of a Jew under the Nazis, whether in Germany or in one of the occupied countries, that of a detainee at Abu Ghraib or Guantánamo Bay, that of Lord Jim on trial—is just like any of the others. Each is unique and incommensurate with any of the others, just as the experience of each of the six millions Jews murdered by the Nazis differs from that of all the others. An analogy is not an identity. Nevertheless, Kafka's account of Josef K.'s trial and execution helps to get some glimpse of what those others at different times and under different regimes of injustice must have experienced or even at the moment I write this are still experiencing, just as Kertész's *Fatelessness* is, as I shall argue, another example of fictional bearing witness.

Doubling and Repetition in The Trial*: The Architecture of the Uncanny*

I must begin my more detailed discussion of *Der Proceß* with a confession, though it has not been wrung out of me by torture or by my inability in any other way than by confessing to deal with an unjust accusation, as Leni advises Josef K. to do. I confess that I do not think I understand Kafka's *Der Proceß*. I am not even sure it is understandable.

By "understanding" I mean achieving a full, totalizing, rational, logical accounting for all *The Trial*'s features and details according to some unifying hermeneutical principle of interpretation. I have discussed in chapter 1 the reasons Kafka had for writing texts that resist verifiable interpretation.

Confronting *The Trial*, I feel more than a little like the man from the country in "Before the Law," the parable the priest tells Josef K. in the chapter of *The Trial* called "In the Cathedral." I stand before the text of *The Trial*. The door is open inviting me to enter the text and understand it, and the door is meant for me. *The Trial* makes a specific demand on me to read it and to understand it. For some reason, however, access is forbidden. I may die before figuring out the law that governs this strange work. Reading *The Trial* again and again in order to write this chapter, after many years since last reading it, I am struck once more primarily by that resistance to understanding.

The Trial is a truly strange work. It is perverse, uncanny. It is uncanny in the strict Freudian sense of *das Unheimliche*. Freud defined the uncanny as the encounter with something unfamiliar that nevertheless seems familiar, like something one has encountered before.[12] The decor, the mise-en-scène, of *Der Proceß*, for example, is like that of an early twentieth-century European city, Prague, for example, but not quite. It is both familiar and strange, for instance, in the way interrogations and court proceedings are held not in government buildings but in rooms hidden away in tenements. Kafka is famous for the unsettling strange familiarity of his urban staircases, corridors, doorways, rooms, and windows. They seem ordinary enough, but not quite. I shall return to the use of this motif in *The Trial*. An uncanny combination of familiarity and strangeness, along with a consequent resistance to rational understanding, is, as the previous chapter suggested, one feature of Kafka's work that makes it a premonition of Auschwitz. This chapter will investigate in detail one salient feature of this foreshadowing. *Der Proceß* dramatizes a breakdown of community. The result, as I shall show, is a disabling of the speech acts on which any lawful community depends for its everyday working, for example, in the legal system.

The motifs of doubling and repetition, fundamental features of the Freudian uncanny, appear repeatedly in *The Trial*, like leitmotifs, as in the doubling of Franz and Willem, Josef K.'s two guards, at the beginning. This initial doubling is matched by the doubling of K.'s two executioners at the end, with many doublings of various sorts in between. What is the meaning of these uncanny doublings? They must have some meaning. No hint of a reason for them is given. It is just the case that two of each exist, like Tweedledum and Tweedledee in *Alice in Wonderland*. This motif is doubled once more in the doubling in *The Castle* of K.'s two assistants, who cause the protagonist so much trouble. The two novels echo one another, like Franz and Willem.

This inscrutable feature of *The Trial* creates a distinct uneasiness in the reader, in me as reader, at least. That no reason is given is what makes the doubling unsettling. This uneasiness is like the disquiet generated by the first sentence of *The Trial*: "Someone must have been slandering Josef K., for one morning, without having done anything wrong, he was arrested" (5e, trans. altered). Another example is the uneasiness generated by the demand made on the reader to accept the famous first sentence of *The Metamorphosis* (*Die Verwandlung*) (1915): "As Gregor Samsa awoke one morning from uneasy dreams he found himself transformed in his bed into a monstrous insect [*zu einem ungeheures Ungeziefer verwandelt*]."[13] The reader will note that the last word in the German original of this sentence echoes the main word in the German title: *Verwandlung*, *verwandelt*. Come on, the reader thinks to herself, you cannot expect me to accept such a transformation!

The resistance is generated in part by the way this shocking and improbable fact is presented in the conventional objective, slightly ironic, language of realist fiction, like the famous first sentence of Jane Austen's *Pride and Prejudice*: "It is a truth universally acknowledged, that a single man in possession of a good fortune, must be in want of a wife."[14] Our incredulity about the opening presupposition, the mise-en-scène, of *The Trial* or of *The Metamorphosis* is analogous to our resistance to accepting plain statements about the Shoah, for example, the following sentence, validated by a Polish archival source, from the *Wikipedia* entry on Kafka: "Ottla [Kafka's beloved sister] was sent to the concentration camp at Theresienstadt and then on October 7, 1943 to the death camp at Auschwitz, where 1267 children and 51 guardians, including Ottla, were gassed to death on their arrival."[15] That cannot be true, the reader thinks. Surely something so monstrous, so *ungeheurlich*, cannot have happened, nor can it be reported now in such cool language. The long *Wikipedia* entry on "Auschwitz" is even more frightful, with its sober discussion of the way the evidence disagrees about whether 2.5 million, or 1.1 million or 1.6 million were killed at Auschwitz. The entry contains objective information about the components of the Zyklon B used in the gas chambers, its manufacturers, and so on. Can this really have happened? the reader asks herself, and yet the evidence is irrefutable.

Even more disturbing, perhaps, are photographs of SS officers at play during time off from their murders. These are to be seen in a recently publicized photo album, the so-called Karl Hoecker Album.[16] Hoecker was adjutant to the commandant of Auschwitz from May1944 to January 1945, during the period, that is, when four hundred and thirty thousand Hungarians, including Imre Kertész and his imaginary hero, Gyuri, were brought by train to Auschwitz. The crematoria, we are told, were overrun. An American soldier brought the Hoecker photo album back to the United States after the liberation of Auschwitz. He fairly recently turned the album over to authorities. What is so troubling about these photographs is how ordinary and how cheerful these bad people look, including their "helpers," the young women who served as their secretaries and mistresses. They look like ordinary German army officers and their pretty girlfriends, though they were guilty of horrible crimes. The album includes even the photographs of two particularly awful people, Dr. Josef Mengele and the earlier commandant of Auschwitz, Rudolf Höß. They look as ordinary as the rest. I urge my readers to search out these photographs on the Internet. The facts about slavery and about postemancipation lynchings in the United States are equally atrocious, equally hard to accept, as my discussion of Morrison's *Beloved* in chapter 7 will show. I have already in chapter 2 given the URL and a book reference for postcard photographs of lynchings. Such photographs were widely circulated in the south during the post–Civil War decades.

Hard to take also is the accumulating evidence of the lies told by the Bush administration to justify invading and occupying Iraq, the facts about the huge number of Iraqis who have died (over one million, according to a reliable estimate) or have been displaced (six million more), details about the torturing of prisoners at Abu Ghriab, Guantánamo Bay, and places of "extraordinary rendition" around the world, the suspension of habeas corpus for these prisoners, the illegal wiretapping of United States citizens, with the connivance of the big telecommunications companies, and so on. Abu Ghraib images are widely available on the Web.[17] Not long ago (June 2008), it was revealed that the guards at Guantánomo Bay were trained in methods of torture with the help of a handbook used by the Chinese to get false confessions from downed American airmen during the Vietnam War. A revision of the Surveillance Act allowing secret electronic surveillance of American citizens was passed on July 10, 2008, by a craven Congress and then happily signed by President Bush. President Obama has not revoked this secret surveillance law, though we may hope it is used more sparingly under his regime and always with a court order. But is it ever justified?

Anyone in America in those Bush days might have heard that knock on the door, as did Josef K., and been arrested without having done anything wrong, with a subsequent nightmarish and unsuccessful attempt to find out what law had been reputedly violated, who had accused you, so you could confront your accusers, as the law requires. This might have led to a "process" or trial culminating in a hugger-mugger execution that preceded the official and public verdict. Josef K.'s experience in *The Trial* anticipates our situation during the Bush years. How could something so *ungeheurlich* have happened without a public outcry, without marching in the streets, without impeachment of the malefactors in order to save our precious democracy and its foundation on the Constitution? Instead we were given bits and driblets of information in the newspaper and on television news. This information aroused little response beyond collective shoulder shrugging. The resonance among the five epochs discussed in this book (the time of American slavery, the interwar years that produced Kafka's premonition of Auschwitz, the postwar period of the three Holocaust novels I discuss, the post-civil-rights, postmodern era of the "rememoring" of slavery manifested in Morrison's *Beloved*, and our present time), is what I mean by calling Kafka's work a foreshadowing not only of the Shoah, but also of the other later epochs I have mentioned.

Kafka already passed judgment on attempts at empire building that might scale heaven, such as ours in the United States. This occurs in the last sentence of a short text that combines, in a wryly ironic and twisted way characteristic of Kafka, "The Great Wall and the Tower of Babel." The Tower of Babel "failed and was bound to fail," a great authority is quoted as saying in this text, "because of the weakness of the foundation" (der Bau an der Schwäche des Fundamentes scheiterte und scheitern mußte).[18] The speaker of this parabolic paradox or paradoxical parable says he cannot understand how the incomplete arc of the Great Wall could form a secure foundation for a tower scaling heaven. "That could obviously be meant only in a spiritual sense [*in geistiger Hinsicht*]. But in that case why build the actual wall, which after all was something concrete, the result of the lifelong labor of multitudes of people?" (*PP*, 27, 26).

All Kafka's work, it might be argued, turns on the impossibility of reconciling material meaning and spiritual meaning. One sign of this is the failure of religious or allegorical readings of Kafka's work to be convincing. The brief text just cited ends with an expression of the inveterate self-destructive penchant of human nature that rivals Jacques Derrida's formulations about the autoimmune tendencies of any human community.[19] Kafka says: "Human nature, essentially changeable [*leichtfertig in seinem Grund*], unstable as the dust, can endure no restraint; if it binds itself it soon begins to tear madly at its bonds, until it rends everything asunder, the wall, the bonds, and its very self" (*PP*, 27, 26). The term *Grund* echoes, of course, the argument about the Tower of Babel's lack of a secure foundation, while *leichtfertig* means "careless, thoughtless, inconsiderate, light-minded, irresponsible; frivolous, wanton, feckless, fickle." The translation omits part of the phrase about "rending everything asunder." The German says: "Mauer, Kette und sich selbst in alle Himmelsrichtungen zerreißen" (*PP*, 26). This might be translated as "to tear everything to pieces and disperse it in all directions, to all points of the compass: wall, bonds, and its very self." The *Himmel* in *Himmelsrichtungen* means "heaven" as well as "sky," the heaven, for example, that the builders of the Tower of Babel wanted to scale. One remaining sign, one might think, of the confusion of tongues, Jehovah's punishment for the tower builders' temerity at Babel, is the continual difficulty of translating into English the nuances of Kafka's German.

Repetition is a variant of doubling, though on a temporal rather than spatial coordinate. Repetition is another disquieting and inexplicable feature of *The Trial*. One example out of many is the way it seems to K., as he listens to the interchange between the lawyer Huld and Huld's client, the merchant Block, as the latter kneels cringing at the bedside of the former, that "he was listening to a carefully rehearsed dialogue that had occurred many times before, and would occur many times again [*ein einstudiertes Gespräch, das sich schon oft wiederholt hatte, das sich noch oft wiederholen würde*], one that would remain forever fresh only to Block" (194e; 264g). The word "rehearsed" (*einstudiertes*), "carefully learned," is an example of the many theatrical references that run all through *The Trial*. One uncanny aspect of a theatrical performance, in my experience at least, is the spectator's awareness that the actors and actresses are performing again, as though it were for the first and only time, an action that they (and perhaps many others) have already performed again and again and will perform again. This hollows out the performance and makes it seem factitious, superficial. This also often is the case with the dialogues in *The Trial*. They seem as if they have been carefully rehearsed for a stage performance. They have been performed many times before or perhaps are somewhere even now being performed over and over perpetually. That "somewhere" is of course within the covers of any copy of *The Trial*.

Another example of repetition in *The Trial* is comic, but at the same time somehow troubling, like a nightmare in which the same apparently senseless thing happens over and over. This is the moment when the painter Titorelli succeeds in selling Josef K. many identical paintings of "a landscape of the heath." Each painting is produced covered with dust from under Tintorelli's bed: "It showed two frail trees [*zwei schwache Bäume*; note the 'senseless' doubling again], standing at a great distance from one another in the dark grass. In the background was a multicolored sunset" (163e; 220g). After having shown K. one such picture, which he buys, Titorelli then produces "a companion piece" which turns out to be identical to the first: "Not the slightest difference [*nicht der geringste Gegenstück*] could be seen between it and the first one: here were the trees, here was the grass, and there the sunset" (163e; 220g). This is followed by a third, "exactly the same landscape," and then by an indeterminate number more. K. buys them all. "I've painted a lot of heath landscapes," says Titorelli (163e; 221g). Why? Why has he done that? What is the meaning of this slightly wacky episode? Titorelli's attic atelier is adjacent to more law offices, and K. gets a lot of information about the legal system from the painter. In spite of this unsettling proximity, reading the episode of the identical paintings made me laugh out loud. Is that its purpose? Why did Kafka put it in? No overt answer is given. It just happened that way and is reported solemnly by the imperturbably serene and only implicitly ironic narrator. The narrator is just giving a truthful report of exactly what happened, whether it seems significant or not, so that nothing will have been left out of the evidence of what happened to Josef K.

I have mentioned already the presence in *The Trial* of Kafka's leitmotif of a wandering through streets, corridors, stairs, landings that leads finally to a door behind which a surprising encounter takes place. In *The Man Who Disappeared* this motif figures Karl Rossmann's starting place of being lost, as when, on the opening page, he loses his way in the ship's depths trying to find his umbrella. Rossmann is on the way to disappearing from the beginning of his arrival in America. In *The Trial* a similar motif appears more than once, but it figures Josef K.'s weird relation to a court system that is both unreachable and ubiquitous. The motif's recurrence increases the reader's sense of what is uncanny about K.'s situation. Whatever he does, he keeps coming back to the same scene. This is like one Freudian example of the uncanny in "The Uncanny." Freud remembers trying to get out the brothel area of an Italian town only to discover that he keeps coming back to the same place, however hard he tries to escape it.

In the first such return of this leitmotif K. answers a somewhat ambiguous call from the court to show up on a Sunday for an "inquiry [*Untersuchung*]" (35e; 49g) at a certain address "on a street in a distant suburb [*in einer Entlegenen Vorstadtstrasse*]" (36e; 50g). K. arrives late, even though he has not been told an exact time to appear. His walk to the appointment is like a bad dream. The street where the address he seeks is supposedly located is a slum scene, with men, women, and children leaning out of windows, the men smoking, the women airing bedding, the children perched on windowsills. Comments are exchanged across the street from window to window, accompanied by loud laughter. The outside of this scene exposes the inside of the way these people live. The building he seeks is a commercial structure with a large courtyard, "with signs bearing the names of firms, some of which K. knew from the bank. Contrary to his normal habit, he was taking close note of all these surface details [*Äußerlichkeiten*], and he paused a while at the entrance to the courtyard. On a crate nearby sat a barefoot man reading a newspaper. Two boys rocked back and forth on a handcart. A frail girl in her night jacket stood at a pump and gazed at K. as the water poured into her jug. In one corner of the courtyard a line with wash to be dried already dangling from it was being stretched between two windows. A man stood below and directed the task with a few shouts" (39e; 54g). Three staircases lead from the courtyard. K. has no idea which one to take but chooses one arbitrarily. He is annoyed that he has not been given more precise directions but remembers having been told by the guard Willem that the court is attracted by guilt. How can he go wrong? He goes from floor to floor of this slum tenement knocking on doors and asking a completely fictitious question of the unkempt people who live in one room apartments with open doors, "Does a carpenter named Lanz live here?" ("Lanz" is the name of his landlady's nephew. *Lanze* means "lance" in German, but a word that sounds almost the same, *Lenz*, is an antithetical word meaning "spring," "prime," "bloom of life," and also [Austrian] "indolence," "leisure," but as an adjective in dialect, *lenz*, it means "dry," "empty." Are any of these connotations relevant? Impossible to tell.) Finally, in desperation, K. knocks on the first door on the fifth floor. He encounters within "a young woman with shining black eyes, who was washing diapers in a tub" (41e; 57g). He asks his absurd question again, but she says, "This way, please," points to the opening door of an adjoining room within which, behold! the court is in full session. Then follows the nightmarish scene in which K., rather than submitting to interrogation, much damages his case by denouncing the examining magistrate and the whole proceeding. I shall return to this. He has arrived too late in any case.

This uncanny leitmotif recurs with all its components (Here we go again!) in a later chapter. K. follows the suggestion made by a manufacturer whom he encounters at the bank where he (K.) works. The manufacturer suggests he might want to visit the painter Titorelli. Though Titorelli's address is at the opposite end of the city from the court just discussed, the approach is uncannily similar, though even grimmer in its disrepair: "It was an even poorer neighborhood, the buildings were darker, the narrow streets filled with filth floating slowly about on the melting snow. In the building where the painter lived, only one wing of the great double door stood open" (140e; 188g). K. struggles up to the third floor, "completely out of breath; the steps were unusually high and the flights unusually long, and the painter supposedly lived right at the top in an attic room [*in einer Dachkammer*]. The air was oppressive as well; there was no stairwell, the narrow stairs were closed in on both sides by walls with only a few small windows here and there, high up near the ceiling [*die enge Treppe war auf beiden Seiten von Mauern eingeschlossen, in denen nur hie und da fast ganz oben kleine Fenster angebracht waren*]" (140e; 189g). K. is waylaid by a group of young girls who are "a mixture of childishness and depravity [*Kindlichkeit und Verworfenheit*]" (141e; 190g). He takes at their direction yet another extremely long and narrow stairway that leads finally to Titorelli's tiny attic room. The long conversation with Titorelli follows. The painter informs K. of the triple bind he is in ("actual aquittal" [impossible], "apparent acquittal" [certain to lead eventually to rearrest], and "protraction" [just putting off eventual condemnation]). I shall discuss these alternatives later. The interview ends with the episode in which K. buys all those identical landscapes in recompense for the painter's promise to help him, or rather it ends when Titorelli opens a small door behind his bed that leads (Behold!) to a corridor lined with court offices and waiting clients. The court is everywhere, in the shabbiest slum attic, and always, it seems, in full session. This mise-en-scène of slum streets, courtyards, and narrow staircases leading to a door, and behind the door to a surprising encounter, establishes the architecture of the uncanny within which Josef K.'s calamitous fate takes place.

The Failure of Hermeneutical Principles of Explanation

The Trial appears strange, I suppose, only if, or especially if, the reader assumes that it ought to be possible to give a rational explanation for all its details and features. Such an explanation might be made according to any number of totalizing external principles of explanation: Kafka's psychology; a certain religious vision influenced perhaps by Kafka's interest in Judaism and in the Talmudic and Midrashic traditions of biblical commentary or in Kabbalah; the conditions of life in Prague at about the time of World War I; the legal system there at the time (a variant of civil law descended from Roman law, as opposed to English common law, which has a separate provenance); habits of everyday conversation and storytelling in Kafka's predominantly Jewish milieu; the conventions of narrative in the newspapers, magazines, and printed books in Yiddish, German, and Czech at that time and place; work by previous writers, such as Goethe, Heinrich von Kleist, and Robert Walser, who influenced Kafka;[20] the conventions of Yiddish theatre in Prague, and so on. All these contextual principles of explanation seem to work to some degree, but none is entirely satisfactory. All of the elements borrowed from these sources are given a hyperbolic twist in Kafka's novels, stories, and other writings. This twist makes them strange to themselves. They are carried to a point where they are both familiar and unfamiliar. Of all these commentaries one might almost say what the priest in "In the Cathedral" says about the text of the parable "Before the Law": "The text is immutable [*unveränderlich*], and the opinions are often only an expression of despair [*Verzweiflung*] over it" (220e; 298g).

The function of explanatory principles is to explain. On the one hand, each of those I have mentioned would lead in one way or another to a symbolic reading in which the reader could say: "This stands for that." "This material detail has that spiritual meaning." Such and such a feature of Josef K.'s behavior or speech, for example, corresponds to features of Kafka's own psychological makeup, as we know it from other sources, or to some other of the contextual determinants I have listed. *The Trial* itself, on the other hand, encourages a hyperbolically literal reading, in which "this stands for itself." Each detail is no more than exactly itself. It cannot, or should not, be read as standing for anything else. Each detail is what it is and does not reach one iota beyond itself. That, however, makes a reading or a work of criticism, such as this one, exceedingly difficult, perhaps impossible. How can I offer a reading without somehow saying, "This means that"?

The Trial's hints about how its own text ought to be read appear in the reproaches the priest in the cathedral chapter makes to Josef K. for not reading the parable "Before the Law" literally enough. "You don't have sufficient respect [*Achtung*] for the text and are changing the story," the priest tells K. (217e; 295g). What, exactly, is a literal reading, letter by letter, *à la lettre*, not adding anything or taking anything away, out of respect for the text?[21] Is such a thing possible? How would one know that one had a truly literal reading in hand? Moreover, after having counseled respect for the text, the priest also admits that even the most literal reading of "Before the Law," according to agreed-upon rules, does not escape from endless unverifiable possibilities of interpretation. That has certainly happened with *The Trial* itself. The novel has received wildly diverse readings, each proceeding according to some version of one or another of the external bases of interpretation I have listed above, or by way of some combination. For every opinion a counter opinion exists, as is the case with what the priest tells K. about the tradition of "opinion" about "Before the Law."

Even more disturbing is the assertion by the priest that "the commentators tell us: the correct understanding [*richtiges Auffassen*] of a matter and misunderstanding [*Mißverstehn*] of the matter are not mutually exclusive" (219e; 297g). If that is true, it is a terrible law, or rather it may be not true but necessary. "No," the priest tells K., "you don't have to consider everything true [*wahr*], you just have to consider it necessary [*notwendig*]," to which K. replies, "A depressing opinion. . . . Lies are made into a universal system. [*Die Lüge wird zur Weltordung gemacht.*]" (223e; 302–3g). This is an odd and not entirely perspicuous comment. Why would something "necessary" be necessarily a lie? Just because it is neither true nor false? How would one ever know which part of one's reading is a correct understanding, which a misunderstanding? A lie, by the way, is a speech act, since its constative value is nil, while its ability to do something with its words may be considerable if the lie is believed. If what Josef K. says is "true," this means that the web of "necessary" lies with which he is surrounded is one gigantic multiplex speech act working toward his condemnation and execution.

K.'s discussion with the priest about the parable, "Before the Law," turns on questions about whether the man from the country, or the doorkeeper, or K. as hermeneut are "deceived." To misunderstand is to be deceived, as the priest tells K. "You're deceiving yourself [*täuscht Du Dich*] about the court," the priest says to K., when the latter tells the priest he trusts him more than any others he has met who "belong to the court" (215e; 292g). The priest then recites "Before the Law" as a parable about that deception: "In the introductory texts to the Law it says of this deception: Before the Law stands a doorkeeper," and so on (215e; 292g).

The only way to avoid being deceived might be to stick to an absolutely literal reading, as the priest seems to recommend. Nevertheless, as the discussion of the parable by the priest and K. demonstrates, endless disagreements can arise even at the level of the most literal readings. How does one know for sure, as I have already asked, that one is reading literally? Moreover, one would need to be as simpleminded as the doorkeeper before the Law (most, but not all, of the "opinions" the priest reports seem to agree that he is simpleminded, but that may be a misunderstanding) not to see that much about *The Trial* encourages the reader to see it as in one way or another parabolic. By saying "parabolic" rather than "allegorical" or "symbolic," I mean that *The Trial* seems to be a "realistic" story about everyday life in a city somewhat like Kafka's Prague (it has banks, a telephone system, cabs, boardinghouses, slums, merchants, law courts, etc.) that nevertheless has a further reference to some form of ultimate truths or, perhaps, merely necessities. In a similar way the parables of Jesus tell stories about farming, fishing, and economic exchange in ancient Judea but are nevertheless about the Kingdom of Heaven and how to get there. If *The Trial* is to be taken as parabolic, however, that only compounds the difficulties of reading it. Kafka had this to say about parables in his parable about parables, "On Parables" ("Von den Gleichnissen"):

> When the sage says: "Go over [*Gehe hinüber*]," he does not mean that we should cross to some actual place, which we could do anyhow if the labor were worth it; he means some fabulous yonder, something unknown to us, something too that he cannot designate more precisely, and therefore cannot help us here in the very least. All these parables [*Gleichnisse*] really set out to say merely that the incomprehensible [*Unfassbäre*] is incomprehensible, and we know that already. (*PP*, 11, 10)

The normal German word for "parable," the word Martin Luther used in his translation into German of the parables of Jesus, is *Gleichnis*. The word literally means "likeness." It is a word far from the Greek overtones of the English word "parable." A "likeness" is a cunning imitation in miniature of something existing outside mimetic media. The gap between the real world and the world designated in parable is absolute, as is the gap between the referential function of words that designate first one, then the other, though the same words are used to speak of each, as when the sage says, "Go over." The two realms are wholly other to one another. Nevertheless, the ultimate goal of human life is to get from one to the other, from the comprehensible to the incomprehensible. No way exists, however, to do this. There is a goal but no way. What we call the way is only wavering, that is, a wandering back and forth not one whit closer to the goal, in fact, probably further from it all the time. Nevertheless, as the little dialogue that ends "On Parables" tells the reader, if we could just bring ourselves to follow the parables literally, we would "go over":

> Concerning this a man once said: Why such reluctance? If you only followed the parables you yourselves would become parables [*ihr selbst Gleichnisse geworden*] and with that rid of all your daily cares.
>
> Another said: I bet that is also a parable.
>
> The first said: You have won.
>
> The second said: But unfortunately only in parable.
>
> The first said: No, in reality: in parable you have lost.
>
> (*PP*, 11, 10)

Figure that out if you can! The words set up an oscillation or feedback loop that defies comprehension. The incommensurability between reality and parable remains absolute. A speech act uttered within reality, that is, in the rational realm within which we distinguish between parabolic language and the ordinary referential or performative language we use in daily life, has no purchase on the realm of parable. If you can say, "I bet that is also a parable" (a performative speech act), you are not yet in the parabolic realm. You have not crossed over, as you would if you just followed the parables, that is, took them literally as meaning you should cross over into some actual place. Bets can only be won in reality because speech acts are only valid in the everyday world. They are always lost in parable, where the incomprehensible remains incomprehensible in the etymological sense of unable to be grasped, *unfaßbar*. We know that already, but as long as we know it, it is a complete obstacle to crossing over into parable or to becoming oneself a parable. However hard we try to take *The Trial* literally, we cannot help also yielding to the temptation to read it parabolically, which means that we are always deceived by it.

Resistances to Interpretation

Just what is it about the stylistic texture or the narrative structure of *The Trial* that so resists logical comprehension? A long list of such features can be identified: for example, the unfinished state of the manuscript, the lack of sequence between one chapter and another, the existence of a series of fragmentary chapters each of which nevertheless has a certain completeness and might be fitted in almost anywhere, the implicit possibility of a potentially infinite number of chapters between what we have and the final chapter of K.'s execution, "The End." The narrative structure or narrative grammar of *The Trial* is anacoluthic. It fails to hang together. It does not cohere as a unified narrative syntax. Or one might also say that each chapter, fragmentary or not, is extrapolative. It reaches out futilely toward a goal that is infinitely distant, whether that goal is thought of as the death of K. or as a direct confrontation with the Law that ultimately, so it seems, condemns him to death for a crime that is never identified and that K. is never aware of having committed.

I say "so it seems" because neither K. nor the reader ever confronts the court or the judge that hands down the verdict, much less the Law with a capital *L*. The verdict actually comes from another direction, as I shall show. It is as though there is a goal all right, namely, K.'s execution or his direct confrontation with the Law, but no way to get to it, only the waverings of a series of chapters potentially infinite in number that do not seem to lead any closer to that goal. Then before the end, in the gap between the penultimate chapter and the ultimate chapter, called "The End" ("Ende"), there is a jump over that infinite distance to K.'s execution.

Another such feature repeats the large-scale lack of cohesion on the small scale of dialogue or of K.'s thoughts as reported in indirect discourse by the narrator. One example of this feature out of many comes near the beginning. K. is told that he has been arrested. Quite reasonably he asks if he can telephone his friend Hasterer, the public prosecutor (about whose friendship with K. we learn in an unfinished chapter). The "inspector" tells him that he doesn't see what sense there is in doing that unless he has some private matter to discuss with Hasterer. "What sense [*Welchne Sinn*]?" cries K. "What sense is there in telephoning a lawyer when I've supposedly been arrested. Fine [*Gut*], I won't telephone." "But do," says the inspector, and he waves toward the hall, where the telephone is. "No," says K. "I no longer wish to" (15e; 23–24g). It's that "Fine, I won't telephone" and what follows that is the characteristic illogical twist. Why won't he telephone? It seems the obvious thing to do. Why does the inspector say it is senseless? Why does K. suddenly no longer wish to call Hasterer?

The whole sequence is weirdly illogical, or rather it exhibits what might be called "kettle logic," of which Kafka is one of the greatest masters. The phrase "kettle logic" is a reference to one of Freud's examples in *Jokes and the Unconscious*: "A. borrowed a copper kettle from B. and after he had returned it was sued by B. because the kettle now had a big hole in it which made it unusable. A,'s defense was: 'First, I never borrowed a kettle from B. at all; secondly, the kettle had a hole in it already when I got it from him; and thirdly, I gave him back the kettle undamaged."[22] As Freud observes, what is illogical or sophistical about this (as well as funny), is that "each one of these defenses is valid in itself, but taken together they exclude one another. A. was treating in isolation what had to be regarded as a connected whole" (62). A.'s error is to say "and" . . . "and," when he should have said "or" . . . "or."

Another way to put this is to say that, as in the case of Kafka's many examples of kettle logic, the contradictory alternatives cannot be dialectically organized to lead toward a synthesis that would allow forward movement. The mind remains stuck fast among the alternatives. They cannot all be true, but there seems no way to choose among them. Freud's own account of jokes, the careful reader will note, exhibits a form of kettle logic. He is sometimes in doubt, or at least pretends to be in doubt, about whether or not one of his examples is really a joke or not. The reason is that "we have no criterion at our disposal before our investigation has given us one. . . . For the fact is that we do not yet know in what the characteristic of being a joke resides" (61). The examples he gives are the basis on which Freud will decide or discover what is the hidden law that makes a joke a joke. On the other hand, he has no way ahead of time to be sure that the examples from which he deduces this law are really jokes. No logical way exists to get from the particular examples to the general law. You can only get to the law by way of the examples, but you can only choose the examples with confidence that they are really jokes if you know the law beforehand. This kettle logic impasse does not prevent Freud from saying with confidence about his next example that it "is an undoubted joke" (61), or of the story of the kettle itself that though it "has been much laughed over" its "right to be called a joke might be doubted" (62). Well, if it has been much laughed over, why is it not then a joke?

Freud tries to get around this impasse in a way that is characteristically cheerful and optimistic. He says we have a kind of intuitive knowledge of the law that defines jokes even when we cannot yet formulate it: "In coming to our decision [about whether a given story is a joke or not] we can base ourselves on nothing but a certain 'feeling,' which we may interpret as meaning that the decision is made in our judgment in accordance with particular criteria that are not yet accessible to our knowledge" (61). A neat trick if you can do it. We know the criteria without knowing them. We have foreknowledge of the law of jokes that gives us a certain "feeling." It is easy to see that this is another version of kettle logic. One either knows or does not know, just as the kettle either has a hole in it or does not have a hole. I may have a "certain 'feeling'" that I am Ludwig von Beethoven, but that claim, or argument, or feeling would hardly hold water, any more than would a kettle with a hole in it.[23]

It is no accident, it may be observed, that Freud's kettle logic story is sandwiched between Jewish marriage broker stories that all turn on the *Schadchen*'s (marriage-broker's) attempt to persuade a reluctant man to accept a defective woman as his bride. A kettle with a hole in it is somehow like a woman with a hump or with one leg shorter than the other. This indicates some obscure, or perhaps not so obscure, connection between kettle logic, jokes, and sexual relations. This is certainly borne out in *The Trial*, where K.'s relations to various women—Fraulein Bürstner, Leni, his mistress Elsa—are curiously entwined with his trial and where large-scale versions of kettle logic on the level of dramatic action show K. distracted from his focus on his trial by his relations to various women. In one of the fragments, K. neglects an urgent phone call from the court summoning him to appear, in order to go to an assignation with Elsa. In another episode he is seduced by Leni, his lawyer's servant, when he should have stayed with the lawyer to take part in a discussion of his case with an important, or perhaps not so important, judge. Leni, possibly, may be a better way to the Law after all. Who knows? These women, and K.'s sexual desire for them, are both a means of access to the Law (many of them turn out to be connected with the court) and at the same time an obstacle to that access, a detour, a delaying force. Each woman K. desires is a distraction, one more childish measuring stick that he will not be forgiven and that he must nevertheless traverse on the infinitely long road between him and the Law, to use a figure I shall discuss in a moment.

Both on a large and small scale *The Trial* everywhere exhibits kettle logic. This makes it both funny and at the same time deeply disturbing, like the kettle logic of the Bush administration's way of dealing with "terror suspects" held indefinitely at Guantánamo Bay. If they are terrorists, why not bring forth the evidence and try them in a regular court of law? No, we were told, that is impossible because it would mean revealing classified information. Such prisoners therefore remain in limbo, perhaps for the rest of their lives. What is disturbing about kettle logic, as about our detention of "terrorists," is that its effect is to freeze forward movement in a dreamlike stasis, an endless hovering among contradictory motives, motivations, feelings, or alternatives that in one way or another forbid K. to get on with it.

Another good example of this pervasive stylistic feature appears in the fragment of *The Trial* entitled "The Building." In one episode of the dream K. has, as he lies resting on the couch in his office at the bank, he sees in the courthouse lobby a man dressed like a bullfighter. As is often the case with K., he becomes fascinated by the details of what he sees, senseless or irrelevant details though they seem to be, since no significance is ever ascribed to them: "He knew all the patterns of the lace, all the frayed fringes, every swing of the little jacket, and still he hadn't seen enough [*sattgesehn*]. Or rather he had long since seen more than enough, or even more accurately had never wanted to see it in the first place, but it held him fast [*es ließ ihn nicht*]" (262e; 350g). Well, which is it, not enough, or more than enough, or would any at all be too much? What he had seen in his dream, in any case, "held him fast," did not let him go. In this case too, kettle logic, with its wavering contradictions, freezes forward movement and leaves K. in paralyzed suspension.

The law that governs such suspensions is expressed succinctly in one of Kafka's "Reflections on Sin, Pain, Hope, and the True Way": "The road is endless, there is nothing that can be subtracted from it or added to it, and yet every one insists on applying his own childish measuring yard. 'Yes, you will have to go the length of that measuring yard as well; it will not be forgiven you'" (*GW*, 287). K.'s frequent absorption in irrelevant details in what is around him functions to make these details both mediators of the goal and obstacles to reaching it, just as the man from the country, in "Before the Law," comes to know even the fleas on the gatekeeper's fur collar. The details become in an odd way inadequate measuring yards.

Why, it might be asked, is the invention and application of one's own measuring yard for the "endless" road something that has to be "forgiven," that is, pardoned as though it were in some way sinful or criminal, though in this case it will not be forgiven? Failed to be forgiven by whom or by what authority? What's wrong with trying to measure the road? Could that attempt to measure be the "etwas Böses," the something bad, that K. has done, or rather not done, or rather has done without knowing he is doing it? Trying to measure the immeasurable with one's own childish measuring yard may be a form of that cardinal sin that Kafka names in another "Reflection": "Perhaps, however, there is only one cardinal sin: impatience. Because of impatience we were driven out [of Paradise], because of impatience we cannot return" (*GW*, 278).

Speech Acts in The Trial

Much more could be said about these features, but out of impatience (another name for which is presumed lack of time) I choose rather, in conclusion, to measure *The Trial*'s strangeness by one yardstick: its use of speech acts.[24] When I first thought of writing this chapter I planned, more or less as a blind hypothesis, to investigate performative language in *The Trial.* Remembering the spectacular example of a "felicitous" performative utterance (felicitous at least in J. L. Austin's sense of doing its work efficiently) at the end of Kafka's first great story, "The Judgment," I assumed that *The Trial*, which after all deals with a supposedly criminal case, would have a complex integument of legal speech acts. The reader will remember that Georg's father, in "The Judgment" ("Das Urteil") declares, "I sentence you now [*Ich verurteile dich jetzt*] to death by drowning [*des Ertrinkens*]!"[25] Georg promptly goes out and drowns himself. One can see, I guess, why Kafka and his friends laughed until the tears ran down their faces when Kafka read this story aloud to them. Surely, I thought, without thinking too carefully about it, there must be parallel examples in *The Trial.*

The realm of lawyers, the law, court cases, arrests, interrogations, trials, with all their complex protocols of swearing witnesses, taking evidence, making depositions, rendering verdicts, and so on is a prime source of the examples J. L. Austin adduces and analyzes in that founding text of speech act theory, *How to Do Things with Words.* A rhythmic counterpoint of multitudinous references to law, lawyers, judges, and courtroom scenes punctuates *How to Do Things with Words.*[26] These serve as an explicit reminder of what is at stake in making performatives work. One of Austin's important essays, "A Plea for Excuses," uses a legal term in its title ("plea") and gives a detailed account of an actual criminal case from the nineteenth century.[27]

Austin's attitude toward law and lawyers is slightly ambiguous. On the one hand, he more than once blames lawyers for their timidity in being unwilling to recognize explicitly the performative dimension of their language: "Of all people, jurists should be best aware of the true state of affairs. Perhaps some now are. Yet they will succumb to their own timorous fiction, that a statement of 'the law' is a statement of fact" (*HT*, 4). Lawyers want "to apply rather than to make law" (*HT*, 32). Lawyers are timorous because they are, understandably, unwilling to acknowledge what Austin sees clearly about judges and juries if not about lawyers, the somewhat terrifying fact that "as official acts, a judge's ruling makes law; a jury's finding makes a convicted felon" (*HT*, 154). By deciding that a given general law applies to a given specific case, the judge makes the law in the sense of defining its applicability. This means deciding what the law really means and is. That is why precedent is so important in the law.

On the other hand, Austin admires the realm of law because it has clear conventions, rules, and protocols to make sure that performative utterances work: "The whole point of having such a procedure [a preordained, ritualized assembly of speech acts and protocols along with infallible ways to identify who is authorized to use them] is precisely to make certain subsequent conduct in order and other conduct out of order: and of course for many purposes, with, for example, legal formulas, this goal is more and more nearly approached" (*HT*, 44). Austin's entire theory presupposes that for a performative to work, "there must exist an accepted conventional procedure having a certain conventional effect, that procedure to include the uttering of certain words by certain persons in certain circumstances" (*HT*, 14).

It can be argued, without much exaggeration, that the underlying purpose and raison d'être of *How to Do Things with Words* is to make it possible for a judge speaking in the proper circumstances to say, "I find you guilty" (*HT*, 58), and to have that speech act work to get the miscreant punished. As Austin recognizes, the circumstances are crucial: "The performative nature of the utterance still depends partly on the context of the utterance, such as the judge being a judge and in robes on a bench, &c." (*HT*, 89).

The ultimate goal of Austin's work is to secure the conditions whereby law and order may be kept. This explains the urgency and determination with which he seeks to establish a sound doctrine of performative utterances. The stability of civil society and the security of the nation depend on it. We must have some justified way to hold people to their promises, to put people in jail for perjury, or for breach of promise, or for bigamy, or for welshing on a bet, and so on. We need ways to be sure that the rules of the game are obeyed, that ships get christened correctly, and that people do not marry monkeys (Austin's examples). "But of course lawyers," says Austin in "Performative Utterances," "who have to deal very much with this kind of thing, have invented all kinds of technical terms and have made numerous rules about different kinds of cases, which enable them to classify fairly rapidly what in particular is wrong in any given case" (*PP*, 3rd ed., 240). A whole book, Dennis Kurzon's *It Is Hereby Performed . . . : Explorations in Legal Speech Acts*, has been devoted to legal speech acts, though it does not quite have Austin's sense of what is problematic about speech acts in general, including legal ones.[28] Judith Butler's *Excitable Speech: A Politics of the Performative* is an extremely subtle and forceful investigation, based on Austin and others, of what is at stake in laws against hate speech and pornography.[29]

Surely, I thought, *The Trial* must be an exemplification of this dependence of a legal system on the just workings of legal performatives, even if Josef K. is condemned unjustly. Dickens's *Bleak House* has more than once been compared to Kafka's *The Trial*.[30] Both deal with a legal system that has gone seriously awry. However monstrously unjust are the delays of Chancery in *Bleak House* that have destroyed the lives of so many of the characters—Tom Jarndyce, Gridley (the Man from Shropshire), Miss Flite, and Richard Carstone—nevertheless this happens through a multitude of speech acts, written and spoken. These are perfectly in order. In that sense they are "felicitous." That their felicity is inhumanly destructive is just Dickens's point. Speaking of the case of Jarndyce and Jarndyce, John Jarndyce tells Esther: "The Lawyers have twisted it into such a state of bedevilment that the original merits of the case have long disappeared from the face of the earth. It's about a Will, and the Trusts under a Will—or it was, once. It's about nothing but Costs, now. We are always appearing, and disappearing, and swearing, and interrogating, and filing, and cross-filing, and arguing, and sealing, and motioning, and referring, and reporting, and revolving about the Lord Chancellor and all his satellites, and equitably waltzing ourselves off to dusty death, about Costs. That's the great question. All the rest, by some extraordinary means, has melted away. . . . Why, yes, it was about a Will when it was about anything."[31] All those participles (swearing, interrogating, filing, and so on), strictly speaking, name different kinds of performative enunciations used in court cases. A will is a paradigmatic example of a performative. Almost the first example Austin gives in *How to Do Things with Words* of a performative utterance is " 'I give and bequeath my watch to my brother'—as occurring in a will" (*HT*, 5). Each of those acts John Jarndyce mentions (swearing, interrogating, filing, and so on) is a specific legal speech act with its own strict rules, obedience to which is necessary for its "felicity." The lawyers are paid to make sure that the swearing and interrogating and filing are done correctly. Surely, I thought, *The Trial* must be similar.

Finally, said I to myself, it is well known that Kafka received advanced training in Czech civil and canon law. He received the doctor of law degree in June, 1906, after having served as a clerk in his uncle's law office while studying law. In 1906–7 he practiced law in the *Landesgericht* (provincial high court) and in the *Strafgericht* (criminal court). He then rose to a relatively high position in the semi-state-owned Workers Accident Insurance Company for the Kingdom of Bohemia in Prague. There he held, among other positions, that of "concipist," or junior legal adviser, and he must have had plenty of opportunity to see the workings of legal speech acts at close hand. He also wrote many legal documents. A good many are now available in translation in his *Office Writings*, discussed briefly in chapter 1 of this book.[32] The fragmentary chapter of *The Trial* entitled "Public Prosecutor" may perhaps be based on Kafka's evening discussions at taverns with legal colleagues. If Kafka had wanted to base *The Trial* on the actual workings of the law in Prague at that time, he could certainly have done so. A whole book, Lida Kirchberger's *Franz Kafka's Use of Law in Fiction*, has been devoted to exploring the ways Kafka's legal training is reflected in his work.[33] For all these reasons, I thought, *The Trial* might be expected to contain many examples of felicitous legal speech acts.

As anyone who has ever tried methodically to read *The Trial* in the light of speech act theory knows, however (if there has ever been such a person before me), the texture of speech acts in Kafka's novel is extremely peculiar, to say the least. Not only are there relatively few speech acts of any kind in *The Trial*, whereas *Bleak House* is full of them, even in the everyday conversation of the characters, but such performatives as there are in *The Trial* are also highly irregular. They are incomplete or incorrectly performed, so that they are all in one way or another what Austin calls "infelicitities" or "misfires." *The Trial* is a large-scale example of how not to do things with words, or of how not to do anything with words, or of how to do nothing with words, how to use words to stop forward movement in a perpetual wavering.

Take, for example, Josef K.'s arrest. In the celebrated first sentence the narrator tells the reader that someone must have been slandering Josef K. ("Jemand mußte Josef K. verleumdet haben"), because without having done anything wrong ("etwas Böses"), he was arrested ("verhaftet") one morning. Kafka first wrote "gefangen," "seized," "taken prisoner," then crossed that out and substituted "verhaftet." The chapter is called "Verhaftung" ("Arrest"). Slander (*Verleumdung* in German) is a speech act. If I publicly tell a lie about you and it is believed, then I have successfully done something with words, especially if the belief leads to action. Saddam Hussein did not have weapons of mass destruction, but the lie was believed and led to the Iraq War. Bush and his cronies were, one might say, slandering Hussein.

An arrest is a paradigmatic example of a speech act: "I arrest you, in the name of the law." That sentence, however, is never pronounced by anyone in *The Trial*. The proceedings of the so-called arrest, moreover, are extremely irregular, illegitimate, one might say even "illegal," as K. himself observes. Two men burst into his bedroom while he is still in bed, as has happened so often in recent times, for example, in arrests made by the Nazis of Jews, or by our "security forces" in Iraq and elsewhere. Four other men (three witnesses and one man described as an "inspector" [*Aufseher*]) are added to the first two when he is ordered into the adjoining room. He is told that he is "being held" [*gefangen*], to which K. replies, "So it appears [*Es sieht so aus*] . . . But why?" His doubled guards, Willem and Franz, refuse to tell him why. "We weren't sent to tell you that," they say (5e; 9g). Only later in the scene is he told that he is "under arrest" (8e; 13g). Completely unsatisfactory answers are given to all K.'s questions, even though, as K. reflects to himself, he "lived in a state governed by law [*in einem Rechtsstaat*], there was universal peace, all statutes were in force; who dared assault him in his own lodgings?" (6e; 11g). No charge is stated. No arrest warrant is produced. The guards have no interest in seeing K.'s identity papers, though at first he can find only his bicycle license, then his birth certificate. He is told only that his arrest must be in order because the court they represent, or rather the "department" of it they represent, "as the Law states, is attracted by guilt [*von der Schuld angezogen*] and has to send us guards out. That's the Law" (9e; 14g). When K. says he doesn't know that law, Franz uses this as an argument against K.'s protestations of innocence: "You see, Willem, he admits that he doesn't know the Law and yet he claims he's innocent" (9e; 15g). How can K. know he is innocent if he does not know the law that might condemn him?

The whole first chapter of *The Trial* is a darkly hilarious nightmarish travesty of a regular arrest, though it is of course, as many commentators have observed, just the sort of thing that happens in a totalitarian country, where people are arrested, taken from their homes, detained, tortured to death, and their bodies dumped in a ditch or simply "disappeared." Jews during the Shoah were treated in just this way. The explanation, however, that the scene of *The Trial* corresponds to a police state does not really work, since *The Trial* takes place, according to K. at least, in a country under the rule of law. I suppose, however, that all totalitarian regimes say that or try to persuade citizens that this is the situation. In any case, it is not the secret police, apparently, but the courts that have jurisdiction over K. Though K. may have been arrested, he is allowed to go on living his normal life, more or less, working at the bank, living in his boardinghouse, visiting his mistress Elsa, and so on. Perhaps *The Trial* corresponds best, prophetically, with the situation under, say, Communist East Germany, when a person could go on living an apparently normal life while a secret dossier made up of the reports of ubiquitous, often slanderous spies was being compiled that would ultimately lead to that person's imprisonment or execution. Even Kafka does not seem quite to have been able to anticipate the torture chambers of the Gestapo, of the KGB, or of the Argentinian regime under Perón, or in the political prison in Montevideo, Uruguay, now a department store, or indeed during the recent war in Bosnia, or, recently, under the jurisdiction of the Los Angeles police, or in many countries in Africa, certainly so under apartheid in South Africa, or in Guantánamo Bay, or in Abu Ghraib. Nor does K. ever doubt the existence somewhere of a sovereign Law that governs all lesser laws and all the infinite gradations of the court. The problem, of course, is that this Law is totally unavailable to K. or to his lawyer or to anyone else in the lower circles of the court. The Law, as goal, is infinitely distant, though all-powerful, in spite of the fact that no way exists, it appears, to reach it.

The remaining chapters after K.'s arrest develop this situation through various confrontations, all of which involve "infelicitous" speech acts, "misfires," as Austin calls them. In the chapter called "Initial Inquiry," K. is summoned by telephone (a highly irregular method) to appear in court on a Sunday (the wrong day, surely, for legal proceedings), for the first of what are promised to be a long series of interrogations (which, by the way, never take place). When he shows up an hour and five minutes late (because he has not been told just where the court is located, only the number of the building on a distant street where it is said to be found), instead of allowing himself to be interrogated in a regular way by the "examining magistrate," K. makes a long speech to the large crowd present. He denounces the court and all its procedures and then leaves the court, only to be told at the door by the examining magistrate: "You have today deprived yourself—although you can't yet have realized it—of the advantage that an interrogation [*Verhör*] offers the arrested man in each case" (52–53e; 72g). I have already discussed the leitmotif of wandering that precedes this highly irregular courtroom scene. When K. returns the following Sunday (though he has not been summoned), he finds the court empty and discovers that what he had thought were law books in the hands of the examining magistrate were really sadistic pornographic narratives, with indecent pictures. One is entitled *The Torments* [*Die Plagen*] *Grete Suffered at the Hands of Her Husband Hans* (57e; 77g). Once more, as in many other places in *The Trial*, sex and the court are curiously intertwined.

When K.'s uncle forces him to engage the lawyer Huld to prepare his defense, K. leaves the room to be seduced by Leni just when Huld, his uncle, and the chief clerk of the court begin a conversation that might greatly help his case. What his lawyer tells him in the next chapter about the court is not at all reassuring. These details uncannily and frighteningly anticipate the procedures followed during the Bush years by the military courts with the "detainees" in our Guantánamo Bay prison and torture house. The detainees are said to be "enemy combatants," therefore exempt from habeas corpus and other constitutional guarantees of a fair and public trial, such as the exclusion of evidence obtained under torture. Waterboard someone or start pulling out her or his fingernails, one by one, and at about the third nail or half an hour of waterboarding that person will confess to anything. When I revised this chapter in June, 2008, the United States Supreme Court, by a five to four decision, had just declared the Guantánamo Bay military courts unconstitutional. Later (November 2009), it was decided that prisoners from Guantánamo Bay are to be tried in a regular civilian court in New York, over the vehement protests of conservatives like ex–Vice President Dick Cheney. Now (November 2010) only one of those civilian trials has happened, and the issue is still controversial. The parallels with Kafka are truly terrifying. Can this be happening in the land of the free and the home of the brave? The proceedings of the court in *The Trial*, like those of our illegal "military tribunals," are all officially secret, so that it is impossible for the accused or his lawyers to get their hands on the indictment. This means, among other things, that no officially sanctioned lawyers exist for this court: "There are no court-recognized lawyers; all those who appear before the court as lawyers are basically shysters [*Winkeladvokaten*]" (114e; 152g).

The result is that petitions (speech acts, of course) addressed to the court are generally useless: "The court records, and above all the writ of indictment [*Anklageschrift*] , are not available to the accused and his defense lawyers, so that in general it's not known, or not known precisely, what the first petition [*Eingabe*] should be directed against, and for that reason it can only be by chance that it contains something of importance to the case. Truly pertinent and reasoned petitions can only be devised later, when, in the course of the defendant's interrogations, the individual points of the indictment and its basis emerge more clearly, or may be surmised" (113e; 152g). Such surmises may or may not be on the mark. No way exists to know for sure. In any case, though K.'s lawyer claims to be working on a petition for K., he never finishes it or submits it: "He was always at work on the first petition, but it was never finished" (122e; 164g). Moreover, as Huld says, even if the petition were to be finished and filed, it would most likely never be read or would be returned at some point as useless, as a performative that has not performed, as empty language without any sort of power to do anything with words: "Then you come home one day," says Huld, "to find on your desk all the many petitions you submitted so diligently and with such great hopes in the case; they've been returned; since they can't be transferred to the new stage of the trial, they're worthless scraps of paper [*wertlose Fetzen*]" (121e; 163g).

Lawyer Huld, like almost everyone else from whom K. learns about the court, seems to think that indirect means are best: the appeal to friends in the court hierarchy, bribery of one form or another, such as offering one's wife or one's servant girl to some member of the court staff as a mistress, "pulling strings," as one says in English, trying every unofficial means to court favor. Nevertheless, as Huld tells K., absolutely no certainty can be had that this will work: "No matter how decisively they [court officials who have been unofficially appealed to] state their new intent, which is favorable to the defense, they may well go straight to their office and issue a decision [*einen Gerichtsbeschluß*] for the next day that conveys the exact opposite, and is perhaps even more severe with respect to the defendant than that which they had at first intended, and which they claimed to have entirely abandoned" (116–17e; 156g). Even if these indirect means function by way of speech acts—appeals, pleas, promises of some quid pro quo—these performatives seem destined to misfire. They will perhaps, or even probably, have the opposite effect from the one that is intended and even promised by the official. That promise is another speech act that misfires.

K. ultimately dismisses his lawyer, as many of the Guantánamo Bay prisoners have done theirs. This is one speech act that works or that seems to work (since Huld never accepts the dismissal), but of course it is a speech act that leaves K. exactly where he was at the beginning, stuck in a state of arrest. Nor does K. ever carry out his determination (or at any rate his consideration of the possibility that he might determine) "to prepare a written defense [*eine Verteidigungsschhrift*] and submit it to the court" (111e; 149g). How could he defend himself against a charge he cannot know? He would need to tell the story of his life in minutest detail, justifying every act in it, in the hope that he might by accident hit on the excuse (another speech act) that would exonerate him. That would be a more or less infinitely long document, therefore impossible to write. K. never gets around anyway even to beginning his defense document. It is another case of kettle logic.

In the next chapter, K. enlists the help of the court painter Titorelli, who appears to be attached to the court, but surely in a way that gives him no official jurisdiction, any more than it makes sense that Titorelli tells K. the motley group of girls (perhaps child prostitutes) who peer through the door and listen to K.'s conversation with the painter are also attached to the court. Titorelli paints even low-level judges perched on a throne as if they were the highest of judges, and behind the throne a figure that combines "Justice and the goddess of Victory in one" (145e; 196g), though to K. it looks "just like the goddess of the Hunt" (146e;

1978). This figure is a fine emblem of the sort of justice that can be expected from a court that assumes the guilt of the accused, is "impervious to proof [*für Beweisgründe unzugänglich*]" (153e; 206g), does not tell the defendant what the charge is, and gives the defendant no means of defending himself or herself.

Every careful reader of *The Trial* will remember the three outcomes Titorelli says are possible ways to avoid condemnation. I have already mentioned these. Each is a strange form of quasi acquittal. An acquittal is of course another speech act. The jury in a trial by jury votes for acquittal, and the judge pronounces the verdict: "You are acquitted," or "This court acquits you." In the case of the strange court that has arrested Josef K., however, three possible forms of this exist, none satisfactory or regular. Together they form another case of kettle logic, since they put K., even though he declares his innocence to Titorelli, in an impossible situation, a situation in which no forward movement is possible. A declaration of innocence is another speech act, but, as I have said, K. has no way of knowing whether he is innocent or not, since he does not know of what crime he is accused. His declaration of innocence is therefore infelicitous.

The first possibility, "actual acquittal [*die wirkliche Freisprechung*]" (152e; 205g) is not really a possibility, since Titorelli, with all his long court experience, has never seen a single instance of actual acquittal: "Ich weiß von keiner wirklichen Freisprechen" (207g). Note that the German word for acquittal stresses the performative aspect of this legal event. It is a setting free by means of a speech act, a *Sprechung*. Actual acquittals may have occurred, but no way exists to know about them, since "the final verdicts [*Entscheidungen*] of the court are not published" (154e; 208g). The second possibility, "apparent acquittal," is no better. In an actual acquittal the records are all destroyed, whereas in an "apparent acquittal" they are saved: "No file is ever lost, and the court never forgets" (Es geht kein Akt verloren, es gibt bei Gericht kein Vergessen) (158e; 214g) The result is that "someday—quite unexpectedly—some judge or other takes a closer look at the file, realizes that the case is still active, and orders an immediate arrest" (158–59e; 214g). "Protraction [*Verschleppung*: a wonderful word]," the third choice, is just as bad. It consists in prolonging the case by various means, so that "the trial is constantly kept at the lowest stage" (der Proceß dauernd im niedrigsten Proceßstadium erhalten wird) (160e; 216g).

Both apparent acquittal and protraction "have this in common: they prevent the accused from being convicted" (eine Verurteilung des Angeklagten verhindern), but "they also prevent an actual acquittal" (161e;

218g), thereby leaving the defendant in a permanent double bind or rather triple bind, caught once more in the tangles of kettle logic. That logic always seems to come in threes. Actual acquittal is unheard of, possible, perhaps, but apparently extremely unlikely, since arrest assumes the guilt of the accused. All that is perhaps possible is either apparent acquittal, which is not acquittal at all but leads sooner or later to another arrest, or protraction, which, as its name suggests, just puts off the evil day. Sooner or later the protraction will come to an end. The culprit who chooses protraction must live in the perpetual *malconfort* of not knowing when that moment will come. He must spend every waking hour protracting the protraction, without a moment's rest.

All three possibilities converge on the ultimate necessity of conviction and execution, just as every human life ends ultimately in death, perhaps today, perhaps tomorrow, perhaps at some far-off time. The presupposition of all three possibilities is that guilt is assumed and innocence impossible to prove. You cannot, logically, pursue all three strategies at once, but all three choices come in the end to the same, though each seems distinct. Each is inhabited by the others as shadows of itself. K. leaves Titorelli without having chosen which of the three to go for, and of course he cannot choose, since any choice would be as disastrous as the others. And so he remains poised, inactive, paralyzed, which is certainly the effect of kettle logic generally. Such illogical logic might be defined as a horrible parody of dialectical reasoning. It is thesis and antithesis with no possible sublating synthesis.

The final speech act in *The Trial* is of course the verdict that seals Josef K.'s guilt and condemns him to death. This performative too is hideously infelicitous. In any sensible court of law the judge would render a verdict, for example, a death sentence, and then the sentence would be carried out. In Josef K.'s case the verdict, absurdly, follows the execution. The two executioners come for K. on his birthday, just a year after his initial arrest. He is waiting dressed in black, as if he somehow expects them to come on that day. The executioners strike K. as being like cheap actors or operatic tenors, hired inexpensively to perform the execution. This is another reference to theater, like those in *The Man Who Disappeared*. It implies the factitiousness of what is happening, as though it were a scene in a play. The two men then lead K. to an abandoned quarry, set him against a rock, and pass a long thin sharp butcher knife back and forth across his body. He understands that he is supposed to grasp the knife and plunge it into himself, but he is unable to do that, which is his "final failure [*letzten Fehler*]" (230e; 312g). Then one of the executioners drives the knife into K.'s heart, turning it twice, in a last example of doubling. As K. passes judgment on his own death ("Like a dog! [*wie ein Hund!*]," he says), "the men drew near his face, leaning cheek-to-cheek to witness the verdict [*Entscheidung*, decision]" (231e; 312g). The verdict does not precede the punishment, but may be, absurdly, witnessed after the fact in the dying gaze of the one who is executed. This verdict is the climactic infelictous speech act in *The Trial.*

What can one say about this cascade of defective performatives that starts with K.'s arrest, occurs repeatedly in different forms in almost every chapter, and culminates in his execution followed by the verdict? I shall give first a succinct formulation of the law whose abrogation determines the infelicity of every speech act in *The Trial.* Speech act theory, including that theory as it has been applied, whether by Austin or by others, to legal acts, depends on the existence of a situation in which law and order are installed, in which the law is codified in comprehensible form available to all. An example is the law of wills that determines whether a given case of saying or writing "I give and bequeath my watch to my brother" will be legally effective. For a legal speech act to work, regular rules and protocols for evaluating the felicity or lack of it of a given legal speech act must exist, be ascertainable, and be agreed upon by the community. Members of the community must have faith in the system that guarantees the felicity of speech acts. The social system presupposed by speech act theory, in short, is rational, fiduciary, and finite. Jacques Derrida expresses these preconditions as follows: "Without the performative experience of this elementary act of faith, there would neither be 'social bond' nor address of the other, nor any performativity in general: neither convention, nor institution, nor constitution, nor sovereign state, nor law."[34]

None of these conditions obtains in *The Trial.* The social system in *The Trial* is irrational and infinite. As the merchant tells K., "Group action is entirely ineffective against the court. . . . There's no sense of community [*keine Gemeinsamkeit*]" (176e; 238g). Speech act theory depends not only, as has often been said by experts, on the stability and continuity through time of the ego that makes promises, files petitions, issues verdicts, passes legal sentences, and so on, but also on the stability, finitude, and comprehensibility of the social system within which, as context, one I or another enunciates a speech act. The context must be "saturable," in Jacques Derrida's word for it in "Signature Event Context," that is, fully identifiable, limited, and totalizable.[35] In *The Trial,* however, the context is radically unsaturable, infinite, immeasurable, impossible to master. As a result, speech acts are powerless. They are doomed to be infelicitous in one way or another. Like *The Trial* itself, the context within which speech acts are enunciated in *The Trial* is anacoluthic. Not only is the (non)community of *The Trial* oriented toward an infinitely distant goal, the Law, but it is also discontinuous, interrupted, incoherent, full of gaps within itself. It is anacoluthic in the etymological sense of a "failure in following." It is nonsequential, inconsequential, like a sentence with abrupt breeches in syntax (the standard linguistic definition of "anacoluthon"), or like the incomplete and broken series of chapters that make up what we have of *The Trial*. Community in *The Trial*, I conclude, is, to recall Nancy's formula cited at the beginning of chapter 1, if not "conflagrated" yet by the Shoah, certainly "dissolved" and "dislocated," "désoeuvrée," unworked and unworkable.

As the parable "Before the Law" affirms, the sovereign Law exists, but it is unknown and unknowable. It is impossible to get access to it. No merely human speech act has any purchase on it. As Kafka asserts in "The Problem of Our Laws," the problem of our laws is that "our laws are not generally known"; "the very existence of these laws, however, is at most a matter of presumption" (*GW*, 254–55). As that brief text says, "It is an extremely painful thing to be ruled by laws that one does not know" (*GW*, 254). You can say that again! There is a goal but no way; what we call the way is only wavering. No better demonstration of that wavering exists in *The Trial* than the consistent failure of speech acts uttered within the narrative ever to be regular or to work. How can K. under any conceivable concept of justice be arrested, secretly tried, convicted, and executed in the name of a Law that is apparently unknown and unknowable?

I began by saying that *The Trial* was a genuinely strange work. One of its strangest aspects is the weirdly askew performative utterances that punctuate it and that determine its most important moments. These moments, however, do not get anywhere. They do not move the action forward. They rather testify by their impotence to the impossibility of moving forward. They do not constitute anything more than a running in place on an infinitely long road.

The Narrator's Felicitous Performatives

I have mentioned the odd self-effacement of the narrator of *The Trial*. He, she, or perhaps best "it," never says "I," never speaks for itself, but just imperturbably follows K.'s actions, speech, thoughts, and experience of the behavior and speech of others, repeating them or expressing them in past-tense third-person language. One additional thing that vanishes with the dissolution of community is the old-fashioned "omniscient" or "telepathic" narrator who speaks for a general togetherness, or *Mitsein*, of all members of a functioning community. The rule in *The Trial* is that the narrator does not have any more direct access to the minds and feelings of the other characters than does K. himself, which is practically zero.

The narrator of *The Trial* is, to borrow a term from a brilliant essay by Jacques Derrida on Henri Thomas's *Le Parjure*, an acolyte.[36] The word "acolyte" is closely related to the word "anacoluthon," though it names a positive following rather than a failure in following. An "acolyte" is someone who closely follows a superior authority. As an acolyte, the narrator of *The Trial* follows Josef K.'s thoughts, feelings, and perceptions closely without ever overtly affirming an authority of his, her, or its own, implicitly claiming a merely constative or truth-telling function. Or rather the narrator of *The Trial* is both an acolyte and an anacolyte. "It" is someone or something, a narrative voice, who, or which, follows closely K.'s every step and thought, but who does not really follow, partly because he, she, or it keeps a quietly smiling, imperturbable, slightly ironic distance, partly because he, she, or it has not been arrested, is not guilty, apparently, like K., of some crime committed inadvertently.

Moreover, the narrator survives K.'s execution to tell K.'s story in the past tense, from some unidentified time in the future. The narrator is nevertheless, like all narrators, to some degree a complicitous witness, if only in revealing something that would not otherwise have been revealed and that perhaps ought to have been kept secret. The last words of *The Trial* are those I have already cited twice: "'Wie ein Hund!' sagte er, es war, als sollte die Scham ihn überleben" ("Like a dog!" he said; it seemed as though the shame was to outlive him) (312g; 231e) This phrasing is echoed in Kafka's *Letter to His Father* and is applied there by Kafka to himself.[37] The outliving of K.'s shame happens through the narration, through the responsible speech acts of the narrator. The narration as a whole is one supremely felicitous performative, though of course it is a bearing witness to the life and death of a fictitious person. *The Trial* is an act of giving testimony performed by the narrator as discreet, effaced, unassertive witness, someone or something that never says "I," but who (or which) is the issuing place for the language that brings it about that K.'s shame outlives him.

The narration as a whole fulfills Austin's definition of a speech act as a way to do things with words. This is so in the sense that reading *The*

Trial causes something to happen in the reader, such as my response as registered in this chapter. Behind the narrator of course is Kafka himself, who wrote it all down, failed to finish it, then in another speech act ordered his friend Max Brod to destroy it along with his other manuscripts after his death (rather than destroying it himself). He then had to suffer the posthumous shame of Brod's refusal to carry out the command in an implicit negative performative: "I refuse to do what I have been enjoined to do."

Does not the narrator, Kafka, Brod, and the reader, any reader, in spite of their collective refusal to admit any shameful guilt, perhaps repeat the crime of which K. may be guilty, the crime of not ever having confronted and so coming to know the Law? Like Josef K. just before he is executed, I end by asking questions that appropriate K.'s final questions just before his execution, as the narrator does in the indirect discourse with which he, she, or it speaks: "Where was the judge he'd never seen? Where was the high court he'd never reached?" (231e; 312g). My initial confession, the confession with which this paper began, my admission that I do not think I understand *The Trial*, may have confessed to more than I knew when I made it. By confessing to you as witnesses my complicity in K.'s ignorance of the Law I hope to pass the responsibility on to you, my dear readers. On your head be it if you do not understand *Der Proceß*, or if you add or subtract from the text when you claim to understand it.

4 *The Castle*: No *Mitsein*, No Verifiable Interpretation

The Castle *and Narratology*

I have already in chapters 2 and 3 indicated the way Kafka's work can be read as a "premonition" of Auschwitz and of our Orwellian situation in the United States today. In this chapter I want to carry this way of reading Kafka further through an investigation of *The Castle* (*Das Schloß*). My founding hypothesis in this investigation is that "community" in its usual sense depends on the assumption that each member of a community has some form of access to what his or her neighbor is thinking and feeling. I also presuppose that if you do not begin with a belief in what Heidegger calls *Mitsein* (being with), or what we call in English "intersubjectivity," you cannot generate that assumption or argue your way into believing it exists.[1]

The narratological presuppositions of *The Castle* are (1) that none of the characters have direct or verifiable access to the minds of other characters and (2) that the narrative voice is limited to partial access to the protagonist's mind, without any direct access to the minds of other characters.[2] *The Castle*'s narrative is controlled by these presuppositions, and they do not change in any of the segments and fragments we have of this incomplete novel. This chapter explores the novel from the perspective of these generative narrative assumptions.

One feature of our relation to Auschwitz, as I have said, is the immense difficulty of imagining just how it could have happened, of imagining just what was going on the minds of those SS officers whose cheerful, normal faces are shown in the photos of the Hoecker photo album. I have given an Internet reference to these extraordinary photographs in chapter 3 of this book. One way in which Kafka's work, for example, *The Castle*, is a premonition of Auschwitz is in the breakdown of community togetherness in his fictions, including belief in the *Mitsein* that, if we had it today, would give us insight into the minds of those SS men and their "helpers." I shall return to the question of communities in Auschwitz in chapters 5 and 6. The dissolution of community in *The Castle* is signaled by K.'s explicitly registered inability to know what those he confronts are thinking.

The presupposition in *Das Schloß* of the other person's opacity is strikingly different from the basic presuppositions of novels by such Victorian writers as Anthony Trollope. In Trollope's novels, for the most part, the characters are explicitly represented as knowing what their neighbors or family members are thinking at a given moment, for example, at the moment of a direct confrontation between two characters. This, in my judgment, is more an ideological or cultural assumption than the realistic representation of a true fact about Victorian society. Kafka presented his fictional characters in a different way. The hero of *The Castle*, K., can only guess what others may be thinking and feeling. The consequence for *The Castle* of this lack of immediate intuition, as this chapter will show, is the impossibility of verifying any interpretation of the data with which the protagonist is confronted. This distressing disability obtains both for K., the hero of the novel, and for the reader or critic, as well as for the other characters in the novel.

One goal of this chapter is to see whether *The Castle* can be shown to foreshadow Auschwitz. Nevertheless, the chapter has been inflected by a question about narratology's value.[3] How useful are narratological modes of analysis in reading and understanding Kafka's *Das Schloß* or, more broadly, twentieth-century Western fiction, fiction written in the years leading up to the Shoah and then in its aftermath? This question might be related to my focus on "fiction before and after Auschwitz" by way of the observation that narratology in its present form was developed after World War II and after Auschwitz as a way of dealing more or less empirically and objectively with narratives. The same thing can be said of structuralism in its relation to its various objects of study. Narratology can be seen as a subdiscipline of structuralism. The social and professional role of professors, in the humanities as in other disciplines, is to account for things, to give an accounting of them, to make sense of whatever data their disciplines have marked out for them to study and teach. Narratology is a post–World War II mode of such accounting. The strategy of both narratology and structuralism might even be defined as a form of defense against the threatening irrationality of modernist and postmodernist fiction or of human cultures generally as recent anthropologists have found them to be, and as modern history has shown them to be, for example (it is more than an example), in the perpetration of the Holocaust. It may not even be an accident that the Porter Institute for Poetics and Semiotics at the University of Tel Aviv, sponsors of the journal *Poetics Today*, is one of the centers of narratology. Narratology works to heal some wounds. It promises clear understanding. That is certainly something all of us who live after Auschwitz need as much of as we can get. Modernist and postmodernist novels, however, may resist such clear understanding, as I am arguing is the case for Kafka's work.

An impressive body of theoretical and practical work in the discipline that calls itself "narratology" exists. This includes work by Gerald Prince, Wayne Booth, Seymour Chatman, Gérard Genette, Shlomith Rimmon-Kenan, Shen Dan, Dorrit Cohn, Mieke Bal, Robert Scholes, Robert Kellogg, Wallace Martin, James Phelan, Jakob Lothe, and many others. Though these theorists differ among themselves, their general goal is to establish a set of terms and distinctions that will allow an objective and verifiable analysis of narrative technique in a given work. Their correct assumption is that technique participates in production of meaning. Some narratologists, skittish about the word "meaning," would prefer to say "production of effect."

The narrative techniques Kafka employed have inspired the more or less unpredictable and variable performative effects of reading his work. By "performative effects" I mean a (sometimes tacit) decision, brought about by reading a novel by Kafka, to do something, for example, to teach the novel or to write about it, to account for it, but also perhaps to change one's behavior in everyday life. Evidence of the variability of these effects is the distressingly contradictory ways of reading Kafka that have developed over the years. Religious readings of many different kinds, autobiographical readings, psychoanalytic readings, political readings, sociological readings, intrinsic readings, and allegorical readings have proliferated, each claiming to "have Kafka right." I call this situation "distressing" because all these readings are, in general, cogently argued but cannot, in my judgment, all be right.

My reading of Kafka in this chapter in the light of the current political situation in the United States and in the world is an example of what I am calling "performative," or, as one might call it, "situated," reading. I propose to read Kafka's work as anticipating our current plight as well as foreshadowing the Shoah that was to take the lives of Kafka's three sisters, as well as of his beloved Milena.

Key terms and distinctions in narratological analysis are "point of view"; "focalization" ("internal," "external," "fixed," "variable," and "multiple focalization," in Gérard Genette's famous classifications and subclassifications); the distinction between reliable and unreliable narrators; the opposition between "extradiegetic" and "homodiegetic" narrators, that is, narrators who are either outside or inside the "reality" narrated in the novel; the opposition between the narrator and the implied author or the real author; the distinction between an omniscient narrator and a narrator with limited knowledge or fallacious knowledge; the discrimination among various forms of indirect discourse, in which the narrator speaks for the character, and so on. These are powerful concepts and distinctions. They work heuristically as aids to interpretation. They do this by leading the interpreter to ask questions: Just who or what is the narrator in this particular case? Just where does the narrator stand in relation to the characters and the action? What means of access does the narrator have to the minds and feelings of the characters? What access do the characters have to one another's minds? Just how does free indirect discourse work in this particular narrative, if it is used at all?

When the narratologist gets answers to such questions, however, her work is just beginning, as most narratologists would agree. It is necessary to go on in each case to show how a particular narrative device is used to get the story told. It is also necessary to show how analysis of the device in question confirms a "reading" of that work by the critic. In the case of Kafka's *The Castle*, for example, the impersonality and ironic reserve of the narrator are not just verifiable facts about the novel. They are essential to the meaning of the narrative and to whatever performative effect it may have on its readers. By "performative effect" I mean, as I have said, an event of reading that leads a given reader to think and act differently, on the basis of the reading.

As other scholars have noted, however, narratological terms and distinctions make some implicit, and even problematic, assumptions. Wayne Booth, a founding father of narratology, for example, notoriously disliked unreliable narrators. The narrator, he tended to think, should be a reliable source of knowledge about a story's characters and their deeds. The narrator should perhaps even pass judgment on what the characters do, so the reader will not be left in doubt.[4] That excludes a lot of powerful narrations, narrations in which the reader is explicitly left to pass his or her own judgment on actions that are as ambiguous as are many actions in real life. Good examples are Henry James's *The Portrait of a Lady* and Toni Morrison's *Beloved*. The latter is discussed in chapter 7 of this book. Did Isabel, in *The Portrait of a Lady*, do the right thing when she went back to her villainous husband, Gilbert Osmond? Did Sethe, in Morrison's novel, do the right thing when she cut her baby daughter's throat with a handsaw so that baby would not be taken back into slavery? In neither case does the narrator explicitly say whether these were good or bad acts. Does that necessarily make them bad novels? In the case of Kafka's *Das Schloß*, the reader might ask whether it is in any way K.'s fault that he makes so little headway toward reaching the Castle and confronting Count Westwest face to face, as he says is his goal. The reader might also ask whether anything in the set of narratological presupppositions Kafka adopted in *Das Schloß* might have made it difficult or impossible for him to finish the novel.

As Shlomith Rimmon-Kenan and no doubt others have observed, moreover, to give another example of what is problematic about narratology, "focalization," like the older term "point of view," is a visual figure. It implies that a narration's characters and events are something spatially displayed to be seen, put in focus, whereas they are actually a sequence of words to be read. These words follow one another in temporal sequence as the reader goes from one printed line to the next and turns the pages. A novel is not a spatial scene open to visual inspection by some virtual optical instrument that can be put into one focus or another, close-up or panoramic. To use the term "focalization," even with full recognition that it is "only a metaphor," begs some questions, to put it mildly.

The term "omniscient narrator," to give yet another example, is, as Nicholas Royle has forcefully argued, misleading. Though we all know it is a metaphor, nevertheless, the term cannot easily be detached from its theological source.[5] The term implies that the narrator is godlike in the sense of being present within the minds and feelings of all the characters at all times and having full knowledge of those. This assumption tends to be contaminated, by way of a confusion between narrator and author, with the quite different notion that the author is godlike in creating the narration. She can create anything she likes, with a sovereign freedom like God's freedom in creating the world. Royle plausibly, but polemically, suggests that the term "telepathic narrator" would be more accurately descriptive. The basic assumption of much novelistic narration is that the narrator has at least intermittent telepathic access to the minds of the characters. Telepathic powers are, moreover, ascribed to characters in many novels, for example, in George Eliot's *The Lifted Veil*, in Charlotte Brontë's *Jane Eyre*, in Virginia Woolf's *Mrs. Dalloway*, and in Salman Rushdie's *Midnight's Children*.

Narratological terms and procedures, finally, tend to beg the question of narrators' and characters' unity over time in a given work. The narrator, like the characters, is assumed to be a person or quasi person who remains the same through time, just as a "real life subjectivity" does.

Das Schloß conspicuously fails to satisfy these expectations. The characters, including the protagonist, K., change bewilderingly from one segment to another, or even from moment to moment in a given segment. The narrative voice is not individualized enough to be measured for its consistency as a "person."

Narratological terms and distinctions in general tend to imply that a good novel is, or ought to be, organically unified, and therefore ought to be open to an unambiguous and verifiable reading. That is yet another dubious assumption. The means of verifying a reading are all those wonderful tools narratologists have invented as aids to interpretation. I shall keep those tools at hand and use them as best I can in my reading of *Das Schloß*, while at the same time remaining suspicious of their perhaps question-begging presuppositions.

Two conspicuous features of *Das Schloß* prima facie put obstacles in the way of a conclusive narratological reading. (1) The novel is unfinished. (2) It is discontinuous, rather than being a straight narrative line going from beginning to middle to end. *Das Schloß* is made up of a sequence of more or less detached segments or fragments that do not follow from one to the other in a linear narrative order leading toward some ending that ties all the threads together. Kafka improvised the various sections of the novel as he went along and as episodes for it occurred to him. Only in retrospect did he assign chapter numbers and establish a definite narrative sequence. That was never done for the later segments, so we do not know just what order they would have had, nor do we know what never-written sections might have intervened. The most authoritative versions of *Das Schloß* in German and English fritter themselves away at the end into a cascade of "fragments" whose planned place in the complete novel is unknown. In spite of reassuring hints that Kafka made to his friend Max Brod, we do not really know how the novel would have ended.

Brod said that Kafka told him: "The ostensible Land Surveyor was to find partial satisfaction at least. He was not to relax in his struggle, but was to die worn out by it. Round his death-bed the villagers were to assemble, and from the Castle itself word was to come that though K.'s legal claim to live in the village was not valid, yet, taking certain auxiliary circumstances into account, he was to be permitted to live and work there."[6] This ending would have been ambiguous enough. K. was to die at the moment he was given permission, so to speak, to live. Kafka did not live to write this or any other ending, though that was not from lack of time. He just set the novel aside at a certain moment. Moreover, Kafka, in promising a quasi-happy ending, may have been charitably beguiling his good friend Brod. Brod had much trouble accepting the bleakness of Kafka's work.

As with his other novels, *The Man Who Disappeared* (*Amerika*) and *The Trial*, for some unascertainable reason Kafka could not proceed beyond a certain point and just stopped work on *The Castle*. The reader or critic can only speculate why. In a letter to Max Brod, Kafka announced that he was pleased by the recent sections of *The Castle* he had written, but in the same letter he said that he could not "pick up the thread" (325e) and had stopped working on the novel. This was perhaps because during that year (1922) he had suffered two nervous breakdowns. After all, he died in 1924. Kafka may only have been trying to reassure his friend in what he said about the projected ending, just as he did in the case of *The Man Who Disappeared* (*Amerika*). I have discussed in chapter 2 the discrepancy between what Brod says Kafka told him about the ending of that novel and what he says in a diary entry. The entry says both Josef K. and Karl Rossman would be pitilessly struck down. The "crime" of Josef K. in *The Trial* seems to be his procrastination in dealing with his urgent case of presumably unwarranted arrest, just as K., in *The Castle*, is perhaps guilty of impatience, of wanting to get to the goal without making his way through any intermediaries.[7] A brief preliminary sketch in the first person of the beginning of *The Castle*, quite different from the "final" version, was written in the diaries in 1914. It has the enigmatic title of "Temptation in the Village." I say the title is enigmatic because it is not at all evident in the incomplete fragment just what the "temptation" is. The narrator does not give his name as K.[8]

The bottom line is that we do not know for sure just how *The Castle* would have ended had Kafka been able to bring himself to finish it. From the chapters and fragments that we do have, the reader can say definitely that Kafka invented dozens of different ways—some in the form of small-scale verbal formulations, some in the form of large-scale narrative segments—to avoid getting on with it. He inexhaustibly concocted new ways to reach yet another dead end or impasse forbidding narrative progress. After each blank wall, the narrative starts over again, from the beginning, on another track K. hopes will lead him to the Castle and to a direct confrontation with Count Westwest. It almost seems as if, for secret reasons, Kafka did not want to get to that unwritten ending, and K. did not want to reach that confrontation either.

The Castle, I conclude, puts up various frustrating barriers to a satisfactory narratological analysis.

Why Read The Castle *Now?*

Before I turn to an attempt to account for what we have of this incomplete novel, I must ask another question: Why is it important, here and now, for me to understand *The Castle* as best I can? Why does interpreting *Das Schloß* seem to me an urgent demand made on me by this text, a responsibility I must shoulder? I first published an essay on Kafka almost fifty years ago. I read Kafka then, and earlier, in graduate school, with a cool and amused insouciance. Mixed with that carefree insouciance, however, was "a twinge of uneasiness." That is Kafka's description, in the old Muir translation, of K.'s fear at "the idea of being caught in the inn by Klamm."[9] Kafka's German is "eine peinliche Unzukömmlichkeit" (46g), which is much better translated by Harman's "awkward unpleasantness" (34–35e). The difference in translation gives me yet another twinge of uneasiness. How can the translations be so different? "Twinge of uneasiness" echoes the phrase about the "uneasiness" that Conrad, in *Heart of Darkness*, has Marlow say is aroused in him by the station manager: "He inspired uneasiness. That was it! Uneasiness. Not a definite mistrust—just uneasiness—nothing more."[10]

My cool and amused insouciance was a result of assumptions that Kafka's picture of the world was "merely literature." Kafka himself was clearly some kind of nut, though an extremely interesting one. Moreover, he lived in another country, belonged to a different culture, and wrote in a different language. Kafka's writings, after all, did not really have anything to do with me or with the world I lived in. My essay was called "Franz Kafka and the Metaphysics of Alienation."[11] I was given to big words in those days. "Metaphysics"! "Alienation"! The effect of these abstractions was to hold Kafka at arm's length and to imply that I had sovereign control of what happens when I read Kafka.

The twinge of uneasiness was a sneaking suspicion that I might be wrong in my assumptions. Nowadays that uneasiness has increased hyperbolically. Today I find reading Kafka, for example, *The Castle*, deeply disturbing, not just because I have the feeling that I am face to face with something uncanny that I can by no means control, not even, I suspect, control by narratological tools, but also, in another form of the *Unheimliche*, because I have the uneasy feeling that the world I live in now is more like the world of Kafka's *Das Schloß* than like the world of almost any other fictive writer whose work I know. I am thinking of the way we in the United States during the George W. Bush years were ruled by elected and appointed officials many of whom who were almost wholly disconnected from reality, who were often liars, treasonous cheats, and even outright criminals. They, for example, obstructed justice, as in the Valerie Plame "outing" case, or ordered the unjustified invasion and occupation of two foreign countries. Matters are better under Barack Obama than they were under George W. Bush, but not yet all that much better. Guantánamo Bay has still not been closed. President Obama has escalated the (in my view) hopeless war in Afghanistan to the tune of another trillion dollars in cost, not to speak of the dead and maimed. His officials are already insisting that no firm timeline for withdrawal be set. Obama has put from the beginning of his term management of the financial crisis in the hands of several of those who caused it. The financial so-called industry (though they do not make anything but money out of money) has created mortgage and banking crises that, along with gigantic budget deficits caused by the Iraq and Afghanistan wars, have put the country in the worst recession since the Great Depression. We are impoverished by wars, global warming disasters like Hurricane Katrina, security contractors, big oil companies, health insurance companies, and pharmaceutical companies, companies like Blackwater, Halliburton, Exxon Mobil, Chevron, Blue Cross and Blue Shield, United Health, Eli Lily, Merck, and their ilk, as well as by the lobbyists for all these. Lobbyists and industry representatives write our legislation in ways that will benefit them. Our legislators have been bought by gifts from corporations working through their lobbyists, and by campaign contributions in the millions for a given legislator that are legal but look like bribes to me. It is absurd to think that these campaign contributors do not expect a quid for the quo. Little has been done to stop outrageous bonuses and executive salaries for the CEOs and their cohorts, financial "experts" who bankrupted their institutions, trashed the economy, and brought untold misery on Americans and other people around the world. The top 1 percent of Americans have more than twice the wealth of the bottom 90 percent. The middle class is vanishing. We are more and more becoming what used to be called "a third world country." The employment rate is officially at almost 10 percent, but actually nearer 20 percent when those who have given up looking for a job are included. By the time this is in print more than a year will have gone by and whatever I say now will be out of date. I fervently hope I am wrong about Afghanistan and in my other forebodings too. We shall see, but at the moment our situation is truly "Kafkaesque."

The villains I have named and the system they run are classic examples of what Derrida calls "auto-co-immunity." This neologism names a community that in the attempt to protect itself turns its immunity weapons against itself in a self-destructive autoimmune response.[12] Our whole airy civic structure has come tumbling down in the form of bank failures, gigantic budget deficits that are bankrupting the country, a big increase in homeland insecurity, a reduction in consumer spending because so many people are out of work or have lost their houses, a much lower stock market even after recent recoveries, soaring health care costs, a refusal so far to do anything serious about manmade global warming, or about our deeply dysfunctional education system, and so on. This collapse is bankrupting or making jobless or impoverished many United States citizens. We are, moreover, victims of unconstitutional electronic surveillance. Habeas corpus has been suspended for our prisoners in Guantánamo Bay and, as a concomitant, implicitly for all United States citizens who might happen to be suspected of terrorism and be arrested one fine day. Many of our prisoners have apparently been apprehended by accident or mistake, or because someone told lies about them and turned them in, like Josef K. in *The Trial* who, "one morning, without having done anything wrong, . . . was arrested."[13]

It has become a cliché to describe someone inextricably caught in an unjust bureaucracy or in a tangle of autocratic governmental impositions as living in a "nightmarish Kafka-like" world. We in the United States live in such a world today. As you can see, I have lost my cool, amused insouciance, both about Kafka and about the "real world" in which I live, if you can call it real and not just another "virtual reality," since it depends so much on the performative power of the media. Virtual realities, however, can hurt you, for example, George W. Bush's belief that he was chosen by God to do what he did, that he had sovereign authority, above the law, and his consequent authorization of universal electronic surveillance, torture of our prisoners, and his signing of laws with the explicit proviso that he had no intention of implementing them. Lies being told, at the moment I am revising this chapter in December, 2009, about the proposed health care reform by the likes of Sarah Palin, the talk show host Glenn Beck, and many senators and representatives are believed by millions and may yet lead to the disaster of not having such reform. These lies have been broadcast widely on radio, television, and in blogs. As a result many people now believe that the democratic health care reform proposals will "pull the plug on grandma" and eviscerate Medicare, both lies. If no serious health care reform is passed, with a robust public option, health care costs will soon constitute at least 20 percent of our total economy. They are already twice that of any other "developed" economy. Nor are we getting what we pay for. The quality and effectiveness of our health care system ranks near the bottom of the list of developed countries. (Addition of May 19, 2010: Happily, a moderately good health care reform bill was passed, over the unanimous opposition of Republican senators and representatives. Many of them have vowed to repeal the law, when and if they retake control of the Senate and House. No public option was included, which will mean continued dramatic escalation of health care costs. Twenty states are suing to have the health care law declared an unconstitutional abrogation of states' rights.) (Addition of March 17, 2011: The Republicans now control the House of Representatives and are doing their best to repeal or defund the health care law.)

K. on the Telephone

The *donnée*, as Henry James would have called it, of *Das Schloß* is simple enough. A young man, who is called K. by the narrator, arrives on a snowy night in a village at the foot of a castle hill. He claims that he has an official appointment from Count Westwest, the Castle's sovereign, as land surveyor (*Landvermesser*) for the village. The novel's segments recount various attempts by K. to get himself accepted by the Castle and by the village. He wants a job and a secure place in a viable community, just as do most United States citizens and illegal immigrants in these bad days. Initial telephone calls to the Castle get ambiguous information. First the Castle authorities say no, and then they say yes. The narrator's account of this is an early example of the exasperating uncertainty of narration in *Das Schloß* and of the weird atmosphere of dreamlike, slapstick irrationality that Kafka excels in producing. K. is awakened at the inn and confronted by a young man named Schwarzer, "in city clothes," "with an actor's face [*mit schauspielerhaftem Gesicht*]" who claims (falsely it turns out) that he is the son of the Castle steward. When K. says he is the land surveyor the count has sent for, Schwarzer telephones the Castle. The telephone is conveniently (or inconveniently) just over K.'s head (1–4e; 9–12g).

This telephone is an example of Kafka's dependence on the latest high-tech means of telecommunication of his time, in this work and in others of his works. The chairman of the village council, in a later chapter, explains to K. that "all those contacts [by telephone] are merely apparent [*nur scheinbar*]" (71e; 90g). That is because you can never be sure the person you are talking to is giving out a true identity. A telephone, says the chairman, is no more useful than "an automated phonograph [*ein Musikautomat*]" (71e; 91g). This seems to anticipate answering machines, automated telemarketing calls, and automated answers from businesses or banks. We spend a lot of time these days "talking" to nonpersons and trying to push the right buttons on our keypads to get the machine to understand a simple yes or no in response to a question, such as "Do you want to sign up today for a free trip to Las Vegas." In *The Castle,* those in the village can hear mostly only "murmuring and singing" on the telephone: "Well, this rustling and singing [*dieses Rauschen und dieser Gesang*] is the only true and reliable thing that the local telephones convey to us, everything else is deceptive" (72e, trans. altered; 91g).[14] This report corresponds to what early telephone users thought they were hearing in telephone background noise. Sometimes people thought they were hearing the voices of the dead behind the "murmuring and singing."[15] At an earlier moment in the novel, K., pretending to be one of his assistants, tries to call the Castle on his own:

> From the earpiece [*Hörmuschel*] came a humming [*ein Summen*], the likes of which K. had never heard on the telephone before. It was as though the humming of countless childlike voices [*Stimmen*]—but it wasn't humming either, it was singing [*Gesang*], the singing of the most distant, of the most utterly distant, voices—as though a single, high-pitched yet strong voice [*eine einzige hohe aber starke Stimme*] had emerged out of this humming in some quite impossible way and now drummed against one's ears as if demanding to penetrate more deeply into something other than one's wretched hearing. K. listened without telephoning, with his left arm propped on the telephone stand as he listened thus. (20e, trans. altered; 30g)

We today "know" that K. is hearing the usual background noise created by the electrical current flowing through the telephone wires and other parts of a purely mechanical apparatus, but Kafka has K. interpret the humming otherwise, in a quite extraordinary series of transformations. These revisions of his "reading" are characteristic of the rhetoric of *The Castle*, as I shall later show. In K.'s reading humming becomes the singing of innumerable childlike voices. Those in turn become heard as a single voice that is both feminine ("high-pitched") and strong, like the authoritative voice of one's dead mother that so many early users of such devices, as Laurence Rickels shows, thought they heard behind the static. The emergence of this single voice is said to be "impossible [*unmöglich*]," though it happens. This high-pitched but strong voice makes demands on K. It seems as if it demands to penetrate deeper into him than his wretched hearing (*armselige Gehör*), presumably into the depths of his selfhood. The passage is an example of what I just said about people's early sense of the telephone, just as is the great passage in Proust about the way Marcel experiences telephone calls from his grandmother as anticipations of her death.[16] Talking to his grandmother on the phone makes Marcel feel that she is already dead, since he cannot see her face, only hear her disembodied voice. Few people these days are bothered any longer by what is truly spooky about the telephone, not to speak of cell phones, e-mail, television, texting, Tweeting, and all the rest of our everyday telecommunication devices or programs. These are more and more "handheld" and seem almost like handily removable body parts. In *The Castle* K. experiences over the telephone the infinite distance of the Castle, its utter transcendence of the village, even though people like Klamm seem to be able to go back and forth from the village to the Castle easily enough. Kafka's point in these passages about the telephone is that in the village/Castle (non)community telephones are a completely unreliable means of communication, or *Verbindung*, "connection," between "down here" and "up there," just as are written letters. Telephones also play a strategic role in *The Trial* and in *Amerika*.

In the opening scene of *Das Schloß*, first a substeward at the Castle, a Mr. Fritz, who answers the phone up there, checks and says no appointment of a land surveyor exists. "Just as I said," shouts Schwarzer, "no trace of a land surveyor, only a liar and a common tramp [*Landstreicher*], and probably worse still" (4e; 12g). Then the phone rings again and, after listening to a lengthy explanation, Schwarzer says, "So it's a mistake? This is most unpleasant. The department head himself telephoned? Odd, very odd! [*Sonderbar, sonderbar.*] And how am I supposed to explain this to the land surveyor?" (5e; 13g).

What is most odd, however, is K.'s response to what Schwarzer says over the phone. It is an early conspicuous example in *The Castle* of the weird contradictory nonlogic that rules K.'s interpretations of what happens to him. These interpretations are governed by a nondialectical, unsublatable "on the one hand" but, at the same time, "on the other hand." Kafka, in a diary entry to be discussed later, gives such formulations the formal rhetorical name "antithesis." The reader might have expected K. to be relieved by hearing that his status is now recognized. Schwarzer now calls him "the land surveyor." He can, one might think, henceforth go on straightforwardly to set himself up in his profession of land surveyor and thereby become an integral part of village and Castle community life. Instead of that, K. interprets what he hears as sinister evidence that the Castle is on to him and is "taking up the struggle with a smile [*den Kampf lächelnd aufnahm*]" (5e; 13g). Struggle? What struggle? This reaction just does not make sense. It seems perverse and self-destructive. It is a non sequitur, like the reaction of a paranoid person who puts the worst constructions on everything. Such a person sees malign intentions in all messages that reach him or her and in everything everyone says, even though these may have the most friendly intent. Such a suspicious attitude is likely to develop under a totalitarian regime in which spies and secret police may be everywhere. K.'s two assistants are clearly spies sent by the Castle, though K. does not seem to grasp that, not, at least, at first. Frieda speaks of them as perhaps Klamm's "emissaries [*Abgesandte*]" (138e; 170g). "Their eyes," she says, "those naïve but sparkling eyes, somehow remind me of Klamm's eyes, yes, that's it, Klamm's glance sometimes leaps from their eyes and goes straight through me [*durchfährt*]" (139e; 171g). The assistants, in spite of their absurd slapstick behavior, are apparently not only Klamm's emissaries, but also mediators of Klamm's panoptic surveillance. It is always possible, of course, that K. has been lying all along and is not a land surveyor with a job appointment. In that case, he has much to fear from a revelation of the truth and from the assistants' penetrating looks. No certain evidence of that either way is given, not even by the narrator, who presumably has telepathic access, some of the time, to some, at least, of K.'s interiority. Some of those our Secret Service authorities have arrested as suspected terrorists may actually be terrorists. You never know for sure, though torturing them, evidence shows, is not the way to find out. Torture in the end makes anyone confess to anything.

The narrative voice's silence on the question of whether K. is lying is evidence of its lack of omniscience or at any rate of its inexplicable reserve about important points. The reader might hypothesize that Kafka the author wanted to keep an impenetrable secrecy about whether or not K. is telling the truth about his appointment as land surveyor. The reader's uncertainty about this might be taken as the generative kernel of the entire fragmented narrative. In any case, everyone, Schwarzer included, from now on refers to K. as the land surveyor, just as they refer to Gerstäcker as "Coachman Gerstäcker." Here, so you can read it for yourself, is the exceedingly peculiar, even somewhat wacky, passage in free indirect discourse, so characteristic of such passages in the novel:

> K. listened intently. So the Castle had appointed him land surveyor. On the one hand, this was unfavorable [*ungünstig*], for it showed that the Castle had all necessary information about him, had assessed the opposing forces, and was taking up the struggle with a smile. On the other hand [*andererseits*], it was favorable [*günstig*], for it proved to his mind that they underestimated him and that he would enjoy greater freedom than he could have hoped for at the beginning. And if they thought they could keep him terrified [*in Schrecken*] all the time simply by acknowledging his surveyorship—though this was certainly a superior move on their part—then they were mistaken, for he felt only a slight shudder [*es überschauerte ihn leicht*], that was all. (5e; 13g)

On the one hand, this passage brings the narrative to a grinding halt by suspending the reader in an endless oscillation among contradictory interpretations. The reader could spend a lifetime pondering this one passage and its various implications, without ever proceeding further with the reading. That would fulfill Kafka's announced goal of writing narratives that would successfully resist interpretation. On the other hand, this passage, by defining K.'s relation to the Castle as an implacable "struggle" between opposing and evenly balanced forces, lays down the program for a narration that would consist, as *The Castle* does, of an endless set of "moves" in a forever-indecisive battle.

The rest of what we have of *The Castle* is made up of episodes in which K. confronts one or another villager or official from the Castle in ever-repeated, ever-unsuccessful attempts to get his appointment acknowledged and, as his failed attempts continue, to get all the way to the Castle and to a direct confrontation with Count Westwest. His quest is the archetypal one of the outsider's or immigrant's effort to find a profession, a wife, a family, and a secure place in a community that he has entered as a stranger.

"Land surveyor," however, is not just an ordinary profession, like the professions of master tanner and coachman that are practiced by Lasemann and Gerstäcker respectively, characters K. meets early in the narration. Being a tanner or a coachman gives a person a designated place in an established community. A land surveyor, on the contrary, has the power to establish property boundaries that may for centuries have been either in perpetually suspended dispute or tacitly accepted without ever having been legally established. To lay these lines down officially and register them bureaucratically has the potential power radically to disrupt or change social relations among the villagers. It is no wonder the village council has concluded that the village does not need a land surveyor and has sent years ago a message to the Castle saying just that. The village chairman tells K., "You were, as you say, taken on as a surveyor, but we don't need a surveyor. There wouldn't be the least bit of work for a person like that. The boundaries of our small holdings have been marked out, everything has been duly registered, the properties themselves rarely change hands, and whatever small boundary disputes [*Grenzstreitigkeiten*] arise, we settle ourselves. So why should we have any need for a surveyor?" (59e; 75g). Of course, the message sent long ago rejecting the appointment of a land surveyor has gone permanently astray, but that is another exemplification of the broken story line and of the broken connections between village and Castle that the telephone does little to repair.

Here We Go Again

I have identified in chapters 2 and 3 the leitmotif in Kafka's novels of a solitary wandering leading to an unexpected encounter behind a closed door that opens to reveal a stranger or strangers. I have claimed in chapters 2 and 3 that works of literature tend to generate in readers an imaginary topography within which the action of the work takes place.[17] The openings of Dickens's *Bleak House* and of Conrad's *Nostromo* are spectacular examples of works that begin with such a stage-setting. In these cases this happens by way of the narrator's overt panoramic description of the scene from an implicit fixed position of sovereign survey. Kafka's version of this motif is special in almost always involving the protagonist's solitary wandering through a spatial scene. The point of view is involved and limited, not external and dominant.

New versions of this leitmotif appear again, not surprisingly, in crucial episodes of *The Castle*. The whole novel is posited on the opening scene in which K. turns off the high road and crosses a wooden bridge to spend the night at an inn in a village covered in deep snow. The imaginary space of *The Castle* is relatively complex, made up as it is of various places in the village: the two inns, the schoolhouse, the dwellings of various people K. encounters, each related to the others by streets and roads. The dwellings have various rooms, doorways, windows, corridors, and staircases. Nevertheless, the whole complicated ensemble is presided over by the brooding presence of the Castle up there on the hill overlooking the village. The Castle is temptingly visible in daylight and in good weather. Nevertheless, it turns out, the Castle is inaccessible to K., even though it looks like anyone could just walk up the hill and reach it. This inaccessibility is strikingly dramatized early in the novel when K., after his first night at the inn, discussed above in "K. on the Telephone," takes a look up at the Castle and decides to walk straight up there and confront Count Westwest face to face in order to take up his post as land surveyor in the village. That seems a reasonable thing to do.

The closer K. gets to the Castle, however, the shabbier it looks. The main tower, for example, is "a monotonous round building, in part mercifully hidden by ivy, with little windows that glinted in the sun—there was something crazy [*etwas Irrsinniges*] about this—and ending in a kind of terrace, whose battlements, uncertain, irregular, brittle [*unsicher, unregelmäßig, brüchig*], as if drawn by the anxious or careless hand of a child, zigzagged into the blue sky" (8e; 17g). On his way, as he believes, to the Castle, K. has a somewhat ominous confrontation with a schoolteacher, who answers his question, "So you don't know the Count?" by saying, "How could I know him?" and then adds loudly, in French, so the schoolchildren standing nearby won't understand, "Keep in mind that there are innocent [*unschuldiger*] children present" (9e; 18g). This is a weird non sequitur. Why would asking about the schoolteacher's knowledge of the Count be something unfit for innocent children's ears? K. then sets out again to walk to the Castle entrance. This turns out to be impossible. K.'s wandering short of the goal reminds me of a similar scene in chapter 2 of Lewis Carroll's *Through the Looking Glass* in which Alice gets further away from her goal (a little hill) the more she tries to go directly toward it.[18]

The reader will note that the streets in *The Castle* are personified. The main street veers off, "as if on purpose," and it is said to be "clinging." The side street "takes him in," with whatever nuances of welcome or betrayal, at least in the English translation. The door "opens itself," as if of its own accord. It is as though the streets are leading him on to get lost and more lost:

> So he set off again, but it was a long way. The street he had taken, the main street in the village, did not lead to the Castle hill, it only went close by, then veered off as if on purpose [*wie absichtlich*], and though it didn't lead any farther from the Castle, it didn't get any closer either. K. kept expecting the street to turn at last toward the Castle, and it was only in this expectation that he kept going; no doubt out of weariness he was reluctant to leave this street, what amazed him, too, was the length of this village, which wouldn't end, again and again those tiny

> little houses and the frost-covered windowpanes and the snow and not a living soul [*Menschenleere*]—finally he tore himself away from this clinging street [*von dieser festhaltenden Straße*], a narrow side street took him in [*nahm ihn auf*], the snow here was even deeper, lifting his sinking feet was hard work, he broke out in perspiration, and suddenly came to a stop and could go no farther.
>
> Well, he certainly wasn't abandoned, there were peasant cottages right and left, he made a snowball and threw it at a window. The door opened [*öffnete sich*] right away—(10e; 19–20g)

The opening door leads the strange scene of K.s encounter with the various people in the interior of this peasant cottage. It is the haouse, it turns out, of Master Tanner Lasemann. K. encounters a woman washing, children playing, men bathing in a steaming tub, a woman wearing an apparently silk dress in an armchair who holds a baby at her breast. K. falls asleep next to the old man who opened the door. When he wakes, he is forcefully ejected, meets outside the two assistants, Artur and Jeremias, who will play such an important role in his adventures, and then, somewhat inexplicably, follows them back to the inn rather than proceeding on toward the Castle. K. has strange fragmentary (non)conversations with these people, one by one, with the two men, with the woman with a baby sleeping at her breast who says she is "a girl from the Castle" (13e; 22g), with Gerstäcker, the man from another house who takes him by sleigh back to the inn, and with the two assistants. The latter say they are the original assistants he has called to help him with his surveying work, but they don't have his instruments and say they know nothing about surveying. They are the same and not the same, and they are ominously doubled, like the guards and the executioners in *The Trial*. Artur looks like Jeremias and Jeremias looks like Artur. These puzzling conversations and everything that happens to K. in this chapter after that door opens are more than a little enigmatic. They are also not at all reassuring to the reader. The events happen according to the somewhat mad or dreamlike nonlogical logic of *The Castle*. The reader has the impression that each small detail may be important. She or he reads the episode over and over, with careful attention to every word, but it still doesn't quite make sense. The whole novel is presided over by this demonstration of the Castle's resistance to direct access and by the strange imaginary space this version of my leitmotif sets up as mise-en-scène for the narrative.

A second version of this paradigmatic event comes near the end of *The Castle* rather than almost at its beginning. This is the description of K.'s wanderings in the corridors of the Gentleman's Inn trying to keep an appointment with Erlanger, secretary to Klamm. Eventually he knocks on a door that opens to reveal not Erlanger but Bürgel. As I shall show later, if K. had not fallen asleep at the wrong moment, Bürgel might actually have given K. what he has sought throughout the novel, access to the Castle. Though he never knows it, K. is as close as he ever gets to reaching his goal. At this point, however, I want only to show how the pages leading up to the encounter with Bürgel are another and anomalous version of my leitmotif. These pages are anomalous in part because K.'s wandering is inside rather than outside and in part because some preliminary encounters precede the opening door that leads to the climactic conversation with Bürgel.

The imaginary space generated by K.'s wandering inside the inn is a strange architectural interiority, like a building one wanders through in a dream. K. first waits with others in the darkness outside the Gentleman's Inn. He and Gerstäcker are called first to meet with Erlanger. A servant leads them across a courtyard into a section of the inn reserved for those from the Castle, a section K. has never before entered. The motif of personification is missing from this description, but K. emphasizes the smallness and delicacy of this interior. It is almost like a self-enclosed underground alternative miniature world. Kafka evidently had a clear vision of this interior in his mind and wanted to recreate that vision in the mind and feelings of the reader by describing it in detail, as I, in my turn, am anxious to do for my own readers:

> In the corridor they were received by a servant who led them along the path already known to K. across the courtyard [this courtyard figures in another scene I shall discuss later] and then through the gate into the low, slightly sloping passageway [*in den niedrigen ein wenig sich senkenden Gang*]. The upper floors were evidently occupied only by the higher officials and this corridor here only by the secretaries, including Erlanger, though he was one of the highest-ranking in their midst. The servant put out his lantern, for there was bright electric lighting in here. Everything here was small, but delicately built [*klein aber zierlich gebaut*]. Full advantage had been taken of the space. The passage barely sufficed for walking upright. On the sides, one door came immediately after the next. The side walls didn't reach the ceiling; this was probably to ensure ventilation, for the little

> rooms in this deep cellarlike corridor surely had no windows. The drawback of these walls that didn't quite meet the ceiling was the noise in the corridor, and therefore, inevitably, in the rooms too. Many rooms seemed occupied, in several of them people were still awake, one could hear voices, hammer blows, clinking glasses. But this didn't leave one with the impression of great merriment [*nicht den Eindruck besonderer Lustigkeit*]. The voices were hushed, one could barely understand a word every now and then, but it didn't seem like conversation, it was probably only somebody dictating something or reading something aloud. (243e; 294g)

The servant peeks over the transom and ascertains that Erlanger is asleep, not to be wakened now. K. then spies his estranged fiancée Frieda "some distance away at a bend in the corridor" (245e; 296g). She has left him, ostensibly because she is jealous of his relations with other women, and now works again at the Gentleman's Inn. She has taken up with one of his assistants, Jeremias. K. tries unsuccessfully to persuade Frieda to return to him. He discovers that Jeremias is at that moment in her bed in one of the rooms opening off a side corridor downstairs. K. then tries unsuccessfully to find Erlanger's room. He finally approaches a door more or less at random. If the room is empty, he fears he "would scarcely be able to resist the temptation to lie down in bed and sleep endlessly. Again he looked right and left in the corridor to see whether anybody was coming who could give him information and make it unnecessary to take such a risk, but the long corridor was silent and empty. Then K. listened at the door, there was not a sound here either. He knocked so softly that the sound couldn't have woken up anyone who was asleep, and since there was no response even then, he opened the door with extreme caution. But he was now greeted by a low cry [*ein leichter Schrei*]" (257e; 310g). The cry comes from Bürgel, who is in the bed but completely hidden by the blanket. Then follows the virtually interminable discourse to K. by Bürgel about the ambiguous feelings of Castle officials toward those in the village, including their sometimes irresistible propensity to help villagers, even though it is against the rules. K., however, falls into a sound sleep at just the wrong time and so misses his chance to reach the Castle by way of Bürgel as intermediary, in this final version of my topographical leitmotif. If the first version from *The Castle* I have discussed expresses the failure of K.'s attempt to go directly to the Castle authorities, this final version expresses the failure of K.'s attempt to get to the Castle authorities by way of some intercessor with a "connection" to the Castle.

Wavering Subjectivities and Intersubjectivities

What presumptions are made in *The Castle* about the way the protagonist, K., exists in himself? How is he related to other people in the village as well as to those he encounters from the Castle? The early chapters of *The Castle* were initially written in the first person. Kafka then decided to write it in the third person. He went back to change every "ich" to "K." Maurice Blanchot, perhaps Kafka's best reader, has noted, in "Kafka and Literature" ("Kafka et la littérature"), that Kafka says he became a writer when he changed *Ich* to *Er*, "I" to "he."[19] The effect of this change is to double the narrative line and to make that double line vibrate with uncertainty. The reader is given the superimposed representation in language of both K.'s putative subjectivity and that of the narrator. The doubling into free indirect discourse from first-person discourse, in the case of *Das Schloß*, gives the reader not only the way things seem to K., but also, at the same time, the effaced narrator's dry, objective report of that seeming. That report enigmatically ironizes what K. says, thinks, and feels. I call the ironizing "enigmatic" because the narrator never explicitly passes judgment on K.'s judgments. K. may be right or he may be wrong. The narrative voice never says anything about that. Indeed, it never says anything at all on its own hook. The narrative voice just transposes first-person present-tense narration into third-person past-tense narration, *Ich bin* into *Er war*.

That narrator, moreover, does not fit very well into any of the usual narratological pigeonholes. Far from being imaginable as any kind of person with one or another "focalization," and identifiable as reliable or unreliable, the "narrator" of *Das Schloß* is almost completely impersonal. The narrative voice is, moreover, almost completely limited in what it says to somewhat restricted access to K.'s thoughts, perceptions, and feelings. This narrative voice is hardly amenable to evaluation as remaining the same from one time of narration to another, so dependent is it on K., particularly since K. does not remain quite the same from one narrative segment to another. Nor do the characters. A spectacular example of this variability is what Olga tells K. about Klamm, K.'s chief possible intermediary for access to the Castle: "They say he looks completely different [*anders*] when he comes into the village and different when he leaves it, different before he has had a beer, different afterwards, different awake, different asleep, different alone, different in conversation, and, quite understandably after all this, almost utterly different [*fast grundverschieden*] up there at the Castle" (176e; 216g).

Ironic discourse is, notoriously, pace Wayne Booth, undecidable in its meaning.[20] The doubling of the protagonist by the narrative voice, as it functions in this particular case, makes *Das Schloß* ironic through and through. The narrator in *Das Schloß* is no more than a spectral, disembodied power of narration. The narrator is a linguistic energy devoted to articulating (or disarticulating) K.'s experiences, thoughts, and feelings. This linguistic energy modulates from episode to episode. The narrative can hardly be called an "organic unity," such as some narratologists expect to be able to find in a good literary work. Of course, someone might object that my claim that no globally unified reading is possible is a globally unified reading. I agree, but answer that this is a conspicuously Kafkaesque aporetic formulation. It is like, for example, what Kafka says about despair, already cited in chapter 2: "Don't despair, not even over the fact that you don't despair."[21]

The narrative texture of *Das Schloß* is made up, for the most part, of three linguistic registers: (1) Dialogue between K. and the characters, reported with minimal objective or descriptive commentary (as opposed to interpretation) by the anonymous narrator. (2) Interpretative speeches about K.'s situation to K. by one of the characters, sometimes going on for many pages, to which K. responds, almost always in disagreement, with interpretative comments of his own. Examples are the long speeches to K. by the landlady, by Frieda, by the council chairman, by Olga, by Bürgel, and by Pepi. The speech by the council chairman to K., in chapter 5, is a marvelous description of a dysfunctional bureaucracy in which messages constantly go astray or are lost within an immense network of offices, agencies, bureaus, and departments, much like the Circumlocution Office in Dickens's *Bleak House*, or much like what almost everyone in the United States has experienced at one time or another in dealings with government or businesses. I shall return later to this topic. (3) The report in free indirect discourse by an unnamed impersonal narrator of things that go on inside K.: thoughts, feelings, interpretations, and sensations. The narrator's access is limited. The narrator often seems not to know things about K. that the reader would like to know, for example, as I have said, whether or not K. is lying when he says he has an appointment as land surveyor.

The strict rule of the narration, moreover, is that neither K. nor the narrator ever has direct access to the minds, feelings, or bodily sensations of the other characters. The landlady boastfully, and I believe fallaciously (on the basis of the evidence), asserts at one point that she can understand K.'s thoughts from within. "If I make an effort," she says, "I can even think my way into your thoughts [*hineindenken in ihre Gedanken*], which make no sense here but are perhaps valid in the foreign lands you come from" (83e; 104g). Even if she were able to think her way into K.'s thoughts, they would not make sense. They would be like the babble of a foreigner speaking in a foreign tongue about strange customs and assumptions. More in correspondence with the evidence is the possibility of generalizing K.'s assertion that "Amalia keeps her motives sealed within her breast, and nobody can drag them from her" (ihre Beweggründe hält Amalia in ihrer Brust verschlossen, niemand wird ihr entreißen) (198e; 242g).

An immense part of the dense local texture of narration in *The Castle* is made up of dialogue between K. and one or another of the characters, sometimes punctuated by long stretches of free indirect discourse recording K.'s thoughts and feelings as he confronts that other person, looks him or her in the face, and listens to what that other person says. The law of these encounters is that K. cannot understand the other, and the other person cannot understand him, as constant notations attest. Good examples of the registration in free indirect discourse of K.'s weird thoughts, as well as good examples of the way K. changes from one time to another, are the long conversation in contretemps with Frieda in chapter 14, "Frieda's Reproach [*Vorwurf*]" (151–61e; 186–98g) and K.'s fantasy in the next chapter of what might have happened if he had not encountered Schwarzer at the inn on the night of his arrival. What he is reported to think to himself in his imaginings, however commonsensical those imaginings are, completely contradicts his claim in the opening pages that he has an appointment from Count Westwest as land surveyor. He thinks of "K. himself knocking on the door at the council chairman's during office hours the following day and registering as a foreign journeyman [*fremder Wanderbursch*] who had already found a place to sleep at a local citizen's [*bestimmten Gemeindemitglied*] and would probably continue his journey the next day, unless, and this was most unlikely, he found work here, but then only for a few days, since he hadn't the slightest intention of staying longer. This is what would have happened, or something of that sort, had it not been for Schwarzer" (165e; 203g).

The word *verschlossen* (sealed) in the passage about Amalia's secrecy reminds the reader of what is implied by the German word for Castle, *Schloß*, a sealed enclosure. The characters of *Das Schloß* are sealed off from one another. Each dwells in his or her private castle, or *Schloß*. Other people's thoughts and feelings must be inferred, always doubtfully and uncertainly, from what they say and from how they look. Those long speeches by other characters give the reader and K. himself indirect access to the idiosyncratic interior worlds of the other characters, but this access is uncertain and unverifiable.[22] They may be dissembling or outright lying. Neither K. nor the reader has any way to check their veracity. The evidence is often contradictory. Of course Kafka as author could have done anything he liked in this domain, but he chose to omit direct access to the minds of the other characters. Their interiorities therefore remain impenetrable secrets.

Kafka is in this in close consonance with Derrida's position or with Husserl at his bleakest and most nearly solipsistic.[23] No Heideggerian *Mitsein* or *Mitdasein* or *Miteinandersein* for Kafka! The result is that no verification of K.'s assumptions about what the other person is thinking or feeling is possible. This law of what Edmund Husserl called "analogical apperception," that is, the unverifiable assumption that the other person must have a mind and feelings analogous to my own, and the consequent uncertainty of interpretation, apply just as much to K.'s reading of the people in the village as to his (mis)understanding of people hypothetically connected to the Castle or representing it. (See note 22.) What K. sees or hears or reads may mean this or it may mean that. No possible way exists to tell for sure. Nevertheless, an urgent need to make correct interpretations defines K.'s situation throughout. His life depends on it.

Unverifiable Acts of Interpretation

The result of this difficulty or impossibility of understanding others is that *The Castle* is made up to a considerable degree of acts of interpretation by K. or by others that often contradict one another in the midst of a sentence. I call them *acts* of interpretation to call attention to the way interpretation is a speech act as well as a constative assertion of meaning. An interpretation says, "I claim this means that," not just "This means that." If what K. sees, hears, and reads were easy to understand, no lengthy work of interpretation would be necessary.

The novel has almost innumerable examples of the law of contradiction that governs interpretation in *Das Schloß*. Unverifiable and inconsistent "exegesis" forms the basic stylistic fabric or texture of the novel. The narrative is not so much the straightforward telling of a story that might be interpreted narratologically, as it is the staging of situations that involve permanently inconclusive acts of reading, always in excess of the data they attempt to read. These readings are, perhaps, allegorical representations of the readers' own acts of interpretation. These, as I have said, have been exemplified by the wildly divergent ways *The Castle* has been read by its critics. In almost all cases the unreadable data are versions of the impossibility for K. to get verifiable knowledge of what is going on, especially in relation to his own situation, up there in the many offices in the Castle. What decisions have they made about K.? What are their intentions in regard to K.?

The acts of interpretation within the novel exist on many different levels and scales. They may take the form of a contradictory interpretation by K. or by another character of some apparently trivial detail in another person's appearance, behavior, or speech. Frieda's hands may be small and delicate or they might be called just weak and expressionless (37e; 50g). The question is important because Frieda, as Klamm's one-time mistress (before she makes love with K. on the floor of the taproom outside Klamm's room), has, or has had, or may have had, a "connection" with the Castle. The contradictions may take the form of extended dialogues in which K. and some other character—Frieda, the village chairman, the landlady, Hans Brunswick, Momus, Barnabas, Olga, Pepi, and the rest—argue at length and inconclusively about some aspect of K.'s situation or about someone else's "connection" to the Castle. These contradictory acts of exegesis may take the form of inconsistencies between the chapters. K. does not seem to be able to stick to any promise or commitment, as he tries, always unsuccessfully, one way after another to reach Klamm, and to go beyond Klamm to the Castle itself. *Weg*, German for "path," "road," or "way," is a key word in the novel. "*Weg*" might be taken as an ironically inappropriate name for the novel's narrative sequence, as it wanders this way and that, always starting over again from the beginning, never finding its way, and never getting any closer to the Castle.

K.'s actions are perversely contradictory and self-destructive. He promises fidelity to Frieda, but then betrays her by turning to Olga, Barnabas, and Amalia. He says at one point that he has left a wife and child at home, but that does not keep him from promising to marry Frieda after he has slept with her. He repudiates the landlady's advice, but later depends on her for information. Instead of getting him closer to the Castle, his dilatory wavering gets him further and further away in the course, or *Weg*, of the novel, as it works its way toward stopping in the middle of a sentence. This sentence was about to report the speech of an apparently peripheral and inconsequential character, Gerstäcker's mother, after previous digressions to Pepi and then to Gerstäcker. It is even doubtful if the word "digression" may legitimately be used to describe *The Castle*'s narrative structure, since no identifiable straight or crooked path to the goal exists, and since we have no certainty even about the nature and location of the goal.

Who knows, however? A given "digression" might suddenly reach the goal, as an exemplification of the law that "the longest way round is the shortest way home," or in analogy with the way Alice gets to the top of the little hill by going resolutely in the opposite direction. As a narrative sequence open to clear and unambiguous interpretation, *The Castle* is distressingly unsatisfactory. A good example of the way a given *Weg* seems at first to be an advance toward the goal but then turns out to be mere wandering is the episode of K.'s sleeping with Frieda in the beer puddles outside Klamm's door in the Gentleman's Inn, where Frieda works. K. perhaps assumes that because Frieda is Klamm's mistress, sleeping with her will be an indirect way of approaching Klamm and a way of going through Klamm to the Castle and to Count Westwest. Instead, he discovers that Frieda's betrayal of her liaison with Klamm puts a complete end to her relation with Klamm. The sexual event, moreover, is described in a powerful passage as a wandering into a strange exile in foreign lands. It is a way of not getting to the Castle, or, perhaps (who knows?), K.'s experience, as he and Frieda make love, of wandering, of getting more and more lost, of suffocating, may be the closest he ever gets to experiencing what it would be like to be up at the Castle:

> Like a child she began to tug at him: "Come, it's stifling down here," they embraced each other, her small body was burning in K.'s hands; they rolled a few paces in an unconscious state from which K. repeatedly but vainly tried to rescue himself, bumped dully against Klamm's door, and then lay in the small puddles of beer and other rubbish with which the floor was covered. Hours passed there, hours breathing together with a single heartbeat, hours in which K. constantly felt he was lost [*er verirre sich*] or had wandered farther into foreign lands than any human being before him, so foreign that even the air hadn't a single component of the air in his homeland and where one would inevitably suffocate from the foreignness but where the meaningless enticements [*unsinnigen Verlockungen*] were such that one had no alternative but to go on and get even more lost [*weiter sich verirren*]. (41e; 55g)

The most extensive connected sequence in *Das Schloß*, several chapters long, is made up by the "digression" of a story within a story. This is the narrative of the ostracism, by what Olga explicitly calls "the community [*die Gemeinde*]" (208e; 254g), of Barnabas's family after Amalia's refusal of a sexual advance from Sortini, an official from the Castle. The novel, both locally and as a whole, has the narrative rhythm of one of those dreams characterized by endless delay and a slowing down of time, as though one were trying to make one's way through deep snow, as K. actually does early in the novel. The reader feels, to boot, as if he or she were getting further and further away from a constantly receding goal. When K. does finally get an interview with someone from the Castle, Bürgel, who says he, Bürgel, would be irresistibly tempted to help K., and explains to K. just what he should do to get to the Castle, K. falls asleep at the crucial moment, so long winded has Bürgel's discourse been. This may be an oblique warning to the reader to keep wakeful, even though the novel does not seem to be getting anywhere. One remembers the notorious occasion when Christ's disciples went to sleep: "What, could ye not watch with me one hour?" (Matthew 26:40). Reading *Das Schloß* is a most exasperating, perhaps even sleep-inducing, experience.

Forms of Contradiction

The verbal contradictions I have mentioned as a chief stylistic feature of *The Castle* may take the form of global descriptions of K.'s life situation. An example of the latter is a passage brilliantly commented on by Henry Sussman at the beginning of his book on the outside, *Idylls of the Wanderer: Outside in Literature and Theory*.[24] K. has been left alone in the dark, snowy courtyard of the Gentlemen's Inn after fruitlessly waiting to waylay Klamm when he comes out to get in his sleigh and return to the Castle:

> All the electric lights went out—for whom should they have shone?—and only the opening above in the wooden gallery remained bright and briefly arrested one's wandering gaze, it seemed to K. as if they had broken off all contact with him [*als habe man nun alle Verbindung mit ihm abgebrochen*], but as if he were freer than ever [*als sei er nun freilich freier als jemals*] and could wait as long as he wanted here in this place where he was generally not allowed, and as if he had fought for this freedom for himself in a manner nobody else could have done and as if nobody could touch him or drive him away, or even speak to him, yet—and this conviction was at least equally strong—as if there were nothing more senseless, nothing more desperate, than this freedom, this waiting, this invulnerability [*und habe sich diese Freiheit erkämpft wie kaum ein anderer es könnte und neiman*

> *dürfe ihn anrühren oder vertreiben, ja kaum ansprechen, aber—diese Überzeugung war zumindest ebenso stark—als gäbe es gleichzeitig nichts Sinnloseres, nichts Verzweifelteres als diese Freiheit, dieses Warten, diese Unverletzlichkeit*]. (106e; 132–33g)

K.'s freedom is here given two contradictory meanings, both of which apply to K.'s sense of his situation, and between which it is impossible to choose. On the one hand, K.'s freedom, the freedom of the outsider, that is, his detachment from all connection (*Verbindung*) to others and from all responsibility toward them, gives him an exhilarating sense of power and invulnerability. He is unique in this freedom, since he has fought for it in a way nobody else could have done. His invulnerability is his complete exemption from the power others in a community are normally felt to have over another member of that community. Nobody can touch K. or drive him away, or even speak to him. On the other hand, this exhilarating sense of sovereign immunity from all responsibility to others is at the same time the most abject feeling, K.'s conviction that his situation is extravagantly, hyperbolically senseless and desperate. That situation is characterized by an endless "waiting" for something or someone, Klamm in this case, who is never going to come, like the waiting for Godot in Beckett's play, or like the waiting for the Messiah in Kafka's striking aphorism "The Messiah will come only when he is no longer necessary; he will come only on the day after his arrival; he will come, not on the last day, but on the very last [*nicht am letzen Tag kommen, sondern am allerletzten*]."[25]

A final contradiction in the passage cited above, characteristic of the stylistic texture of *Das Schloß* throughout, is between its material specificity and the high level of at least implicit generality that has led readers almost irresistibly toward interpreting the novel in one way or another allegorically. It cannot, we readers feel, mean just what it says, which in this case is no more than that K. has failed to get a chance to confront Klamm face to face and consequently has an inner feeling of freedom or of detachment or of being outside everything and everyone. This feeling is at one and the same time exhilarating and senseless, desperate. This passage shows K. enisled with a vengeance. No clue, however, is given that might verify an allegorical reading. It might be better to stick to a "literal" reading, as the priest in *The Trial* counsels Josef K. to do in interpreting the story the priest tells, "Before the Law": "You don't have sufficient respect [*Achtung*] for the text and are changing the story. . . . The text is immutable [*unveränderlich*], and the opinions are often only an expression of despair [*Verzweiflung*] over it."[26]

Many locutions that take the form "X and not X," or "X and at the same time Y," or "perhaps this but also perhaps that" occur throughout *Das Schloß*, in many different ways and at many different scales. Here are some examples of this syntactic paradigm that occurs throughout *Das Schloß* in so many different forms and at so many different scales. The translations carry over quite well the complex syntax and semantics of the German originals:

> "Just as I said," he shouted, "no trace [*Spur*] of a land surveyor, only a liar and a common tramp, and probably worse still." . . . "So it's a mistake [*ein Irrtum*]? This is most unpleasant. The department head himself telephoned? Odd, very odd! And how am I supposed to explain this to the land surveyor?" (4e, 5e; 12g, 13g)
>
> On the one hand [*einerseits*], this was unfavorable [*ungünstig*] for him. . . . On the other hand [*andererseits*], it was favorable [*günstig*]. (5e; 13g)
>
> A bell up there rang out cheerfully [*fröhlich*], a bell that for a moment at least made one's heart tremble as if it were threatened—for the sound was painful [*schmerzlich*] too—with the fulfillment of its uncertain longings. (15e; 26g)
>
> He was obliged to repeat what he had just said out of malice [*Bosheit*], only this time out of compassion [*Mitleid*]. (16e; 26g)
>
> Were staring [*zusahen*] at him but then again not staring at him. (22e; 32g)
>
> Perhaps they really wanted something from him but just couldn't say what it was, and if that wasn't it, perhaps it was merely childlike behavior on their part. (25e; 37g)
>
> "I don't know whether such a decision was reached in your case—there is evidence both for and against [*manches spricht dafür, manches dagegen*]." (68e; 87g)
>
> "I think that the hopes of Hans's relatives were neither completely justified [*Recht*] nor completely unjustified [*Unrecht*]." (84e; 105g)

The only consolation [*Tröstliche*], it seemed, was that it wasn't Klamm, or was that actually cause for regret [*zu bedauern*]? (104e; 129g)

"Perhaps [*Vielleicht*] you aren't initiated into Barnabas's affairs, and that's good [*gut*] . . . but perhaps you are initiated . . . and that's bad [*schlimm*]." (170e; 208g; here the values of the alternatives are clearly stated. The uncertainty is in that "perhaps.")

This was not yet entirely clear and the opposite [*in Gegenteil*] could eventually prove true. (177e; 217g)

"For instance, Klamm has a village secretary here called Momus. . . . A powerful young gentleman, isn't he? And so he probably doesn't look at all like [*gar nicht ähnlich*] Klamm. And yet you can find people in the village who would swear that Momus is Klamm [*Momus Klamm ist*] and none other than he." (181e; 222g)

So they certainly are, as you say, entirely different cases [*grundverschiedene Fälle*; Frieda's and Olga's], but they're similar too [*auch ähnlich*]." (195e; 238g)

"One doesn't know whether she is speaking ironically or seriously [*ironisch oder ernst*], it's mostly serious, but sounds ironic." "Stop interpreting everything! [*Lass die Deutungen!*]," said K. (205e; 251g)

"If we stressed their importance [*Wichtigkeit*; of the messages from Klamm to K.] we would make people suspect that we were overrating something that was obviously so unimportant [*Unwichtiges*] merely so as to recommend ourselves to you as the bearers of this news. . . . But if we didn't attach much importance to the letters we should make ourselves suspect. . . . And staying in the middle, between the exaggerations, that is, weighing the letters correctly is impossible, their value keeps changing, the thoughts that they prompt are endless [*die Überlegungen, zu denen sie Anlaß geben sind endlos*]." (231e; 279–80g)

"You're right, it can never happen. But one night—who can vouch for everything—it does happen." (268e; 323g)

> "That is how the world corrects its course and keeps its equilibrium [*Gleichgewicht*]. It's certainly an excellent arrangement, always unimaginably excellent [*vorzügliche*], even if in certain other respects hopeless [*trostlos*]." (271e; 326g)

Such expressions certainly are calculated to exasperate the reader. Why cannot K. or the narrator tell us which alternative is the correct interpretation? These expressions of unresolved contradictions, of negations without dialectical negativity or possible sublation, are either citations from speeches by one or another of the characters or reports in free indirect discourse of something K. thinks to himself. The subjective situation of all the persons who dwell in the village beneath the Castle is to be caught in the double bind of a permanently unverifiable either/or, or perhaps this/perhaps that, or both this and that, though matters of the utmost importance, to the characters at least, are at stake in these undecidable oscillations between contradictory interpretations. The characters in *Das Schloß* all waver this way and that, often in a single sentence, because they can find no solid external ground of sure knowledge to support deciding one way or the other.

The notorious run-on sentences that make up much of *Das Schloß*, long sequences of phrases or complete sentences bound together by commas or perhaps by semicolons, a stylistic feature that Max Brod "corrected" in the first edition, and that was also suppressed in the Muir translation, mimes this side-by-sideness, in nonhierarchical and nondialectical dispersal, of contradictory judgments or interpretations, just as I have mimicked this dispersal, in my turn, in this present sentence.

This limitation in human possibilities of knowledge can be defined as the impossibility of verifiable interpretation. This impossibility, paradoxically, is what keeps the narrative of *The Castle* going. Strangely enough, interpretative uncertainty, according to Kafka, makes the world go round and keep its balance. The last exemplary passage just cited asserts this in a characteristically contradictory way by saying it is an unimaginably excellent arrangement while at the same time, in certain other respects, hopeless. Well, which is it, unimaginably excellent (*vorzügliche*), or hopeless (*trostlos*)? One would like to know. How can it be both at once?

In an important entry in the *Diaries*, a characteristically strange and hyperbolic notation made on November 20, 1911, Kafka reflected on his fateful penchant for "antitheses," as well on as his distaste for them. "My repugnance for antitheses is certain," he says. He then goes on, predictably, to express this antipathy in a spectacular example of the way his thinking proceeds by way of (or, rather, gets hung up on) antitheses that turn round and round. Though this circling seems to lead to endless vistas, Kafka's antitheses always conclude by turning back on themselves in a self-enclosure that offers no leads for going any further in any direction. No dialectical synthesis is possible for Kafka's antitheses. They just proliferate a cascade of further antitheses. The "wheel of life" referred to in the following citation is, a footnote asserts, "a toy through which one perceived the successive positions of a figure affixed to a revolving wheel. It thus created the illusion of motion."[27] The "wheel of life" was a primitive motion picture machine. It went round and round, repeating the same illusory motion:

> My repugnance [*Widerwillen*] for antitheses is certain. They are unexpected, but do not surprise [*überraschen nicht*], for they have always been there; if they were unconscious, it was at the very edge of consciousness. They make for thoroughness [*Gründlichkeit*], fullness, completeness, but only like a figure on the "wheel of life" [*Lebensrad*], we have chased our little idea around the circle. They are as undifferentiated as they are different, they grow under one's hand as though bloated by water, beginning with the prospect of infinity [*Aussicht ins Grenzenlose*], they always end up in the same medium size. They curl up [*rollen sich ein*], cannot be straightened out, give no guiding principle [*geben keinen Anhaltspunkt*], are holes in wood, are immobile assaults, draw antitheses to themselves, as I have shown. If they would only draw all of them, and forever.[28]

Why These Unresolved Contradictions?

Yes, if we could just gather all antitheses in one sequestered bundle and let them keep quietly circulating there forever, then all might be well. Unfortunately, in Kafka's writing new antitheses are constantly appearing, outside the circle. Reading *Das Schloß* is certainly exasperating! It is exasperating because it "proceeds" (if that is the right word; "skips" would be better) from one antithesis to another, while remaining still stuck in the same place the narrative begins—in the village, at the foot of the Castle hill. Why so much equivocation? Why so little narrative progress?

Let me look in a little detail at one apparently trivial such passage. K. reflects, when he first meets Frieda, that "her hands were indeed small and delicate, but they could also be called weak and expressionless"

(37e). (Ihre Hände allerdings waren klein und zart, aber man hätte sie auch schwach und nichtssagend nennen können [50g].) The effect of such sentences on the reader, on me at least, is extremely odd. Well, which is it, small and delicate, or weak and expressionless? Why cannot K. and the narrative voice, which here speaks for K. in free indirect discourse, make up their minds? It is perhaps important to know, since K. is about to enter into a long-term liaison with Frieda, and thereby obtain an indirect relationship, he hopes, to Klamm, and through Klamm to the Castle. The odd effect is generated to a considerable degree by that phrase "man hätte sie . . . nennen können," "one could have called, or named, them." Called by whom? Named by whom? K.? The narrator? Kafka? Anyone under the sun ("one"; *man*)?

Kafka himself, the reader may suddenly reflect, is the ultimate responsible party. He is making the whole thing up. He could call Frieda's hands whatever he likes, small and delicate, weak and expressionless, or anything else he chooses. The language of *Das Schloß* is not constative or referential, since no extralinguistic referent exists against which it can be measured, but performative or constitutive. The word *nennen* calls attention to the constructive power of performative language in a literary fiction. It calls attention indirectly to the way the whole novel represents examples of the perpetual either/or or both/and of performative invention and its subsequent (mis)interpretation. Since no possible access to any external referent exists, you, K., the narrator, *man* in general, can call those imaginary hands anything they like. The situation of the characters, K. especially, doomed as they are to perpetual undecidable acts of interpretation, mimes the reader's own situation. The reader too is engaged in a difficult, or perhaps impossible, act of exegesis. The storyline follows this unsuccessful attempt to understand as it pursues its wandering and discontinuous way.

Interpretation of Others' Speech: Kafka and Midrash

I have spoken of K.'s "reading" of other people's faces and looks as acts of interpretation. Much of the novel is taken up by even more literal acts of interpretation, that is, interpretation of written or spoken language. A large part of *Das Schloß* is made up of dialogue. K. tries to figure out just what Frieda, or Barnabas, or the village council chairman, or the landlady, or the teacher, or Olga, or the enigmatic voices on the telephone from the Castle mean by what they say. What they say most often takes the form of mysterious and contradictory interpretations of K.'s situation. These need to be perpetually analyzed anew by K., "read" by him, that is, subjected to exegesis. The chapters make a slow round of face-to-face confrontations as K. engages character after character in the give-and-take of conversation.

It is as if, in *Das Schloß*, the famous nitpicking rabbinic interchanges of Talmudic or Midrashic readings had been applied to ordinary human conversation. The difference is that Talmudic or Midrashic interpretations are even more extravagant. Their exegesis, moreover, is often applied to passages from Jewish sacred scripture, not to specific secular details, so the assumption is that Jehovah must have meant something definite, even though that something may be hard to interpret. In addition, the goal of Talmud and Midrash, often at least seemingly reached, is reconciliation, harmony, elucidation, resolution of apparent contradiction.

The transfer of something like Talmudic or Midrashic procedures to K.'s never-successful attempt to understand the people around him, to find out how to get an audience with Klamm, and how to get through Klamm to the Castle, produces something exceedingly strange and unsettling. The reader is led, as K. warns Olga against doing with Barnabas's reports, to "scrutinize his every word as though it were a word from Revelations [*jedes seiner Worte wie ein Offenbarungswort untersuchen*] and make one's own happiness in life depend on the interpretation [*und von der Deutung das eigene Lebensglück abhängig machen*]" (183e; 224g). Are Frieda's hands small and delicate or should they just be called weak? An interminable interrogation of the evidence appears destined not to reach a verifiable conclusion, since no access is possible to solid, extratextual, authoritative evidence that would justify deciding one way or the other.

I thought at first that I might have been the first to notice that *The Castle* is a novel about the interminable undecidabilities of interpretation in a situation in which ultimate verification is impossible, and the first to suggest that this might be compared to Midrash. As I might have expected, however, my insight, such as it is, has been corroborated by more than one scholar.[29] Maurice Blanchot, in what is surely one of the most brilliant essays on *The Castle*, "The Wooden Bridge (Repetition, the Neutral)" ("Le pont de bois [la répétition, le neutre]"), describes this essential feature of the novel with brilliant succinctness.[30] Blanchot does not, however, stress self-contradiction as a basic feature of *Das Schloß*'s style, nor does he note, as I do, that a perpetually unverifiable process of exegesis is applied to interpretations of at least seemingly trivial aspects of the people K. meets. (Are Frieda's hands delicate or just weak and expressionless?) Nor does Blanchot note that these uncertainties derive from the basic narrative presupposition that the subjectivity of the other person (if the other really is a "person") is never directly accessible. Such access would be necessary to verify the speculations about other persons that K. and others make. K.'s isolation is such that any guess he makes about other people's subjectivities "could never be proved, never be refuted [*der sich niemals nachweisen, niemals widerlegen ließ*]" (115e; 144g).

Much attention in *Das Schloß* is paid to written documents and to the difficulty of interpreting them. In one salient example, not only K., but also the village chairman and his wife read Klamm's letter to K. this way and that. They never agree on the right way to read it. Is it an official letter or an unofficial one? Which would be better for K.? Is it friendly or unfriendly? Does it give K. an authorized position in the village or not?

The hardworking Castle authorities and their representatives in the village spend much time producing, storing, and interpreting huge assemblages of documents. An example is the comic description of the search for one lost document (the Castle's original decree stating that a land surveyor is needed) by the chairman's wife, Mizzi, and the two assistants, in the closet full of documents in the chairman's room (60–62e; 76–79g). This is followed by the seriocomic account of what happened to the misdirected file about the decision to hire or not to hire a land surveyor (62–64e; 78–82g). Another example is the putative description by the chairman of Sordini's office, with its piles of documents that are constantly falling down with resounding thuds in rapid succession (66e; 83–84g). The description is necessarily putative because no one the reader encounters from the village has actually been there or ever seen Sordini.

Sordini's office reminds me of Borges's story "The Library of Babel." That story, in turn, reminds me of the mind-boggling proliferation of databases, files, e-mail, and websites on the Internet, and of the never-wholly-successful attempt by Google or Yahoo! to keep them searchable. The World Wide Web already in 2005 had more than 600 billion pages![31] It must be immensely larger now, in 2010. That boggles or googles the mind. A similar problem exists in *The Castle*. Not only do the Castle officials fail to keep up with the piles of new documents, but also if a document goes astray, it is almost impossible ever to find it again, as is the case with large bureaucracies in the real world. Files sent on the World Wide Web, such as e-mail attachments, are broken up into relatively short "packets," then routed by sometimes quite different trajectories and nodes to their destination, where they are reassembled in order. One can imagine a packet that gets lost and circulates endlessly in cyberspace without ever reaching its goal. Something like that happens to the village chairman's response to word from the Castle that a land surveyor should be appointed. The village chairman consults with the village citizens and responds that the village has no need of a land surveyor. That document, however, gets mistakenly sent to Department B rather than to Department A. Department B has no idea what to do with it. The folder is mysteriously empty anyway. Years and years go by before the mixup is sorted out. The delay is exacerbated because no functioning mechanism exists in this bureaucracy, in a way similar to that of many bureaucracies, for admitting that an error has been made, even though a Control Department exists. This endless delay in getting documents sent to their right addressees is one example of the nightmarish temporality I mentioned earlier as a basic feature of narration in *Das Schloß*.

The reader of *The Castle*, faced with all this treatment of documents and their interpretation, may suddenly at some point realize that he or she is at that moment engaged in an act of interpretation that is mirrored by those in the novel. The text of *Das Schloss* and its various translations are by no means unequivocal in meaning. Kafka died leaving the novel unfinished. It stops in the middle of a sentence. It is tempting to believe that it was in principle impossible to finish. K. makes no headway at all in getting closer to the Castle. If anything, he is further away at the end than he was in the beginning. The chapters do not progress forward chronologically toward reaching the Castle. The chapters rather move laterally, as K. encounters one dead end after another, only to retrace his steps and start again. It may be that Kafka gave up writing the novel because he was, as Blanchot asserts in "Kafka and Literature," committed to writing as a way to make headway toward the goal of his own salvation by way of literature and discovered to his dismay that writing cannot be used in this way. Literature in general, perhaps, only leads to endless wandering. Or it may be, as Walter Benjamin and Werner Hamacher have asserted, that Kafka deliberately wrote his works so that they would successfully resist interpretation, in order to keep them from having a malign performative effect.[32]

No Passageway; No Connection

For Kafka, as for Derrida, in a passage already cited in chapter 1, "between my world, the 'my world'; what I call 'my world,' and there is no other for me, every other world making up part of it, between my world and every other world, there is initially the space and the time of an infinite difference, of an interruption incommensurable with all the attempts at passage, of bridge, of isthmus, of communication, of translation, of trope, and of transfer."[33] *The Castle*, no reader can doubt, is a potentially endless variation on the theme of failed "attempts at passage." K. wants, or says he wants, to come face to face with the highest Castle authorities, with Count Westwest himself, in order to demand and get official authority to practice in the village his "calling" of land surveyor. He repudiates every mediation in the name of unmediated direct encounter. His sin is impatience. He wants to find a pathway to the inside of the inside of the Castle. He finds over and over again that he can attain only mediated access to people who have some sort of equivocal distant "connection [*Verbindung*]" to the Castle, or perhaps only appear to do so.

Verbindung is a key word in the novel. It occurs again and again in different contexts, for example, in Bürgel's description of himself as "a connecting secretary [*Verbindungssekretär*]" (259e; 313g). Bürgel is a self-proclaimed mediator, a connector. In another example, much earlier in the novel, the landlady tries to persuade K. to make a deposition [*Protokoll*] to Klamm's village secretary, Momus. The passage repeatedly speaks of the deposition as the only path (*Weg*) to Klamm. "But the hope I have in mind," says the landlady, "has to do with your possessing through the deposition a kind of connection [*eine Art Verbindung*], perhaps a kind of connection, with Klamm" (114e; 142g). K., however, stubbornly refuses, over and over, to have anything to do with such intermediaries, even though the landlady assures him, in quasi-theological language, that Momus is "filled with [Klamm's] spirit [*von seinem Geiste erfüllt ist*]" and that Momus is "an instrument [*ein Werkzeug*] upon which Klamm's hand lies" (115e; 144g). K. believes that all such intermediaries are also "blocking agents," obstacles in the pathway. K. discovers in the course of his failed attempts to reach the Castle that, as one of Kafka's crucial aphorisms, cited more than once in this book, puts it, "There is a goal but no way; what we call the way is only wavering."[34] (Es gibt ein Ziel, aber keinen Weg; was wir Weg nennen, ist Zögern.)[35]

This pattern is repeated over and over in the incomplete novel. It might have gone on being repeated interminably in more and more chapters, without ever reaching that hypothetical deathbed scene with which Kafka told Max Brod he intended to end the novel.

It is not so much contrariness as an instinctive rejection of all mediation that leads to K.'s refusals. As the narrator says, apropos of one of those refusals, speaking for K. in free indirect discourse, "Far be it from him to feel admiration or even envy [for Momus] since it was not closeness to Klamm in itself that was worth striving for but rather that he, K., and he alone, not anybody else with his wishes, or anybody else's, should approach Klamm, and approach him not so as to rest there with him but to get past him and go on into the Castle [*nicht um bei ihm zu ruhen sondern um an ihn vorbeizukommen, weiter, ins Schloß*]" (111e; 138g).

(Non)Community in The Castle

How is this unfortunate situation, and its concomitant, the irremediable isolation of K.'s consciousness, reflected in *The Castle*'s assumptions about community? After all, the "conflagration of community" is supposed to be my main topic in this book. In order to answer my question constructively, I need first to ask how assumptions about community can be related to the narratological questions I began this essay by saying would be one of my guiding paths. I answer that assumptions about community in a given novel are consonant with its assumptions about the narrator (or "narrative voice"), about narrative continuity, and about all the other questions that narratology might lead the critic to ask.

Anthony Trollope's novels, for example, one of his big multiplotted novels like *The Last Chronicle of Barset* (1867), tend to assume (1) that a viable, stable, community remaining the same through history, and supported by universal ethical norms and values, exists in the world of the novel and in the real world the novel implicitly claims faithfully to represent; (2) that the members of such a fictional community have a quasi-telepathic knowledge of what other members are thinking and feeling; this is in part because you can assume your neighbor will in a given situation think and feel as you would; (3) that the intertwined life stories of both men and women in such a community can be told by a narrator who embodies the collective consciousness of the community. Such a narrator has a telepathic insight into the minds and hearts of all the characters and can recount their life stories as a continuous sense-making drama that goes from beginning to middle to end. The end, for those charming English maidens who are the central figures in so many Trollope novels, is a happy marriage that is celebrated by the whole community. This marriage will lead to the birth of children who will carry that community on into future generations.

In spite of Nicolas Royle's persuasive argument for seeing narrators in Victorian novels as "telepathic," the Trollopean storyteller can plausibly be labeled with the old-fashioned term "omniscient narrator." He (clearly it is a "he") is to some degree a surrogate for the Christian God. Trollope's narrator is implicitly modeled on the Christian notion of divinity. God, like the omniscient narrator, is omnipotent, omnipresent, and knows what is going on in the most secret regions of a given person's heart and soul at any moment, in a panoptic surveillance. I was taught in Sunday school that God has such omniscient power over each of us "in real life." "Watch out, God knows what you are thinking, what your most secret motives are." As Jesus said, "Whosoever looketh on a woman to lust after her hath committed adultery with her already in his heart" (Matthew 5:28). God, who knows everything, knows when you have this hidden desire. The deity's universal spying power is expressed in Saint Augustine's definition of God as "interio intimo meo et superior summo meo" (more inward to me than the most inward part of me; and higher than my highest reach).[36]

Well, how does the agglomeration of people in Kafka's *The Castle* measure up to this ideal community? For Raymond Williams, in *The Country and the City*, a hierarchical class structure destroys community.[37] As soon as a squire's country house is built in one of Williams's ideal (and always imaginary) egalitarian rural communities (in their untouched form a presage of the classless society to come in the Marxist millennium), community is destroyed. It might seem at first that the village in Kafka's *The Castle* is such an egalitarian community, with a fixed role for everybody who is "from the village." All the inhabitants of the village seem to have known one another since childhood and to share the same assumptions. The Castle, it might seem, is also a true community, the community of those who are "from the Castle." K. is unique, as the landlady tells him: "You're not from the Castle, you're not from the village, you are nothing [*Sie sind nichts*]. Unfortunately, though, you are something, a stranger [*ein Fremder*], one who is superfluous and gets in the way everywhere [*einer der überzählig und überall im Weg ist*; there is "*Weg*" again!], one who is a constant source of trouble [*Scherereien*]" (48e; 63g). K. is, uniquely among all the characters, "a stranger," someone "from away," as my native-born neighbors in Deer Isle, Maine, put it, or even an "illegal immigrant." K. is repeatedly identified as such, for example, by the landlady in the passage just cited, or by the chairman in K.'s discussion with him (65e; 82g). To be from away, to be neither from the village nor from the Castle, is to be "nothing," since to be something is to be one's community placement.

It is easy to see, however, that matters are not so simple. Just as in Williams's paradigm, so in *Das Schloß*, relations among people in the village are poisoned by the way each villager has some relation to the Castle. Messengers and officials from the Castle are constantly entering the village. The villagers' lives, it turns out, are almost entirely determined by people from the Castle. Barnabas's family is ruined by his sister's refusal of the sexual invitation made by Sortini, a man from the Castle. The lives of both Frieda and the landlady are decisively determined by their sexual liaisons with Klamm. K. thinks he can reach Klamm, and through Klamm, Count Westwest, by making love to Frieda. People in the village are full of jealousy, suspicion, and antagonisms that are caused by their relations to what are most often, at least apparently, obscure lower members of the Castle hierarchy.

Those from the Castle, moreover, are members of an immensely complex hierarchical bureaucracy that hardly fits any normal definition of community. A passage in *Der Proceß* speaks of the Court in that novel as an endless hierarchy of ranks and grades. The bureaucracy in *Das Schloß* differs from that in *Der Proceß* in proliferating sideways as well as vertically. Departments A and B are apparently on the same level, even though innumerable other departments may exist above them, just as an indeterminate number of intermediaries exist below them. This means, to paraphrase what Jacques Derrida says, in disagreement with Jacques Lacan, about Poe's "The Purloined Letter," that in *Das Schloß* a letter or message sent from low to high or high to low is almost certain never to reach its destination.[38] It will most likely end up in the wrong department and become part of an ever-increasing pile of unread and unanswered documents. If the landlady says the truth about K. when she says he is "nothing" because he comes neither from the village nor from the Castle, even those who have always been from the village are deprived of any community membership of the sort Williams imagines. They are deprived of this by their "connections" (and everybody has a connection) to the Castle. Kafka's hierarchy of Castle functionaries already has the bureaucratic complexity and tangle of texts and functionary powers that made the Shoah possible and that today characterize the global financial system, or the Internet, or government bureaucracies.

In one illusory moment of self-satisfaction K. imagines that he is a member of the village community and that it is a real community. What he says gives a good definition of what he (and perhaps Kafka) thought of as the normal and proper way to belong to a local community:

> I have in a sense increased in scope [*Ich habe gewissermaßen an Umfang gewonnen*] and that already says something; trivial though all this is, I do after all have a home, a position, and real work, I have a fiancée who takes over my professional work whenever I have other business to attend to, I shall marry her

> and join the community [*ich werde sie heiraten und Gemeindemitglied werden*]; I also have, besides an official connection [*Beziehung*] to Klamm, a personal one, which I have admittedly not yet been able to take advantage of. Now surely that is more than a little? [*Das ist doch wohl nicht wenig*?]. (198–99e, trans. altered; 242–43g)

Unfortunately, what K. boasts of having is just what he does not have. His position as school janitor is extremely precarious, insecure, and temporary. He does not have a "home" in any valid sense of the word. Frieda is about to leave him for one of the assistants, Jeremias. He and Frieda will never marry. No valid community of which he might ever become a part exists in the village, since the villagers' manifold "connections" to the Castle keep them permanently at odds with one another. Moreover, they are as much lacking in intuitive understanding of one another as K. is of the villagers. Each man and woman in the village is an island, a monad, without any certain isthmus or passage to any of his or her fellow villagers.

The consequence of this lack of community is that no narrator such as tells the stories of Trollope's protagonists is possible for Kafka, no "omniscient narrator," not even a narrator with universal telepathic powers, no narrator as the expression of the community's collective consciousness. What is possible for Kafka is a disembodied narrative voice that is almost completely limited to entering just one mind, K.'s. The narrator is restricted to ironically miming in free indirect discourse what goes on in that mind or to naming objectively what that mind saw, heard, and felt. Kafka himself, in an often-quoted statement in the diaries, expressed this constitutive narratological doubling as follows: "What will be my fate as a writer is very simple. My talent for portraying my dreamlike inner life has thrust all matters into the background."[39] This dreamlike inner life is, in *The Castle*, Kafka's imagination of K.'s adventures after he enters the village on that snowy night. Kafka's "talent for portraying" that dreamlike inner life is manifested in his genius as a storyteller and inventor of unsettling dialogue, behavior, and settings, as well as in the change from *Ich* to *er* that generates the doubling of protagonist by the detached, slightly ironic, narrative voice.

Kafka's *Das Schloß* suggests that a writer's assumptions about the possibility of access to other minds is consonant with (I do not say "causes") that writer's assumptions about community or the lack of it. It is consonant also with the sort of narrative voice that is possible for a given writer, along with his or her choices for the other structural features of storytelling that narratologists study. *Das Schloß*, in its dramatization of an endless unsuccessful search to escape isolation and join a community, suggests, in addition, that if you begin with an assumption, such as Kafka's or Derrida's, of each ego's essential isolation, you cannot think or feel your way out of that presumption to some concept of Heideggerian *Mitsein* or Williamsian togetherness, transparency, and mutual loving-kindness. You must begin with it ever to have it. Husserl's failure ever to satisfy himself that the ego has anything more than an anological apperception of the other's interiority is mirrored in K.'s inability to penetrate others' minds and in his concomitant endless unsuccessful search for a secure authorized place in the (non)community at the foot of the Castle mount.

K. and I

I conclude, though with fear and trembling, that Kafka's presentation of K.'s experience in the village at the foot of the ever-mysterious and unreachable Castle hill has an uncanny and disquieting resemblance not only to the situation of Jews under the Nazis, but also to my situation today as United States citizen living under the Patriot Act and in the new world of global teletechnomilitaryindustrialeconomicocommunications. The genius of *Das Schloß* is to have shown that the sad situation of his hero is, in part at least, the result of not having direct access to other people's mind and feelings. This means that, for Kafka, each person's situation vis à vis other people is the confrontation of a proliferating network of signs. The interpretation of those signs, or, more precisely, their reading, their exegesis, is both urgently necessary and at the same time impossible or, even more precisely, always possible (it's a free country), but never open to certain verification. We can read the signs others emit, but we can never be sure we have read them right. That is what Isabel Archer, by way of the narrator's indirect discourse, says to herself about Gilbert Osmond in Henry James's *The Portrait of a Lady*: "—she had not read him right."[40] James, however, reassuringly implies that Isabel does now finally read Osmond right, whereas Kafka never, ever, gives the reader that kind of reassurance.

This impossibility of verifiable right reading generates the special narrative devices, such as the effaced ironic narrator, the narrative discontinuities, and the impossibility of finishing the story, that are distinguishing features of *The Castle*. I have been led on a zigzag or somewhat wandering path of my own by following out the clues uncovered by my initial narratological questions. Especially productive have been those questions having to do with the narrator and with the narrator's knowledge of the characters, and theirs of one another. *The Castle* is exemplary, and more than exemplary, in dramatizing the consequences for human life of the impossibility of being sure what the other person is thinking and feeling, whatever she or he says, and whatever her or his eyes, face, and bodily gestures seem to indicate. The consequences are premonitions of Auschwitz in the sense of registering the community's breakdown and the concomitant difficulty, perhaps the impossibility, of finishing any narrative, of giving it narrative continuity and rounding it off with a satisfactory ending. Kafka seems to have known already that, after Auschwitz, to write a poem, in the sense of a unified, organic literary work, is barbaric. Some inkling of that may have inhibited him from finishing any of his novels, though it also may have been, as I suggested in an earlier chapter, that he feared his nightmare vision might come true just because he had finished writing it down, in a terrifying version of that performative power of fictions of which I have more than once spoken.

Part Three | Holocaust Novels

Prologue: Community in Fiction after Auschwitz

Niemand
zeugt für den
Zeugen.
Paul Celan[1]

I have experienced a considerable, clearly overdetermined, resistance to writing this section. Perhaps my epigraph testifies to that. An epigraph is a way of appealing to a higher or outside authority, a way of placing the blame on someone else. My epigraph declares that my project of bearing witness to witnesses of the Shoah is doomed to failure, since I am, precisely, trying to do what Celan says is impossible. I would never have thought of writing on this topic except out of obligation to Jakob Lothe and to the research group he led several years ago in Oslo and Berlin, of which I have been a member. I do not think my resistance is exceptional. Each person's reluctance to write about the Shoah, however, or about Holocaust literature, probably takes a specific form. I can identify four reasons for me in particular to be anxious.

1. An enormous body of Holocaust literature and of secondary literature about it exists.[2] How can I have confidence that I have something new to contribute to this field?

2. Adorno's warning that writing a poem after Auschwitz is barbaric, discussed in the preface to this book, still has persuasive cogency. How can a novel about the Shoah, an avowedly fictional reconstruction, be other than an aestheticizing cover-up, a bogus or sham bearing witness that can serve as an apology or as an escape from encounter with true witnessing? True witnessing would be testimony from people who were actually there at Auschwitz, Buchenwald, or another of the camps, testimony such as makes up almost all of Claude Lanzmann's *Shoah*. No such thing exists, one might argue, as witnessing at second hand. "No one bears witness for the witness." Witnessing cannot be passed from one person to another. I can only testify to what I myself have seen and experienced. My visit to Buchenwald on a warm sunny day in the fall of 2009 does not count for much. Moreover, if writing a poem after Auschwitz is "barbaric," how much more barbaric must be cool, analytical "literary criticism," such as, for example, "narratological criticism," of what is called, perhaps in an oxymoron, "Holocaust literature." I shall return to these issues at the beginning of chapter 6. Nevertheless, it may be my responsibility to do what I can from the position in which I find myself and to say, on the basis of the evidence, including fictional reconstructions, that I do believe that these horrors occurred. I have an obligation to say, "I hereby bear witness to my belief and to my conviction that we must never forget."

3. Another source of my resistance is that I am not exactly an uninvolved bystander, someone who can say, "This has nothing to do with me. It was terrible, but I didn't do it. I can't imagine doing it." I have an uneasy sense of complicity or even of guilt, even though I tell myself that it is nonsense to feel that way. Many survivors testify to the same sense of guilt. "Why did I survive, when all those others died?" Disturbing rates of suicide exist among survivors. A more universal sense of complicity and guilt may be a sense that these were human beings, like me, lots of them, who committed the atrocity of genocide. I too am a human being. How can I be sure I would not be capable of similar acts? I am old enough to have been alive when the Shoah was occurring and when six million Jews (along with Gypsies, homosexuals, political prisoners, and others) were being murdered in the camps. Though it does not detract from the exceptional horror of the gas chambers and the crematoria, or from the horror of the Nazis' aim to kill all Jews everywhere, it is worth remembering that the Nazis and their accomplices in occupied countries killed outside the camps, usually by gunshot, about as many Jews as were killed in the gas chambers. Moreover, the Shoah happened in the context of mass killings by Germans and Russians of about fourteen mil-

lion Jews and non-Jews, especially by gunshot and by starvation, during the years 1933–45. This mass slaughter was perpetrated by both the Nazis and the Soviets especially in eastern Poland, the Baltic states, and such Soviet areas as the Ukraine and Belarus. David Denby, in "Look Again: 'Shoah' and a New View of History,"[3] asserts that "by the time of the Wannsee Conference in Berlin, in January, 1942, in which the Final Solution was openly plotted by the S.S., perhaps a million Jews had already been killed, mainly by shootings in the places where they lived, the bodies dumped into pits and buried." Denby juxtaposes the current new release in the United States of Claude Lanzmann's celebrated nine-hour *Shoah* (1985) to Timothy Snyder's *Bloodlands: Europe between Hitler and Stalin*.[4] The latter gives chilling facts about the slaughter of Jews and non-Jews during the period of the Holocaust. As far as I can remember, I was not aware of these awful events while they happened, even though they happened during my lifetime. Snyder's book contains information not known even up to now by most people in the United States, including me. My partial knowledge began when I was in my late teens and the camps were liberated. I can still remember seeing those awful photographs, in, if I remember correctly, *Life* magazine, of stacked corpses and skeletal survivors. I believed then, and believe now, that those photographs were truthful testimony. I can testify to having seen them. I know now, moreover, that we in the United States turned away a boatload of Jewish refugees during the Nazi period (just as we are refusing now to take in any more than a tiny handful of the two million Iraqi refugees who have fled Iraq already, of the four million homeless our invasion of Iraq has caused). The United States was in other ways complicit in what was happening during the Shoah.

My involvement does not quite stop there, however. I have known during my lifetime several concentration camp survivors, at least one person who escaped Germany by way of the *Kindertransport*, and at least one member of the SS. The latter was Hans Robert Jauss, with whom I had a painful conversation the last time I saw him, during a long walk beside Lake Constance. He tried at length to justify himself by saying he just did work as a translator. How can I be sure he was not telling the truth, or that I would not have done the same as he did, whatever that was, if I had been in his place? My ancestors, moreover, were Germans from Hesse who were impressed into the English army during the American Revolutionary War. They surrendered at the Battle of Saratoga, were imprisoned in the United States, and then settled here as the "Pennsylvania Dutch," subsequently moving south into Virginia as farmers. How can I know for sure that some distant German cousin of mine, entirely unknown to me, was not a part of the exterminating crew at some camp or other?

4. Though nothing, finally, is really "like" the Holocaust, though it is difficult to represent it or to testify to it, nevertheless we can understand it a little by way of likenesses, metaphors. James Young affirms this, in a passage cited by Deborah R. Geis in defense of the animal figures in Art Spiegelman's *Maus*: "To leave Auschwitz outside of metaphor would be to leave it outside of language altogether: it was known, understood, and responded to metaphorically at the time by its victims; it has been organized, expressed, and interpreted metaphorically by its writers; and it is now being remembered, commented upon, and given historical meaning metaphorically by scholars and poets of the next generation."[5] I would use the term "catachresis" rather than "metaphor." The Holocaust resists representation. It can be represented perhaps best in catachresis, that is, the imposition of words from other realms on what intrinsically resists representation. I shall in chapter 6, helped by an essay by Jean-Luc Nancy, "Forbidden Representation," discuss further the question of representing the Shoah. Is it impossible to represent it? Is it, perhaps, forbidden to represent it? Or do we perhaps have an obligation to bear witness to it by trying to represent it, even if doing so is impossible? Can't we, or shouldn't we, or should we represent the Shoah? No one can doubt that the sheer magnitude of the Shoah (six million dead!) is part of its horror and part of what is hard to think or represent about it. Death, however, even the death of one person, is perhaps intrinsically unthinkable and unnamable. Every death is, to borrow Jacques Derrida's title for his big book of memorial essays for dead friends and associates, "chaque fois unique, la fin du monde" (each time unique, the end of the world).[6]

The only thing at all comparable to the Shoah, in American history, is slavery. The condition of slaves on a Southern plantation before the Civil War was not entirely unlike the condition of prisoners in concentration camps in Germany, including the barbaric extermination of many slaves by mistreatment, lynchings, and burnings, as well as the sexual abuse of female and male slaves. Toni Morrison's *Beloved* eloquently and graphically testifies to this in a novel based on a historical event. *Beloved* is dedicated to the "Sixty Million and more." Morrison wavered a little in what she said was the referent of that figure. In an interview with *Newsweek* on September 28, 1987, she said she meant all those Africans who died in Africa after being captured to be sold as slaves or on the Middle Passage, that is, those who never even made it to the United States. A week later, she told the *Washington Post* she meant also to include those slaves who died in America. As many other critics have observed, the figure is, perhaps not accidentally, just ten times that of the roughly six million who perished in the Shoah. *Beloved*, in its moving testimony to the historical facts of slavery in the United States, bears a disquieting similarity to the procedures by which what is sometimes said to be unspeakable, what Morrison in *Beloved* calls "unspeakable thoughts, unspoken,"[7] is nevertheless spoken of in novels about the Shoah or about slavery in America.[8] Morrison's novel is the subject of this book's chapter 7. I agree with Naomi Mandel that the difficulty of speaking about slavery or about the Holocaust does not make them "unspeakable," either in the sense that one cannot speak of them or that one should not speak of them. These issues are discussed in my chapter 6 below, apropos of Jean-Luc Nancy's essay "Forbidden Representation."

Another reason for my anxiety in writing about the Shoah or about Morrison's *Beloved* is that I share in what C. Vann Woodward called "the burden of Southern history."[9] Two of my great-grandfathers were in the Confederate Army. A maternal great-uncle was killed in the Second Battle of Bull Run, also called Second Manassas, a terrible carnage. The Shoah and United States slavery are by no means the same, but the disturbing similarity helps me, a little, to understand the Shoah, though it does not make me at all easy in my mind about it. The sins of the fathers are visited on the children, even to the third generation.

5. The final reason for my resistance to writing about the Shoah is the extremely disquieting similarity between the run-up to the Nazi period in Germany and what has happened in the United States in the last decade and is still happening to some extent today. Other parallels would include Rwandan genocides, or South Africa under apartheid. I am thinking most anxiously, however, of the legitimizing of torture and of indefinite incarceration at Guantánamo Bay, with no right of habeas corpus granted the prisoners, and of the possibility, under the Orwellian-named Patriot Act, that any American citizen can be arrested, subjected to "extraordinary rendition," and then tortured in some secret prison somewhere in Eastern Europe or in Egypt. Some moves toward ameliorating these intolerable abuses have been made under President Obama, but Guantánamo Bay has yet to be closed as I review this in March 2011. Abu Ghraib and Guantánamo Bay sound in some ways remarkably like those Nazi labor camps, such as Buchenwald, that made little or no use of gas chambers but killed many prisoners in one way or another. One big difference is that Guantánamo Bay holds only two hundred prisoners, but each abuse there is an unforgivable crime. During the Shoah, most ordinary German or Polish or Hungarian citizens, with some noble exceptions, did little or nothing as the Jews were rounded up and sent to the

camps. Should we just be standing by watching our civil liberties disappear in the United States? Certainly this analogy is a big reason to try to face up to the Shoah and to the fact that people like you and me perpetrated it. Reading and thinking about Auschwitz fiction may help with that. When all the pros and cons are balanced out, I believe it is a good thing to read these novels, especially if we see the Shoah as to some degree a foreshadowing of our own situation today or of what we might, even yet, possibly become.

5

Three Novels about the Shoah

I shall in this chapter test out what I have said in the prologue to this part by way of three quite different Holocaust novels, Thomas Keneally's *Schindler's List*, Ian McEwan's *Black Dogs*, and Art Spiegelman's *Maus: A Survivor's Tale* (if you can call that a novel). The next chapter discusses Imre Kertész's *Fatelessness* at greater length. Let us suppose, as I presume is true, that the project of all of these works was to bear witness in an honorable and honest way to the Shoah, or at least to pass on the facts about it to readers. These authors wanted to transmit this witnessing to their readers, in defiance of Celan's assertion that no one bears witness for the witness. All four works are subject to the double obstacle, or even what might be called a double double bind or double blind alley to fulfilling this project. I have identified this complex "aporia" in the first chapter of this book:

1. The facts of the Holocaust, it may be, are inherently unthinkable and unspeakable, by any means of representation. Witnessing, after all, as Derrida has abundantly argued, is a performative, not a constative, use of language. It has an implicit "I swear that I saw this with my own eyes" attached to whatever it says, but that seeing may not be transmissible.

2. Turning the Holocaust into a fiction of any kind, "aestheticizing" it, is inherently a deeply suspect operation.

The more successful a novel is as a novel the further away it may be from the Holocaust. Perhaps. Performing a "rhetorical reading," with close attention to the text, to the way it operates its performative magic of testifying to the Holocaust, may just compound that shame. Perhaps.

The four works I shall discuss attempt to deal with these obstacles in quite different ways and from quite different initial "subject positions." *Maus* is different from the other three, not just in the medium it uses, but in other ways too. I want to approach the question of community in these works by way of a claim that the closer the authors of my four works were to actual experience of the Holocaust, the more complex and interesting, somewhat paradoxically, their narratological procedures are. Whether or not this can be enunciated as a law, "Miller's law," or is just an accident, is impossible to tell from so small a sample. All four of these are admirable works, worthy of the most careful readings, so my discriminations among them should not quite be taken as value judgments.

Schindler's List

Schindler's List (copyright 1982) is by someone whose subject position is not too different from my own. Keneally is dependent on the testimony of others, as I am; that is, he is dependent on all those documents he studied, plus his interviews of fifty Schindler Jews. His narrator speaks from that perspective. That narrator is a third-person, detached assembler of documentary evidence into a narrative sequence. *Schindler's List* is as much a documentary as it is a novel. *Schindler's List* is written by someone who was furthest, of my four authors, from actual direct witness of the Holocaust. Thomas Keneally is an Australian who was living in California (where he later taught creative writing at the University of California, Irvine) when he met by accident, in 1980, one of "Schindler's Jews" in a luggage shop in Beverly Hills. Keneally became fascinated by the story of Oskar Schindler's heroic saving of as many Jews as he could from the gas chambers and crematoria. Schindler was a war profiteer and the director of two factories, first in Poland and then in the Sudetenland, where the workers were from labor camps. With great cunning and at great risk to his own life he managed to keep many of his workers from being sent to Auschwitz or to some other extermination camp. The back page of the novel asserts that "Oskar Schindler came to save more Jews from the gas chambers than any other single person during World War II."

Schindler's List more or less explicitly defies Celan's claim that no one bears witness for the witness. Or, rather, it might be better to say that in its self-description or self-justification *Schindler's List* claims, pace Nancy, to "think by way of History," that is, to give accurate constative, verifiable, information about the Shoah through a historical reconstruction based on documents, photographs, and interviews. Original photographs from the Yad Vashem collection in Jerusalem, along with others obtained from Leopold Pfefferberg, Keneally's initial informant, punctuate the text. These are photographs of prisoners carrying heavy burdens, of Nazis smiling or carousing, of Oskar Schindler himself. Keneally's "Author's Note" at the beginning of *Schindler's List* specifies that he interviewed fifty Schindler survivors "from seven nations—Australia, Israel, West Germany, Austria, the United States, Argentina, and Brazil."[1] He also visited the locations that figure prominently in the novel: Cracow, Płaszów, "the scene of Amon Goeth's foul labor camp" (9–10), Zablocie, where Schindler's "factory still stands" (10), and Auschwitz-Birkenau, to which most Holocaust fictions sooner or later return. Keneally also did research in the abundant Schindler archives at Yad Vashem, the Martyrs' and Heroes' Remembrance Authority, in Jerusalem. A long list of those who helped Keneally is given at the end of the author's note.

Though Keneally defines *Schindler's List* on the cover of the paperback and in the author's note as "a novel," he justifies using that form by arguing that this is "because the novel's techniques seem suited for a character of such ambiguity and magnitude as Oskar" (10). This claim is a little odd, if you think of it. It seems to claim that there are certain truths, in this case Schindler's "character," that can only be expressed in fiction. This is the exact opposite of Adorno's claim that poetry after Auschwitz would be barbaric. Schindler is in the passage just cited somewhat curiously referred to by his first name, as though Keneally had known him as an intimate friend. Perhaps after studying all that evidence and writing his novel, Keneally did feel that way about Oskar Schindler. Keneally gets around the evident fact that he has invented conversations and incidents for which no direct historical record exists by claiming that he has firm indirect historical evidence:

> I have attempted, however, to avoid all fiction, since fiction would debase the record, and to distinguish between reality and the myths which are likely to attach themselves to a man of Oskar's stature. It has sometimes been necessary to make reasonable constructs of conversations of which Oskar and others have left only the briefest record. But most exchanges and conversations, and all events, are based on the detailed recollections of

> the *Schindlerjuden* (Schindler Jews), of Schindler himself, and of other witnesses to Oskar's acts of outrageous rescue. (10).

"Based on" is a weasel word here, since it could mean all sorts of proximity to and distance from what actually happened or was said. The same can be said for "reasonable constructs." The passage turns on a version of the distinction between performative (as in "witnesses") and constative (as in "record" and "detailed recollections"). The distinction is important because "witnessing" can be justified as a speech act that in effect swears that this did indeed happen because "I" saw it with my own eyes, whereas the constative is "reasonable" and "based on" the historical record, not on personal witnessing. The danger is that the recounting, constatively, at second hand, of awful events, such as the shooting of the Jewish women in one episode, just before liberation, testified to by "M" and referred to below, may have a purely sensational effect. Such segments may encourage readers to luxuriate in violence and horror, such as are the everyday staple of film and television, even of "scientific" "nature" shows on television, with their inevitable shots of lions eating gazelles or crocodiles eating monkeys.

Moreover, what Keneally says minimizes the degree to which he has, necessarily, deviated from "reality" into "fiction." What is said in the author's note about "avoiding all fiction" clashes weirdly with the ritual disclaimer on the verso of the title page, probably put there by the publisher to ward off lawsuits: "This book is a work of fiction. Names, characters, places, and incidents either are products of the author's imagination or are used fictitiously. Any resemblance to actual events or locales or persons, living or dead, is entirely coincidental" (6). This disclaimer completely contradicts the claim of historical accuracy made in the author's note. Well, which is it, a complete fiction or a truth-telling documentary? I do not see how it can be both.

Schindler's List, it appears, is a work of fiction that is not a work of fiction. It is that strange hybrid form sometimes called a "historical novel," or, perhaps more accurately, a "documentary" fiction. *Schindler's List* goes to a lot of trouble to persuade the reader that though this is a novel it is a novelistic rendering of historical fact, carefully researched and verified. The names are all those of real people. A footnote in the novel itself reminds the reader of this documentary basis, as when a note says that such and such a "source" is named only by the letter "M" because that person wanted to preserve anonymity: "Now living in Vienna, the man does not want his real name used" (191).

Schindler's List is for the most part straightforwardly chronological. This happened and then this happened and then this happened. Its narrator writes in a reserved literal style of the most appalling facts, for example, of the way Amon Goeth, camp commander at Płaszów, would shoot with a rifle a prisoner or two at random every morning from his balcony, as they carried out their work in the yard below. That memorably horrible recurrent scene is the closest to a leitmotif for *Schindler's List*, such as the one I identified for Kafka's novels in the chapters on those. Goeth's wantonly inhuman murders can stand emblematically for all the sadistic violence toward Jews from which Schindler is doing his best to save as many as he can. That "Goeth" is "Goethe" minus the final "e," adds to the irony. How could someone with a name like that be so evil? This leitmotif is spatial, like the others. In this case, Amon Goeth's sovereign domination of the prisoners is expressed in his location on a balcony overlooking the work yard. The prisoners' subordination is expressed in their submission, willy-nilly, to his panoptic surveillance of them from his balcony.

Another example of a factual account of lethal violence is the description, in a few laconic sentences, based on "M's" account, of the murder of a group of young Jewish women apparently caught with false Aryan papers. They "intone[d] the *Shema Yisroel.*" "Then, huddling for modesty and the bite of the spring air, they were all shot. At night the Ukranians took them away in wheelbarrows and buried them in the woods on the far side of the Chujowa Górká" (191). A few sentences before, "Chujowa Górká" had been explained as the name of a hill "on whose crest stood the Austrian fort" (191). This is a good example of the scrupulous use in *Schindler's List* of place-names, people's names, and names of Nazi ranks. An appendix lists all the "SS Ranks and their Army Equivalents," from *Oberst-gruppenführer* (general) through *Untersturmführer* (second lieutenant), *Oberscharführer* (sergeant) down to *Rottenführer* (corporal) (398). All these ranks, you will note, end with the word *Führer*. *Führer* means "leader." The power of the top man, Der Führer himself, extends all the way down through the SS ranks to the lowest corporal. It does this by way of a magical communion of authority and leadership, a mystic Aryan blood brotherhood (*Blutbruderschaft*).

The constant, sometimes obtrusive, stylistic deployment of what used to be called "irrelevant detail," contributes, no doubt, to the appearance of historical verisimiltude. It is as though the narrator were saying, "The exact name of this hill is not a matter of great importance, but I am going to tell it to you anyway, so you won't think I'm making anything up."

The narrator's tone is like that of an objective historian who leaves it to the reader, for the most part, to pass judgment, though he does utter such judgments as "Amon Goeth's foul labor camp."

Schindler's List is relatively uncomplicated from a "narratological" point of view. This formal feature no doubt functions to sustain the appearance of cool, objective, documentary, historical accuracy. The narrator is a third-person "omniscient" objective spokesperson in the past tense for "what really happened," as extraordinary as it was. Little in the way of time shifts or recurrent terms and figures exist, few stylistic features that the critic, I, for example, can get hold of for purposes of "rhetorical analysis." The reader is beguiled by the narrator's quiet assumption of authority into not noticing how much of the text goes beyond anything Keneally could have known directly from any of his sources, for example, what Schindler thought at a given moment, or what was actually said in crucial conversations. Keneally's claim that he has attempted "to avoid all fiction" is surely a misleading understatement, when it is set against the actual texture of the text.

A further problematic feature of *Schindler's List* is Keneally's choice to tell the story of one of the relatively few "good Germans" about whom we have a lot of historical information. Oskar Schindler was an extremely courageous man who saved a good many Jews from likely death. He is, however, hardly typical of German behavior during the Shoah. The happy ending of the novel and, especially, of the film made from the novel, which concludes in a triumphant celebration of togetherness by the Schindler Jews and Schindler himself, is likely to mislead readers and viewers.[2] They may take it as a representative picture of Germany during the Shoah. Even though *Schindler's List* tells a moving and historically accurate story, it may perhaps lead readers and viewers to forget Auschwitz. Keneally would probably respond by saying that Schindler's exceptional courage and goodness is just the point his story makes. Even in those terrible times, some unlikely people did good, against all odds. Oskar Schindler, as an exceptional example of this, deserves being remembered and celebrated.

Black Dogs

Ian McEwan's *Black Dogs* (1992) is closer to direct experience than *Schindler's List* and somewhat more complex narratologically and rhetorically. The narrator bears witness to an experience of evil by someone who was a close member of his family, his mother-in-law. That evil is indirectly related to the Shoah. The narrator of *Black Dogs* discovers the way someone he knows, his mother-in-law, someone who was not in a camp, was nevertheless decisively affected by the deportation and extermination of European Jewry and by the German occupation of France. The novel is told in the first person. It is the story of the narrator's gradual discovery of his mother-in-law's traumatic experience. *Black Dogs* is not so much a novel about the Shoah as such as it is about the effects of Nazism even on people who were only tangentially related to it. No intimate details about life and death in Auschwitz here. *Black Dogs* is testimony to Auschwitz at a considerable remove, but it is a kind of testimony nevertheless. It is somewhat easier, though perhaps naive, to believe the disclaimer on the copyright page of *Black Dogs* than to believe the absurd claim made for *Schindler's List*. "All of the characters in this book are fictitious," the reader of *Black Dogs* is firmly told, in a disclaimer that varies significantly from the one at the beginning of my copy of *Schindler's List*, "and any resemblance to actual persons, living or dead, is purely coincidental."[3] Nothing anywhere in the text itself testifies to any basis in reality. Nevertheless, such disclaimers, as any novel reader knows, are often lies. The presentation of the characters and events in *Black Dogs* is so circumstantial, so particular, so plausible, that the reader suspects, perhaps wrongly, that real people and happenings may be "the basis" of this novel. The preface contains a sentence that might seem to assert that this is the case: "In this memoir I have included certain incidents from my own life—in Berlin, Majdanek, Les Salces, and St. Maurice de Navacelles" (xxiii). This assertion, however, the reader realizes, is made by the fictional first-person narrator, Jeremy. Ian McEwan of course may be ventriloquizing his imaginary narrator, speaking through him about his own experience. To say that, however, would be a wild and unverifiable guess, with no textual support.[4] The last, unnumbered, page of the novel is a firm disclaimer, signed "I.M.": "The places mentioned in this novel correspond to actual French villages, but the characters associated with them are entirely fictional and bear no resemblance to persons living or dead. The *Maire*'s story [that the black dogs are Gestapo beasts trained not only to kill but to rape] and the *Maire* himself have no basis in historical fact." That sounds pretty definitive, unless, of course, McEwan is lying in order to protect real people. He doth protest a bit too much, but *Black Dogs*, like fiction in general, keeps its secrets.

Black Dogs, however, is far from being a straightforward "documentary," like *Schindler's List*. It has all the thematic trappings and employs many of the narrative techniques of a sophisticated "postmodern" novel. It also exemplifies not so much the moral ambiguity that is sometimes said to be a feature of postmodern fiction as an inability to decide how the evil of the Shoah can be understood or explained. This undecidability is neatly summed up in what the narrator says in the preface about those incidents in his own life he has incorporated into his "memoir." These incidents, says the narrator, "are open equally to Bernard's and to June's kind of interpretation. Rationalist and mystic, commissar and yogi, joiner and abstainer, scientist and intuitionist, Bernard and June are the extremities, the twin poles along whose slippery axis my own unbelief slithers and never comes to rest" (xxiii). Bernard and June are the narrator's parents-in-law, central figures in the story.

Black Dogs' narrative procedures are much more complex than those of *Schindler's List*. The narrative of *Black Dogs* is consistently limited to what its first-person narrator gradually, through time, saw on his own, as well as heard and learned from the testimony of others. It is constructed as a series of episodes, each told in considerable elaboration, with time breaks between that create dramatic juxtapositions. This is a technique not unlike that used in modern cinema, though Victorian novelists like Dickens and Hardy also used montage. Unlike *Schindler's List*, however, *Black Dogs* also makes elaborate use of time shifts, sudden flashbacks inserted in the midst of consecutive chronological episodes. It would be easy enough to rearrange the episodes in strict chronological sequence, since many dates are given, but McEwan apparently wants the effect of gradual revelation achieved by flashbacks. An example of time shift is the break in the sequence describing the narrator's visit with his father-in-law to Berlin the day after the fall of the Berlin Wall, followed by his trip by plane to the south of France to open his family summer place in the country there. That chronological sequence is interrupted by something his father-in-law says that triggers the narrator's memory of a trip in 1981 to Warsaw as part of a cultural delegation. He remembers his side trip to visit the Majdanek concentration camp with a woman member of that delegation, Jenny Tremaine, after which they made love in a Lublin hotel and were married ten months later. The narrative then returns to the "now" of the narrator's trip to the south of France. Though the narration is apparently governed in its sequences by the vagaries of the narrator's subjectivity, the author has of course cunningly contrived the sequence for maximum dramatic effect.

The visit to Majdanek, a labor camp turned extermination camp outside Lublin in Poland, is the closest *Black Dogs* gets to a quasi-direct confrontation of the Shoah.[5] The passage describing the visit by Jeremy and his new acquaintance Jenny Tremaine to the camp is moving in its specificity, for example, in its description of the immense piles of shoes, including children's shoes, still present at the camp. These were left after the victims were stripped before they were gassed and cremated. The passage ends, however, with a numbness and an obscure sense of shame not unlike my experience at Buchenwald in the fall of 2009. My friends and I were tourists who could come and go freely, as the camp commander could, whereas tens of thousands entered and died there. That freedom insidiously puts visitors to these sites today on the side of the "dreamers of the nightmare":

> We followed a party of schoolchildren into a hut where wire cages were crammed full of shoes, tens of thousands of them, flattened and curled like dried fruit. In another hut, more shoes, and in a third, unbelievably, more, no longer caged but spilling in their thousands across the floor. I saw a hobnail boot beside a baby shoe whose nursery lamb still showed through the dust. Life turned to tat. The extravagant numerical scale, the easy-to-say numbers—tens and hundreds of thousands, millions—denied the imagination its proper sympathies, its rightful grasp of the suffering, and one was drawn insidiously to the persecutors' premise, that life was cheap, junk to be inspected in heaps. As we walked on, my emotions died. There was nothing we could do to help. There was no one to feed or free. We were strolling like tourists. Either you came here and despaired, or you put your hands deeper into your pockets and gripped your warm loose change and found that you had taken one step closer to the dreamers of the nightmare. This was our inevitable shame, our share in the misery. We were on the other side, we walked here freely like the commandant once did, or his political master, poking into this or that, knowing the way out, in the full certainty of our next meal. . . .
>
> We met up with the children again and followed them into the brick building with a chimney. Like everyone else, we noted the maker's name on the oven doors. A special order promptly filled. We saw an old container of hydrogen cyanide, Zyklon B, supplied by the firm of Degesch. On our way out, Jenny spoke for the first time in an hour to tell me that in one day in November 1943 the German authorities had machine-gunned thirty-six thousand Jews from Lublin. They made them lie in gigantic graves and slaughtered them to the sound of amplified dance music. (88, 89)

This passage is not so much a comprehension of the Shoah as an expression of the failure to comprehend it. Comprehension fails even in the presence of the victim's shoes, the gas chambers, and the crematorium that remain as signs of what once happened there. On the one hand, Jeremy and Jenny's visit to Majdanek seems to confirm that no one bears witness for the witness. On the other hand, Jeremy's honest account of his experience is a form of (fictional) bearing witness. Jeremy and Jenny did see the shoes and the rest of what is left of Majdanek, just as I saw the crematorium and the torture cells at Buchenwald. Their response was to make love for the first time that evening in a hotel in Lublin. That seems an odd reaction to the sight of all those children's shoes. It can, however, be seen as an affirmation that love is able to conquer even the worst evil.

Three different stories are elaborately intertwined in this achronological sequence: (1) The story of the narrator's extremely slow recovery from the trauma of his parents' death in an automobile accident when he was eight. He was saved by various foster mothers on whom he imposed himself, for example, mothers of his friends or wives of his teachers, and by his eventual happy marriage to Jenny Tremaine. (2) The story of the narrator's gradual discovery of the reasons why his parents-in-law's marriage has failed and of his decision to write his mother-in-law's "memoir." He makes shorthand notes of his interviews with his mother-in-law, as she lies dying in a nursing home, in preparation for that writing. The novel is not the memoir itself but rather the story of the accumulation of material for the memoir, though one could say that the novel turns out, paradoxically, to make that memoir unnecessary or to be itself, in a manner of speaking, the memoir that the end of the novel leaves the narrator still intending to write. (3) The story of the confrontation, primarily by way of the second story, of two contradictory ways of explaining human evil, as represented by the Shoah. One way is the religious one represented by the narrator's mother-in-law. The other is the rationalist, atheist, or at least resolutely agnostic, one represented by his father-in-law. That disagreement has led to the couple's lifelong separation, even though they still love one another. Though human evil, for example, the Shoah, is resolutely judged as evil, the narrator remains unable to decide between these two ways of explaining it. Human evil does take some explaining.

The climactic episode dramatizing the presence of evil took place forty years earlier, when Bernard and June were on their honeymoon in the south of France, soon after World War II. That event is hinted at throughout the novel in the title and by recurrent enigmatic mentions of "the black dogs," but the event itself is only told at the end of the novel, in the work's most extravagant reversal of chronological time. The narrator's mother-in-law, as a young bride on a long hike with her new husband, was momentarily separated from him. Two huge, now-wild, black Gestapo dogs left behind by the retreating Nazis attacked her. The dogs were trained, so the nearby village's mayor claims, to attack and rape women, though some doubt is cast on the veracity of this assertion by June's husband Bernard. June drives the dogs off by stabbing one with a pocket-knife. Throughout the rest of her life she dreams, just before falling asleep, of the two dogs moving off across the valley and up the mountain on the other side, one dripping blood on the white stones. She experiences a religious conversion as a result of this event, leaves the communist party, and thinks differently from her husband ever after. "Jeremy," she tells the narrator a month before she dies, in the summer of 1987, in a passage cited by the narrator two pages from the end of the novel , "that morning I came face to face with evil. I didn't quite know it at the time, but I sensed it in my fear—these animals were the creations of debased imaginations, of perverted spirits no amount of social theory could account for. The evil I'm talking about lives in us all. It takes hold in an individual, in private lives, within a family, and then it's children who suffer most. And then, when the conditions are right, in different countries, at different times, a terrible cruelty, a viciousness against life erupts, and everyone is surprised by the depths of hatred within himself. Then it sinks back and waits. It's something in our hearts" (147). The narrator then imagines Bernard, his father-in-law, answering, "'Face to face with evil'? I'll tell you what she was up against that day—a good lunch and a spot of malicious village gossip! As for the inner life, my dear boy, try having one of those on an empty stomach. Or without clean water" (147–48).

The reader is left to decide for herself between these two alternative explanations of evil, though the religious one is perhaps more dramatically presented. On the one hand, the narrator remains on the whole true to his description of himself: "I had no attachments, I believed in nothing. It was not that I was a doubter, or that I had armed myself with the useful skepticism of a rational curiosity, or that I saw all arguments from all sides; there was simply no good cause, no enduring principle, no fundamental idea with which I could identify, no transcendent entity whose existence I could truthfully, passionately, or quietly assert" (xxii). On the other hand, the narrator says firmly in the preface, "But I would be false to my own experience if I did not declare my belief in the possibility of love transforming and redeeming a life" (xxiv). This is presumably a reference to his love for Jenny and her love for him, as well as their parental love for their four children and Jeremy's love for his niece Sally. That love is not based on principles, ideas, or on any transcendent entity. It just happens. Nevertheless, it transforms and redeems Jeremy's life. "Amor vincit omnia," even the affectless anomie of someone who did not believe in anything. That seems to be the ultimate message of *Black Dogs*. It is a theme persisting through all its narrative complexities.

The novel ends, however, with the narrator's admission that those black dogs now haunt him too: "But it is the black dogs I return to most often. They trouble me when I consider what happiness I owe them, especially when I think of them not as animals but as spirit hounds, incarnations . . . fading as they move into the foothills of the mountains from where they will return to haunt us, somewhere in Europe, in another time" (148, 149). That scene of the black dogs fading into the foothills, one dripping blood, is the presiding leitmotif of *Black Dogs*. It sticks in the mind as an emblem of the obscure persisting evil that motivated the Holocaust and that will never go away. Like the leitmotifs I have identified in others of my novels, this one is a spatial emblem. The dogs are watched from "here," as they disappear into the foothills "over there," as if they were spirit hounds, incarnations of evil. In speaking of the happiness he owes to the black dogs, Jeremy means the happiness that ensued by way of the tangle of circumstances that left him married to June's daughter Jenny. He also ends, with his family, in possession of the *bergerie*, the shepherd's house, now turned summer house, that June Tremaine bought the next day after the attack and would not have bought if she had not encountered the black dogs.

I have in my comments on *Black Dogs* juggled three of the four balls I am trying to keep in the air in this book: the question of whether a novel can testify to the Shoah; the question of narrative form in relation to whether fiction can be testimony; the question of our relation today to the Shoah. That leaves the question of what sort of community, if any, is imagined in *Black Dogs*. I shall say something about that in the next chapter.

Maus

Maus: A Survivor's Tale (1973–91) is closer to an experience of the Holocaust than either *Schindler's List* or *Black Dogs*. The father and mother of this graphic novel's narrator-creator are survivors of Auschwitz. *Maus*, however fictional, is composed from the perspective of what its author actually is: the son of concentration camp survivors. The narrator is primarily dependent on his father for such knowledge as he has. Survivors' children are a special class. Many clinical studies have been made, for example, in Canada, of such people and of the way the traumas of the parents are transmitted to the children. Art Spiegelman, if we are to believe that *Maus* is straightforwardly autobiographical (perhaps a dangerous assumption), has been in a mental institution (just as had his mother for post-partum depression before the war). In a time during the composition of *Maus*, the narrator goes regularly to a "shrink," who is also a survivor. Artie's psychiatrist helps him deal with the complex feelings of guilt that are said to be typical of the children of survivors. I use "Artie" for Spiegelman's representation of himself in *Maus*, since that is what his father calls him, and "Spiegelman" for Art Spiegelman, the creator of *Maus*, in order to maintain that narratological distinction. Artie is shown on his way to his "shrink," walking through the imaginary naked bodies of all those dead in the gas chambers. Artie's second-generation guilt spreads out in fading concentric rings even to such peripheral persons as me, the author of this book. This part's prologue uneasily attests to that.

Many distinguished essays have been written about the graphic and narrative complexity of *Maus*, and about the ways Spiegelman manipulates the conventions of "comix," underground comic books. [6] *Maus*'s subtitle, for example, *A Survivor's Tale*, parodies in the word "tale" in other such titles or subtitles in comic books and graphic novels. Whether a pun on "tail," as in mouse's tail, is faintly present can hardly be decided. *Alice in Wonderland* uses that pun in a graphic representation of the mouse's tale in tail form winding down the page. "It *is* a long tail, certainly," says Alice.[7] Some commentators have also been made anxious by the temerity involved in representing the Shoah in a comic book. I would respond that the format is an ironic distancing that works to make it more likely that the reader will confront the stark facts of Vladek and Anja Spiegelman's almost unimaginable suffering. The other side of this is that the graphic rendering of these atrocities makes them, paradoxically, all the more powerful and disturbing, more powerful and more disturbing, in my view, than the staged reenactments of violence in the film of *Schindler's List*. The paradox is that the film, to my eye, looks like the playacting it is, whereas the comic book renderings have the more direct force of graphic art.

Comic book though it is, *Maus* is a work of genius. Almost any reader will be instantly beguiled, taken in, and will read on and on with fascinated attention, as I have, down to the last frames, with their painfully ironic claim by Vladek that when he was miraculously reunited with his wife Anja after the liberation, they then lived happily ever after, in a fairy-tale ending. The third frame from the last shows Vladek embracing his wife and exclaiming, "Anja, Anja, my Anja," while Vladek's taped commentary (reported in a square box at the bottom) says "More I don't need to tell you. We were both very happy, and lived happy, happy, ever after" (296). In fact, Anja has committed suicide after they have moved to America, and the father is at this point extremely ill with a heart condition, as well as having become a pathological miser. For example, Vladek leaves the free gas oven in his rented house on all day so he won't have to use another wooden match to start it when he needs it. He steals paper towels from men's rooms so he won't have to buy them. His habit of "saving" is one of the things that "saved" him at Auschwitz, since he always had a bit of bread left to eat or share, or a bit of jewelry to use for bribes or in exchange for food. His present condition leads his son Artie at one point to say to his wife, when she says his survival was a "miracle": "But in some ways he *didn't* survive" (250).

Whether Spiegelman intended, in picturing Vladek's match-saving technique, the allusion to the gas ovens in Auschwitz is impossible to tell. Perhaps not. Perhaps it was just another circumstantial fact about his father. In the last frame of all, Vladek, in a moving confusion, addresses Artie, born in Sweden after the war, by the name of the first son he and Anja had had, in Poland, Richieu: "I'm *tired* from talking, Richieu, and it's enough stories for now." (296). The woman who was keeping Richieu in supposed safety during the Holocaust poisoned him, herself, and two other children she was caring for when the news came that they were about be taken to almost certain death in Auschwitz. The latter did happen to Kafka's sister Ottla and the children she was caring for. A photograph of Richieu, a beautiful child, is placed at the beginning of the second part of *Maus*. A photograph of Vladek in clean prison garb provided by the photo shop after the liberation, looking handsome and well fed, is inserted near the end. A photograph of Artie's mother and himself, when he was a boy, in 1968, is put at the beginning of the interpolated first underground comic book Spiegelman published, *Prisoner on the Hell Planet: A Case History* (102). This is the story of his mother's suicide and his reaction to it. *Maus* is hardly a story that ends "happy, happy, ever after."

Just what are the narratological complexities that contribute to *Maus*'s force? Almost all are a brilliant exploitation for unconventional purposes of conventional features of ordinary comic books I read as a child: *The Lone Ranger*, *Flash Gordon*, *Superman*, *Mickey Mouse*. Spiegelman has dared to represent his father and mother, himself, and all the other characters as having animal heads and human bodies, mice heads for Jews, pig heads for Poles, frog heads for French people, cat heads for the Germans, the brutal Nazi guards and SS officers, amiable-looking dog heads for American liberating soldiers. Sometimes these heads are shown as masks over human faces, when the scene has shifted to the present in the United States, for example, in the sequence of Artie's visit to his shrink. This reminds the reader-viewer that all these animal faces are masks.

This "animalization," as it might be called, may be modeled on Mickey Mouse, Donald Duck, Krazy Kat, and the rest. Nevertheless, it has a great and somewhat ambiguous power. It compares the differences among different races and nationalities to the differences among animals, as though they were natural, not conventional. At the same time it shows these differences as artificial conventions, as artificial as showing people as animals in the first place. Neither Richieu nor Vladek looks conventionally "Jewish," whatever *that* is, as prejudices presuppose, in his photograph. Portraying Nazis as cats and Jews as mice carries over the implacable brutality of even the gentlest house cat toward mice, including the way they enjoy killing their prey by inches, as the Nazis often did by gradually moving Jews to the gas chambers, humiliating, starving, beating, and raping them first.

Comics are called "comic strips," in reference to the minimal number of frames in a horizontal line in newspaper comics. *Maus* puts usually eight frames on a single page, two on each line, often juxtaposing them ambiguously so the reader-viewer does not know whether to move down, across, or both, from the one on the upper left-hand corner. Each frame is a moment frozen in time, though conventional means of representing movement in that time are standard in comic strips, for example, in giving the give-and-take of speech and response. Spiegelman makes the frames of different sizes, superimposes them on one another (22), and divides them occasionally from one another in ways other than the conventional straight line. An example is his representation of the two sides of a telephone conversation by a zigzag electrical line with the distant parties on either side, in separate frames (23). Spiegelman makes ironic use of comic book clichés, as in the title of the second chapter of part 2: "Auschwitz (Time Flies)" (199). Sometimes a single picture overlaps several frames, as in a big picture of Vladek that overlaps four frames to match a sequence of four stages in his narration of what happened to various members of his family (most died in the Shoah) (276). The most powerful use of a convention, however, is the doubling of the picture by a narrating voice represented inside its own separate square box (as opposed to the conventional round boxes ["balloons"] with arrows pointing to the person who is speaking the words). Often these words are speech of the primary narrator, as in the box in the first frame: "It was summer, I remember I was ten or eleven" (5), accompanied by a drawing of him as a child roller-skating. Sounds are represented, as is usual in comic books, by superimposed words, as in "SLAM!" in large letters for a slamming door (23). Sometimes a picture without caption conveys forcefully part of the story, as in the recurrent frames showing the famous crematoria chimneys with black smoke billowing out of them, a silent graphic comment on Vladek's recurrent statements, such as "Abraham I didn't see again . . . I think he came out the chimney" (187), or "Thousands—hundreds of thousands of Hungarians were arriving there at this time" (215). Here is a moment when Vladek's story overlaps with that of the narrator of Imre Kertész's *Fatelessness*, since the latter was one of those Hungarians. Vladek and Imre Kertész may have been at one point within a short distance of one another, if we take *Fatelessness* as more or less autobiographical (a problematic assumption). *Fatelessness* is the subject of the next chapter.

Most dramatically, Spiegelman's square boxes enclose the speech of Vladek Spiegelman, the father-survivor, either speaking directly as his son Artie interviews him, or as listened to later on a tape recording, for example, in the last sequence, when Vladek is already dead and only his son's notes or the tapes exist as his acts of bearing witness to his experiences at Auschwitz. These boxes are then matched by Artie's imaginary representation, in comic book style, of what his father is describing. An example is the representation of four Jewish men hanged in the public square "for dealing goods without coupons." "They hanged there one full week," says Vladek in the box at the bottom of the picture (85). Artie at one point exclaims to his psychiatrist, who has mentioned his book, "My book? Hah! What book? Some part of me doesn't want to draw or think about Auschwitz. I can't visualize it clearly, and I can't BEGIN to imagine what it felt like" (206). In spite of this disclaimer, the graphic representations look pretty plausible to me. They clearly use other sources to increase their accuracy, for example, the detailed drawings of the gas chambers and crematoria ostensibly based on Vladek's seeing them with his own eyes when, as a "tinsmith," he was ordered to dismantle their machinery, just before the Russians came. As boxes within a picture of the undressing room report Vladek as saying, "They came to a big room to undress their clothes what looks so, yes [he must be looking at Artie's drawings]—there is a place so like they say. If I saw a couple months before how it was all arranged here, only ONE time I could see it!" (230), meaning he would have been gassed a few minutes later. Other examples of Spiegelman's use of outside evidence are the aerial maps of Auschwitz and the adjacent Auschwitz-Birkenau or the representation of the gate into Auschwitz, with its famous inscription in the arch overhead, *Arbeit Macht Frei*, and with SS men with dogs and clubs crowding around the swastika-marked trucks bringing Vladek and a hundred or more others to the camp (159). This big frame has no edges and fills a whole page with three small frames superimposed. The square boxes report Vladek saying, "And we came here to the concentration camp Auschwitz, and we knew that from here we will not come out anymore. . . . We knew the stories—that they will gas us and throw us in the ovens. This was 1944. . . . We knew *everything*. And here we were."

"And here we were." Vladek's words have an admirable laconic simplicity. This depends in part on their quaint foreign syntax. They also have, partly through that simplicity, a magic ability to generate vivid images in Artie's mind, in a kind of internal theater that he can virtually see, hear, and feel, and then, in another magical operation, render admirably in comic strip format on his drawing board. At least it seems quasi-magical to me. I have said that *Maus* is a work of genius. Its genius lies partly in this double transformation, enacted before the reader-viewer's eyes, from Vladek's words, to Artie's imagination, to the artful arrangement of enframed words and pictures on the page. The genius lies also in Spiegelman's brilliant economy in getting so much information, in the combination of word and text, verbal and graphic, within a given frame, and in the rapid tempo that moves each episode forward from frame to frame. *Maus* advances in a brisk presto that capitalizes on skipping what is left out between one frame and the next, by way of the discontinuities proper to the "comix" medium. Nietzsche might have admired this rapidity, just as he admired Stendhal's rapid tempo.

I have attempted, for each of my novels, to identify what I have called a "leitmotif," a recurrent spatially deployed paradigm that corresponds to or expresses the imaginary inner space the novel generates in the reader. I have also mentioned how problematic and hard to pin down the concept of "imaginary inner space" is. In *Maus* the leitmotif is the ubiquitous matrix of a conventional comic book page that allows Spiegelman, in page after page, to express so much in so little. He does this by juxtaposing, on a given page, different places, different times, and different levels of discourse, as indicated by graphic and verbal signs: the now of the drawing, the time of Vladek's recounting of his experiences to his son, the past of Vladek's experiences as imagined by Artie on the basis of what his father says, the time of listening to the interview tapes after Vladek's death, maps, photographs, schematic topographical drawings, conventional representations of sounds, some in balloons, many not ("PSHT," "SLAP" [234]; "SPLASH," "KBANG! KBANG!" [267]), and so on.

Most of *Maus*'s readers will have been "reading" comic strips since early childhood. They will be already so adept at interpreting comics as to be unaware of the extreme temporal and spatial complexity their conventions generate. As used in manifold ways in page after page of a masterwork in comic book matrix like *Maus*, that matrix detaches itself in the mind of the attentive reader and becomes itself a recurrent leitmotif, a quite unusual form of the "Here we go again!" that accompanies our recognition of a recurrent leitmotiv in a Wagner opera.

A final narratalogical complexity will complete my repertoire. Like *Black Dogs*, though in a somewhat different way, *Maus* is made up of three intertwined stories. The difference is that the three stories in *Maus*, unlike those in *Black Dogs*, are told in more or less straightforward chronological order, though with time shifts back and forth from one to the other. All three are governed and controlled by the explicit or implicit presence of a "reliable" narrator, Artie Spiegelman. The primary narrative is Vladek's "survivor's tale," as the subtitle has it, his circumstantial account of his life before the Holocaust, during it, and after. One of the most important aspects of *Maus*, for me at least, is its circumstantial account of the prolonged persecution and suffering of Polish Jews under German occupation *before* they were sent to Auschwitz. Most, but not all, non-Jewish Poles collaborated in this persecution. It must have been truly horrible, day after day and week after week of fear and privation. *Maus* is the most vivid and circumstantial account I know of what preceded Auschwitz for Jews in a city like Sosnowiec.

Maus is a harrowing story of continual hair's-breadth escapes from the death that took six million other Jews. This story is presented in discontinuous units, as Artie is able to persuade his father, from time to time, to tell the story. It is a witnessing that is not so much borne witness to by Artie as recorded and passed on as accurately as possible. It is a story not only of Vladek's courage and cleverness, but also of the sheer good luck that allowed him to survive. Artie says to his psychiatrist, "Well . . . sure. I know there was a lot of luck involved, but he was amazingly present-minded and resourceful," to which the psychiatrist replies, "But it wasn't the BEST people who survived, nor did the best ones die. It was RANDOM!" (205).

Though this is the primary story, it is subordinated, as a kind of story within a story, to the account of Artie's life now as a successful graphic artist, his difficult relation with his father, his determination to get his father to tell his story and his success at that, his sorrow over his mother's suicide, his happy marriage to a French woman who converts to Judaism, the gradual deterioration of his father's health, his father's battles with his new wife Mala, all in the successive "nows" of the narration, themselves made of discontinuous episodic blocks. Artie's story can even be said to be the primary narration.

The third narrative strand is the story of how *Maus* got composed. Crucial moments in the book comment on that. These are remarkable acts of what used to be called metanarrative or self-reflexivity. Artie is periodically shown at his drawing board, composing *Maus*, listening to the tapes of his father's accounts. Example are on pages 201 and 207. The former shows Artie at his drawing board at the beginning of chapter 2 of the second part, wearing a mouse mask, thinking of his father's death in 1982, the suicide of his mother in May 1968, the expected birth of his child by Françoise in May 1987, the hundred thousand Hungarian Jews gassed in Auschwitz between May 16, 1944, and May 24, 1944, and the international critical success of the first part of *Maus*. An imaginary pile of naked dead bodies with mouse heads lies beneath his drawing board.

This is followed by a sequence in which Artie is interviewed by the media sitting at his drawing board. He is made more and more depressed by their inane questions and made to feel more and more infantile, shrinking in size in his drawing-board chair and crying to the assembled reporters and photographers, "I want . . . ABSOLUTION. No . . . No . . . I want . . . I want . . . my MOMMY!" (202). In another place, just after the confession, cited above, of inadequacy for the whole project to Pavel, his psychiatrist, he says his father worked in a tinshop near Auschwitz and he has no idea "what kind of tools and stuff to draw. There's no documentation." Pavel, who worked in a tool and die shop in Czechoslovakia as a youth gives him some information, and as he walks home, he thinks, "Maybe I could show the tin shop and not draw the drill press. I hate to draw machinery" (206). On the next page, we see his drawing of Vladek at work with a tin cutter. Near the beginning of *Maus*, Artie tells his father, "I want to tell YOUR story, the way it really happened" (25). In another place, after Vladek has broken off an interview, Artie says, "Okay, good idea. . . . My hand is sore from writing all this down" (42).

The father's narrative is punctuated with moments when Artie tries to get his father to stop complaining about his wife, Mala, and to get back to what it was like in Auschwitz: "ENOUGH! Tell me about Auschwitz"

(207). In another, earlier, frame, he exhorts his father, "WAIT! *Please*, Dad, if you don't keep your story chronological, I'll never get it straight. . . . Tell me more about 1941 and 1942" (84). At one point, he worries that his father is "in some ways . . . just like the racist caricature of the miserly old Jew" (133). In one sequence he shows his father part of what he has drawn ("the black market Jews they hanged in Sosnowiec") (135). His father tells him he'll be famous like Walt Disney, and Artie says, "I've just GOTTA write this conversation down before I forget it" (135). Artie worries about whether he should represent his French wife Françoise, who has converted to Judaism, with a frog face or a mouse face (172). In two later panels he says to his wife, in explanation of a sigh: "Just thinking about my book . . . It's so PRESUMPTUOUS of me. I mean, I can't even make any sense out of my relationship with my father. . . . How am I supposed to make any sense out of *Auschwitz*? . . . of the *Holocaust*? . . ." (174).

Maus is continually punctuated, at irregular intervals, arhythmically, in periodic syncopes, by such metanarratological comments. This third narrative allows me to say that *Maus* is not only Vladek's story and Artie's story. It is also the story of how the comic book we are in the act of reading came to be written. It is a running narrative of the special difficulties entailed in telling in comic book format the story of a Holocaust survivor. This brilliantly works to forestall objections the reader may have to doing this. Spiegelman knows those objections already and expresses them forcefully through Artie's rueful comments.

Compared to *Schinder's List* or *Black Dogs*, *Maus* is much closer to direct testimony to the horrors of the Shoah. In one sense, *Maus* bears witness for the witness by transforming what Vladek has told his son into the overtly conventional form of a graphic novel, but in another sense Spiegelman is transmitting to the reader-viewer, word for word, the direct testimony Vladek gave to his son. The son faithfully transcribed that testimony in his notes and tapes. They were then transferred to *Maus* in the words in the graphic frames. This technique of bearing witness is not entirely unlike the filmed interviews that make up Claude Lanzmann's *Shoah*. Film is, after all, a medium too, with its conventions and distortions, as Lanzmann certainly knows. Once Auschwitz was liberated, all testimony to it was in one way or another indirect, mediated in one way or another.

I shall in the next chapter comment further on degrees of distance among my four Holocaust novels and on the question of communities in the four novels. At this point I observe that the closer these first three novels are to the Shoah the more complex, paradoxically, their narrative techniques are. *Maus* is a masterpiece that magnificently exploits and appropriates the conventions of comix novels. *Schindler's List* and *Black Dogs*, good as they are, are relatively less original in the narrative forms they employ. Whether this apparent paradox is generalizable to Holocaust novels in general, or whether it is an accidental feature of the series I have chosen to discuss, must remain an open question for now.

6 Imre Kertész's *Fatelessness:* Fiction as Testimony

The survivors bore witness to something it is impossible to bear witness to.
Giorgio Agamben, *Remnants of Auschwitz: The Witness and the Archive*

A novel about Auschwitz is not a novel—or else it is not about Auschwitz.
Elie Wiesel, preface to *Day*

We read books on Auschwitz. The wish of all, in the camps, the last wish: know what has happened, do not forget, and at the same time never will you know.
Maurice Blanchot, *The Writing of the Disaster*[1]

Preliminary

Imre Kertész is a Hungarian Jew who was born in Budapest on November 6, 1929. At age 14 he was deported to the death camps along with hundreds of thousands of other Hungarian Jews, most of whom died in the camps. Kertész probably survived, like the hero of his novel, *Fatelessness*, by lying about his age, since all those under sixteen were immediately gassed and cremated. Those old enough and strong enough were separated out at the initial *Selektion* and sent to work camps instead. Kertész was imprisoned at Buchenwald. After the liberation of the camps he returned to Budapest and became a writer.

Kertész's first novel, *Sorstalanság* (*Fatelessness*) was published in 1975, that is, thirty years after his liberation from the camps, though the novel had been completed earlier.[2] Kertész has insisted that the novel is not autobiographical and that it is not even a novel. Nevertheless, the story it tells of a fifteen-year-old boy from Budapest who is transported to Auschwitz and survives there obviously bears some relation to Kertész's own experience. It also looks like a novel to me, whatever Kertész says. It employs sophisticated novelistic techniques, and it is apparently not just a transcription of history. *Fatelessness* was first translated into English, as *Fateless*, in 1992, and then, in a translation by Tim Wilkinson, as *Fatelessness* in 2004. I cite the latter translation in this essay.[3] A film based on *Fatelessness* was made in Hungary in 2005, with a script by Kertész.[4] Kertész has published in Hungarian numerous other works since then, many of which have been translated into English. The best-known other work is probably *Kaddis a meg nem született gyermekért* (1990) (*Kaddish for an Unborn Child*).[5] Kertész's work was initially not greatly successful in Hungary. He moved to Germany and now resides in Berlin, though he continues to write in Hungarian. In 2002 Kertész was awarded the Nobel Prize in Literature.[6]

Fatelessness (1986) is the only work of my four Holocaust novels written by someone who is a survivor, in this case a survivor of Auschwitz and Buchenwald. *Fatelessness* is in the first person, like *Black Dogs* and like *Maus*. *Maus* uses the first person in a more complex way than *Black Dogs*, since in *Maus* both Vladek and Artie speak in the first person, as if to indicate that only an I can bear witness to the Holocaust. Such bearing witness cannot be done in the third person. This is true of testimony in general.

Fatelessness is the story of incarceration and survival told "in his own words" by a Hungarian teenager. Exactly where he is now located as he speaks or writes in the first person and to whom he is to be imagined as addressing his words are uncertain. The reader, as in most first-person narrations, is an overhearer or even someone granted in imagination access to another person's interior monologue. The reader supposes that this story bears some relation to what the author, Imre Kertész, experienced, but it would be a mistake to identify the two. Kertész's protagonist, Gyuri, is an invented personage in a novel.[7] *Fatelessness*'s basis in Kertész's own experience, nevertheless, makes it the only one of my four examples that is an almost direct act of bearing witness, even though it is a fictional one, while all three of the others, even *Maus*, in different ways and with different degrees of authority, defy Celan by bearing witness for witnesses.

Is it so certain, however, that *Fatelessness* is no more than a straightforward autobiography, as some critics have assumed? Somewhat against what one might expect, *Fatelessness* is, even more than *Maus*, the most complex and challenging of my four works from a narratological perspective and from the perspective of "rhetorical criticism." This bears out my proposed "law" that the closer my examples get to direct witnessing and the closer to a large-scale "conflagration of community," the more complex and subtle they get stylistically and narratologically. *Fatelessness* is, in any case, a moving and distinguished masterpiece. It certainly justifies the awarding of the Nobel Prize to Kertész.

A First Look at Fatelessness

Fatelessness is closest of all my examples to the Holocaust, since it is by a survivor and is the story of a survivor told in the first person, with no relay by way of another person, as happens in *Maus*. In another sense, however, *Fatelessness* is the furthest away from direct representation of the Shoah. It is conspicuously "fictional." It deploys masterfully the aesthetic conventions of modernist fiction, for example, Albert Camus's *L'étranger* (1942). *Fatelessness*'s local stylistic texture gives the literary critic much to "analyze," much more than either *Schindler's List* or *Black Dogs*. As I am uneasily aware, however, the more I analyze, the more I perhaps may aestheticize and anaestheticize Auschwitz, that is, get further away from it. Perhaps. Perhaps, however, the use of complex narratological and rhetorical techniques of storytelling is the only way to grant the reader any proximity to what the experience of concentration camp inmates was like. Perhaps. This double "perhaps" is thematized in the novel itself, as I shall show.

Fatelessness begins with sentences that to my ear sound like a muted echo of the beginning of Camus's *The Stranger*. *Fatelessness* also has some echoes of Kafka, including Kafka's characteristic doubling of the protagonist's experience with the cool ironic objective recording of what happened to the hapless protagonist, such as waking up to find that he has been turned into a gigantic cockroach, or being arrested one fine day, or, in *Fatelessness*, being rounded up on another fine day and sent to a concentration camp. György, the actual first name of Kertész's protagonist, is at least distantly related to Gregor, the first name of the protagonist of Kafka's *The Metamorphosis*. I have no idea whether Kertész has read either Camus or Kafka, though it seems likely. The similarity, however, may be a sheer accident, a matter of fatelessness.

Kafka's *The Trial* begins: "Someone must have slandered Joseph K., for one morning, without having done anything wrong [*etwas Böses*], he was arrested."[8] *The Stranger* begins, "Mother [the intimate *Maman* is used in the French original] died today. Or, maybe, yesterday; I can't be sure." (Aujourd'hui, maman est morte. Ou peut-être hier, je ne sais pas.)[9] *Fatelessness* begins: "I didn't go to school today. Or rather, I did go, but only to ask my class teacher's permission to take the day off" (3). In both *The Stranger* and *Fatelessness* an expected or "normal" emotion is deflected to an apparently peripheral and trivial uncertainty: Did she die yesterday or today? Did I go to school or did I not go to school today? In the opening of *The Stranger*, the reader is shocked at the narrator's apparent coldness about his mother's death. In the opening of *Fatelessness*, the question of whether Gyuri did or did not go to school today, in a kind of nitpicking uncertainty, is a mask for the real event of chapter 1. That event is the preparation for the narrator's father's enforced departure the next day to a Nazi labor camp at Mauthausen. The reader finds at the end of the novel that he has died there, as so many did in the camps, even in the labor camps (*Arbeitsläger*, such as Buchenwald), as opposed to the extermination camps (*Vernichtungsläger*, such as Auschwitz).

Each novel begins in a quite strange present tense. *The Stranger* is not all enunciated on the day of Meurseult's mother's death (or the day after), nor is *Fatelessness* all enunciated on the day Gyuri's father prepares to go to Mauthausen, but the opening sentences sound like that is going to be the case. The conventional assumption is that all novels are narrated from the perspective of the end. The speakers in the opening sentences, we assume, must already be at the end, but that is not congruent with the way both novels do not end on that initial "today." Both novels soon return to a more conventional past tense, though with periodic shifts back to what is sometimes called the "historical present tense," such as is used throughout for the third-person narrator's half of Dickens's *Bleak House*. An example of more present tense narration is the opening sentence of chapter 2 of *Fatelessness*: "Already two months have passed since we said good-bye to Father" (27). I am assuming that Wilkinson accurately translates the tenses used in the Hungarian original.

The effect of these initiating present tense sentences is to plunge the reader into a kind of eternal "today," the happening and re-happening, either in language or in the implied memorial consciousness of the narrator, of the event recorded: "Mama died today." "I didn't go to school today." The whole narrative, in both cases, is colored by the effect of these initial sentences. The events in both novels do go on happening within the covers of the two books, ready to be brought back into the reader's present whenever she or he picks up the book and reads. The critic's instinctive use of the present tense in talking about the novel is implicit testimony to that. An example is my usage in this present essay. See "is" in the next sentence below.

The central event of *The Stranger* is Meurseult's gratuitous shooting to death of an Arab on a beach in Algiers. "It was because of the sun," he says during his trial (130). Meurseult is arrested, tried, condemned to the guillotine, and, at the end of the novel, awaiting execution. Just as Charles Baudelaire in "Fusées," no. 17, says, "When I have inspired universal disgust and horror I shall have conquered solitude,"[10] so Meurseult's last words are: "For all to be accomplished, for me to feel less lonely, all that remained to hope was that on the day of my execution there should be a huge crowd of spectators and that they should greet me with howls of execration" (154). Just where is Meurseult located when he utters or writes these past tense words? Does he speak from after or before his death? It is hard to imagine him writing down the words in the condemned cell. As in the case of *Fatelessness*, the effect is of being present at the moment-to-moment consciousness of the protagonist, miraculously transformed by some anonymous power into words on the page.

Just before the last sentence, Meurseult has looked up at the starry sky and has asserted that he has been happy and is still happy: "For the first time, the first, I laid my heart open to the benign indifference of the universe. To feel it so like myself, indeed, so brotherly, made me realize that I'd been happy, and that I was happy still" (154). This moment is perhaps echoed in the scene in *Fatelessless*, discussed below, when Gyuri, near death, looks up at the sky, as well as in what Gyuri says at the end of the novel about having been happy in the concentration camps. What intervenes between the first and last sentences of *Fatelessness* is of course quite different from the central events of *The Stranger*. *Fatelessness* is the minute and circumstantial account of György Köves's arrest and deportation first to Auschwitz (for just three days), then to Buchenwald and Zeitz, and then back to Buchenwald. He somehow survives, through a combination of courageous strategy and luck that is similar to Vladek's means of survival in Spiegelman's *Maus*. Nevertheless, *Fatelessness*, like *The Stranger*, ends with an assertion that one can be happy even in extreme circumstances, in this case "the happiness of the concentration camps" (262).

Can One Testify to Auschwitz in a Work of Fiction?

The central questions of this chapter are the following: Is it possible to bear witness to the Holocaust in a work of fiction?[11] If so, just how might that be done, by what narrative procedures? Does *Fatelessness* succeed in performing that work of testimony? What should I do after reading *Fatelessness*, if anything? Is a critical analysis of the novel's narrative procedures an appropriate response, or would some other action be better to perform? Just what does critical or narratological analysis contribute by mediation to what might be called the performative force of *Fatelessness*? I mean by "performative force," the novel's ability to do something with words, for example, possibly to bear witness to Auschwitz? Final question: What is the fate of community in *Fatelessness* and in my other three novels about the Shoah?

The writing of *Fatelessness,* like the writing of any novel about Auschwitz, was subject to a double obstacle, or even to what might be called a double double bind or double blind alley. This impasse is a complex "aporia" standing in the way of bearing witness to Auschwitz. I have named somewhat different versions of this aporia in earlier chapters, but need to elaborate further here. *Aporia* means in Greek a dead end or no thoroughfare. An aporia is an impasse in an argument in which two conclusions follow from the premises, but contradict one another, though neither can be chosen over the other. The aporias in this case perhaps block the project of bearing witness to Auschwitz in a novel or indeed in any other form of words, even the most factual or autobiographical. Kertész, like anybody who writes about the Holocaust, was confronted with these obstacles. The narrative form *Fatelessness* took, this chapter argues, was his way of dealing with this double obstacle and of making his way forward in spite of it. Here are the aporias I have in mind:

First aporia: The facts of Auschwitz are, it may be, inherently unthinkable and unspeakable, by any means of representation. One must be careful, however, in using such terms, since, if they are taken in one possible way, they assimilate Auschwitz, illicitly, to a species of negative theology. They imply that just as God is unthinkable and unsayable, so is Auschwitz. Taken another possible way, saying Auschwitz is unthinkable and unsayable plays into the hands of the Nazis and into the hands of the deniers, the revisionists. The Nazis taunted their victims by telling them that what the SS was doing was so awful that no one would believe the few who might survive to bear witness. It would be easy to pass it off as Allied propaganda.[12] The bare facts of Auschwitz—the *Selektion*, the deadly gas, the crematoria, the approximate number of those murdered, the starvation and forced labor that turned so many prisoners into *Muselmänner*, just what the term *Muselmann* means, and so on—can be said in so many words. Those facts are irrefutable because they are backed up by so much documentary evidence. Nevertheless, as almost every survivor agrees, bearing witness to the actual experience of the camps presents big linguistic, and more than just linguistic, difficulties. These difficulties involve questions of life and death, the distinction between the human and the inhuman, what it means to "represent" the concentration camps, and so on. Episodes at the end of *Fatelessness*, discussed below, dramatize these difficulties.

Jean-Luc Nancy, in a characteristically complex and challenging essay, "Forbidden Representation," has approached these questions from the perspective of ambiguities in the word "representation," rather than, as I do, from the perspective of questions about the conflagration of community and about the possibility of testifying to the Shoah.[13] Nancy sees Auschwitz as representing a decisive turning point in Western notions of representation: "The Shoah is, then, an ultimate crisis of representation" ("FR," 34). He claims that both the argument that the Shoah is impossible to represent and the argument that it ought not to be represented are dangerously wrong. The Shoah is neither "ineffable," as in some conceptions of God, nor does the biblical prohibition against making graven images apply to the Shoah. "Not only," says Nancy, "is the 'representation of the Shoah' possible and legitimate, it is, in fact, urgent and necessary—on the condition that the idea of 'representation' be understood in the strict sense that is its own" ("FR," 29).

What is that "strict sense"? The prefix "re-" in "representation" does not, according to Nancy, indicate repetition, a new presentation of something that has already been presented. "Re-" in this case is rather an intensive, or what linguists call a "frequentative." "Representation" can mean "to make observable, to expose with insistence" ("FR," 36). It has a quasi-theatrical sense. In a theatrical representation, people, along with their words and actions, are present to the audience's eyes and ears. Nancy sees "representation" in the Western tradition as having a Jew-Greek origin. Representation is both a biblical and a Platonic-Aristotlean concept. It is, moreover, riven in another way. "The entire history of representation—that entire fevered history of the gigantomachies of *mimesis*, of the image, of perception, of the object and the scientific law, of the spectacle, of art, of political representation—is thus traversed by the fissure of absence, which, in effect, divides it into the absence *of* the thing (problematic of its *re*production) and the *absense* [*sic*] *within* the thing (the problematic of its [re]presentation)" ("FR," 37). *Absense* is Nancy's neologism for an absence of sense and an absence *tout court* at the heart of the thing represented, in this case, the Shoah.

Why then was the Shoah "an ultimate crisis in representation"? According to Nancy, this was because Nazi ideology wanted to make the Aryan race the ultimate self-contained representation of "humanity," "present and with a complete presence" ("FR," 40). They defined Jews (and Gypsies, homosexuals, twins, dwarfs, etc.) as representations, in the bad sense of insubstantial mimicry. Adolf Hitler said, in a statement cited as an epigraph to *Maus*: "The Jews are undoubtedly a race, but they are not human."[14] Since Jews pretend to be human, and thereby challenge the notion that only Aryans are human, they must be exterminated. This must happen so that the Nazi goal can be unequivocally reached. The all-too-real process of killing six million Jews, however, put the SS-Totenkopfverbände units, with their death's head insignia, face to face with their inverse mirror images, the dead or dead-alive prisoners, the latter typified by the *Muselmänner*, about whom I shall say more later in this chapter. "At Auschwitz," says Nancy, "the space of representation was shattered and reduced to the presence of a gaze appropriating death for itself, filling itself up with the dead gaze of the other—a gaze filled with nothing other than a dense emptiness within which the [Nazi] *Weltanschauung* in its entirety came to implode" ("FR," 46).

Death, the Nazis inadvertently discovered, is just what cannot be appropriated for any representation. That is what Paul de Man means when he says: "Death is a displaced name for a linguistic predicament."[15] Nancy would say rather that death is a predicament for representation in any medium—language, film, painting, sculpture, music. Nancy cites a horrible statement by Himmler in a speech to his top lieutenants: "Most of you know what it means when 100 corpses lie there, or when 500 corpses lie there or when 1000 corpses lie there" ("FR," 41). The Nazis, Nancy replies, could make and confront thousands, millions, of corpses and yet never look death in the face, never really "know what it means." And so they had to kill yet thousands more, and yet more, millions all told, in the impossible attempt to incorporate death into the Nazi Aryan presence of humanity to itself. "At Auschwitz," says Nancy, "the West touched the will to present to itself that which is outside presence. Hence, it also touched the will to a representation without remainder, without hollowing out or withdrawal, without a line of flight. To that extent, it is the exact opposite of monotheism, as well as of philosophy and art" ("FR," 43). I suppose Nancy means that monotheism, like philosophy and art, always involves an absent or invisible God, a *deus absconditus*, or the absent existence of some underlying ground that is not open to direct confrontation, only to indirect representation.

In the Shoah's dreadful symbiosis of executioner and victim, multiplied six million times, the gap in the West's double conception of representation became "an opening—interval or wound" ("FR," 49), that is, a decisive crisis in representation. This does not mean that representations of Auschwitz are not both possible and urgently necessary, but that such representations, whether in novels, films, memoirs, taped recollections, or scholarly analyses, must respond to the "demand: that such an opening—interval or wound—not be shown as an object but rather that it be inscribed right at the level of representation, as its very texture, or as the truth of its truth" ("FR," 49). You will note that Nancy speaks entirely of constative representations, of telling the truth of the Shoah's truth. I would shift what Nancy says from the constative register to the register of that performative enunciation called "witnessing." Seeing the paradoxical representation of a fissure, gap, or wound in representation, opened by the Shoah, as an act of testimony, a speech act, as a bearing witness to something to which it is impossible to bear witness, will allow another step beyond what Nancy says. This will be a step further toward understanding what is at stake in all representations of Auschwitz. This chapter tries to take that step.

Jean-François Lyotard succinctly identifies a core aspect of Auschwitz that resists being said and transmitted to others: "To have 'really seen with his own eyes' a gas chamber would be the condition which gives one the authority to say that it exists and to persuade the unbeliever. Yet it is still necessary to prove that the gas chamber was used to kill at the time it was seen. The only acceptable proof that it was used to kill is that one died from it. But if one is dead, one cannot testify that it is on account of the gas chamber."[16] Kertész's hero comes up against this impasse when he confronts an Auschwitz denier on his return to Budapest, as I shall show. This impasse may be at least part of what Giorgio Agamben means when he says that witnesses to Auschwitz must bear witness to something to which it is impossible to bear witness. That does not mean, however, that such bearing witness should not be attempted, in the teeth of its impossibility, as Nancy forcefully argues. *Fatelessness* tries to do that.

Jacques Derrida, in an interview by Antoine Spire in *Paper Machine*, "Others Are Secret Because They Are Other," reframes this impasse in a hyperbolic way. This happens in a discussion of the question of forgiveness in its relation to bearing witness. "Forgiveness" is *pardon* in French. *Par* has many meanings: "by," "with," or "across," "out of," or "through." *Don* means "gift." *Pardon* is close to the combination in the English word "forgive" but not an exact match. Both reveal themselves to be strange combinations of syllables, if you think about them. Spire puts Derrida's assertion that only the unforgivable demands forgiveness in the context of Auschwitz: "You also say that forgiveness comes from the fact that we live together in the same society. We do indeed live under the same sky as the Nazi torturers [*bourreaux*], the Algerian murderers, those guilty of crimes against humanity, and so on."[17] Derrida, in response to Spire's asking whether the survivors can forgive "in . . . place" of the dead, says only the victims can forgive. The survivors cannot forgive: "No! Only the victims might at some point have the right to forgive. If they are dead, or have disappeared in some way, no pardon is possible" (*PMe*, 161; *PMf*, 396). This is a transposition to forgiveness of Celan's assertion that no one bears witness for the witness. No one can pardon but the victims of the unpardonable. In the case of Auschwitz, those murdered are no longer around to forgive, just as they are no longer around to bear witness. In response to Spire's further question, "But in what respect is it unforgivable?" Derrida answers, somewhat evasively or indirectly, by saying that in any scene of face-to-face forgiveness, the only kind possible, even if only two persons are present, a third is always, even if only virtually, present:

> Another aporia: it's all very well for the scene of forgiveness [*pardon*] to require the singularity of a face-to-face encounter between the victim and the guilty party, but a third person is active from the start. Even if there are only two of you, in the tête-à-tête, forgiveness implies a third person [as endorsing, countersigning witness—JHM] as soon as it goes by way of a speech or some generally iterable trace. So, for instance heirs (and the third person is in the position of heir, he preserves the trace) have a sort of right to speech [*une sorte de droit à la parole*]. So the scene of forgiveness can and even must be prolonged after death, contradictory as that appears in relation to the requirement for the face-to-face encounter between two living people, the victim and the criminal. (*PMe*, 162; *PMf*, 397)

Matters are not quite so simple as Lyotard says, however, or even as Derrida says. One significant class of prisoners was the *Sonderkommandos*, or "special squads." These were prisoners, usually Jews, who were, horrifyingly, conscripted by the SS to perform the dirty work of the gas chambers, that is, to kill and then cremate their fellow prisoners, sometimes their own relatives or friends. Though the SS made a point of periodically sending the *Sonderkommando* teams themselves to the gas chambers and replacing them with a new batch, so that no witness would remain, nevertheless a few did leave written records or did survive to testify to their inhuman experience. These survivors had seen the gas chambers at their work of extermination with their own eyes and so could escape Lyotard's impasse.

Second aporia: Turning the Nazi genocide into a fiction of any kind, "aestheticizing" it, is inherently a deeply suspect operation. On the one hand, the more successful the novel is as a novel the further away it may be from Auschwitz. Perhaps. That is what Elie Wiesel says in my second epigraph. On the other hand, Imre Kertész may have been right when he said more than once in a recent oral communication that all testimony to Auschwitz, even the most overtly autobiographical, is "fiction."[18] He certainly did not mean that the Holocaust is a fiction in the sense meant by Holocaust deniers who say the Shoah never happened. Quite the reverse. It is crucial to be clear about this. I think Kertész meant that any narrative of the Holocaust is a selective and ordered sequence. I extrapolate on my own from what Kertész said to affirm that any narrative of a concentration camp experience by a survivor, from the most autobiographical to the most fictional transposition, is a putting together of somewhat arbitrarily chosen details to make a story out of them. This "putting together" is not inherent in the details themselves. Any narrating puts the facts in constructed form, though the facts remain facts. I would express this by saying that Auschwitz narratives, whether autobiographical or fictional, are not just an ordering of facts, but an interpretation of them, a passing judgment on them, in short, a bearing witness to them.

I make two claims about these aporias: (1) that the form of storytelling Kertész employs in *Fatelessness* made it possible for him to bear witness to Auschwitz more effectively than he could otherwise have done, and (2) that the novel itself dramatizes within itself the reasons for this.

Performing a "rhetorical reading" or a "narratological reading" of a novel like *Fatelessness*, with close attention to the text, to the way it operates its performative magic of testifying to Auschwitz, may just compound the possible shame of writing fiction about Auschwitz. It may be an act of unforgivable temerity. Perhaps. I distinguish between the two forms of reading I have named here and earlier. A rhetorical reading, in the sense I mean it, especially attends to patterns of tropes, to the function of recurrent terms (such as "naturally" in *Fatelessness*), to stylistic features like irony. A narratological reading concerns itself with narrators, points of view, plot structure, and other matters of narrative form. My reading somewhat uneasily combines these two. They cannot in any case be sharply divided or, perhaps, ever be seamlessly reconciled. Either form or any combination may be subject to the obstacle Maurice

Blanchot identifies in *The Writing of the Disaster*: "All theories, however different they may be, constantly change places with one another, distinct each from the next only because of the writing which supports them and which thus escapes the very theories purporting to judge it."[19]

How can we in good conscience perform either sort of theory-based analysis, or any combination, with something so serious as bearing witness to Auschwitz? On the one hand, analytical commentary, with its scrupulous distinctions, such as I am performing here, is perhaps just a way to protect oneself from the affective force of *Fatelessness*, so disabling its testimonial force. The story this novel tells is certainly hard to take. The reader resists confronting it directly. On the other hand, can a critical analysis of a novel that bears witness to Auschwitz be itself a form of testimony or at least a form of testimony's effective transmission, in defiance of Paul Celan's assertion, mentioned often in this book, that no one bears witness for the witness?[20]

Impediments to Bearing Witness to Auschwitz

The obstacles to testifying to Auschwitz are inscribed in the novel itself. This happens in the displaced form of the difficulties Kertész's protagonist, Gyuri, has in getting his experiences understood by those he encounters on his way home after being liberated from Buchenwald and when he first arrives back in Budapest. These encounters dramatize the problems Kertész himself may have felt he faced in trying, a good many years after his experience in the camps, to write a novel that would work as a successful testimony to Auschwitz. Though these episodes come at the end of the novel, I need to discuss them now in order to establish the obstacles to bearing witness to the Shoah as Kertész's protagonist experienced those when he returned from Buchenwald after its liberation. I hope the reader will forgive my metalepsis, putting the cart before the horse. My procedure may be especially unforgivable, and therefore in need of forgiveness, because Kertész himself follows such a strict chronological order in his narration. The logic of my argumentation, the story I am telling, is different, however, from that of the novel itself. Expressing cogently my reading of the novel necessitates turning at this point to the end of Gyuri's story.

My hypothesis is that the choice of writing a work of fiction, rather than a memoir, and the choice of the narrative strategies Kertész employs in *Fatelessness*, were his solutions to an experience of blank incomprehension by other people on his return, such as the experience he ascribes to Gyuri when he comes home from Buchenwald after its liberation. I must now show how that incomprehension is dramatized by displacement to a fictional protagonist. After that, I shall move on to consideration of the function of irony and other stylistic features in the novel and then to the way Kertész's narrative strategies are employed in the climactic episode of the novel, its peripeteia, or turning point: Gyuri's almost becoming what was called in the camps a *Muselmann*, that is, someone near death from starvation, overwork, and abuse. That episode includes another example of the way Gyuri's cool irony serves an essential narrative function in this fictional testimony. I shall return finally to an explanation of the title and the title's relation to Kertész's choice of a strictly chronological narration as the right way to testify to the Shoah. These sections are approaches from different perspectives toward giving an account of *Fatelessness*, that is, testifying to its effect on me as reader.

At the end of the novel, Gyuri, having miraculously survived until the liberation of the camps, makes his way back to Budapest, penniless and still wearing his prison uniform. Along the way and when he reaches his native city, he has four confrontations that bring home to him the difficulties of communicating what he has experienced, five if you count the meeting with his mother he is starting toward as the novel ends and which he anticipates as though it were fated to happen in a certain way. The reader is not told how that reunion comes off, though Gyuri says, "My mother was waiting, and would no doubt greatly rejoice over me" (262).

The first encounter takes place on the way home, in an unnamed city where Gyuri hears "a lot of Hungarian being spoken as well as Czech" (240). A stranger in the street, as Gyuri waits for the next train, approaches him and asks whether he "personally, however, did not ascertain this [the existence of the gas chambers] with your own eyes." When he answers, truthfully, "no," since, as he says, he would be dead if he had, the stranger says, "I see," and walks away "unless I was very much mistaken, satisfied in some manner" (242). "Unless I was very much mistaken" is one of those either/or reservations characteristic of Gyuri's narration. The significance of these is discussed below. The implication is that the man who interrogates Gyuri is an Auschwitz denier whose refusal to believe will now be confirmed. That implication is less explicit in the film version, since the sentence I have just quoted about his interlocuter's satisfaction is, naturally, missing, because it is part of the narrator's report of Gyuri's thoughts. You cannot film thoughts or interior monologue, except by the extremely awkward and anticinematic device of a disembodied voice-over. In the film we have only the denier's facial expression to go by, but that conveys a lot.

The second confrontation is with Bandi Citrom's sister and mother in their apartment on Forget-Me-Not Road in Budapest. Bandi was Gyuri's only true friend in the camps, though he abandoned Gyuri when the latter was on the way to becoming a *Muselmann*. Bandi had spoken with nostalgia about what a wonderful place Forget-Me-Not Road was, though Gyuri finds it shabby enough when, even before going home, he goes to Bandi Citrom's house to see if Bandi has survived and made it home. The painful confrontation with Bandi's sister and mother reveals that Bandi has not returned and that almost certainly he has died in the camp. Gyuri makes no attempt to tell Bandi's sister and mother what the camps were like.

The third confrontation is a most unsatisfactory conversation with a journalist. Gyuri meets this reporter on a tramcar on his way home from Bandi Citrom's house. This man tries, unsuccessfully, to get Gyuri to acquiesce to a whole set of clichés about the camps, such as "Can we imagine a concentration camp as anything but a hell?" (248). The journalist is greatly annoyed when Gyuri says he knows nothing about hell, but the difference, he guesses, is that it is impossible to be bored in hell, whereas he was sometimes bored, even in Auschwitz. He tells the journalist that his primary feeling, now that he is back home in Budapest, is "hatred" (247). Hatred of whom? "Everyone" (247). Finally, the journalist says, "No, it's impossible to imagine it" (250), with which the narrating Gyuri remembers being in silent agreement. He soon ends the conversation, though the journalist wants to help him write up and publish his memories of the camps.

The implication is that journalistic clichés about the camps are not a successful bearing witness, while the narrative strategies Kertész uses in *Fatelessness* may possibly succeed, for example, in the passage the reader is at that moment reading. Writing a novel about Auschwitz rather than a factual account within the constraints of journalistic conventions is here implicitly defended as the right way to bear witness, in blank contradiction to what Elie Wiesel was later to assert, as cited in my epigraph.

The fourth encounter is an equally unsatisfactory meeting with two members of what is left of Gyuri's original community. His father has died at Mauthausen, and his stepmother has remarried. An impassioned speech from Gyuri only angers his Uncle Fleischmann and his Uncle Steiner. (They are apparently not blood relatives, but are called "uncles" because they are intimate friends and neighbors of his family.) Uncle Fleischmann asks him about his plans for the future. Gyuri answers that he has not given it much thought, whereupon Uncle Steiner tells him,

"You must put the horrors behind you . . . in order . . . to be able to live" (256). "Live freely," adds Uncle Fleischmann. Gyuri reacts negatively to these suggestions. For one thing, he says, he would be unable to forget unless he were to suffer some injury or disease that would affect his mind. Moreover, he does not want to forget.

This painful confrontation is the climax of Gyuri's discovery that though he feels an obligation to testify to his experiences, a direct account of them seems to convey nothing. It confirms, rather, the second half of Blanchot's contradictory injunction in my third epigraph: "Know what has happened, do not forget, and at the same time never will you know." Gyuri's explanatory speech to his uncles just makes them angry. His visit to them is broken off in a recognition that they have understood nothing and do not want to understand anything: "But I could see they did not wish to understand anything, and so, picking up my kit bag and cap, I departed in the midst of a few disjointed words and motions, one more unfinished gesture and incomplete utterance from each" (261). This is the hyperbolic climax of Gyuri's experience of the difficulty of testifying to Auschwitz.

Ironic Narration as Witnessing

The narrative strategies of *Fatelessness* repay with interest minute rhetorical and narratological analysis. Just what is that interest? It comes back as a kind of supplementary repayment, a plus value, for close attention to the words on the page. That plus value may include a deeper understanding of what is at stake in trying to bear witness to Auschwitz in a fictional work.

As I said above, a powerful film of *Fatelessness*, with a script by Kertész, called just *Fateless*, is available on DVD. This chapter does not give this admirable film the extended analysis it deserves. Moving and disturbing as the cinematic version is, however, partly through putting before the viewer's eyes the atrocities and sufferings the reader of the novel must imagine on the basis of the words on the page, the film has great difficulty finding graphic equivalents for the verbal complexities of Gyuri's narration in the novel proper. These are essential to the novel's meaning. As is always the case, the juxtaposition of novel and film has great value as a means of identifying distinctive features in each medium by way of differences between one and the other.

The film makes intermittent and quite effective use of the protagonist's speech in voice-over. That disembodied voice repeats some important things that are said by the first-person narrating I or by the experiencing

I in the novel. Nevertheless, only part of this level of discourse is given. The pervasive irony of the novel is more or less missing, naturally, from the film. I say this is natural because irony is essentially a linguistic effect, not a visual one, though of course something like irony can arise from the juxtaposition of images. What is given in the novel as Gyuri's sharp vision of things, a vision that makes him a kind of camera eye, becomes in the film the actual "camera eye" vision, often a vision of Gyuri's silent and more or less impassive face, seen, naturally, from the outside, something the novel nowhere presents. The explicit theme of the *Muselmann*, so important in the novel and in my reading of it later in this chapter, is absent, oddly, from the film, though the film powerfully presents Gyuri's near death in a way that closely follows the novel.

I have seen the Hungarian original of the novel. As I said in a footnote above, it was in 2007 available online, though the site is now unavailable. Happily, I downloaded it in time. The Hungarian original has been helpful to my reading, as I shall show, even though I do not know Hungarian. My ignorance means it is an act of chutzpah to pretend to be able to talk intelligently about this novel. A painful inability of Gyuri to understand what is being said around him in the camps, since so many different languages are spoken there, is one of the ways the survival of community is endangered in *Fatelessness*. To compare great things with small, my inability to read *Fatelessness* in the original Hungarian may possibly give me a vague idea of what it must have been like for Kertész (or Gyuri) to be surrounded by a Babel of languages he did not understand. The difference, and it is a huge difference, is that a failure to understand in Auschwitz was likely to be a matter of life or death, whereas nothing more is at stake in my linguistic inability than my scholarly competence to write about *Fatelessness* at all.

Kertész's solutions to the aporias I have identified included his choice of a first-person mode of narration and his use of irony as the basic form of discourse in that narration. The narratological presupposition of *Fatelessness* is to tell in the first person the story of a fifteen-year-old Hungarian Jewish boy's experiences of arrest in Budapest in 1944, near the end of World War II, his deportation to Auschwitz along with hundreds of thousands of other Hungarian Jews, most of whom died, and then his survival in the labor camps at Buchenwald and Zeitz, that is, the Wille subcamp of Buchenwald, near the town of Zeitz. Zeitz was a labor camp for work in the synthetic oil factory in that town. The story Kertész's hero tells matches closely many details about life in the camps given, for example, in the overtly autobiographical accounts by Primo Levi in *Survival in Auschwitz* and by Elie Wiesel in *Night*.[21]

Gyuri is presented as a "cool," detached, ironic, more or less affectless teenager, who nevertheless (or perhaps as a result) has an extremely sharp eye for details of what he witnesses, for example, what other people look like. He also has an extraordinary ability to put what he has seen into words, a sharp intelligence devoted to figuring things out for himself, and a quiet "stubbornness" (138) that contributes to his extremely unlikely, and in many ways fortuitous, survival. "Stubborness" is an important word in the novel, as I shall show.

Gyuri's experiences are narrated in strict chronological order. No confusing time shifts for Kertész. The novel narrates one vivid present after another, in "fateless" sequence. I shall identify later the significance of this narratological choice. The past is rarely explicitly remembered in the present by the protagonist whose story the narrator is telling, the experiencing I, and the future is almost completely unpredictable to him.

I call the hero *then* "the protagonist," or "the experiencing I," and the hero *now* narrating his past experiences, "the narrator," or "the narrating I," in this first-person novel. Protagonist and narrator are two aspects of the same person, separated by the gulf between the unidentified present of the narration and the past of what is narrated. They are also separated by the fact that the narrator knows that he survived to return to Budapest, while the protagonist lived from moment to moment aware that he was in danger of imminent death. The narrator is granted, apparently, the ability to remember everything, as is a common convention of first-person novels. These differences between the narrating I and the experiencing I require distinguishing, as with most first-person novels, the language of the protagonist *then*, from the language of the narrator *now*. That may, however, sometimes be difficult or even impossible to do. This is parallel to the ambiguities of telling whose language is being used in free indirect discourse, that of the protagonist or that of the narrator who speaks in the third-person past tense on the protagonist's behalf. Periodic use of the present tense in *Fatelessness* (as in the opening sentence, "I didn't go to school today" [3], discussed earlier) play an important role in reinforcing the experiencing I's absorption in the present moment when the events now narrated in retrospect actually took place.

Gyuri is granted by Kertész an extremely active mind. That activity is devoted to interpreting what he sees, hears, and feels, even when starvation and infections bring him to the brink of death, bring him almost to the state of the *Muselmänner* in the camps. The basic narrative assumption of *Fatelessness* is that Gyuri has no understanding of the details of what he sees and hears until he figures them out at first hand for himself. He is fooled into thinking he is leaving Hungary for work, not to be starved, beaten, and most probably gassed and cremated. Many other deportees were similarly fooled. This is analogous to the naïveté of Kafka's protagonist in the final episode of *The Man Who Disappeared* (*Amerika*), discussed in chapter 2 of this book. The reader knows, the retrospectively narrating Gyuri knows, and Kertész knows, but the experiencing Gyuri does not at first know, that the strange smell at Auschwitz is the burning bodies of the gassed in the crematoria. He thinks at first that those chimneys with billowing black smoke are tanneries. He does not at first understand that those sent to the right-hand group in the initial *Selektion* at Auschwitz will be immediately gassed and cremated, including boys in the group that was arrested with him who are too fat, or who have poor eyesight, or who have weak muscles. However, Gyuri figures all this out by the end of his first day in Auschwitz. His understanding is based on the evidence of his senses and on what he hears other prisoners say. Part of the force of the novel depends on presenting these unspeakable atrocities, as understanding of them gradually replaces the ignorance and innocence of an intelligent and observant teenager. The reader knows these atrocities already in a general way, but seeing them in this new form, through the eyes of someone who was from moment to moment in mortal danger and who only gradually realized this, brings these horrors home to the reader, proves them on his or her pulses, in a particularly unforgettable way.

Three stylistic features dominate Gyuri's narration, or at least may be singled out as of special importance to the expression of just exactly what is meant by "fatelessness." A full rhetorical reading of the novel would require a long, minute, stylistic and thematic analysis. That would be necessary, for example, to decide whether Gyuri's perspective changes in the course of the novel. It is not at all easy to be sure about that either one way or the other, though it is an important question. Gyuri certainly *knows* more at the end, and he becomes more eloquent, but does his *affective* stance really change? I think it does not change all that much, not enough to fit *Fatelessness* easily within the paradigm of all those first-person novels about growing up and losing innocence that leave the protagonist at the end a sadder but wiser man or woman. Such first-person discourse is governed by a "Then I was ignorant; now I know."

I limit myself here, however, to brief discussions of three important stylistic aspects of *Fatelessness*. Other important features are omitted, such as Gyuri's gift for grotesque metaphor, as when he says that his grandmother's nearly blind eyes, through her thick glasses, "looked just like two peculiar, perspiring insects" (24), or when he describes the hand of an older prisoner hesitantly offering a bribe as "like some big, sparsely haired spider or, even more, some kind of smaller sea monster that was, as it were, seeking the crevice that would allow it to scuttle under the jacket" (52), or when he says Uncle Steiner's hand, as the two uncles are about to tell him his father is dead, "slowly lifted and set off in the air before settling like a cautious, aging bat on my arm" (254). Such metaphors, or, strictly speaking, similes, are splendid examples of what Kenneth Burke called "perspective by incongruity." They also contribute much to the irony that is my first stylistic feature.

Gyuri's Irony

Fatelessness is told throughout in a mode of ironic understatement that matches Gyuri's detached observation. Irony is an aspect of Gyuri's teenage coolness. The entire stylistic texture of *Fatelessness* is ironic throughout, from that first sentence on: "I didn't go to school today." The irony often surfaces overtly, however, as when Gyuri says of something extremely ominous, the evidence he has that it is dangerous to be in the infirmary at Zeitz, that these bits of evidence "did not exactly boost one's confidence" (173). In another place he "disinterestedly," as Kant says we should do with artworks, admires the statue at the entrance to Buchenwald. This shows a prisoner carrying on the run a heavy rock. Gyuri then draws himself up to think about this further: "But then it crossed my mind that it no doubt also carried a message, though that message could not be considered exactly auspicious, if one thought about it" (123).

In an extended overt irony, Gyuri says the carefully planned procedures of the bathhouses, gas chambers, and crematoria of the camps "all somehow roused in me a sense of certain jokes, a kind of student prank" (111). He goes on, in a passage cited in chapter 2, to imagine the German officials thinking up one by one the gas chambers, the bathhouses, the soap, the flower beds outside, the soccer field, the soothing music, and so on, and congratulating one another for their inventiveness. This is disturbingly close to what must actually have happened at the famous Wahnsee Conference, in which the "final solution" was worked out in detail: "Some of the ideas may have provoked more prolonged discussion and amendment, whereas others would have been immediately hailed with delight, the men jumping up (I don't know why, but I insisted on their jumping up) and slapping one another's palms—this was all too readily imagined, at least so far as I was concerned. By dint of many zealous hands and much to-ing and fro-ing, the commanders' fantasy then becomes reality, and as I had witnessed, there was no room for any doubt about the stunt's success" (111–12).

To speak of the murder of six million Jews in the Holocaust as a students' prank is a savage irony indeed, but it forcefully brings home to the reader what Hannah Arendt called the "banality of evil." Gyuri has "witnessed" with his own eyes the results of the incredibly evil fantasies of the "final solution" as the Nazi leaders thought it up, smoking cigars, slapping hands, and laughing at each new diabolical invention. Irony, however, as everyone knows, or ought to know, is a two-edged sword. It cuts both ways, and, as Friedrich Schlegel asserted, turns especially against those who presume to have mastered it.[22] This unmastering may include Kertész, who chose to ascribe to his imaginary protagonist a pervasively ironic way of thinking and talking, as well as that protagonist, Gyuri, and any reader, such as the author of this essay, who pretends to explain what *Fatelessness* means.

Irony exists on several planes in *Fatelessness*. It exists as dramatic irony, the clash between what the reader or the author knows and what the protagonist knows, as when Gyuri momentarily thinks the crematoria chimneys, with their sickeningly sweet-smelling smoke, are tanneries, whereas the reader, as well as Kertész, already know they are the notorious Auschwitz crematoria. Irony also exists as the more or less controlled irony of Gyuri's self-conscious discourse, his apparent saying one thing and meaning another, as when he calls the planning for the final solution a student prank. Gyuri's ironies, however, do not really just say one thing while clearly meaning another, as a hypothetical (though never real) "controlled irony" or "perspicuous irony" would do. Gyuri's ironies say both things at once, though those things are logically incompatible. The final solution, in its hideous moral irresponsibility, does have a chilling resemblance to a student prank. To call it that is a brilliant insight into the banality of evil. It does not take too much imagination to suppose that similar conferences took place at the highest levels in Washington, D.C., in recent years, as Abu Ghraib, Guantánamo Bay, extraordinary rendition, limitless electronic surveillance, and other such perfidies were planned in detail.

Kertész's choice of irony as a pervasive mode of Gyuri's discourse turns against the author by rendering the novel fundamentally "undecidable" in meaning. The novel is an example of what Friedrich Schlegel called a "permanent parabasis," a permanent suspension of a single identifiable meaning. "Parabasis" is a Greek rhetorical term for the moment in a stage play when the illusion is broken by a character who comes forward and speaks of the play as a play. An example is the end of Shakespeare's *The Tempest.* Irony is a "permanent parabasis," as opposed to a momentary one, because it suspends the illusion of straightforward representation of external events and people from one end of an ironical discourse to the other. It is impossible to know, for example, whether Kertész endorses, as a proper moral stance, on the basis of his experience, Gyuri's assertion to the journalist that his primary feeling on returning home is "hatred," hatred not of his captors, but of "everyone," on hearing which the journalist "[falls] silent, this time for a longer period, before starting up again" (247). Readers want to know whether or not Kertész believes in "fate" or in "fatelessness."

Irony, to put it mildly (or ironically), tends to turn people off, to perplex, annoy, and even enrage them. We want clear knowledge and judgment. A good novel about Auschwitz, we think, ought to provide that. Critics will go through remarkable contortions to satisfy their desire for certainty and to resist irony's permanent parabasis of such certainty. The difficulty of reaching such certainty on the basis of the textual evidence, the words on the page of *Fatelessness*, may explain the resistance to this novel and the low marks some critics give it among Holocaust novels, as in Efraim Sicher's remarks, cited below. I claim, contra Sicher, that irony is essential in two contradictory fashions to the way *Fatelessness* bears witness to Auschwitz. Gyuri's ironic narration provides enough distance from the horrible events he represents to bring them vividly home to the reader. The irony breaks down the reader's resistance to confronting the Shoah. At the same time the uncertainty or undecidability generated by Gyuri's irony constitutes, in this text, that fissure of absence or "ab-sense," that gap in representation, that Nancy says is an essential feature of the crisis in representation the Shoah brought about. Another name for that gap is death, the deaths of those six million victims of the Holocaust.

Perhaps This, Perhaps That

The irony is related to another salient stylistic feature of *Fatelessness*. This feature is a discursive counterpart to the distressing performative uncertainty of the trope that is not a trope, irony. Irony is a way of doing something with words, but that something is to put the reader in a suspended condition of uncertainty. If irony says two incompatible things at once, cutting both ways, Gyuri's explicit judgments, though they are based on his stubborn innate commitment to seeing clearly and to understanding correctly, are also an enunciation in cognitive terms of ironic suspension, or parabasis. Gyuri registers his cognitive uncertainty as part of his truth-telling testimony.

Gyuri is systematically unwilling or unable to make any straightforward unequivocal judgment about anything he sees. He is, moreover, too honest to pretend otherwise. Even though he more than once says "no two ways about it" (154), as if to put an end to his "either/or" uncertainty, his judgments are characteristically accompanied by an often extraordinary series of qualifications, provisos, revisions, contradictions, and assertions of uncertainty. For Gyuri, there are "two ways about" more or less anything he sees. A frequent locution is something like "from yet another angle, though," or "from another angle, though" (250, 135). Gyuri remains, in James Joyce's admirable phrase in *Finnegans Wake*, in "twosome twiminds."[23]

Dozens of examples could be adduced of this habit of qualification, or dubiety, or outright self-contradiction, all forms of twimindedness. I cite a few. Gyuri speaks of the expression of satisfaction on the face of the guard who tells him to say he is sixteen (a lie that saves his life): "Another thing I noticed, though it was more just a fleeting observation and perhaps mistaken at that . . ." (86). The faces of those who have been chosen for the good side in the *Selektion* at Auschwitz express "success, if I sensed it correctly" (86). On a later occasion he says, "That was my impression, right then at least, though that might have been mistaken, of course" (100). About the question of whether their guards are human beings like Gyuri and his fellow captives, he asks himself, "Were these beings proceeding here by our side deep down, despite everything, basically similar to ourselves, fashioned, when it came down to it, from much the same human material? But then it occurred to me that my way of looking at it might be flawed, since I myself was not, of course, one and the same" (122). Later he says, "From another angle though—and this is also true" (135); "at least that was my experience . . . that, by and large, was how I grasped it" (135–36). Of the occasional suicide in the Zeitz camp he says it was "in some ways hard to explain, maybe slightly frivolous, maybe even slightly honorable, but in any case premature" (136). He speaks of the chanting of the Kaddish, by the assembled lines of witnessing prisoners for their three hanged fellows, as "the final, sole, and perhaps, I could not help realizing, in some ways slightly forced, I might almost say prescribed and in a certain sense fixed, so to say imposed, and, at the same time, useless mode of stubbornness (for it altered nothing up at the front: apart from the last few twitches of the hanged men, nothing moved, nothing wavered at these words)" (161–62). Gyuri, a little to his regret, cannot participate in the chanting, since he is not a believer, though in the film he does. Two more examples: "unless I was mistaken" (206); "I would likewise have been mistaken on that score, too" (207).

Another example of twimindedness is worthy of slightly extended commentary "I noticed that the emotion gratified them, gave them some sort of pleasure, the way I saw it. Indeed—and I could have been mistaken of course, though I don't think so" (213). This qualified assertion is movingly ironic, since it comes as part of an episode in which one of the doctors who are treating Gyuri in the camp hospital gets him to tell the story of how he was arrested and sent to Auschwitz. The doctor then passes that story on to other doctors and patients. The emotion in question is pity: "In the end, I found that people on all sides were looking at me, heads shaking, and with a most singular emotion on their faces, which was a little embarrassing because, as best I could tell, they were feeling sorry for me. I felt a strong urge to tell them there was no need for that after all, at least not right at that moment, but I ended up saying nothing, something held me back, somehow I couldn't find it in my heart to do so, because . . ." (213), and then follows the passage already cited: "I noticed the emotion gratified them," and so on.

Gyuri doesn't say anything not because he thinks pity for him is justified, but for the strange and ironically dissonant reason that he cannot bring himself, in this concentration camp hospital, to deprive the doctors, orderlies, and patients of the pleasure of feeling sorry for him. He is not even sure that he is right about the emotion he thinks they are feeling but says they were feeling sorry for him, "as best I could tell." In saying this Gyuri is being true to one important law of this first-person narration. This law decrees that no direct access is possible to the minds of other people, such as an omniscient or telepathic third-person narrator might have.

The sequence is a good example of the ironic disjunction between the language of the experiencing I and the language of the narrating I. It also exemplifies the difficulties of distinguishing with certainty between those two languages, particularly in a narrative that is ironic through and through. "I noticed that the emotion gratified them, gave them some kind of pleasure, the way I saw it" must be, the reader thinks, if she thinks about it at all, the narrating I reporting in the past tense what the experiencing I noticed and saw. "I could have been mistaken of course, though I don't think so," the reader assumes, must be the narrating I's present judgment on the accuracy of the experiencing I's judgment. But is this absolutely certain, plausible as it seems? "I noticed that the emotion gratified them," and the rest, could be either the narrating I putting words in the experiencing I's mouth, or it could be a transposition into the past tense of Gyuri in the past thinking to himself in the present tense: "The way I see it, the emotion gratifies them, gives them some sort of pleasure. I could be mistaken of course, though I don't think so." After all, the narrating I has earlier in the sentence said in the past tense about the pity the experiencing I discerned in those who have just heard his story: "as best I could tell." That seems clearly to be a reporting after the fact of the experiencing I's evaluation. Still, "I don't think so" seems indubitably a statement of the narrating I's judgment in the present of what the experiencing I saw and judged in the past. This linguistic mixture corresponds to the psychological or phenomenological mixture within any person's consciousness at a given moment of features that belong to the past and features that belong to her or his present memory of the past. It is hard to tell, in a given sample of first-person narration, whether the words on the page reflect the experiencing I's transformation of perhaps initially wordless thoughts, feelings, and observations (if there are such things) into words that accompanied them, in that endless dialogue with ourselves that we carry on all the time, or whether the narrating I has given language to what was originally, *then*, a wordless event of experiencing.

Gyuri's ironic understatement functions powerfully to generate pity in me too. What has happened to Gyuri is truly atrocious. The Aristotelean tragic emotions of pity and fear are appropriate responses. Something not entirely dissimilar has happened today in response to learning about those who have been unjustly imprisoned in Guantánamo Bay or who have been subjected to "extraordinary rendition" and then torture in a foreign jail. Kertész has given a name by displacement to the emotion the reader should feel when reading *Fatelessness*, though he has also warned the reader against taking too much pleasure in that feeling of pity.

James Phelan, in *Living to Tell About It*, identifies three main functions of narrators: reporting, interpreting, and evaluating.[24] Gyuri as narrating I certainly performs all those functions, but it is not always easy to be sure just which Gyuri is doing the performing of these linguistic acts, or whose language the reader is encountering. Kertész's narrating I in this novel appears to be that happy thing, a reliable narrator. He is restricted, however, to reporting, interpreting, and evaluating Gyuri's experiences in the camps from Gyuri's perspective. This exemplifies another of Phelan's narratological terms: "restricted narration." Kertész's narrator can only show the way events appeared to other characters by means of what they say. Direct access to the minds of others is forbidden. This means that both Gyuris may conceivably be mistaken. The narrating I may conceivably have forgotten something important. The reader has no way to know for sure, since no other perspective is given. We do not have access to any outside confirmation of the testimony the narrating Gyuri proffers.

No way out of this uncertainty is possible within a first-person narration. Testimony is a performative enunciation, not a constative one. Any testimony is, like that of a witness in a court case, implicitly prefaced by a performative oath: "I swear this is what I saw with my own eyes and heard with my own ears." The one who hears the testimony, a jury member, for example, must believe, without being able to prove, that the witness thinks he or she is telling the truth. Even if what the witness says is demonstrably wrong, that does not mean she does not think she is right. The possibility of forgetting what the camps are like, even by a survivor, is named in the last sentence of the novel, in a moving conclusion, to which I shall return.

For Gyuri, in any case, I mean for both the experiencing I and the narrating I, in their often inextricable entanglement or superimposition, there often are "two ways about" anything he experiences. The ironic suspension of certain knowledge characteristic of Gyuri's narration is expressed in the locutions I have cited.

I complete my repertoire of these discursive equivalents of the trope irony, the spelling out in so many words, so to speak, of the perpetual uncertainty that an ironic stance generates, with a slightly more extended example. The reader will see how given to circumlocution Gyuri's statement in this example is, how punctuated and delayed by reservations and qualifications that resist saying anything definite and unequivocal: "I suspect," "one could even say," "so to say," "so it seemed," "at least the way I saw it." Gyuri is trying to understand why prisoners from other parts of the camp risk so much to visit their friends in the hospital, against all the rules and knowing that rule breakers could be beaten, starved, shot, or hanged:

> Indeed, I suspect, and on the basis of a fair bit of experience would venture to assert outright, that the risk in itself, that stubbornness, one could even say defiance, was to some extent part of the event, or at least that is what I gathered from their expressions, hard to read as they were but, so to say, lighting up with the successful completion of some piece of rule-breaking, as if (or so it seemed) they had thereby managed to change something after all, to punch a hole in or chip away at something, a particular

> order, the monotony of the daily routine, to a small extent at nature itself, at least the way I saw it. (217)

The kernel of what Gyuri "ventures to assert outright" is the claim that the internal affect, stubbornness or defiance, forms, "to some extent" at least, part of the event. It is not just what the prisoners do that counts, but the way that doing actualizes stubbornness and defiance, makes it real, and therefore to a small extent changes nature itself. The nature in question is the implacable rules the Nazis have established, as though they were laws of nature, not arbitrary human laws. At least that was the way Gyuri saw it.

The conceptual climax of this pervasive impossibility of verifiable cognition is the incoherent confusion of Gyuri's speech to his uncles about fate and freedom. I discuss this below. No final certainty can be obtained about these ultimate issues (and what could be more important to know for sure than whether I am free or fated?). Even the most immediate and apparently simple event, the event that is happening right now, before one's very eyes, is not open to definitive judgment. As a result, ironic suspension of judgment before what one sees from moment to moment is the most appropriate stance. In addition, irony is the most appropriate mode of narrative language for writing about Auschwitz. It is easy to see why some readers are exasperated and dissatisfied with what Gyuri says, as is the journalist Gyuri meets and as are Uncles Fleischman and Steiner.

"Naturally"

The final stylistic feature of *Fatelessness* I shall discuss is even more micrological, so to speak, and more apparently trivial. Nevertheless, it is an essential part of the novel's verbal texture. It is also not all that easy to read correctly. One word appears over and over in Gyuri's discourse. It is used dozens and dozens of times (eighty-three, to be exact), almost as an idiomatic tic, as certain Americans say "you know," over and over, in a kind of verbal hiccough. Gyuri's tic is the word "naturally," *természetesen* in Hungarian. The word only appears a couple of times in the film, much less often than it appears in Gyuri's narration in the novel.

I have identified the Hungarian word for "naturally" and the number of times it appears in the orginal text from the online version of *Sorstalanság*, now no longer available, alas. One online English to Hungarian to English dictionary tells me "naturally" is in Hungarian either *természeténél fogva* or *természettõl fogva*.[25] Another online dictionary adds *természetesen* to the list.[26] The latter, I initially assumed, is most likely the word Kertész used, since it sounds (to my untrained ear) more conversational and idiomatic, less formal and scientific. Nevertheless, to use a Gyuri-ism, I thought at first I could be mistaken. It was just a guess. A check of the online version of *Sorstalanság*, however, shows that *természetesen* is used consistently in the places where "naturally" appears in the English translation.

The word *természetesen* is said in the second online dictionary to mean "artlessly," "naturally," "of course," "to be sure," and "unconventionally." "Unconventionally" is the odd man out in this list, since at first it seems to be the antithesis of "naturally," "of course," or "to be sure." At first I thought *természetesen* might be a double antithetical word in Hungarian, like *unheimlich* in Freud's famous account, in "Das Unheimliche," of the way that German word means both familiar and strange; "homely" or "homey," and at the same time "uncanny," "ghostly," "ghastly."[27] My Hungarian informant, Susan Suleiman, however, firmly denies that this is the case. I conclude that *természetesen* means "unconventionally" in the sense of artless "naturalness," that is, in the sense of acting naturally rather than acting according to conventions. Nevertheless, I still stubbornly maintain, it often takes a lot of self-consciousness art to act unconventionally. *Természetesen* looks like a complex word to me.

It is not all that easy for me to get a sense of the subtle nuances conveyed by "naturally," especially, naturally enough, since I am working through the double-thick fog of translation and my ignorance of Hungarian. I will cite later in a different context more examples of "naturally," but here are a few for now: Gyuri says anything could happen as the next step in a sequence from the present moment on, but that what happened did happen, and something different "in reality . . . didn't [happen], naturally" (258). In answer to his uncles' question about what they could have done to keep his father from being sent to his death at Mauthausen, Gyuri says, "Nothing, naturally, . . . or rather anything, . . . which would have been just as senseless as doing nothing, yet again and just as naturally" (258). The reader can see that "naturally" as a recurrent locution in *Fatelessness* is intimately tied to the novel's pervasive irony. To call something as "unnatural" as the inhuman depravities in the camps something that occurred "naturally" is a savage irony. The word "naturally," by way of its meaning of "of course" and at the same time "unconventionally" is also tied to the novel's rhetoric of an either/or that is simultaneously a both/and. The word *természetesen* is also related to the novel's constant versions of some unsublatable expression of a thesis and an antithesis that are both simultaneously true, though illogically contradictory, and between which it is impossible to choose the right one.

The word "unnaturally" is also a kernel expression of Gyuri's cool detachment, his wry lack of affect. It also concentrates in a single word that theory of fateful fatelessness and perpetual inalienable human freedom that gives the novel its name. Neither doing nothing nor doing anything will have any effect, naturally, since the father was bound to go to the labor camp, though something might have conceivably been done to stop that. The father could have gone into hiding. Though each moment has an absolute openness to an unpredictable future, what happens, naturally, is just what does happen, fatefully. Even in English, "naturally" has this ironic double meaning.

I give now a further cascade of some of the salient examples of "naturally," *természetesen*, in *Fatelessness*. To count them, as the search engine in the online Hungarian version of the novel did for me, would be pedantic, naturally, but there are a great many. They recur in a kind of diabolically ironic refrain, or like a dead sound or thud at the end of a sentence or phrase. "Naturally" exists in two registers, naturally enough. Some are retrospective comments by the narrator speaking or writing now about something he experienced, did, or felt then. Some are part of statements made by the protagonist in the now of some past event. "Naturally" occurs a little more often as the novel progresses, as though in relation to some change in Gyuri's discourse, perhaps in response to his experience of the camps, though the increase in frequency may just mean that Kertész is warming to the task of exploring the nuances of the word. He does this by showing the strikingly different contexts in which his protagonist can naturally, and at the same time unconventionally, say "természetesen." Following this word through is a way of tracing the trajectory of Gyuri's experiences in the camps, from initial arrest to liberation and return home.

My first example uses the word "natural," not "naturally," as occasionally happens. Of the moment when Gyuri sees his father and stepmother sitting silently side by side holding hands, "looking intently at one another, the way men and women do," at the family party before the father's departure for Mauthausen, Gyuri says: "I have never cared for that, and this time too it made me feel awkward. Though the thing is basically quite natural, I suppose, I still don't like it" (14). A little later, when his father asks him if he will miss him, the father, Gyuri says only one word: "Naturally" (19), not exactly a warm response. When he gets an identification card allowing him to work in an oil refinery outside Budapest, his stepmother is satisfied because the ID "testifies that I am not alive on my own account but am benefiting the war effort in the manufacturing industry, and that, naturally, puts it in an entirely different light" (28). After an unsatisfactory visit to his natural mother, he says, "Naturally I could not allow her to go on supposing that I didn't love her," and "Of course I am attached to my mother, and naturally it bothered me that again I could do nothing for her today" (31).

Here are more examples, taken sometimes out of context: "I also wanted to win the argument, naturally" (36). "I could see straightaway that he [the Hungarian policeman who arrests him and the other boys from the buses taking them to work, the first step in their journey to Auschwitz] had nothing against us—nor indeed could he have, naturally" (41). When Gyuri decides to accept the lying invitation to go to work in Germany, he says, "So most people, myself included, saw it as obvious that we might do better for ourselves, naturally enough, the first way" (63), that is, by going now rather than later. He believes they are going to "a more sensible lifestyle more to my liking than the one here in Hungary, just as was promised and as we boys, quite naturally, pictured it when we talked among ourselves" (64). When they get to Auschwitz, he says, "I was glad, very naturally" (77). When he is entering Auschwitz and is asked by the Yiddish-speaking Jewish prisoners who meet the train, "Willst di arbeiten?" (Do you want to work?), he answers, "Natürlich" (79). When he is told about the medical examination that will decide which prisoners are fit for work, he says, "It was mentioned, though naturally I did not find it hard to appreciate, that this was obviously a matter of grading, of screening for suitability for work" (82). What he does not yet know is that those who are not judged suitable for work will be immediately gassed and cremated. That the guards all have weapons "is only natural, of course, when it comes down to it" (84), though the leather whips they also carry are a little ominous. "Other boys also arrived [into the good group after the *Selektion*], one after the next, and now I too was able to join in the greeting they received, naturally" (86). When he sees Gypsies in Auschwitz, he remembers that almost everyone back home, "naturally enough," was "guarded" "in their opinion of Gypsies" (109). "Fancyman," who has actually had sex with a girl, is looked at "with a certain measure of respect, which I didn't find so very difficult to understand, naturally" (112). He says "ghastly" "is not the word, that is not precisely the experience—for me at any rate, naturally—with which I would truly characterize Auschwitz" (117). Other uses of the word are on pages 119, 143, 145, 151, 153, 158, 162, 166, 168, 174–75, 183–84, 185, 207, 216, and 235–36.

In case the reader has not noticed the recurrence of the word "naturally," Kertész in one place calls explicit attention to it and to its ironic double meaning. This happens in the episode of Gyuri's conversation with the journalist, if it can be called a conversation, since the journalist does not appear to "get" anything Gyuri says. The journalist is exasperated by Gyuri's responses and resists them. Gyuri often remains mute, offering no response at all to something the newspaperman says. The journalist's impatience functions as an expression of the reader's own exasperation and resistance, at least those of some readers. Such readers want clear judgments, naturally, so they can sum up the novel and have done with it. The journalist suggests that Gyuri "had undergone a lot of deprivation, hunger, and more than likely they had beaten [him]," to which Gyuri replies, "naturally." The journalist, on hearing this almost loses his patience. He exclaims: "Why, my dear boy, . . . do you keep on saying 'naturally,' and always about things that are not at all natural?" When Gyuri replies that "in a concentration camp they *were* natural," the journalist replies, "Yes, of course, of course, . . . they were *there*, but . . . ," and he then breaks off, "hesitating slightly," "but . . . I mean, a concentration camp in itself is *unnatural*" (247), to which Gyuri does not bother to say anything. His silence and the journalist's momentary hesitation before passing a final reassuring univocal judgment express the blankness of an uncertainty that may not be univocally articulated, but only expressed in ironic equivocations. What is natural in one context is, viewed from another angle, unnatural. Naturally is unnaturally, and vice versa.

That might be said to be the last word about *Fatelessness*, though, naturally, I could go on and on expanding my reading more or less indefinitely. One evidence of the "conflagration of community" brought about by Auschwitz, it can be argued, is the way it makes impossible from now on any straightforward narrative discourse. Auschwitz does something horrible and irreparable to language. This might be taken as one further meaning of Adorno's "After Auschwitz to write even a single poem is barbaric." This does not mean poetry is impossible but that Auschwitz imposes something like Celan's almost impenetrable complexity of poetic language, or Kertész's ironically suspended "naturally."

The Muselmann *and His Witnessing Survivor*

I want now to identify one last important feature of *Fatelessness* as a fictional bearing witness to Auschwitz. Everything I have written so far has been preparation, staging, mise-en-scène, for this section of my argument. The denouement of Gyuri's story, its resolution or untying, is his return home, his four encounters with uncomprehending people who have not been in the camps, his development of his concept of "fatelessness," and his turning away in silence from his "uncles," when they do not understand, to make his way toward his mother. The peripeteia, or turning point, of *Fatelessness* is the moment, earlier in the narrative, when Gyuri returns to life, so to speak, after almost becoming a *Muselmann*. I say "almost" because once one becomes veritably a *Muselmann*, as witnesses testify, return is almost impossible and rarely occurs. Gyuri retains his lucid vigilance even in this extremity, when he is nearest to death, as, we are told, the true *Muselmänner* did not. This stubborn, unquenchable lucidity and Gyuri's return from the *Muselmann* condition are two of the quasi-miraculous features of *Fatelessness*, along with all the other "miracles" that allow him to become a survivor, against all odds.

Muselmann was a name given by prisoners in the camps to those other prisoners who, through starvation, overwork, beatings, and repeated abuse, both physical and verbal, by the SS guards, became reduced to walking corpses, zombies, "mummy-men," dead-alive nonhuman persons who had lost the will to live. Such prisoners may have been called *Muselmänner* because they swayed their upper bodies rhythmically back and forth as they stood in place, or stumbled forward, or crouched on the ground, like Muslims at prayer time. Those who came back from this living death, however, claim that they made this movement to avoid getting pneumonia. Almost all the *Muselmänner* were gassed, or simply died of starvation or abuse, but a few survived. Giorgio Agamben, at the end of *Remnants of Auschwitz*, cites some of the moving testimony of those who can say, "I was a *Muselmann*."[28] Feliksa Piekarska, for example, writes, "I personally was a *Muselmann* for a short while. . . . I completely collapsed as far as my psychological life was concerned. The collapse took the following form: I was overcome by a general apathy; nothing interested me; I no longer reacted either to external or internal stimuli; I stopped washing, even when there was water; I no longer even felt hungry" (166). The other survivors of the camps testify that those who were not *Muselmänner* left the *Muselmänner* strictly alone, as if nothing more could be done to help them. They were outside the human community.

Agamben argues, in his admirable chapter "The *Muselmann*," in *Remnants of Auschwitz* (41–86), that perhaps even worse than the millions of murders in the gas chambers was the reduction of so many living human beings, before they were actually killed, to the dead-alive, human-inhuman state of the *Muselmänner*: "The *Muselmann* is not only or not so much a limit between life and death; rather, he marks the threshold between the human and the inhuman. . . . There is thus a point at which human beings, while apparently remaining human beings, cease to be human" (55).

The *Muselmann* chapter of Agamben's *Remnants of Auschwitz* is centrally devoted to developing what he calls "Levi's paradox." It is a version of the paradox I cited from Lyotard at the beginning of this chapter. On the one hand, Primo Levi asserts categorically that "we survivors are not only an exiguous but also an anomalous minority: we are those who by their prevarications or abilities or good luck did not touch bottom. Those who did so, those who saw the Gorgon, have not returned to tell about it or have returned mute, but they are the 'Muslims,' the submerged, the complete witnesses, the ones whose deposition would have a general significance. They are the rule, we are the exception."[29]

"No one bears witness for the witness." No one but the *Muselmänner* can testify to what it was like to be a *Muselmann*. On the other hand, the *Muselmänner* could not, cannot, speak for themselves. Only those who did not fully become *Muselmänner* and survived can bear witness by proxy for these exclusively privileged witnesses. But the *Muselmänner* had nothing to say for themselves, any more than did those who were gassed and cremated. It is impossible to bear witness for them. That is what Agamben means by saying that "the survivors bore witness to something it is impossible to bear witness to" (13). Here is Primo Levi's formulation of this in *The Drowned and the Saved*:

> We who were favored by fate tried, with more or less wisdom, to recount not only our own fate but also that of the others, indeed of the drowned [Levi's word here for the *Muselmänner*]; but this was a discourse "on behalf of third parties," the story of things seen at close hand, not experienced personally. The destruction brought to an end, the job completed, was not told by anyone, just as no one ever returned to describe his own death. Even if they had paper and pen, the drowned would not have testified because their death had begun before that of their body. Weeks and months before being snuffed out, they had already lost the ability to observe, to remember, to compare and express themselves. We speak in their stead, by proxy.[30]

This speaking by proxy, however, is impossible. It is an absurd project. As Agamben says, "And yet to speak here of a proxy makes no sense; the drowned have nothing to say, nor do they have instructions or memories to be transmitted. They have no 'story' . . . , no 'face,' and even less do they have 'thought.' . . . Whoever assumes the charge of bearing witness in their name knows that he or she must bear witness in the name of the impossibility of bearing witness" (34). Agamben's book ends with the claim that the survivors who can say, "I was a *Muselmann*," do not refute Levi's paradox, but utter its most extreme and verifying formulation: "I, who speak, was a *Muselmann*, that is, the one who cannot in any sense speak" (165). As Agamben asserts, Levi's paradox "implies two contradictory propositions: 1) 'the *Muselmann* is the non-human, the one who could never bear witness,' and 2) 'the one who cannot bear witness is the true witness, the absolute witness' " (150). The paradox enunciated by Levi and Agamben is analogous to that "fissure of absence" in representation Jean-Luc Nancy identifies in the essay by him discussed earlier in this chapter.

The hero of *Fatelessness* suspends, or, rather, expresses in a unique way, Levi's paradox by combining in one person both the narrator, the narrating I, and the protagonist, the experiencing I, both the "complete witness," the *Muselmann*, and the proxy who bears witness to what it is impossible to bear witness to. Kertész's evasion of Levi's paradox is perhaps one that is only possible, for him at least, by way of a particular exploitation of the conventions of fictional representation. Kertész's genius, I claim, was to understand that, and to give *Fatelessness* the form of a first-person novel. Like all first-person novels, *Fatelessness* has a narrative language that combines two persons, the Gyuri who had the experience of the camps and the narrating Gyuri who has survived that experience to tell the tale. It is as though Kurtz and Marlow, in Conrad's *Heart of Darkness,* were combined in one person. Or rather, the experiencing Gyuri is already doubled into the almost *Muselmann* and a lucid vigilance that is still aware of what is happening to him and that can therefore survive into a future remembering. That doubling is then doubled again by the narrating I in the present looking back and reporting on what the experiencing Gyuri experienced. What distinguishes Gyuri, as I have already emphasized, is his extremely sharp eyes, ears, nose, and touch, his observation of sights, sounds, and tactile sensations, along with an exceptional ability to turn these into succinct, vivid language that carries them over to the reader.

Essential to the meaning of *Fatelessness* is that Gyuri, in defiance of the standard descriptions of the *Muselmänner* and even against physiological probability, retains his remarkable lucidity even when he almost becomes a *Muselmann*. He is able to tell the reader in retrospect just what it felt like to be almost a *Muselmann*. That wakeful vigilance is mirrored, at least for sight and sound, and without the narrator's ironic commentary, by the camera eye and the recording microphone in the film version of *Fatelessness*.

The *Muselmänner* first appear in *Fatelessness* soon after Gyuri arrives at Zeitz. His description of them is as vivid and specific as any other testimonies to their existence in the camps that we have. Describing certain of the prisoners from Riga, Gyuri shifts from the present tense, a kind of eternal present maintained in existence by testimony, to the past tense, in the midst of a sentence, and then returns to the present tense, at least in the translation. He also uses his characteristic ironic understatement, for example, "a little disconcerting," as well as his gift for startling but apt metaphor:

> Among them one can see those peculiar beings who at first were a little disconcerting. Viewed from a certain distance, they are senilely doddering old codgers, and with their heads retracted into their necks, their noses sticking out from their faces, the filthy prison duds that they wear hanging loosely from their shoulders, even on the hottest summer's day they put one in mind of winter crows with a perpetual chill. As if with each and every single stiff, halting step they take one were to ask: is such an effort really worth the trouble? (138)

Gyuri's new Hungarian friend Bandi Citrom warns him away from the *Muselmänner*. "You lose any will to live just looking at them," he says (138). In the next chapter, chapter 7, many pages later, Gyuri recounts his own transformation almost into a *Muselmann* and his quasi-miraculous recovery from that state. Note that I say "almost." If he had gone all the way, he would not have returned to tell his tale. Gradually reduced to lassitude, weakness, and semiconsciousness, he stops washing or in other ways taking care of himself. He gets, in short, almost in the state of those *Muselmänner* he had looked at so curiously when he first entered the work camp:

> I can report that, after so much striving, so many futile attempts and efforts, in time I too found peace, tranquility, and relief. For instance, certain things to which I had previously attributed some vast, practically inconceivable significance, I can tell you, lost all importance in my eyes. Thus, if I grew tired while standing at *Appell*, for example, without so much as a look at whether

> it was muddy or there was a puddle, I would simply take a seat, plop down, and stay down, until my neighbors forcibly pulled me up. Cold, damp, wind, or rain were no longer able to bother me; they did not get through to me, I did not even sense them. Even my hunger passed; I continued to carry to my mouth anything edible I was able to lay my hands on, but more out of absentmindedness, mechanically, out of habit, so to say. As for work, I no longer even strove to give the appearance of it. If people did not like that, at most they would beat me, and even then they could not truly do much harm, since for me it just won some time: at the first blow I would promptly stretch out on the ground and would feel nothing after that, since I would meanwhile drop off to sleep. (171–72)

Bandi Citrom tells Gyuri he is "letting himself go" and forcibly washes him. Bandi can tell from Gyuri's face, however, when he asks him "did I maybe not want to get back home" (172), that Gyuri is becoming, or has already become, a *Muselmann*. True to the "opinion he had once expressed about Muslims" (173), and true to what other survivors say about the way the *Muselmänner* were ignored, given up for lost, Bandi Citrom abandons Gyuri henceforth. After Citrom turns him over to the infirmary, they never see one another again. The rest of the chapter describes with extreme precision Gyuri's experiences in various infirmaries and hospitals inside Zeitz and eventually back again in Buchenwald.

A good example of the superimposition of the two experiencing Gyuris is a passage in which he describes himself lying outdoors in the rain after his return to Buchenwald, waiting to be taken to the hospital. On the one hand, he is practically in a *Muselmann* state: "It seemed I must have lain there in that way for some time, and I was getting on just fine, peacefully, placidly, incuriously, patiently, where they had set me down" (186). On the other hand, Gyuri, even in that extremity, has a clear and precise vision of what he can see above him: "the low, gray, impenetrable sky, for instance, or *to be more precise* the leaden, sluggishly moving wintry cloud-cover, which concealed it from view" (186, my italics). This sky is shown in the film version, as a shot of what Gyuri sees as he lies motionless on the cold, wet ground. The passage in the novel goes on to name, in a style that shifts from realistic description toward allegorical picture, the way the leaden sky is intermittently "parted by an unexpected rent, with a more brilliant gap arising in it here and there for a fleeting moment, and that was like a sudden intimation of a depth out of which a ray was seemingly being cast on me from above" (186). That ray seems to Gyuri like "a rapid, searching gaze, an eye of indeterminate but unquestionably pale hue—similar to that of the doctor before whom I had once passed, back in Auschwitz" (186). The sky's metaphoric gaze reminds Gyuri of the searching gaze of the doctor in the *Selektion* at Auschwitz. That doctor probably knew Gyuri was lying when he said he was sixteen but saved him from immediate gassing nevertheless. This memorable scene does not function as a recurrent leitmotif, such as I have identified in Kafka's novels, since it does not recur. It does work, nevertheless, as perhaps the best spatially deployed scene serving as an emblem encapsulating Gyuri's temporally extended experience in *Fatelessness*.

Sure enough, this moment is followed a couple of pages later by Gyuri's arrival in a handcart with other dead-alive *Muselmänner* inside Buchenwald. He gets a whiff of the familiar turnip soup of the camp, weeps a few tears from his dried-out eyes, and, in a moment that is emotional for the reader too, recovers, senselessly, his will to live. This is without doubt the turning point of the novel. Gyuri describes it with characteristic irony: "Despite all deliberation, sense, insight, and sober reason, I could not fail to recognize within myself the furtive and yet—ashamed as it might be, so to say, of its irrationality—increasingly insistent voice of some muffled craving of sorts: I would like to live a little bit longer in this beautiful concentration camp" (189).

In the topsy-turvy world of those who have been reduced to the condition of *Muselmänner*, the natural will to live is unnatural. What would be most natural, sensible, and reasonable, would be the will to die. Two pages earlier, as he and other prisoners lay there in the rain, a camp guard had quizzically asked one of Gyuri's fellow prisoners, the man whose refrain is still, in his extremity, "I p . . . pro . . . protest," "Was? Du willst noch leben?" (What? You still want to live?) (187). The return of Gyuri's will to live is the novel's moment of reversal. It marks the instant of Gyuri's exit from an almost-*Muselmann* state that has always been shared with another Gyuri, the one who, even in his extremity, can see his condition and his surroundings with sober, ironic clarity, can look up in the rain toward the gaze of the distant judging sky, and later on, as the narrating I, can report in precise language what he so vividly remembers.

Gyuri is able to solve Levi's paradox or at least to live his life in an acute demonstration that it is impossible to solve. During all of chapter 7 Gyuri is both almost the complete witness and the proxy witness who testifies on that witness's behalf. This is so even though it remains impossible to bear witness either to the experience of being gassed or to having become one of the "drowned," to have seen the lethal Gorgon's face that turns the viewer to stone (to echo Primo Levi's figures in *The Drowned and the Saved*), to have crossed the border into the state from which there is no return, the state of the *Muselmänner*.

The Conflagration of Community in Fatelessness

The genius of *Fatelessness* is the way in which Kertész has been able to combine in one person the *Muselmann* and his proxy witness, in a novel that bears witness to something to which it is impossible to bear witness. That "something" has as one of its components "the conflagration of community." Bearing witness depends on the survival of community along with the legal and conventional forms of obligation and togetherness, or *Mitsein*, that community entails. No community, no bearing witness. The Nazis deliberately destroyed, as best they could, Jewish communities both in the ghettos and then in the extermination camps. Nevertheless, *Fatelessness* and other testimonies report the continuation even in the camps of, for example, clandestine groups of orthodox Jews who held secret services.

Gyuri experiences, however, the paradox of being treated as an outsider, as a Gentile, by Jewish groups in the camps, for example, because he does not know Yiddish: "Di bisht nisht kai yid, d'bisht a shaygets" (You're not a Jew, you're a Gentile kid) (139–40). The diversity of languages in the camps made difficult the establishment of even fragile communities among the prisoners, many of whom had to betray friends for a scrap of bread if they were to survive a little longer. When Gyuri returns to Budapest he finds that the community of family and neighbors he left behind no longer exists. *Fatelessness* itself, however, it might be argued, creates the community of its readers, those who across several languages and in different national locations nevertheless come together in their shared experience of this novel's testimony to Auschwitz. Unless we forget. I shall return at the end of this essay to my sense of this community's limitations. It is no substitute for what we have traditionally meant by a community, that is, people who live together in the same place and know one another by name.

Why Call It "Fatelessness"?

Gyuri at the end of his unsatisfactory encounter with his "uncles" develops a striking emblem for the temporal sequence that makes up a human life. Gyuri's impassioned speech to his uncles about fate just makes them angry when they understand that he is accusing them of being responsible in some measure for what has happened, rather than agreeing that they have been passive and innocent victims. Gyuri transposes that to an affirmation of his own responsibility for his fate. Since this speech and the coda that follows it are the denouement of the novel, they must be read with care, micrologically, with close attention to detail. The figure of a step-by-step movement through time, with a new decision being required at every moment, suggests why Kertész employs a strictly chronological method of narration in *Fatelessness*. It is another example of the way narrative form follows function and contributes essentially to meaning, in this novel as in literary texts in general, and as in this chapter.

Just as those in the lines waiting for the *Selektion* at Auschwitz move forward step by step toward "the point where it is decided whether it will be gas immediately or a reprieve for the time being" (257), so I and all the rest of us human beings, Gyuri says to his uncles, move moment by moment, and step by step, through life. This comparison is shocking to his "uncles" and to his so-called aunt, the wife of Uncle Fleischmann. They saw their life in Budapest during the Nazi occupation as a series of happenings that just "came about." Gyuri argues that each of those moments was both determined by its contingent contexts, in that sense "fated," and at the same time free, so that we are responsible for what we make of whatever situation in which we find ourselves. Each moment is detached from the ones before and after, and each is the opportunity for endless new possibilities. "There are only given situations and new givens inherent in them" (259). "It was not quite true," Gyuri reports himself as having said, "that the thing 'came about'; we had to go along with it too. Only now, and thus after the event, looking back, in hindsight, does the way it all 'came about' seem over, finished, unalterable, finite, so tremendously fast, and so terribly opaque. And if, in addition, one knows one's fate in advance, of course" (257). Only by way of the falsifications of hindsight or of an impossible foresight does one's life congeal into a "fate": "Whether one looks back or ahead, both are flawed perspectives, I suggested" (258).

Life as it is actually lived, from minute to minute, is always open to an unpredictable future that might radically change the past: "Every one of those minutes might in fact have brought something new. In reality it didn't, naturally, but still, one must acknowledge that it might have; when it comes down to it, each and every minute something else might have happened other than what actually did happen, at Auschwitz just as much as, let's suppose, here at home, when we took leave of my father" (258). His family, for example, might have hidden him and have helped him escape to another country. His uncles are angered at what Gyuri says and ask what they could have done on behalf of his father. "Nothing, naturally," he answers, " . . . or rather anything, . . . which would have been just as senseless as doing nothing, yet again and just as naturally" (258). Note the three uses of "naturally" (*természetesen* in Hungarian) in the two citations just made from what Gyuri says to his uncles.

It is on the basis of a quite specific and quite sophisticated theory of human time and freedom that the reader can understand the meaning of the novel's strange title. What Kertész has Gyuri say is perhaps influenced, however indirectly, by Sartrean existentialism, but with a twist toward "postmodern" undecidability, as in what Gyuri says about being neither winner nor loser, about cause and effect, and about being both wrong and right. Just what does it mean, "fatelessness" (*sorstalanság)?* Gyuri tries to answer this question in what he says to his uncles:

> Why did they not wish to acknowledge that if there is such a thing as fate, then freedom is not possible? If, on the other hand—I swept on, more and more astonished myself, steadily warming to the task—if there is such a thing as freedom, then there is no fate; that is to say—and I paused, but only long enough to catch my breath—that is to say, then we ourselves are fate, I realized all at once, but with a flash of clarity I had never experienced before. . . . It was impossible, they must try and understand, impossible to take everything away from me, impossible for me to be neither winner nor loser, for me not to be right and for me not to be mistaken that I was neither the cause nor the effect of anything; they should try to see, I almost pleaded, that I could not swallow that idiotic bitterness, that I should merely be innocent. But I could see they did not wish to understand anything. (259–61)

This passage comes just before the end of the novel. It is the nearest the reader gets to a conceptual explanation for the either/or, both/and, neither/nor, maybe this/maybe that ironic rhetoric that characterizes Gyuri's discourse throughout the novel. It also helps to explain Kertész's choice of a chronological recounting of Gyuri's life. Anything positive that can be said can also be plausibly negated, as in the antinomies of freedom and fate.

Surely Efraim Sicher oversimplifies, in his otherwise fine book *The Holocaust Novel*, to say that Gyuri "followed a fate given to him, minute by minute, day after day, step after step."[31] This could be too easily read as a return to the religious explanation offered by Gyuri's Uncle Lajos. That explanation is clearly repudiated by Gyuri's irony. Uncle Lajos, at the beginning of the novel, tells Gyuri that "you too . . . are now a part of the shared Jewish fate." This fate, says Uncle Lajos, was one of "unbroken persecution that has lasted for millennia." This suffering must be accepted "with fortitude and self-sacrificing forbearance," because "God has meted it out to them for their past sins" (20). It is true that Gyuri says at one point in his eloquent but, as he puts it, "a little incoherent" (259) speech to his uncles that "I too had lived through a given fate. It had not been my own fate, but I had lived through it, and I simply couldn't understand why they couldn't get it into their heads that I now needed to start doing something with that fate, needed to connect it to somewhere or something; after all, I could no longer be satisfied with the notion that it had all been a mistake, blind fortune, some kind of blunder, let alone that it had not even happened" (259). Note that Gyuri says this was not "his fate," even though it had been "given."

Gyuri does not want to break off his life in some impossible way, and start life afresh, as his uncles counsel, but to go forward step by step in continuity with what has happened: "We can never start a new life, only ever carry on the old one" (259). This means accepting responsibility for the steps you have already taken and going forward on the basis of those. Gyuri's ultimate resolution is expressed in a Blanchotian or Beckettian aporetic formulation: "I was already feeling a growing and accumulating readiness to continue my uncontinuable life" (262). Gyuri's attempt to convey to his uncles that they were not passive victims but to some degree responsible for what has happened just makes them angry: " 'So it's us who are the guilty ones, is it? Us, the victims!' I tried explaining to them that it wasn't a crime; all that was needed was to admit it, meekly, simply, merely as a matter of reason, a point of honor, if I might put it that way" (260).

Gyuri's contradictory formulations, for example, "impossible for me not to be right and for me not to be mistaken," mark this novel as "post-Auschwitz" in its suspension of unequivocal assertion. In these days, for many people, it has become impossible to pass definitive judgment. Everything may be neither this nor that, or this and that at the same time. Gyuri's impassioned demand that his uncles recognize that no one is just an innocent victim, that we are all responsible for our fates, even if our fate is to be sent to Auschwitz, is met with incomprehension by Gyuri's uncles, expressed in a sentence already cited twice: "But I could see they did not wish to understand anything" (261). The uncles are clearly proxies for you and me, dear reader. Do we too perhaps not wish to understand anything, or are we able to accept Kertész's belief that we are responsible for our fates, even though we cannot rationally comprehend the mixture of freedom and fate in our lives?

An equivocation, one can see, exists in the word "fate," as Kertész uses it and as it is traditionally used. "Fate" can either mean, as in the Homeric epics or in Uncle Lajos's discourse, a transcendent, divine force that predestines people to live their lives in a certain way, or it can mean no more than that in retrospect one can see that things happened as they did happen, in a combination of contingencies and free steps taken one by one, from moment to moment. This happens according to the theory of human time Gyuri so eloquently expresses. He took steps in response to the options that the contingencies he encountered allowed, such as getting arrested and finding himself deported to Auschwitz just because he happened to be on a certain bus at a certain time. Gyuri seems to be using more this second sense of fate than Uncle Lajos's when he says: "I took the steps, no one else, and I declared that I had been true to my given fate throughout" (259). This means, as he says on the next page, that "we ourselves are fate."

"Fatelessness" in the title of Kertész's novel refers, in my judgment, to Gyuri's experience that things happen as they do happen, in a mixture of randomness and steps taken as free responses, within the limits of the given situation, to what happens. We do not have preordained fates. An example is the steps Gyuri takes to keep himself alive in the three camps. His survival is the result of an astonishing series of quite implausible or even "miraculous" events. Why did the doctor believe his lie when he said he was sixteen, not fifteen, as he actually was, at the preliminary *Selektion* at Auschwitz? Why, when he was near death from abscesses on his knee and hip at Zeitz, was he more or less tenderly cared for at a succession of hospitals rather than just allowed to die, since he would be of no more use for work? Why did the *Pfleger* (male nurse) Bohoosh, from the building next to the hospital at Buchenwald where Gyuri lay near death, choose to keep Gyuri alive by bringing him bread and tinned sausage for no recompense, and at great danger to himself? These events, and many others equally crucial to Gyuri's survival, against all odds, just do not make sense. Gyuri makes only highly tentative attempts to explain them. In one place, when he has reached comparative safety in a hospital bed in the surgical ward in Buchenwald, where he is actually given fairly good medical attention, he says, "After all, if I took a rational view of things, I could see no reason, I was incapable of finding any known and, to me, rationally acceptable cause for why, of all places, I happened to be here instead of somewhere else" (207). "I have to say," he comments near the end of his account, "that over time one can become accustomed even to miracles" (225). That Gyuri survives at all justifies the term "miracle," when so many millions, in just his situation, died.

The human condition, Gyuri's experience confirms, is one of fatelessness. You cannot blame anything on fate, at least in the sense of a benign or malign force pulling strings behind the scenes. Gyuri's ultimate wisdom, perhaps, is that every positive judgment has an equally plausible counterjudgment and that, as he says of his day-to-day existence in Zeitz, "The main thing was not to neglect oneself; somehow there would always be a way, for it had never yet happened that there wasn't a way somehow. . . . For example, your first device is stubbornness" (136, 138). "Stubbornness" (*makacsság* in Hungarian) is the name Gyuri gives to taking such steps as you can take, even when you are moving forward in the line toward the moment of the *Selektion*. "Stubbornness" is the best explanation Gyuri can give, for example, of Bohoosh's kindness, since that kindness is a recalcitrant and extremely risky defiance of camp rules.

If there are no atheists in foxholes, there appear to be relatively few true believers in God, in Kertész's view, in concentration camps. The camps appear to have tended to take away, to some considerable degree, shared religious belief as a form of community togetherness, along with the rest of such forms. In the film Gyuri joins in the prayer for the dead when the prisoners stand at attention watching the escaped and recaptured prisoners dangle from the gallows, but this does not occur in the novel. The narrator in the novel says, rather, "For the first time, I now somewhat regretted that I was unable to pray, if only a few sentences, in the language of the Jews" (162). Vladek, in Art Spiegelman's *Maus*, hears in Auschwitz a friend in extremity calling on God. He comments to Artie, when telling the story in retrospect, "But here God didn't come. We were all on our own."[32] *Fatelessness* seems to be saying something similar, in its own way. "Apart from the last few twitches of the hanged men, nothing moved, nothing wavered at these words [the Kaddish]" (162). That may be one reason why, as Sicher comments, Kertész "has not been easily accepted in the canon of Hungarian literature, where critics have not always welcomed his pessimistic self-irony."[33]

"Pessimistic self-irony" does not quite seem to me an adequate descriptive summing up of Gyuri's attitude. *Fatelessness* ends, as does Albert Camus's *The Stranger*, with an appeal to happiness that seems to me moving and plausible, not pessimistic or self-ironizing. I suppose "self-irony" means "self-deprecating" irony, irony directed at oneself.

Gyuri's persistent attitude or tone, surfacing explicitly at the end, is rather of irony against, for example, the journalistic clichés that assume the camps were unmitigated "hell," that no one was ever bored or happy there. Anticipating his future postwar life fulfilling his mother's hopes for him to be "an engineer, a doctor, or something like that" (262), Gyuri says, in a powerfully counterintuitive formulation, that not "fate" but "happiness" will be watching over his future, as it has watched over him in the camps:

> No doubt that is how it will be, just as she wished; there is nothing impossible that we do not live through naturally, and keeping a watch on me on my journey, like some inescapable trap, I already know there will be happiness. For even there, next to the chimneys, in the intervals between the torments, there was something that resembled happiness. Everyone asks only about the hardships and the "atrocities," whereas for me perhaps it is that experience which will remain the most memorable. Yes, the next time I am asked, I ought to speak about that, the happiness of the concentration camps. (262)

That, however, is not quite the end. Two characteristically qualifying sentences follow, given a separate final paragraph to themselves: "If indeed I am asked. And provided I myself don't forget" (262). Such is the fragility of testimony, based as it is on the vagaries of memory and on being in a situation in which one is called upon to bear witness.

Recapitulation

I have shown in this chapter that Kertész's fictional testimony to the Shoah is made possible by the specific narrative devices he brilliantly employs in *Fatelessness*: the ironic discourse of the narrator, the combining of narrator and protagonist, the narrating I and the experiencing I, within the same imaginary personage, and the double doubling of the I in the *Muselmann* episode and throughout. Gyuri's ironic testimony to his experiences in the camps somewhat paradoxically not only distances the events being narrated but also allows the reader to see them more vividly than a sentimental or melodramatic telling might have done. The combining in one voice of a narrating I and an already doubled experiencing I means that the *Muselmann* and the proxy witness who survives the *Muselmann* can be combined in a single ironic doubly doubled vision. This provides a fictional solution to Levi's paradox. The strictly chronological narration, finally, corresponds to the concept of fatelessness as a series of step-by-step decisions in given circumstances.

My commentary in turn is not so much a bearing witness for the witness as it is a facilitating of reading by what might be named a "calling attention" to the testimonial work the novel enacts. My chapter, however, also has a dimension of performative testimony. It is a declaration of what has happened to me when reading and rereading the novel. A reading in the sense of analytic commentary, if it works, can help open a literary work to other readers. It will thereby perhaps contribute to the creation of a community of readers who may, if not know, at least not forget Auschwitz. I would not, however, put too much stress on this idea of "a community of readers." Such a community, if it exists, is fairly abstract, since it is made up of people who, for the most part, do not know one another. A "community of readers," as I said earlier, is quite different from a traditional community of people living together from generation to generation in the same place and sharing the same culture, such as the Jewish communities the Nazis so systematically destroyed.

Community in Auschwitz

None of the four works I have discussed is, strictly speaking, about the deaths of those six million Jews and others in the Holocaust. Each work, rather, in a different way in each case, is about those who lived for a shorter or longer period in imminent danger of death from the Nazis—and survived to tell the tale. Henry James was right when, in a quite different context (commenting in the preface to *The Wings of the Dove* on the death of Milly Theale), he said, "The poet essentially *can't* be concerned with the act of dying. Let him deal with the sickest of the sick, it is still by the act of living that they appeal to him, and appeal the more as the conditions plot against them and prescribe the battle."[34] About the experience of those who died in the gas chambers no witness, naturally, survives, and no valid testimony can be proffered. *Maus*'s Vladek testifies to this, as does also Kertész's Gyuri when, after he has made it back to Budapest, he tells the Holocaust denier who asks if he had seen the gas chambers, "If I had, we wouldn't be standing around talking now" (241). No way exists to "present" or "represent" the death of one person or of six million persons. From that bourn no traveler returns. That is what Paul de Man meant by calling death, in a phrase cited earlier that has scandalized many, "a displaced name for a linguistic predicament,"[35] or what Jacques Derrida meant when he said, "At the origin of the *graphein* there is debt or gift rather than representational fidelity. . . .

The just measure of 'restoring' or 'rendering' is impossible—or infinite. Restoring or rendering is the cause of the dead, the cause of deaths, the cause of a death given or requested. [*Rendre, c'est la cause des morts, de la mort donnée ou demandée.*]"[36] One meaning of "render," the reader will remember, is the separating of fat from meat by cooking it out, as happened with all those bodies burned in the crematoria. Rendering is certainly in that grisly sense the cause of death. Derrida, naturally, also means "cause" in the sense of what is at stake or at issue, as a legal case before a court is called a "cause," and "rendering" refers to the reciprocity demanded of a gift. What Derrida calls "the gift of death," "le don de la mort," can, however, never be repaid, rendered back, as is the case with any gift, if there is such a thing, "s'il y en a," in Derrida's locution.

My title promises that I shall approach all the works I discuss through the problematic of community. Why is that a good way to enter them? My epigraph from Nancy to chapter 1 of this book gives a clue. I now circle back to what I say there about Nancy's sentence. The odd word in Nancy's formulation, which is the opening sentence of *La communauté désoeuvrée*, is, as I said, "conflagration." "The gravest and most painful testimony of the modern world," says Nancy, ". . . is the testimony of the dissolution, the dislocation, or the *conflagration* of community" (my italics). History is constative, a statement of the facts. An example is the reliance on documents in Keneally's *Schindler's List*. Witnessing is performative. It is, as Derrida argued at length in his seminars on witnessing, a special kind of speech act. Testimony is always prefaced by an explicit or implicit: "I swear to you that I saw this with my own eyes, that I am telling the whole truth about what I saw."

Surely Nancy's word "conflagration" is an oblique reference to the Holocaust. "Holocaust" means "sacrificial fire," a burnt offering, from a Greek word meaning "burnt whole." Our gravest and most painful testimony, or that of "the modern world" in general (whatever, exactly, *that* means; presumably it means all us survivors collectively, or perhaps "the modern world" means social conditions in the West after Auschwitz), is to the conflagration of community. I take it that this is a way of saying something analogous to what Adorno said. Just as poetry after Auschwitz would be "barbaric," so the Holocaust burned up community in the great conflagrations of the crematoria. No communities after Auschwitz.

Certainly the Nazis deliberately and systematically destroyed all the Jewish communities that existed throughout Europe and that even persisted in the camps, as in the group of Orthodox Jews Gyuri witnesses in the camp hospital holding dangerous secret religious services. In another episode, a crowd of a sick prisoner's friends appears in the hospital to gather around his bed and comfort him. A lemon and a knife are miraculously produced, an example of precious food secretly and communally shared in the camps. The sick friend who has brought them together dies, however, before their eyes. The momentary community gathering "start[s] to drift away in their ones and twos, just as they [have] come" (219). Though the destruction of Jewish communities was perpetrated primarily through extermination, the conditions in the camps tended to destroy community even for the survivors. As Artie's father, Vladek, says on an early page of *Maus*, when Artie complains of being mistreated by his friends, "*Friends*? Your friends? . . . If you lock them together in a room with no food for a week. . . . THEN you could see what it is, friends!"[37] The community to which Gyuri belonged before he went to the camps no longer exists when he comes home, as his final encounters testify.

It is not even certain that it is always, or ever, a good thing to live in a community. Though we (I at least) tend to think that the normal and good human condition is to dwell immersed in a community, surrounded by family, friends, and neighbors who think the way I do, share my "values," and live by the same judgments, it may well be that this is not the case, or at least that matters are not quite so simple. The Nazis appealed to the *Blutbruderschaft* of the German *Volk*. Calling on *Gemeinschaft*, the community of Aryans, was a fundamental part of Nazi ideology. It was an essential feature of the justification for "purifying" Europe of all Jewish "vermin." Today we would call that "ethnic cleansing." It was also the justification for the suicidal wars of the Third Reich. Goebbels and Hitler rejoiced when the bombs began to rain down on German cities because collective death would be the fulfillment of German *Volksgemeinschaft*.[38] Even Heidegger, notoriously, spoke of the German *Volk*, just as United States right-wing politicians today claim to speak in the name of "the American people" when they say, "The American people do not want universal health care," or "The American people are willing to give up civil liberties in order to be protected from 'the Terrorist Threat,'" or "The American people want illegal immigrants sent back where they came from." Derrida, who suffered from French anti-Semitism in Algiers as a schoolboy, resisted calling Nancy's "unworked community" or Blanchot's "unavowable" one "communities." "Why call them communities?" he asked. He went on to say, "If I have always hesitated to use this word, it is because too often the word 'community' resounds with 'common' [*commun*]. The as-one [*comme-un*]."[39] On a later page of *A Taste for the Secret*, Derrida speaks eloquently and hyperbolically of his resistance to being "one of the family." Can this resistance have been not simply a carefully worked-out philosophical position (which it certainly is), but in some way a reflex result of Derrida's experience as a Jew in Algeria and later in Paris during the Nazi period? The narrator of Kertész's *Fatelessness* is closest of the protagonists of my four novels to Derrida's intransigent position, in a passage cited at length in chapter 1, when he says, "I'm not one of the family."

Well, what about communities in my three novels and in *Maus*? Here, in conclusion, I enunciate an important corollary or essential concomitant of what might be called "Miller's law." If Holocaust novels get more complex, more "interest bearing," narratologically and rhetorically, the closer the author was to direct experience of the camps, at the same time the rendering of the conflagration of community becomes more pronounced. Those novelists further away are most likely to want somehow to affirm that community survived the conflagration of the crematoria. Who, naturally, would not wish to be able to believe that?

Thomas Keneally is furthest away, of my four authors, from actual experience of the Holocaust. *Schindler's List* has a happy ending in the collective celebration of their survival at the war's end by "Schindler's Jews," those he has courageously saved from the gas chambers. They make him a ring made of gold tooth fillings that one prisoner has somehow preserved. (The Nazi guards violently extracted most teeth with gold fillings, or took them from the corpses of the gassed.) The Schindler Jews crowd around him to cheer and embrace him as he flees in a borrowed convict uniform to escape reprisal as a collaborator with the Nazis. This scene of community restored is particularly vivid in the Hollywood film version. The novel ends with information about Schindler's later life and about the way he was honored and memorialized in the newly formed state of Israel. I am not saying these things did not happen in history. They are well documented. These events, however, are by no means typical. More typical was the collaboration in evil by so many non-Jews, to which survivors bear witness. Keneally has taken a strikingly exceptional case, an extraordinary story of courage and defiant cunning, in the midst of unspeakable evil, by a "good German." Testimony that such good Germans existed is of course the attraction of *Schindler's List*.

Black Dogs is a bit closer to the Holocaust. The Wikipedia entry indicates that McEwan's life has been adventurous. He grew up in East Asia, Germany, and North Africa, where his father was posted as an army officer; his first wife absconded with his thirteen-year-old son after a court granted him custody; he discovered in 2002 that he had a brother who had been given up for adoption during World War II. The events in *Black Dogs*, however, do not appear to be directly autobiographical or based on someone's real experience, though I may be wrong about that, as Gyuri might say. Certainly the events in *Black Dogs* have a convincing immediacy. Nevertheless, in a note following the last page of *Black Dogs* and signed with his initials McEwan forcefully compounds the ritual publisher's disclaimer that appears on the obverse of the title page. The note asserts that the characters in *Black Dogs* are "entirely fictional and bear no resemblance to persons living or dead" (151). I have cited this note in the previous chapter. Of course McEwan may be lying. Moreover, he does not exactly say that the main characters have no basis in historical fact. The disclaimer is explicitly directed at the local French people, the mayor, and so on, who figure in the novel, but it is stated in inclusive terms.

The conflagration of community appears in *Black Dogs*, as in McEwan's other novels, as an almost universal breakdown of that essential component of community, the stable nuclear family. The cause of this is identified as World War II and the Holocaust, however tangentially or immediately they may have been experienced. An eloquent page describing the shoes of the victims remaining still at Majdanek and the narrator's experience of growing numbness and shame on seeing them, also cited in the previous chapter, dramatizes the narrator's sense of what the Holocaust was like, his sense of it, that is, during his visit to Majdanek, and just before he makes love with his future wife, Jenny Tremaine, for the first time, that afternoon (88–89).

The passage not only asserts that the sheer numbers murdered make the Holocaust unimaginable, but also implies that each of those millions died alone, like that baby with the nursery lamb on his or her shoe. Long after her encounter with the black dogs, when she is on her death bed, June Tremaine laments her inability to belong to any society: "Why should I expect millions of strangers with conflicting interests to get along when I couldn't make a simple society with the father of my children, the man I've loved and remained married to?" (30) After Auschwitz no nuclear families.

Black Dogs is not quite so simple, however. Though the first-person narrator has lost his parents in an automobile accident when he was quite young, and though the result of this is a condition of anomie, an inability to finish university, keep jobs, or have stable relations with friends or lovers, and though his mother-in-law, June, has been permanently detached from her husband and from any community in the normal sense of the word by her experience of being attacked by the black Gestapo dogs, the novel does reestablish community in the miniature form of the narrator's happy marriage to June's daughter, Jenny. He has a happy family life with his four children. This is the case even though, as he says in the last paragraph, he remains haunted by those black dogs, as is the reader, this reader at least.

Maus is closer yet to actual testimony, since its author/artist is the son of a survivor, and since much of *Maus* is made up of Vladek Spiegelman's own words and of comix pictures of him speaking of his experiences in Auschwitz. What he says springs magically into visibility in Spiegelman's powerful drawings above Vladek's speech enclosed in white rectangles in each box. Community is only tenuously present in this novel, however, since so many members of Vladek's family and of the Jewish community he lived in before the war have been killed. Even in the safety of Rego Park, New York, community has not been reconstituted, not for Vladek at least, nor for his son Artie. Vladek's wife has committed suicide. He does not get along at all with his new wife, even though she is a survivor too. His pathological miserliness makes him unfit for community life. Father and son have a terrible relation, even though the son has moved away and has an apparently happy marriage to a French woman, someone not a survivor, someone who has only nominally converted to Judaism. Vladek's family isn't much of a community. The camps seem to have disabled him for communal belonging.

Kertész and Kertész's protagonist are closest of all to the Holocaust, since both are survivors, one real, one fictional. Gyuri is closest of all the protagonists of my novels to Derrida's intransigent "I am not one of the family," and even closest to something like Derrida's reasons for claiming that such detachment is a good thing. Gyuri bears direct witness to his experience, telling his (fictional) story in the first person, with no recourse to second-hand "history," such as Spiegelman evidently used, for example, in his map of Auschwitz. Gyuri bears witness to the conflagration of community, not only in his own detachment, the "twosome twimindedness" that characterizes his discourse, and in his ironic descriptions of "the myriad petty nuisances, annoyances, and vexations that, it appears, are inevitably bound up with communal life of that kind" (59), meaning life in mortal danger as a prisoner of the Nazis, but also in his testimony that the gas chambers put an end to families and communities, even to that minimal kind of "communal life" the captives have while they are still alive. The chambers destroy all that by a process that is, in the most literal sense, a conflagration.

Even at home in Budapest, before he is deported, Gyuri does not feel solidarity with the Jewish community to which his family belongs. A moving episode describes the traumatic discovery by the older sister of Gyuri's first adolescent girlfriend that she is "Jewish." She cannot understand what that means. "I attempted," says Gyuri, "to explain to the girl that they did not really hate her, that is to say not her personally, since they have no way of knowing her, after all—it was more just the idea of being 'Jewish.' She then said she'd been thinking the same thing right before, because when you get down to it she doesn't even know exactly what 'Jewish' is" (35). Jewishness, this episode argues, is not an "essence," though the Nazis and other anti-Semites think it is.

This episode in *Fatelessness* parallels Derrida's report, in "Abraham, the Other," that his first true experience of what it means to be "Jewish" was when French anti-Semitism in Algeria led to his being expelled from his school, one fine day, with no forewarning.[40] This was a decisive trauma for Derrida. This trauma, it may be, led Derrida to feel that he belonged to no community and to choose to say "I am not one of the family," just as Kafka felt outside any family or community. Kafka tirelessly explored, in his stories, novels, and other writings, what that feels like. Just as Sethe, in Toni Morrison's *Beloved*, is expelled from the black community of free African-Americans in Cincinnati just before the Civil War, so Kertész's Gyuri feels himself in exile from any family or community, with the sole exception of his fragile and temporary community of two with Bandi Citrom, who is ultimately swallowed up by the Shoah. The Yiddish-speaking community of Jews in the camps, for example, deny him membership in their group. The result for Gyuri is an odd and distressingly ironic experience of reverse discrimination. In Budapest, he felt isolated from the normal community because he was Jewish. In the camps he feels isolated from the normal community because he feels, paradoxically, "as if [he] were somehow Jewish" (140) in relation to the real, Yiddish-speaking Jews, as if they were the norm and he the outsider. It is, he goes on to say, "a rather odd feeling to have after all, I reckoned, in the midst of Jews, in a concentration camp" (140). "Jew," it appears, is a universal name for someone who is declared to be outside, for someone who is a stranger. As Gyuri says, the experience of being excluded from community is not something abstract. It makes your skin crawl.

Whether my "law," with its hypothesis of a double contradictory movement toward narrative complexity and toward the unworking of community, the closer one gets to the Holocaust, would be confirmed by investigation of a wider selection of Holocaust novels remains to be seen. My sample is too small to constitute proof. I might be right or I might be wrong. I claim, however, that it is a useful hypothesis. It raises important questions. It is, like any good scientific hypothesis, open to testing and to possible disproof.

Part Four | Fiction after Auschwitz

7 Morrison's *Beloved*

Beloved *as Postmodern Masterpiece*

I have already in earlier chapters suggested that slavery and its aftermath in continuing racism is the closest thing we have in United States history to what the Shoah is for the German historical legacy (although the genocide of Native Americans is is another obvious analogue).[1] By "aftermath" I mean, for example, the approximately 3,500 lynchings of black people in the United States from 1880 to 1930, that is, well after emancipation. Many photographs of lynchings have survived. I have indicated the Internet URL for one in chapter 2 of this book, apropos of Kafka's possession of such a photograph. Their survival is evidence that Sethe, the protagonist of *Beloved*, is right to say that once something happens it never dies. It goes on happening somewhere in some medium, or reachable by some medium in another, related, sense of that word.

By "aftermath" I mean also the continued racism and racial inequality in the United States from the Civil War to the present (2011). I have attempted in this book to keep in the reader's mind a continuous parallel among four topics: slavery and its aftermaths; Kafka's novels; Holocaust·novels; and our situation today, that is, a situation in which the Guantánamo Bay detention camp can still exist.

The aim of Toni Morrison's great novel *Beloved* (1987) is, to use her own word, to make sure we "rememory" slavery, even though it might seem healthier to forget. "In trying to make the slave experience intimate," writes Morrison in the foreword to *Beloved*'s Vintage International Edition of 2004, "I hoped the sense of things being both under control and out of control would be persuasive throughout; that the order and quietude of everyday life would be violently disrupted by the chaos of the needy dead; that the herculean effort to forget would be threatened by memory desperate to stay alive. To render enslavement as a personal experience, language must get out of the way."[2] I shall try later to identify what Morrison means by the odd phrase, "the needy dead." I see what she means by saying language must get out of the way, but surely language, as direct and transparent as possible, in a novel about slavery, is the essential means of "rendering slavery as a personal experience." Morrison's *Beloved* belongs to two different historical moments, 1987, the date of its first publication, and the time in American history just before and after the Civil War.

Though *Beloved* sticks closely to its task of remembering what slavery was like in the United States just before the Civil War, it does, after all, have a specific historical context of its own. The novel was published in 1987, just two years before the fall of the Berlin Wall. This event is often said to have signaled the end of the Cold War. The Berlin Wall's fall figures prominently in McEwan's *Black Dogs*, discussed in chapter 5 of this book. In 1987 Ronald Reagan was President of the United States. Apartheid was in full force in South Africa, with the covert support of the United States, just as the later genocide in Darfur took place with little effort on our government's part to stop it. Morrison in the foreword identifies the women's movement of the eighties as an essential context for her novel: "In the eighties the debate was still roiling: equal pay, equal treatment, access to professions, schools . . . and choice without stigma. To marry or not. To have children or not. Inevitably these thoughts led me to the different history of black women in this country—a history in which marriage was discouraged, impossible, or illegal; in which birthing children was required, but 'having' them, being responsible for them—being, in other words, their parent—was as out of the question as freedom. Assertions of parenthood under conditions peculiar to the logic of institutional enslavement were criminal" (xvi–xvii).

1987 was also the heyday of what is called "postmodernism." It was the moment of recognition that a new way of living had developed after World War II. This new social experience was being registered in new forms of architecture, film, visual arts, and narrative, as well as in new forms of everyday life. Fredric Jameson's influential essay "Postmodernism; or, The Cultural Logic of Late Capitalism," is a description and somewhat ironic celebration of this new style and new mode of social existence. It was first published in 1984 in *New Left Review*,[3] just three years before *Beloved*'s publication. I have elsewhere argued that "postmodernism" is to some degree a bogus historical category.[4] It mixes our new cultural and economic situation under post–World War II late capitalism with formal features of novels by writers like E. L. Doctorow or Thomas Pynchon. These formal features already exist in Cervantes's work, so the mixture is heterogeneous.

What, then, are the special features of so-called postmodern narratives? I would alter Jameson's categories a bit to list the following as the most salient features of postmodern narrative: pastiche, that is, an incoherent mixture of styles from different periods (as opposed to parody); allusion; mixing of genres; depthlessness; a making problematic of the assumption that selfhood is fixed and unitary; lack of affect (or, I should prefer to say, a shift to that peculiar kind of ironic affect called "cool"); attenuation of the "omniscient narrator," or, to put it more precisely, use of a telepathic narrator who does not pass judgment or proffer interpretation; discontinuity, that is, narration through short episodes separated by breaks; "preposterous" (in the etymological sense) time shifts by way of metalepsis, prolepsis, or analepsis, flashbacks, and flashforwards; use of interpolated stories, usually told by one or another of the characters; abrupt changes or shifts in register or tone; a high degree of indirection, so that the real story is told offstage, as it were, by hints and innuendos, as a story beneath the story; a degree of hallucinatory antirealism, or "surrealism," or what has more recently been called "magical realism," in which impossible, "magic" events are told in a straightforward "realistic" style; or, to put this in a slightly different way, an odd sort of half-ironic, but only half-ironic, persistence of the religious, the superstitious, the magical, the supernatural; an exuberant, hyperbolic use of comedy, farce, or anarchic social explosions; the use of one sort or another of a frame story that both controls, interprets, and at the same time ironically undercuts the story proper; a focus on the experience of outsiders or underdogs, the "wretched of the earth"; a sense of the community as turned against itself, self-sacrificially, or in a suicidal way, in what Derrida calls a process of autoimmune self-destruction; a problematic sense of what it means to make an ethical decision or to take ethical responsibility; some direct or indirect calling attention to problems of fictionality or virtuality, that is, a turning of the narrative back on itself to raise questions about its own mode of existence and about its social function; resistance to unequivocal interpretation because of some fundamental ambiguity or moral undecidability.[5]

The economic conditions of the "postmodern period" are decisively new, but the formal features of postmodern fiction Jameson lists can, as I have said, already be found in, say, Cervantes. I have added, among other features, a problematic fascination with the supernatural to Jameson's list. The presence of the supernatural in postmodern fiction tends to generate embarrassed silence in critics. "Surely," critics are likely to think, "we are not meant to take seriously this stuff about ghosts and revenants." The supernatural is a feature of Cervantes's *The Dogs' Colloquy*, one of his *Exemplary Stories*, as well as of *Beloved* and of work by Thomas Pynchon such as "The Secret Integration," not to speak of his *Gravity's Rainbow*. One should always be suspicious of attempts to periodize literature by means of supposedly distinctive formal and thematic traits. The apparently new features such attempts name can almost always be found in other epochs. Cervantes's work makes big problems for setting periods for the Western novel, as does Sterne's *Tristram Shandy*.

In spite of these endemic problems with periodization, *Beloved*, no one can doubt, is that portentous thing, a postmodern novel. It is a pastiche of many different genres: slave narrative, Middle Passage story, reconstruction of an actual historical event, ghost story, repetition with a difference of several biblical stories, quasi-anthropological dramatization of the beliefs and behavior of a "marginal" ethnic culture. An example of the quasi-anthropological is the ascription to the protagonist, Sethe, of a belief that once something has happened it cannot cease going on happening, over and over, in the place where it first occurred, until finally it may be purged. This parallels a similar Irish folk belief registered in W. B. Yeats's poem "The Curse of Cromwell" and in his plays *The Words upon the Windowpane* (1934) and *Purgatory* (1939).[6] In the first and last of these texts a ruined house periodically lights up with the reenactment of tragic, unpurged events that happened there. In *The Words upon the Windowpane* Swift, Stella, and Vanessa return at a spirit séance to reenact a moment of their tangled relationship. Here is the way Sethe expresses her belief to her daughter Denver:

> Someday you be walking down the road and you hear something or see something going on. So clear. And you think it's you thinking it up. A thought picture. But no. It's when you bump into a rememory that belongs to somebody else. Where I was be-

> fore I came here, that place is real. It's never going away. Even if the whole farm—every tree and grass blade of it dies. The picture is still there and what's more, if you go there—you who never was there—if you go there and stand in the place where it was, it will happen again; it will be there for you, waiting for you. So, Denver, you can't never go there. Never. Because even though it's all over—over and done with—it's going to always be there waiting for you. That's how come I had to get all my children out. No matter what. (43–44)

Denver says, "That must mean that nothing ever dies," and Sethe answers, "Nothing ever does" (44). Not only does nothing ever die, but also such "rememories" are transferable from one person to another. They are outside any one person's memory. This motif reappears much later in the novel when Denver fears to go outside 124 Bluestone Road, Sethe's house in Cincinnati: "Out there where there were places in which things so bad had happened that when you went near them it would happen again. Like Sweet Home where time didn't pass and where, like her mother said, the bad was waiting for her as well" (287). Sethe's belief is fulfilled in Beloved's apparent return as a ghost. Beloved seems to be the baby Sethe has murdered. After all, she calls herself "Beloved," the name on the murdered baby's tombstone. This return of the dead exemplifies the supernatural theme that, as I have said, tends, somewhat unexpectedly, to appear in postmodern fiction. Beloved's return also underlies the theme of "rememory," so important in *Beloved*, as I shall show. It also echoes, somewhat unexpectedly, the postmodern theme of the past as "simulacrum" or image. Forgetting can never be complete or certain, however desirable it may be to forget, and memory is involuntary, spontaneous. Memory is always "rememory," that is, one repetition in an endless sequence of rememberings or reassemblings of the past. Whatever has once happened, particularly acts of violence, injustice, or betrayal, such as schoolteacher's mistreatment of slaves at Sweet Home (Sethe's plantation in Kentucky), or the murders at Auschwitz, can never cease happening somewhere. They are always open to a resurrection or return from the dead, like those horrible photographs of Auschwitz or like Morrison's raising again the ghost of the historical Margaret Garner from that old newspaper clipping she happened to see. The past returns as ineffaceable image.

Like much other postmodern fiction, *Beloved* contains a lot of sex and violence, though of course those were already abundantly present in work by a modernist novelist like William Faulkner. The difference may be that in postmodern fiction, as in our films and television shows, hideous violence and explicit sex are more casual and more constant. We have become inured to both, in part, perhaps, by the sight of all those stacked corpses in the photographs of concentration camps taken at the time of their liberation. Seeing those photographs in *Life Magazine*, in 1945, when I was seventeen, was certainly a defining moment in my own life. Think, by comparison, of Anthony Trollope's high-Victorian novels! No sex and no violence, beyond a couple of examples I can think of: Melmotte's suicide with a penknife in *The Way We Live Now* (1875) and Lopez's flinging himself under a train, in *The Prime Minister* (1876). Generally speaking, the violence in Trollope is all psychological: the Reverend Josiah Crawley's suffering in *The Last Chronicle of Barset* (1867), for example, when he is unjustly accused of having stolen a check for twenty pounds, or the silent suffering of all those Trollopean girls who are secretly in love but may not speak their love out of maidenly decorum, or who are persecuted by their parents for openly loving what they see as the wrong man. Postmodern novels show the sex and violence in graphic detail. Adaptations of Victorian or other premodernist novels for cinema or television, for example, tend to add sex and violence that are not there in the original texts. One case is the scene of Charlotte and the Prince making love in the recent cinema version of James's *The Golden Bowl* (originally published as a novel in 1904; the film appeared in 2000). A major point in the novel proper is that Maggie does not have eyewitness evidence of this event, and neither does the reader. In the film we see it with our own eyes.

"Postmodern" though it is, *Beloved* employs a mixture of modes of narration borrowed from high-modernist writers like Faulkner, Conrad, and Kafka: an abrupt enigmatic beginning, hallucinatory realism mixed with supernatural events, dreamlike interior monologue, confusing shifts in point of view, obscure or inexplicit allusions, striking discontinuities and time shifts, a narrative structure that moves forward in time in order to recover and "rememory" a past that, as in a detective story, is hidden from the reader at the beginning except in puzzling hints. This spectrum of incompatible ways to tell a story is employed higgledy-piggledy, as each seems to be needed, just as a postmodern building mixes, in pastiche, incongruous architectural styles, to produce a strange, depthless stage-set effect. All these big guns of narrative technique are employed, however, in a novel whose announced goal is to repair that "crisis in historicity" Jameson laments as a feature of postmodernism. *Beloved* attempts to bring the reader to understand the degree to which our present condition in the United States is a result of the institution of slavery in pre–Civil War America, just as the Shoah conditions Germany today, and just as the Cultural Revolution is a still a determining event for Chinese culture now, in 2011.

The Way We Live Now

A lot of water has gone over the dam since 1987, the year *Beloved* was published, to put it mildly. The Cold War is over. It seems in retrospect a minor skirmish in increasingly global confrontations of large conglomerations of nations such as George Orwell foresaw. The United States is now, in 2011, still bogged down in seemingly endless wars of occupation in Iraq and Afghanistan, and in the interminable so-called War on Terror, though President Obama promises that all combat troops will soon be withdrawn from Iraq and in a year or two from Afghanistan. We'll see about that. The teletechnological revolution that potentially links everyone everywhere in the world in instantaneous communication by e-mail, the Internet, iPhones, and the like has transformed most people's lives and made "globalization" a reality. The greed and chicanery of our government and its allies, the banks and large corporations, have pushed the United States and the whole world into a recession that mixes the bursting of the housing bubble, the consequent near collapse of the global financial system, and extremely high unemployment. We have piled up gigantic budget deficits. We have widened the gap between rich and poor to unprecedented levels. We had for eight years the worst and most unpopular president in our history, George W. Bush. Our reputation abroad was, during his rule, at a low ebb, so that, for example, a German novelist, Christoph Peters, could write in 2008, in an essay translated as an op-ed piece in *The New York Times*, with a calm certainty that millions of people outside the United States would agree with him, the following: "George W. Bush's contempt for the rules and institutions of international politics, his revival of preventive war, with all its unforeseeable consequences, his abrogation of the rule of law in his own country, and his ignorance of every issue related to environmental conservation have become, for me and for the vast majority of Germans, synonymous with a high-handed, ugly America. This state of affairs has provoked not only rage and horror, but also great sadness, for the United States has always been the symbol of freedom, democracy and law."[7]

Since the election of Barack Obama as our president our situation in the United States has somewhat improved, but the job of repair on so many fronts Obama faced when he took office will require years of Herculean effort: disastrously expensive health care, with over forty million uninsured, environmental destruction and unchecked global warming, an inequitable tax code, huge budget deficits, a seemingly endless state of war, our banking system and housing markets a shambles, skyrocketing oil and food prices, unconstitutional destruction of our civil rights, a Supreme Court with a conservative majority that seems bent on destroying one by one all the advances toward social equity made since Franklin Roosevelt's time. Most recently, in January, 2010, the Supreme Court overturned a hundred year precedent prohibiting corporations from political advertizing. This ruling will tilt the United States even further toward being a postdemocracy, a plutocracy, in which financial institutions and large corporations (especially oil, gas, pharmaceutical, and health care companies) run the country.

Nor have matters been markedly improved as yet under the leadership of Barack Obama, I regret to say. His State of the Union address of January 27, 2010, however, did give me some hope that he may eventually fulfill his campaign promises, if he can only get Congress to act on his proposals. A big if, since many members of Congress seem determined to do nothing. Though the withdrawal from Iraq of all combat soldiers appears to be taking place on schedule, nevertheless Guantánamo Bay still imprisons a good many prisoners, two hundred at the last count, fifty of whom have been judged both too dangerous to be set free and at the same time not able to be tried. This is presumably because their "confessions" have been obtained under torture. Secret detention centers still apparently exist, as do warrantless wiretapping and e-mail reading, as well as harsh interrogation techniques, though Obama claims he has outlawed torture. Nothing serious has yet been done to regulate the banks and other financial institutions, so they are already on the way to bringing about another financial meltdown. As I revise this book (June 2010) the Senate and the House are still at work reconciling the two financial reform bills they have passed. Lobbyists for banks and other financial institutions are spending millions to persuade legislators to block the regulation they dislike, for example, supervision of "derivatives" that are a form of gambling at best and fraudulent Ponzi schemes at worst. Though a moderately good health care reform law was passed by Congress and signed by President Obama, it is so compromised by features favorable to the health insurance "industry," as well as to pharmaceutical companies, and by the killing of the "public option" that the cost of health care will almost certainly continue to spiral out of control. Many more people will have health care, however. Nothing serious has yet been done by the United States government to combat global warming, or to prevent environmental catastrophes like the British Petroleum Gulf oil spill, still going on as I write this sentence (July 2, 2010). Obama has, in an extremely problematic move, escalated the probably unwinnable war in Afghanistan. His advisers include people like Ben Bernanke, Timothy Geithner, and Lawrence Summers, who were among those who caused the financial meltdown in the first place. Practically nothing has been done to increase jobs for the almost 10 percent unemployed (an artificially low figure, since it omits the millions of part-timers and those who have simply stopped looking for a job), or to prevent millions more Americans from losing their homes through foreclosure.

Now (December 2010) the Republicans have taken over the House of Representatives in the recent election. Their goal is to repeal the recent health care law, reduce and privatize Social Security, weaken Medicare, and defeat Obama in the next presidential election. It is not prima facie evident that reading *Beloved* is any help whatsoever to bring us in 2010 to face up to our current frightening situation and to do something about it. The most urgent intellectual and ethical challenge today is to understand, and then act responsibly on, a recognition that our present world condition is determined by the complex interactions, antagonisms, overlappings, and interdependences among three great forces. These are tele-techno-scientifico-military-medico-mediatic-globalized transnational capitalism; Evangelical, apocalyptic, fundamentalist, rapturous Christianity; and radical "terrorist" transnational Islamic fundamentalism. Of course many people are to some degree outside these forces, for example, large numbers of the Chinese and Indian populations who are Buddhist, or Americans who are secular or who are Christians more given to tolerance and loving-kindness than some of their so-called Christian neighbors, or Islamists who are moderate, but even these are increasingly under the sway of scientific-teletechnological-capitalism. The new media exert increasing political influence, so that Glenn Beck and Rush Limbaugh are often said to be the real leaders of the Republican Party in the United States. China and India will soon become two of the globally dominant capitalist countries. Both China and India, moreover, have large numbers of Christians and Muslims. Nor am I unaware of the existence of large numbers of moderate Jews, Christians, and Moslems who constitute various combinations of religious belief and scientific rationalism. Nevertheless, such movements as the vigorous attempt these days to get evolution taught in United States schools as no more than an unverifiable hypothesis puts one in the position of apparently having to choose. The Christian Bible certainly does not appear to support evolution.

Either the Bible or the scientists, it seems to me, must be wrong, on this point at least.

Each of the three knowledge/faiths I have mentioned is an integrated system made up of a combination of knowledge and belief. Each depends on the others, though it is to some degree antagonistic to them. Each is unthinkable without understanding its relation to the others. From a certain scientific, rational, enlightened perspective, some extreme Christian Evangelical beliefs (that the end of the world is at hand, that the saved will be rapt into heaven from Jerusalem, leaving the streets below running in blood) are no more sensible than Islamic beliefs (that a suicide bomber will become an Islamic martyr going straight to heaven to enjoy a thousand virgins, and by his or her martyr death ensuring the eventual triumph of a worldwide Islamic religion and the defeat of infidel Christians and Jews).

The three great Western "religions of the book," Christianity, Judaism, and Islam, are at war with one another, though each traces its origins to the story of Abraham and Isaac. From the perspective of either Christian fundamentalism or Islamic fundamentalism, certain scientific ideas, such as belief in evolution, or in a woman's right to choose, or in the evidence of global warming, are works of the devil. These three belief systems, in their inextricable interrelation, are determining world history these days, for example, the wars in Iraq and Afghanistan, global terrorism, the War on Terror, and the defensive attempts of Iran and North Korea to develop nuclear weapons, now successful in North Korea. What would you do if you were declared to be part of the Axis of Evil and threatened with unilateral "preventive" "regime change"? I think you would get ready to defend yourself as best you can.

Terrorism, the War on Terror, and nuclear weapons, however, would not be possible without science, global capitalism, and the new techno-tele-communications. What made 9/11 a so-called major global event was not the physical occurrence of over two thousand sudden deaths, but the transmission everywhere in the world, by the media, of those films showing the disturbingly double phallic World Trade Center twin towers falling. (I say "disturbingly double phallic" because of Freud's assertion that the doubling of the phallus equals castration, as happened symbolically for Western capitalism when the twin towers fell.) Both the terrorists and the Bush administration, then in the act of declaring the War on Terror, wanted the image of the towers falling shown everywhere and often, but so did the media themselves. They wanted it partly in order to make more money from advertising, that is, by running ads interwoven with the endless repetition of films showing the towers collapsing. Those films are still occasionally shown, whenever an opportunity arises. The terrorists employ the technological devices they deplore, as in the use of airplanes as bombs, or as in the use of the media to broadcast defiant warnings from Osama bin Laden, or as in the use of cell phones to communicate with one another, or to detonate "improvised explosive devices." The American religious right employs both the media (in talk shows, "tele-Evangelical" sermons, websites, and blogs), and, through their influence on our government, high-tech weapons like drone strikes, such as those used against the Taliban, Al Qaeda, and, as "collateral damage," the Iraqi, Afghan, and Pakistani people. Evangelicals' complicity with global captalism and with the military is well known, as in the leadership of the notorious Blackwater (now Xie) Group of civilian-contractor mercenary guards who operated in Iraq. That complicity was fully embodied in the make-up of the Bush administration. That administration mixed, at various times over its disastrous eight years, religious fanatics, like John Ashcroft, and ex-CEOs of oil companies, like Richard Cheney and Donald Rumsfeld, along with neoconservatives like Douglas Feith. George W. Bush combined Evangelical religious belief with political neoconservatism and corporate roots, though he was pretty much a disaster as an oil company executive. Moreover, one does not imagine him reading Carl Schmitt on sovereignty of an evening, whatever may be said about the authenticity of his born-again Christianity. He said the jury is still out on evolution. Only with extreme reluctance was he forced into admitting the existence of climate change, though he and his allies in government and industry resisted every attempt to do anything beyond "voluntary compliance" to slow it down. That attitude still persists to a considerable degree even under Barack Obama's presidency, so powerful are the oil and coal lobbies, just as the lobbyists for the health insurance companies and the pharmaceutical companies have succeeded in getting Congress to craft a health care reform bill that is a gigantic giveaway to their clients. Senators on both sides of the aisle have taken millions from these companies that are labeled legal "campaign contributions" but that look like bribes and vote buying to me.

I add one more essential feature of the way we live now that is crucially relevant to my topic of the conflagration of communities. The rise since 1987 of the Internet and the ubiquity of devices like cell phones, iPods, and iPhones have made the postmodern literature of the 1970s and 1980s, such as Morrison's *Beloved*, or E. L. Doctorow's novels of those decades, as well as reflections on that literature like Jameson's "Postmodernism, or, The Cultural Logic of Late Capitalism," seem to some degree quaint and old fashioned, voices from a now-vanished world of the past in which printed books still mattered greatly. Such communities as we now have are likely to be the strange online communities of collective computer game players or of participants in blogs. A given blog site can be read and contributed to by hundreds of thousands of participants on a given day. It is a strange form of *Mitsein*, since the members of online communities may choose not to use their real names. Nevertheless, such communities may have big cultural and political effects. A spectacular example is Charles Johnson's blog *Little Green Footballs*. A fascinating *New York Times Magazine* essay of January 24, 2010 by Jonathan Dee, "Right-Wing Flame War!" gives details about the way Johnson developed his blog into a major right-wing operation, daily read and participated in by hundreds of thousands of fellow sympathizers.[8] After that Johnson moved quite suddenly far to the left and then turned against Fox News, Rush Limbaugh, Sarah Palin, and his former colleagues. The result was been an immense "flame war," that is, insults traded back and forth online between Johnson and his former extremist collaborators. Now right-wing people like Pamela Geller denounce Johnson as "a traitor, a turncoat, a plant." All these good people belong to an extremely curious kind of community in cyberspace. As Dee observes, one feature of this teletechnological virtual community is that unless something is deliberately erased, all those blogs go on existing simultaneously on the Web, in a defiance of time and in electronic fulfillment of Sethe's claim that "nothing ever dies." Johnson's earlier reactionary rants are still available on his site, posted side by side with expressions of his recent change to being a believer in climate change, and juxtaposed with expressions of his recent change to opposing the extremist Belgian party "Vlaams Belang" (Flemish Interest), a group he used to support. Such "virtual realities" may seem too immaterial to have effects in the "real world," but they do affect the way people vote and other forms of their behavior. The current right-wing populist Tea Partyers in the United States are bound together by the Internet. Not long ago they helped persuade the people of Massachusetts to elect Scott Brown to the United States Senate, where he has promised to stop health care reform, support waterboarding, oppose cap and trade of carbon emissions, and block regulation of banks and other financial institutions, in an apotheosis of the Republicans' commitment to resolutely "just say no."

By the time this book appears in print, the shift to Republican control of the House will be having its effect, along with other national and global changes. Time will tell which way the balance tips.

I permit myself, however, the audacity of hope.

What Good Is Reading Beloved?

What good is literature in understanding this situation and in perhaps being led to act to ameliorate it? My example is Toni Morrison's *Beloved*. Should we read it or teach it or write about it? If so, why? *Beloved*, as I have said, was first published in 1987, four years before the appearance of the book version of Fredric Jameson's *Postmodernism, or, The Cultural Logic of Late Capitalism* (1991). A reader might therefore plausibly assume, as I have done, that *Beloved* is a postmodern work, whatever that might mean, beyond being no more than a chronological designation. Does so-called postmodern literature help readers in any way to face up to our world situation today? The ethos of most United States citizens today is not determined by "literature," whether canonical or not, but by films, television news, talk shows like Glenn Beck's on *Fox News*, television programs like *American Idol* or *The Biggest Loser*, popular music, computer games like *World of Warcraft*, and Internet blogs, twitters, tweets, and flickrs. It is no wonder that "cultural studies" have so largely replaced "literary studies" in humanities departments in our colleges and universities. Paying close attention to a literary work, even so recently written and so manifestly distinguished a one as Morrison's *Beloved*, seems increasingly out of it, otherworldly. This book attempts to show otherwise, but doing so is a big challenge.

The central event of *Beloved*, as the reader gradually discovers, is Sethe's killing, eighteen years before the novel opens in 1873, of her baby daughter in order to keep that daughter from being taken back into slavery. She also tried to kill her other three children and herself. The novel circles around this event, hinting at it, resisting it, coming back to it, until finally it is directly described in horrifying detail. Or rather Sethe with her dying baby daughter in her arms is described, at one point from schoolteacher's perspective: "Inside, two boys bled in the sawdust and dirt at the feet of a nigger woman holding a blood-soaked child to her chest with one hand and an infant by the heels in the other" (175). The actual cutting of the baby's throat with a handsaw is only referred to indirectly. This "indescribable," or at any rate "undescribed," event is the leitmotif for *Beloved*. It is the endlessly recurrent "rememoried" offstage event that organizes all the narrative, just as a scene of solitary walking down corridors that lead to a confrontation behind an opening door organizes Kafka's novels, or just as Gyuri lying in the rain looking up at a cloudy sky rent by a sunbeam serves as an emblematic summarizing scene for Kertész's *Fatelessness*.

All these leitmotifs have a complicated spatial structure setting people in relation to one another across a gap. These imagined spaces express the life situation of the protagonist, as I shall show later for *Beloved.* They are all in this like Jacques Lacan's famous "stade du miroir" (mirror stage) in which the little boy identifies himself with his reflection in a mirror and can thenceforth say "I."[9] Though the leitmotifs in my novels are not, strictly speaking, a coming face to face with one's mirror image, they are nevertheless defining self-discoveries. They happen by way of a confrontation with another person across a separating space. For these events it is not so much "I identify myself with my mirror image, therefore I am" as "I confront another person behind an opening door or across an intervening distance, therefore I am."

Beloved is based on a real event that Morrison had learned of by accident from a newspaper article, though Morrison changed the historical facts. The original of Sethe, a woman named Margaret Garner, was sent back into slavery, as Sethe is not. Scholars have identified other differences. Morrison justifies these as follows: "The historical Margaret Garner is fascinating, but, to a novelist, confining. Too little imaginative space there for my purposes. So I would invent her thoughts, plumb them for a subtext that was historically true in essence, but not strictly factual in order to relate her history to contemporary issues about freedom, responsibility, and women's 'place'" (xvii).

Did Morrison's Sethe do the right thing? That is the big ethical question the novel raises. Would I have done the same thing in her place, or ought I to have done the same thing? Kant says I should always act in such a way that what I do could make a universal law for all mankind. That is the only truly ethical act. Is Sethe's infanticide an act of that sort? Morrison, in an interview with Bill Moyers, was asked whether she herself would do the same thing with her own children in similar circumstances. Her answer makes explicit the comparison of American slavery with the Holocaust that I have proposed.[10] She then claims, as Holocaust survivors have often asserted, that only the victims, those who died in the gas chambers, would be in a position to pass judgment and enunciate forgiveness. I have discussed "Levi's paradox" in chapter 6 of this book. Morrison's invention of the apparent return of Sethe's daughter as a spiteful and unforgiving ghost gets around this paradox by having a victim of slavery both dead and alive at the same time. Morrison, finally, in her response to Moyers, proposes a paradox of her own, or rather, a borrowed one, in a formulation about what judgment we should pass on Sethe's infanticide. Moyers asked Morrison, "Did you ever put yourself in her position and ask, 'Could I have done that to my two sons?'" Morrison answers:

> I ask it a lot. As a matter of fact, the reason the character Beloved enters the novel is because I couldn't answer it. I don't know whether I would do it or not. You hear stories of that in slavery and Holocaust situations, where women have got to figure it out—fast, really fast. But the only person I felt had the right to ask her that question was Beloved, the child she killed. She could ask Sethe, "What'd you do that for? Is this better [meaning her life in the grave or as a ghostly revenant]? What do you know?" For me it was an impossible decision. Someone gave me the line for it at one time which I have found useful. "It was the right thing to do, but she had no right to do it."[11]

How can we understand that contradictory judgment? What does it mean to do the right thing but to have no right to do it? Is it just another example of what is often called "postmodern ethical undecidability"? Certainly Sethe disobeys in a particularly shocking way the commandment "Thou shalt not kill." To kill one's own dearly beloved baby daughter, to cut her throat with a handsaw! How can that be condoned or forgiven, either by us or by Beloved herself?

Sethe, in her account to herself of her justification for what she did, emphasizes (1) that she acted to save her children and herself from return to slavery; (2) that she was confident killing them would take them all to the "other side," where they would be "safe," and where they would join Sethe's dead mother-in-law, Baby Suggs; (3) that the decision was her own autonomous one, analogous to her decision to send her children to freedom in Ohio on the "underground railway," and then follow them herself; (4) that she is unable to explain or justify what she did to someone who does not spontaneously understand it: "And if she thought anything," the narrator says, speaking for Sethe in free indirect discourse, "it was No. No. Nono. Nonono. Simple. She just flew. Collected every bit of life she had made, all the parts of her that were precious and fine and beautiful, and carried, pushed, dragged them through the veil, out, away, over there where no one could hurt them. Over there. Outside this place, where they would be safe" (192). Two pages earlier, she says to Paul D, "I did it. I got us all out. Without Halle [her busband] too. Up till then it was the only thing I ever did on my own. Decided. And it came off right, like it was supposed to. We was here. Each and every one of my babies and me too. I birthed them and I got em out and it wasn't no accident. I did that" (190). The murder too is her decision, spontaneous though it is. "I took and put my babies where they'd be safe," she tells Paul D. "It's my job to know what is and to keep them away from what I know is terrible. I did that" (193, 194).

Like all genuine ethical decisions, the murder is not based on any preexisting law or prescription that programs decision and makes it automatic. For that reason, a true decision cannot be explained to anyone who does not get it. It is an "impossible decision," like all true decisions. "Sethe knew," the narrative voice says, "that the circle she was making around the room, him, the subject, would remain one. That she could never close in, pin it down for anybody who had to ask. If they didn't get it right off—she could never explain" (192).

Sethe's breaking of the commandment against killing may be compared to the founding moment of Judaism, Islam, and Christianity, the three great religions of the book. That moment was Abraham's willingness to sacrifice Isaac. Perhaps that story was somewhere in Morrison's memory when she wrote *Beloved*. The differences between Sethe's and Abraham's acts are as important as the similarities. Both, however, are acts of sacrifice that are above or outside any law, in that sense "impossible." Both are initiatory, inaugural. They mark a break from what came before. They are the basis for what comes after in the community.

The differences are as significant as the similarities, however. In one case, it is a father/son sacrifice. In the other, it is mother/daughter sacrifice, reflecting Morrison's feminist concerns in *Beloved*. Jacques Derrida asks in *The Gift of Death*, a book to a considerable degree about the Abraham and Isaac story: "Would the logic of sacrificial responsibility within the implacable universality of the law, of its law, be altered, inflected, attenuated, or displaced, if a woman were to intervene in some consequential manner [*de façon déterminante*]? Does the system of this sacrificial responsibility and of the double 'gift of death' imply at its very basis [*au plus profond de lui*] an exclusion or sacrifice of woman? A woman's sacrifice or a sacrifice of women, according to one sense of the genitive or the other?"[12] Morrison's *Beloved* is implicitly an answer to these questions. Her answer, unlike John D. Caputo's belief in a softer, more feminine model of sacrifice if women were in charge, is that women might be even more resolute and violent in their willingness to carry out the sacrifice of what is dearest to them, what is most beloved.[13]

Abraham has a clear mandate from God to sacrifice Isaac, though only he hears that command. He keeps silent about it to everyone, to his wife Sarah, to his family, and to Isaac himself. Isaac asks his father, not unreasonably, "Behold the fire and the wood: but where is the lamb for a burnt offering?" Abraham answers equivocally: "My son, God will provide himself a lamb for a burnt offering" (Gen. 22:7–8). Sethe, though she too at first keeps silence, has no such direct command from God as calls Abraham. She makes her own autonomous decision, establishes her own law. In the biblical story, the angel of the Lord stays Abraham's hand at the last moment, as he raises the knife to sacrifice Isaac. A ram caught by the horns in a thicket miraculously appears as a substitute for Isaac. Sethe, on the contrary, does carry out the murder of her daughter. Those are big differences, to say the least. Setting the two stories side by side is primarily useful as a way not only to identify a clear, but ironic, precedent, but also to see clearly what is distinctive about Sethe's act. What she does is perhaps more to be explained by Morrison's feminism than by biblical precedent.

"Behold, here I am," says Abraham, when he hears Jehovah call him by name (Gen. 22:1). Abraham's willingness to obey Jehovah's terrible command paradoxically makes it possible for Abraham and Isaac to father innumerable generations down even to the House of David and to Jesus Christ himself: "By myself have I sworn, saith the Lord, for because thou hast done this thing, and hast not withheld thy son, thine only son: That in blessing I will bless thee, and in multiplying I will multiply thy seed as the stars of the heaven, and as the sand which is upon the sea shore; and thy seed shall possess the gate of his enemies; And in thy seed shall all the nations of the earth be blessed; because thou hast obeyed my voice" (Gen. 22:16–18). That is quite a promise! Because you were willing to kill your only son and cut off your lineage, I promise your lineage will be as numerous as the stars in the sky and the grains of sand on the seashore.

Sethe's Story

The result of Sethe's decision, on the contrary, is her ostracism from the community, the haunting of 124 Bluestone Road in Cincinnati by the ghost of her dead baby, and all the other events that make up the present action of *Beloved*. That present action must be set against the events previous to the murder. Those are called up from time to time in the present as often involuntary and undesired "rememories." Far from having children that bless all the nations of the earth, Sethe's two sons run away because the house is haunted. She has killed her daughter Beloved. Only Denver, of her four children, stays within the community, perhaps to carry on her line. The novel does not say anything definite about that, though it shows her in a brief moment near the end with "her face looking like someone had turned up the gas jet" when a young man comes "running toward her, saying, 'Hey, Miss Denver. Wait up'" (315).

Moreover, while Abraham's obedience to God, madness though it is from the perspective of ordinary morality, is exemplary for all Jews, Christians, and Muslims, the black community of Cincinnati universally condemns Sethe's solitary decision and act. Baby Suggs can only ask God's pardon for what Sethe has done. She eventually takes to her bed and dies. The community shuns Sethe when she comes back from jail, judging her a dangerous woman, someone too proud to admit she did wrong. Worst of all, she is condemned and abandoned by her lover, Paul D, when he finds out from Stamp Paid what she has done. "What you did was wrong, Sethe," says Paul D in response to her proud and defiant "I did that." As he gets ready to leave the house, he accuses her of having acted like an animal: "You got two feet, Sethe, not four" (194). She finds that an unforgivable insult. An instant forest of estrangement grows up between them. Nothing of Abraham's redemptive or initiatory power seems present in Sethe's infanticide.

Matters are not quite so simple, however. *Beloved* has, somewhat unexpectedly, a happy ending. More or less. It depends on how you feel about Beloved, the embodied specter. The novel tells the story of the interruption and then reconstitution of a community and of a family within that community. The reader will see that in following the story of Sethe's relation to Beloved I am making a linear narrative of what is presented in discontinuous fragments and out of chronological order, as if they still exist simultaneously in some place, that "other side" where "nothing ever dies." The narrative voice has access to this place and can speak in telepathic omniscience, in any order it likes, for everything that goes on happening there, interminably, including all the thoughts and feelings the characters have ever had. The reader will also note that in following through a reconstruction of one thread of the collective narrative about slavery Morrison writes, I am omitting many other stories that are interwoven in the telling with Sethe's story, for example, Baby Suggs' story, Stamp Paid's story,[14] or the moving story of Sixo's love for the Thirty Mile Woman and his murder by schoolteacher, the slave overseer at the Sweet Home plantation, or the story of the white girl, Amy Denver, who helped Sethe give birth to Denver in the leaky rowboat with one oar, still on the wrong, Kentucky, side of the Ohio River, or the story of Paul D's journey north after emancipation and the end of the Civil War. All these are interpolations, or stories within the main story about Sethe. They exist side by side in that place where nothing ever dies. They are told discontinuously and out of temporal order by a variety of narrators and by way of a variety of narrative techniques. The reader, if she or he wishes, is left to reorder the events into their chronological sequence, as the characters, obsessed with their private memories and resisting these memories, tell their pasts on one occasion or another. A good example is Denver's reconstruction of the story of her birth, at Beloved's request. Beloved is fascinated by the story and wants to hear every detail, even invented ones: "Denver spoke, Beloved listened, and the two did the best they could to create what really happened, how it really was, something only Sethe knew because she alone had the mind for it and the time afterward to shape it" (92). The telling shifts abruptly from Denver's narration to the telepathic, ubiquitous, omniscient narrator's telling. Morrison is a wonderfully moving storyteller. Taken together, the various stories she tells make *Beloved* a powerful fictional testimony to what slave life was like in the United States, as powerful a fictional testimony as Kertész's *Fatelessness* is to the Shoah. *Beloved* keeps us from forgetting what it is so painful to remember.

Morrison describes eloquently the community Sethe belongs to for twenty-eight days after she makes it with the newborn Denver to 124 Bluestone Road and is reunited with her mother-in-law and with her other three children, whom she has sent on ahead to get them free from slavery: "the twenty-eight days of having women friends, a mother-in-law, and all her children together; of being part of a neighborhood" (204). It is a true togetherness, a *Mitsein*, a community of mutual understanding and love, with shared beliefs, values, and reciprocal obligations. Baby Suggs, with her great heart and her preaching power, is to a considerable degree the center of this community. The house at 124 Bluestone is where everybody meets to leave messages, to pick up messages, and to talk. It is a station on the Underground Railroad, so escaped slaves pass through frequently.

As the topics of the community's talk indicate, however, it is a precarious community. It is a black community situated in Cincinnati, just across the Ohio River from Kentucky, a slave state. Many members of this community are, like Sethe and her children, runaway slaves. They are therefore in constant danger of being captured and sent back into slavery under the provisions of the Fugitive Slave Bill. They live between "sighing at a new betrayal" and "handclapping at a small victory" (204). Here is Morrison's list of what they talk about, in "discussions, stormy or quiet": "the true meaning of the Fugitive Bill, the Settlement

Fee, God's Ways and Negro pews; antislavery, manumission, skin voting, Republicans, Dred Scott, book learning, Sojourner's high-wheeled buggy, the Colored Ladies of Delaware, Ohio" (204).

The community is disrupted, its worst fears confirmed, when schoolteacher, the overseer for Sethe's owner back in Kentucky, the local sheriff, and two other men, armed with the proper documents, as well as with rifles, come to take Sethe and her children back to slavery at the ironically named Sweet Home in Kentucky. Sethe's murder of her baby keeps that from happening. She goes to jail. The Colored Ladies of Delaware (women again, this time as politically effective) and others, including the white Bodwins, brother and sister, make a great and successful effort to keep Sethe from being hanged. When Sethe returns with Denver from jail, the baby's ghost comes back to haunt the house. Baby Suggs, once the center of the community, takes to her bed and dies. No one comes to 124 Bluestone anymore. Sethe and the rest of her family are ostracized, not so much for what she has done as for her proud refusal to admit any wrong in what she did. After Paul D chases the baby's ghost away and moves in with Sethe, it comes back, apparently, in the embodied form or spirit possession form of the fetch or "haunt" of a teen-aged woman who says her name is Beloved. Paul D leaves when he finds out about the murder, but also because Beloved moves him out by the force of the subtle psychological pressure ghosts have. Things then go from bad to worse, with a mutually destructive symbiotic relation developing between Sethe and Beloved. Sethe starves herself so she can fatten Beloved, loses her job, and spends all their money on food and on gaudy clothes to try to please Beloved:

> Denver thought she understood the connection between her mother and Beloved: Sethe was trying to make up for the handsaw; Beloved was making her pay for it. But there would never be an end to that, and seeing her mother diminished shamed and infuriated her. . . .
>
> And no one, nobody on earth [Denver imagines Sethe thinking], would list her daughter's characteristics on the animal side of the paper [as schoolteacher had done with the slaves at Sweet Home]. No. Oh no. . . .
>
> This and much more Denver heard her say from her corner chair, trying to persuade Beloved, the one and only person she felt she had to convince, that what she had done was right because it came from true love.

> Beloved, her fat new feet propped on the seat of a chair in front of the one she sat in, her unlined hands resting on her stomach, looked at her. Uncomprehending everything except that Sethe was the woman who took her face away, leaving her crouching in a dark, dark place, forgetting to smile. . . .
>
> . . . It was as though Sethe didn't really want forgiveness given; she wanted it refused. And Beloved helped her out. (295, 296, 297)

I have mentioned "undecidability" as a fundamental formal feature of so-called modern and postmodern fiction, for example, novels by Kafka and Kertész in their different ways. In *Beloved* this takes a spectacular form in the impossibility of deciding whether Morrison or her unnamed and impersonal narrator believes in the religious, ghost story dimension of the book or is just presenting it as a historical feature of the ostensibly Christian culture of ex-slaves in Cincinnati in the period just before the Civil War. I say "ostensibly" because the Christianity of Sethe and her community is mixed with remnants of African religion and African matriarchy. Examples are the role of Baby Suggs as someone who can preach the pods off the chestnut trees and the role of the community's black women as the ones who have power to exorcise Beloved.

Moreover, as other readers of *Beloved* have persuasively argued, Beloved may not be the ghost of Sethe's murdered baby at all. She may be, as a good bit of evidence in the novel suggests, a young black woman who has survived the Middle Passage only to be sexually enslaved by a white man from whom she finally escapes by murdering him. She then appears in black Cincinnati rising up out of a stream and walking into the yard at 124 Bluestone: "A fully dressed woman walked out of the water. She barely gained the dry bank of the stream before she sat down and leaned against a mulberry tree. All day and all night she sat there, her head resting on the trunk in a position abandoned enough to crack the brim in her straw hat" (60). Beloved may, mistakenly, identify Sethe as the mother who abandoned her on the slave ship. It is, perhaps, Sethe and the others who take Beloved, again mistakenly, as the material embodiment of the ghost that has been causing such havoc in the house, that is, the ghost of Sethe's murdered baby, now grown up to the age she would have been had she lived. The powerful account of Beloved's experiences on "the other side," in the grave (248–56), can be read at the same time as a representation of the horrible conditions on a slave ship on the Middle Passage from Africa to the United States, experiences being remembered by the young woman who has escaped from slave bondage and sexual abuse in the United States. She then walks up out of the river to enter Sethe's life and that of the others in Sethe's community. Beloved remembers, it appears, the dead being thrown into the sea from the slave ship (253). A great painting by J. M. W. Turner (*Slavers Throwing Overboard the Dead and Dying—Typhoon Coming On ["The Slave Ship"],* exhibited 1840) is testimony to what that was like.[15] The painting shows shapes in the foreground water of the dead and dying who have been thrown overboard. Further back, in a tiny vignette, is what looks to me like a mother rescuing her child momentarily from the waves.

In my judgment, it is impossible to decide which way to take Beloved. The evidence is deliberately ambiguous. Beloved is a little too much a fleshly presence to be a ghost. Those new work shoes she appears wearing are just the sort an escaped slave might have stolen. On the other hand, her hands have no lines on their palms, a sure sign in that culture that she is a supernatural revenant. Many other details can be read both ways, like a Gestaltist duck/rabbit. Critics have tended to think it is necessary to choose. My own conclusion is that Morrison intentionally left the question unanswerable. Beloved may be both at once: a real person possessed by a ghost. *Beloved* is perhaps explicable by way of the belief that nothing ever dies and that things that have once happened as some human being's experience can migrate to another person as a "rememory." Certainly the horrible events of slavery recounted in *Beloved* have entered indelibly and unforgettably into my own memory. For those reasons, it may be, Morrison chose, in the great passage of Beloved's interior monologue, to render Beloved's experience of being dead and buried, crowded in a dark place with the other dead, in terms transferred from the experience of slaves crowded in the holds of slave ships on the way to the New World in the Middle Passage. Beloved has apparently had that experience as a baby. She remembers seeing her mother throw herself into the sea to join the dead and dying slaves who have been cast overboard. Beloved insists her mother was not pushed. She sees her mother's death as a betrayal of her obligation to her baby. Beloved then sees in Sethe the face of her mother and takes her *as* her mother, in a living figurative transfer motivated by psychological need. Sethe, however, takes Beloved as her daughter come back from the dead at just the age she would have been had she lived, in another living figurative transfer, also motivated by need.

This would be a plausible, somewhat rationalizing, rhetorical reading. But then how would you explain Beloved's smooth palms and the scar like a second smile under her chin? What about the evidence in the opening episodes that 124 Bluestone is haunted: the food dishes thrown on the floor, the moving furniture, and so on? Which reading is right? Go figure, or rather, read for yourself, and then figure. The thirty women of Sethe's community are sure that Beloved is a dangerous embodied ghost that must be exorcised. They believe that "Sethe's dead daughter, the one whose throat she cut, had come back to fix her" (300). The neighborhood women do successfully chase her away by means of "the sound." The sound is that paradoxical thing, a wordless but efficacious speech act, something possible only for black women: "The voices of women searched for the right combination, the key, the code, the sound that broke the back of words. Building voice upon voice until they found it, and when they did it was a wave of sound wide enough to sound deep water and knock the pods off chestnut trees" (308). "Sound" here is a double word meaning both a noise and the measuring of the distance to the bottom of a body of water.

Why does the thirty women's ritual of exorcism work? The last page of the novel hints that Beloved has disappeared back into the water of the nearby stream from which she emerged to haunt 124 Bluestone. That would mean that she has all along been a haunting specter, a strange sort of water sprite:

> Down by the stream in back of 124 her footprints come and go, come and go. They are so familiar. Should a child, an adult place his feet in them, they will fit. Take them out and they disappear again as though nobody ever walked there.
>
> By and by all trace is gone, and what is forgotten is not only the footprints but the water too and what it is down there. (324)

Beloved is certainly a case of the "undecidability" said to be a feature of postmodern narrative.

Denver breaks the impasse of Sethe's attempt to get forgiveness for the unforgivable from Beloved, taken unequivocally by Sethe, as by the women in her community, as the incarnation of her murdered daughter. At the same time, paradoxically, as Denver understands, Sethe wants to get the limitless reproach and accusation that is the refusal of forgiveness. She wants both, both at oncc, and it is rapidly killing her. It is as though Abraham had actually killed Isaac on Mount Moriah and Isaac had come back to haunt Abraham, charging him day and night with an infinite, unrepayable, irredeemable crime.

Denver one day leaves the house and goes out to seek help from the community, offering to work at any kind of job in recompense. The community starts leaving food at 124 Bluestone. Denver gradually gets to know different members of the Cincinnati black community when she goes to return the empty dishes and to say thanks. She gets a night-time job with the Bodwins, the white brother and sister who helped Baby Suggs years before and gave her 124 Bluestone to live in.

In a highly cinematic climax, Edward Bodwin comes with his cart to pick up Denver for her first night's work at the same moment the thirty women come to exorcise the ghost with "the sound." Sethe sees Bodwin's hat and thinks it is schoolteacher come again to return her to slavery, whereas the Bodwins are abolitionists. They moved heaven and earth years before to keep Sethe from being hanged. Sethe rushes to attack Bodwin with an ice pick. She is knocked senseless by Ella, in a repetition with a difference of Sethe's reaction when, years before, schoolteacher and his posse came: "It is when she lowers her eyes to look again at the loving faces before her [of the thirty black women come to conjure Beloved away] that she sees him. Guiding the mare, slowing down, his black hat wide-brimmed enough to hide his face but not his purpose. He is coming into her yard and he is coming for her best thing. . . . And if she thinks anything, it is no. No no. Nonono. She flies. The ice pick is not in her hand; it is her hand" (308, 309).

The difference between the two episodes is crucial. The first time Sethe attacks her children and intends to kill herself. The second time she attacks the man she thinks is schoolteacher. The first act led to her ostracism from the community. The second is accepted and leads ultimately to her survival and to her reintegration into the community. Beloved disappears, successfully banished, though perhaps still haunting the stream under the bridge. Paul D comes back take care of Sethe in love and sympathy.

The community, along with Sethe, Denver, and Paul D as members of it, is now healthy and safe because it has not only exorcised the ghost, but also gradually forgotten the whole thing, in what one might call a successful mourning. A central theme in the novel is the inevitable return of the repressed, the impossibility of not remembering what you make every effort to forget. Now, at last, forgetting is possible, in a triumph of the collective wisdom that says, in a significant permutation of tenses, speaking first in the past tense for the community's decision to forget Beloved's story, and then as the narrator speaking in the present about the novel we have just read: "It was not a story to pass on. . . . It was not a story to pass on. . . . This is not a story to pass on" (323, 324). Of course what *Beloved* does is precisely to pass it on, in defiance of its ultimate claim that it would be better to forget it. "To pass on," as Katrina Harack, in a brilliant unpublished dissertation chapter, has argued, can be read in two ways.[16] It can mean to pass the story on to others, to transmit it, and it can mean to let it pass, to forget it. Morrison's formulation is double or antithetical. It says two opposing things at once.

The last segment of the novel, however, is told partly from Beloved's perspective. From that viewpoint, being forgotten is horrible, a "loneliness that roams," that cannot be "rocked" into appeasement (323). Beloved, in a moving and disturbing paragraph at the end of the novel, thinks of herself as nameless and forgotten, permanently buried alive, her parts dispersed and eaten by the "chewing laughter." The passage is in free indirect discourse spoken by the telepathic narrator, whose powers, as I have said, reach even into the grave or over "to the other side," if indeed that is where Beloved now is. The passage explains what Morrison means by the phrase "the needy dead," cited earlier from the preface:

> Everybody knew what she was called, but nobody anywhere knew her name. Disremembered and unaccounted for, she cannot be lost because no one is looking for her, and even if they were, how can they call her if they don't know her name? Although she has claim, she is not claimed. In the place where the long grass opens, the girl who waited to be loved and cry shame erupts into her separate parts, to make it easy for the chewing laughter to swallow her all away. (323)

The fear of being eaten alive is an important aspect of the fear of being buried alive, as *Robinson Crusoe,* for example, shows. Both are terrifyingly dramatized in *Beloved.* A "claim" is a performative, a speech act. Beloved's claim is not felicitous. It is not responded to. Unless, that is, Morrison's novel can be taken as responding to Beloved's claim by bearing witness to it in a work of fiction. That "work" remembers. It does the work of reassembling Beloved's dispersed members. "Beloved" can here be the word for what Sethe's dead baby is called, or the word for what the girl who survived the Middle Passage calls herself when she first appears at 124 Bluestone, or both at once, each the figure of the other.

The last word of *Beloved*, or almost the last word, however, is given to the community, the community that is returned safe and sound to health and self-enclosed integrity by forgetting Beloved. Health and safety for the living seems consist in being cut off wholly from the "other side," closed in on themselves, sequestered, indemnified, and protected from any haunting. "They forgot her like a bad dream," says the narrator. "After they made up their tales, shaped and decorated them, those that saw her that day on the porch quickly and deliberately forgot her. It took longer for those who had spoken to her, lived with her, fallen in love with her, to forget, until they realized they couldn't remember or repeat a single thing she said, and began to believe that, other than what they themselves were thinking, she hadn't said anything at all. So, in the end, they forgot her too. Remembering seemed unwise. . . . So they forgot her. Like an unpleasant dream during a troubling sleep. . . . By and by all trace is gone" (323–24).

What at first seemed hints of Beloved's continued presence, the "rustle of a skirt" or "knuckles brushing the cheek in sleep," come to be taken as natural phenomena, "not the breath of the disremembered and unaccounted for, but the wind in the eaves, or spring ice thawing too quickly. Just weather. Certainly no clamor for a kiss" (324). The novel seems to end with an unequivocal assertion that the community is good, healthy, and viable now because it has forgotten Beloved completely. Forgetting, laying the ghosts of the past, is the price of survival. This might be taken even to claim that it is best not to remember the awful details of slavery in the United States, the sufferings of those "Sixty Million and more" who died under slavery or on the way from Africa to the United States, to whom Morrison's novel is dedicated, though, as I have said, that would mean it is better not to read *Beloved*, whether we are black or white, if we want to get on with it. "This is not a story to pass on."

Beloved ends, however, with a single word set off after a space and given a paragraph to itself:

> Beloved. (324)

How should we take this enigmatic repetition? Is it constative or performative? Is it a name constatively reported, the name of the novel and the name of its principle character? Actually, "Beloved" is what the doubled ghost is "called," since no one knows her given name, not the living characters or the narrator or the reader, though Sethe must know what she named her baby. Or is that final word, "Beloved," a perlocutionary cry, a rememory, an invocation or conjuration, by the narrative voice, beyond all forgetting, of the absent ghost? It seems as if the narrative voice could not bear to forget, even though the community has forgotten and may even be justified in doing so. Does that narrative voice not perhaps speak, and has it perhaps not always spoken, from the first words of the novel on, from "the other side," that is, from the realm where nothing ever dies? A novel is, after all, something that generates its reality from the medium of words on the page. Those words are a material reality with performative force. By means of those words, nothing ever dies in the specific sense that it is resurrected anew every time the novel is read by anyone, anywhere, in a growing community of readers. It is impossible to be sure just how to read this final word. It is another example of the ironic undecidability that characterizes all the fictions before and after Auschwitz I have "read" in this book. The word just hangs there on the page, surrounded by empty space:

> Beloved.

One thing is sure, however: the final word, "Beloved," invites, or even coerces, the reader to remember what the narrative has just told her or him it is a condition of sanity, health, and safety to forget.

What Kind of Community Does Beloved *Dramatize?*

I have reached the end of a brief reading of *Beloved*, but I have not yet fulfilled my promise to show how reading this novel can be of any use to us today in helping us to understand and to act, in response to what is happening to us in this age of globalization, of all-embracing, all-dispersing cyberspace, and of the endless War on Terror. I shall now keep my promise. As Kant says, it is fundamentally unethical to make a promise intending not to keep it. To do this is a particularly malign form of lying. I claim (note that word again!) that the wonderfully brilliant, moving, unsettling, and dense verbal texture of *Beloved* allows the reader to understand what may be a universal structure of all communities, including those dramatized by Kafka and Kertész.[17]

Beloved may also allow the reader to see that this structure, or what might be called the paradoxical or aporetic "logic" of community, is fractal. It reconstitutes itself anew, in ever new and differentiated forms, in larger and smaller community agglomerations. This happens in a pattern of repetition with a difference, or of what mathematicians call "self-similarity," though it is similarity with a difference. This pattern exists on the global scale of that implacable battle among the three interpenetrating beliefs I named earlier: fundamentalist Christianity, fundamentalist Islam, and tele-techno-global-mediatic-military-capitalism. None of these can exist without the others, without its appropriation of the others or contamination by them. The structure exists on the smaller scale of the relation of each of these global entities to itself. It exists on the yet-smaller scale of each individual nation-state, insofar as sequestered nation-states still exist. It functions in the still-smaller form of whatever local communities maintain themselves within each nation. It exists, finally, on the scale of family relations, and, smaller yet, on the scale of each individual's relation to himself or herself. Each individual, these days or in any other days, is, we know, not a unity, but a community of many warring forces, each struggling for domination.

Just what is this structure? *Beloved* exemplifies its logic on several different scales. Reading the novel carefully helps the reader to understand what the structure in question is and how it works, since it is active and transformative, not just a static pattern. The word "structure," with its implication of a fixed and static spatial pattern, is not a satisfactory or apt term for something so dynamic and complex. Similarly, "web" or "space" or "network" is not an apt term for what interconnected computers, servers, and distributed databases have created by prestidigitalization. What I am talking about can be called a "structure" only if the word is used against its semantic grain, anasemically, as Nicolas Abraham and Maria Torok call it.[18]

The largest version in *Beloved* of this structure-that-is-not-a-structure would be the United States as a whole before, during, and after the Civil War. "A house divided against itself cannot stand," said Abraham Lincoln, citing Mark 3:25. The United States was a house divided against itself, then as now, now when only 51 percent of Americans voted for George W. Bush in the election of 2004, while the rest voted against him and were, many of them, me included, vehemently opposed to him and to his policies during the eight years of his regime. A paradoxical and, strictly speaking, unthinkable, or illogical, logic characterizes this structure on all scales. This nonlogic involves, among other features, a breakdown of clear inside/outside distinctions.

On the one hand, the Civil War was fought between slave states and free states, between the Confederacy and the Union. On the other hand, as the folklore about the Civil War attests, it was an internal war, a "civil war," a war with brother fighting against brother, son against father, each killing what was dearest to him.

On the next-smallest scale, southern society was itself a house divided against itself. It was a community made up of the symbiosis of white slave owners and black slaves, each dependent on the others, economically and culturally, each both at home with the other and fearful of the other night and day as radically alien, other. Though white people brought black slaves to America, many viewed them (and still view them) as alien presences. An example is the current widespread conspiracy theory belief by "birthers" that Barack Obama was not really born in the United States. He would therefore not be qualified to be president, since he would not be a "natural born citizen," as the Constitution requires. Think what it was like to be a white plantation slaveholder living in the big house with as many as a hundred or so slaves, field slaves and house slaves, living close by in the slave cabins. The slave owners must have been, in part of their minds at least, scared to death all the time, fearful, all the time, that they would be killed or their wives and daughters raped. The slaves were simultaneously inside and outside the white community. One can understand, though by no means condone, what motivated the sexual abuse of the slaves, their whippings, tortures, and mutilations, their lynchings. It was an unsuccessful attempt to get the aliens away or to subdue them thoroughly. At the same time every slave they lynched was the destruction of a valuable piece of their property.

On a still smaller scale is the structure of the black "community" itself, if it can be called that, riven as it was by the breaking up of families and by the systematic destruction of any unified togetherness that might develop within a given group of slaves and so become a threat to the whites. This deliberate undoing of community happened according to the normal behavior of enslavers, colonizers, and imperialist conquerors, as, for example, with United States behavior in occupied Iraq, where whatever clan loyalties there may have been were deliberately destroyed as much as possible to make way for the "freedom" of Western-style democracy. The relation of Cincinnati's black community to itself is the main subject of *Beloved*.

On a lower scale still is the relation of each of the characters to the family group, and, finally, the relation of each character to himself or herself. Both these final two versions of this fractal pattern of self-similarity must include another inside/outside relation, namely, the relation of the black "community" as a whole to the "other side," the unseen other world of the dead that is assumed to impinge with physical presence and even violence on this world. Accepting that for these people the existence of the other side is a given is essential to understanding the behavior of *Beloved*'s black community, as in their laying to rest of the ghost of Sethe's slain baby, so they assume. It is essential also to understanding the behavior of individuals within that community, as in Sethe's "impossible" decision to cut her baby daughter's throat so she can get her to safety on the other side, that is, to kill the best part of herself. In a similar way, the behavior of Islamic "terrorist" suicide bombers only makes sense if we take into account their belief that they will become holy martyrs and go straight to a glorious life in heaven, just as the behavior of George W. Bush and company only made sense in the context of their belief that the end of the world was at hand and that only the Christian faithful would be saved, and just as, Derrida observes, the techno-capitalist system depends on faith in the working of more and more complicated machines and software programs whose functioning we do not understand.[19] My e-mail program, when it cannot "get through," gives me a message that says, "Connection terminated because the other side is not responding." Cyberspace too, like Morrison's black community, has a this side and another, ghostly, spectral, phantasmatic side.

On all these scales the structure is like that of the body's immune system repelling foreign invaders and then turning its immune system against itself in what is called "autoimmunity." I take this figure from Jacques Derrida's brilliant exploitation of it in "Faith and Knowledge" ("Foi et savoir") and elsewhere.[20] I owe to W. J. T. Mitchell, however, the recognition that there is something strange about this figure, namely, that it is a figure of a figure, whichever way you look at it.[21] Biologists appropriated an entire social and political vocabulary, including the notion of aliens to the community or foreign invaders who must be repelled, to name the operation of the body's immune system and the disaster of autoimmunity. The medical terms are then reappropriated by Derrida to describe a feature of human communities.

Derrida's strikingly original insight, made with the exuberance and even wildness characteristic of "the late Derrida," is the claim that both immunity and autoimmunity in one way or another characterize every community. "We feel ourselves," says Derrida, "authorized to make this expansion and to speak of a sort of general logic of autoimmunization. It seems indispensable to us today for thinking the relations between faith and knowledge, religion and science, as well as the duplicity of sources in general."[22] It follows that community cannot be understood except by way of this structure. Derrida emphasizes that immunity and autoimmunity operate in any community mechanically, spontaneously, inevitably, willy-nilly, not as a result of choices members of the community make or that the community collectively makes. Every community strives to keep itself pure, safe, "sacrosanct," uncontaminated by aliens.

A spectacular example of this is the German anti-Semitism that led to the Shoah, to the attempt to kill every last Jew, men, women, children. At the same time, every community is inhabited by a suicidal tendency to shoot itself in the foot, as we say, in the act of trying to shoot the invader. The German Holocaust was in the end a suicidal self-destruction of the Third Reich. This was true even in the sense that they killed innumerable potential scholars, scientists, artists, poets, as well as innumerable good ordinary people, in murdering those six million. They also ensured the end of their regime by relentlessly pursuing their extermination project and by their attempts at imperialist expansion. The Shoah was an autoimmune act with a vengeance.

In a somewhat similar way, Franz Kafka's attempt to avoid what he saw as the potentially malign performative power of his work to help bring about the Shoah that he vaguely foresaw was thwarted by Max Brod's refusal, after Kafka's death, to carry out his friend's command that he burn Kafka's manuscripts. What Kafka wrote, once it was saved and published, had the unintended result he feared, even if only in the sense of being open to being read, as I have done in this book and as others have done before me, as premonitions of Auschwitz. Kafka's "In the Penal Colony," for example, dramatizes suicidal autoimmunity in the way the officer who operates the machine (*Apparat*) that kills the condemned prisoner then kills himself with his own execution apparatus.[23]

It is easy to see both these tendencies at work in the United States' "War on Terror." We spend billions on "homeland security" while at the same time sacrificing the lives of thousands of our citizens in the Iraq and Afghanistan wars, not to speak of the tens of thousands of soldiers who return with post-traumatic stress syndrome. We have also become war criminals in our torture of prisoners and by causing the deaths of one million Iraqis and the displacement or exile of millions more. We often direct our immunity army, the FBI, the CIA, and the more hidden security forces, against our own citizens or against refugees or immigrants to whom we ought to owe hospitality. We do this under the authority of the Patriot Act. This is an Orwellian name if there ever was one, since the Patriot Act is designed to take away the civil liberties of all patriotic United States citizens, as well as of the alien "terrorists" we are taught to assume we must be harboring in our midst, like ghosts who have invaded the homeland. Our government and its corporate and financial-sector sponsors succeeded in the eight short years of the Bush regime in nearly bankrupting the United States with gigantic deficits; in putting our banking and manufacturing systems on the verge of collapse, so that almost a trillion taxpayers' dollars had to be spent to bail them out; in bringing about the worst recession since the Great Depression, accompanied by high unemployment and other miseries, such as mortgage foreclosures, for millions; in putting our reputation around the world at a low ebb; in allowing global warming to continue unchecked; and in allowing over forty million of our citizens to go on living without health insurance. If these people had gone about deliberately to wreck the country they could not have done a better job of it. If they ever regain political power, they will just continue the self-destructive work they began under Bush's presidency (as they are already doing [March 2011]).

It is easy to see, in the light of what I have said already about *Beloved*, how that novel exemplifies, in its own specific way and at various fractal levels of self-similarity, the strange logic of what Derrida calls "*auto-co-immunity*," "community as *com-mon auto-immunity*."[24] In the War Between the States, the United States turned its self-protective apparatus against itself. In the institution of slavery in the South, the slave owners, in order to keep themselves safe, had to destroy their own property, in lynchings, burnings, rapes, tortures. This was the property on which their economic livelihood depended. When schoolteacher shoots Sixo he does so regretfully, not because he is any more compassionately reluctant to kill a slave than he would be to kill a dog, or a horse, or a cow, or a pig, but because Sixo has done valuable work for the farm and he recognizes now that he is no longer useful for that work: "This one will never be suitable," says schoolteacher before they shoot Sixo after having begun to burn him alive, in a horrible scene in which Sixo laughs as they torture and then shoot him (266–67). Schoolteacher has the same regret when he confronts Sethe with her dead baby in her arms and realizes there is no point in taking her or her surviving children back to slavery: "Right off it was clear, to schoolteacher especially, that there was nothing here to claim. . . . Now she'd gone wild, due to the mishandling of the nephew who'd overbeat her and made her cut and run. Schoolteacher had chastised that nephew, telling him to think—just think—what would his own horse do if you beat it beyond the point of education. . . . See what happened when you overbeat creatures God had given you the responsibility of—the trouble it was, and the loss. The whole lot was lost now. Five. . . . Because the woman—something was wrong with her. She was looking at him now, and if his other nephew could see that look he would learn the lesson for sure: you just can't mishandle creatures and expect success" (175, 176).

I have said that Sethe's murder of her baby daughter and attempt to kill her other children and herself is the leitmotif of *Beloved*, the event around which the whole narrative circles, in a repeated act of rememorization. The actual murder of Beloved is never presented directly, in so many words. It is the absent center of the novel. It is approached from several perspectives, from Sethe's viewpoint when she tries to figure out how she can explain what she has done to Paul D, from Paul D's perspective, from that of Beloved herself, and, in the passage just cited, as it was seen by schoolteacher. The spatial distance between schoolteacher and Sethe with her dying baby in her arms is an example of the significance of spatial deployment in all my leitmotifs. Sethe and schoolteacher face one another across the unbridgeable gap between slave and slave owner, each defining the "subject position" of the other.

In an earlier version of my reading of Morrison's novel, "Boundaries in *Beloved*," I have identified some of the frontiers that structure the novel: the Mason Dixon line that divided free states from slave states at the time of the Civil War, the Ohio River as the boundary dividing Kentucky, a slave state, from Ohio, a free state, the line between this world and the supernatural "other side" that is so important a presupposition in this novel, the separation between slave and slave owner, marked by fences and doors, on a plantation like Sweet Home.[25] In the scene in which schoolteacher confronts Sethe with her dying baby in her arms, that boundary is concretely figured not only in the entrance to the woodshed where the murder was committed, the threshold schoolteacher crosses to face Sethe, but in the fence at the edge of the yard beyond which Sethe first sees schoolteacher's hat and knows he has come to take her and her children back into slavery. When Sethe comes back to 124 Bluestone Road from serving her jail sentence, she notices with relief that the fence is gone (192). The entire spatial layout of 124 Bluestone Road is established early in the novel: its rooms (such as the "keeping room," adjacent to the kitchen, where Baby Suggs takes to her bed and dies and where Denver nurses Beloved back to health), windows, the white staircase Sethe's "crawling-already?" (110) baby had so loved to climb, doors, porch, and environs (yard, field, woods beyond, and stream beyond the woods; road out front leading in one direction to Cincinnati). This complex dwelling place serves the reader as a mise-en-scène. For the reader it is an imaginary mental space within which much of the novel's action "takes place," in the strong sense both of happening in a man-made spatial milieu and of making space a humanized place. An early passage, for example, describes the last part of Denver's route back to the house from her secret room in the woods formed of a circle of five boxwood bushes that have grown together both around and overhead: "There was only one door to the house and to get to it from the back you had to walk all the way around to the front of 124, past the storeroom, past the cold house [a separate small house to store meat, milk, and other perishables in hot weather, in those days before refrigerators], the privy, the shed [where Beloved was killed], on around to the porch" (36). *Beloved* is full of accurate notations of what houses, furnishings, clothes, food, and so on would have been like in a house on the edge of Cincinnati at the time of the Civil War and in the decades after.

I can vouch indirectly for that accuracy because all these details are so much like what the houses in rural Virginia of my grandparents on both sides were still like in the 1930s.

The relation between slave owners and slaves, the reader can see, is a terrifying example of autoimmunitary logic, as is the relation between Nazis and Jews during the Holocaust. The black community within itself, for example, the black community of Cincinnati, as an entity somewhat artificially thought of as separate from the white community, repeats the logic of autoimmunity on another scale. In order to keep itself safe, unscathed, pure, exempt from danger, it must first ostracize Sethe and thereby lose Baby Suggs as its maternal center, and then eventually exorcise Beloved, then gradually forget her, in order to reassimilate Sethe and Denver, the survivors, into the community. It could be argued that the surviving community has only temporarily secured its safety by expelling what is other to it. The apparent celebration of that successful forgetting, that completed mourning for the dead, on the last two pages of the novel is ironized and undercut by the final word, "Beloved." That word, for the reader at least, remembers once more and opens the safe enclosure here to the "other side," over there.

The most salient example of immuno-auto-immunitary logic in *Beloved*, however, is Sethe's relation to Beloved. Two overlapping inside/outside permeable frontiers determine Sethe's life. She makes it to what she believes will be safety and freedom by crossing with the newborn Denver from Kentucky to the other side of the Ohio River, to her mother-in-law's house, to the black community of Cincinnati, and to reunion with her three other children. When she kills her third child, she does so in order to send her, she believes, to sanctuary and safety in another "other side," the realm of death. She intends to send all four of her children and herself there.

In both intentions, she fails. The Fugitive Slave Law makes it possible for schoolteacher to come into a "free state," capture her, and return her to slavery. Far from remaining in sequestered safety in the realm of death, Beloved comes back as a spiteful and unforgiving ghost, first as an invisible mischief maker haunting the house and then, so it appears to Sethe, in the embodied form of the avenging Beloved. Beloved both loves the mother who has killed her and at the same time cannot forgive her for her act. Could you forgive, if you were to have your throat cut by your mother and were to survive death, or to survive in death, and be able to return from the other side to this side, each side so close to the other, in obedience to the law that says those who die badly do not rest in their graves? That assumption, by the way, is an extremely widespread religious and folk belief, appearing, for example, in Yeats, as in the examples I cired earlier in this chapter. It serves as the fundamental given of Shakespeare's *Hamlet* and of Dickens's *The Christmas Carol*, ghost stories both.

The double logic of immunity and autoimmunity governs Sethe's behavior in relation to Beloved and to her other children. On the one hand, she wants safety, enclosure, purity, indemnity, immunity from harm, for herself and for her children, according to her presumption that their life in safety and freedom are worth more than anything in the world to her. Their life is beyond price, priceless. On the other hand, just because they are priceless, she is prepared to sacrifice them in order to save them, to get them to a place of true safety. That sacrifice, moreover, is explicitly described as an act of suicidal autoimmunitary killing. Sethe repeatedly says, in justifying her act to herself, to Paul D, and to Beloved, that her children are the best part of her, the only pure and clean part, her "best thing," her life beyond life. Therefore she must kill them when their purity and cleanness is endangered. Much later in the novel, Denver imagines Sethe's reasons for fearing Beloved might leave their house:

> Leave before Sethe could make her realize that worse than that [having her throat cut]—far worse—was what Baby Suggs died of [her loss of all her children and her abuse as a slave], what Ella knew [she has been sexually abused by the father and son who owned her], what Stamp saw [his wife being sexually abused by their white owner's son] and what made Paul D tremble [he was forced by schoolteacher at Sweet Home to wear a bit, like a horse]. That anybody white could take your whole self for anything that came to mind. Not just work, kill, or maim you, but dirty you. Dirty you so bad you couldn't like yourself anymore. Dirty you so bad you forgot who you were and couldn't think it up. And though she and others lived through and got over it, she could never let it happen to her own. The best thing she was, was her children. Whites might dirty *her* all right, but not her best thing, her beautiful, magical best thing—the part of her that was clean. (295–96)

Morrison is relentless and almost unbearably specific about the sexual and physical abuses slaves suffered, as specific as Kertész, Primo Levi, and others are about the abuses concentration camp prisoners endured. Morrison does not want us to forget what being a slave in the American south was like. Sethe has had her breast milk drunk by schoolteacher's two nephews as schoolteacher watches and takes notes. She has also been savagely beaten before she escapes Sweet Home and makes her way north toward Cincinnati and what she hopes is safety. In order to get the word "Beloved" carved on her murdered baby's tombstone, she has to yield her body for ten minutes to the stone engraver as she stands with her legs spread leaning against a gravestone in the cemetery. Calling her child a "thing" is a powerful irony, since it is because she is Sethe's best thing, the only clean part of her, that Sethe turns her into a thing, that is, into a cadaver. In killing her daughter, Sethe kills, according to her own assertions, herself. Sethe's motives and action follow strictly the double autoimmunitary logic that Derrida claims is a universal, the double source of morality and religion:[26] the impulse toward saving pure and clean life and the impulse toward sacrificing it.

Can We Approve Sethe's Act?

I began by asking whether we can approve of Sethe's murder of her daughter, whether we can see it as ethical, as something we could make a universal law for all mankind. On the one hand, it almost seems as if I am asking the wrong question. If Sethe acts according to the mechanical compulsions of autoimmunitary logic, the logic that also governs the behavior of terrorists and counterterrorists alike and makes suicide bombers today, like George W. Bush during his reign, sometimes seem like somnambulists or robots, zombies manipulated by forces of which they are not aware, then she would seem to be beyond praise or blame. She does what she must do. On the other hand, Sethe says she "decided." She takes responsibility for what she has done by saying defiantly, "I did that" (190). She claims she acted spontaneously but deliberately to get her children to safety on the other side: "I took and put my babies where they'd be safe" (193). Though the community blames Sethe, she never blames herself. She speaks of what she has done as a free, autonomous choice. I think we must have it both ways, illogically and according to the illogical logic of autoimmunity as a doubly displaced metaphor. Though in the body the workings of the immune system are not voluntary, in the social world, the original source of the figure, autoimmunitary acts take place as an irresponsible/responsible response to a demand to decide.

One might even argue that what Sethe does, like Abraham's offering to sacrifice his dearly beloved only son, are exemplary ethical acts, precisely because they are programmed by no moral or community law. They are beyond the law, or outside the law. They exemplify an ethics beyond ethics, or they are religious as opposed to ethical, according to the distinction Kierkegaard makes in *Fear and Trembling* and elsewhere, though Derrida does not follow him in this. The solitude and autonomy of Sethe's decision, its uniqueness, makes it exemplary of all true ethico-religious acts. Such decisions cannot be justified by any appeal to preexisting standards. Judged by such standards, Sethe is guilty of that horrible crime, infanticide, just as Abraham is guilty of being willing to kill his only son. The community is right not to condone what she has done, and Beloved is right not to forgive her mother's treachery. It is not the case that what Sethe does can be made the basis of a universal law for all mankind. What would a community be that made infanticide a universal ethical law, justified, even if only in extreme circumstances? On the other hand, Sethe's act provides a model for the solitude and uniqueness, the singularity, the incommensurability with moral law, the terrifying invidiousness, of every true ethical decision and act. She does the right thing, even though she has no right to do it. The distinction between male and female ethical responsibility and relation to sacrifice breaks down in the light of this insight. Each man and each woman are equally alone when making true ethical decisions. Nevertheless, the social circumstances of men and women are historically different. In early biblical times, it was unlikely that a woman would have been given Abraham's choice, and unlikely under the conditions of American slavery that a man could have been in just Sethe's situation when she had to decide in an instant whether or not to kill her beloved baby daughter. The reader will remember that in Spiegelman's *Maus* it is the woman who has charge of Vladek's beloved son Richieu who poisons him, her own children, and herself in order to keep them from being sent to certain death in the gas chambers. Like Sethe, this woman has to make an instantaneous decision. This exemplifies the comparison between slavery and the Holocaust Morrison herself makes in the interview with Bill Moyers cited earlier.

Jacques Derrida, in *Donner la mort* (*The Gift of Death*) expresses with striking hyperbolic force this dilemma of all ethics beyond ethics or all religio-ethics:

> As soon as I enter into a relation with the other, with the gaze, look, request, love, command [*la demande*], or call of the other, I know that I can respond only by sacrificing ethics, that is, by sacrificing whatever obliges me also to respond, in the same way, in the same instant, to all the others. I offer a gift of death, I betray [*je parjure*], I don't need to raise my knife over my son on Mount Moriah for that. Day and night, at every instant, on all the Mount Moriahs of this world, I am doing that, raising

> my knife over what I love and must love, over the other, this or that other to whom I owe absolute fidelity, incommensurably. Abraham is faithful to God only in his absolute treachery [*dans le parjure*], in the betrayal of his own and of the uniqueness of each one of them, exemplified here in his only beloved son.[27] He would not be able to opt for fidelity to his own, or to his son, unless he were to betray the absolute other: God, if you wish.[28]

In Sethe's case the combination of treachery and fidelity might be expressed by saying that by transporting her baby safely to the other side, she is faithful to that baby and to her boundless love for her, but she is faithful only to her baby as dead, as sacrificed, as the recipient of the "gift of death." Toward that baby as alive, she has committed the worst treachery and betrayal. The revenant that Sethe and the others take Beloved the teenage visitant to be cannot forgive her for that, for having, as she thinks to herself, "taken away my face." The young woman who returns and says her name is "Beloved" may, in the alternative reading, be unwilling to forgive the mother who abandoned her on the slave ship. As a baby on the slave ship she saw her own face in the mother's face, in a strange kind of Lacanian "mirror stage." She then sees that face again years later in Sethe's face.

In order to act rightly, to save her baby from slavery, Sethe must act wrongly. She does not hesitate for a second to make her choice and to send her child to safety on the other side, but that unquiet, spiteful, and unforgiving ghost, so she thinks, comes to reproach her for the irredeemable, infinite debt of her crime against the sanctity of life in the living, her disobedience of the prime biblical injunction, "Thou shalt not kill." Faced with an impossible choice between a live baby in slavery and a dead baby safe on the other side, Sethe chooses the dead one, chooses to give her baby the gift of death, but she pays, inevitably, for that choice.

I claim to have shown that reading *Beloved* is, somewhat surprisingly, useful or even indispensable as an indirect way to understand the mechanisms that govern our present-day world, the world of "terrorists," the War on Terror, the wars in Iraq and Afghanistan, cyberspace, and global tele-techno-military-capitalism. Why, it might be asked, is careful reading of *Beloved* perhaps even better than direct discussion of current politics, in the light of suicidal-auto-immunitary theory, such as Derrida performs in *Philosophy in a Time of Terror* (*Le "concept" du 11 septembre*) and elsewhere?[29] I answer that both are good, but that a small-scale version of the fractal pattern can be seen in more concrete detail. The autoimmunitary logic is expressed in *Beloved* with the affective semantic richness and specificity literature especially has. This linguistic richness will mean, or should mean, that what we call literature will or should survive in one way or another its disappearance into cyberspace. Expressing the pattern in literature proves it on our pulses, as Keats puts it, better than any abstract analysis, however eloquent. The moving story of Sethe's life and Beloved's death brings this logic home to the reader not as an abstract argument, but with an emotional vividness that may make it more likely we shall not only understand, but also take responsibility in our turn to act as best we can on our own Mount Moriahs. God forbid that any of us should be faced with just Sethe's choice, though it may be that we are making such choices all the time, in one way or another, choosing fidelity to some "other" or other, and thereby necessarily choosing to betray the demand some other other makes. As Derrida says, all of us stand at every moment on some Mount Moriah with a knife or a handsaw poised over what we love most, our "best thing."

Coda

This book has been based on several assumptions: (1) That a work of fiction or a work of criticism can be a valid testimony to such events as Auschwitz, or as slavery in the United States, or as our wars in Iraq and Afghanistan and other recent United States catastrophes. (2) That a work of fiction can, after the fact, be seen as proleptic, as a premonition or foreshadowing of later happenings, as Kafka's writings, I claim, anticipate the Shoah. (3) That valid fictional testimonies tend to be more complex narratologically in direct proportion to the closeness of the author to the historical events to which the fiction bears indirect witness. Parts of some of my chapters are in a rather uneasy dialogue with so-called narratology. Most of all, however, I have attempted to present readings of eight novels that will work as adequate testimony to what happened to me when I read them. I also hope they might function as speech acts to instigate others to read these novels for themselves.

Kafka, Keneally, McEwan, Spiegelman, Kertész, Morrison—my test cases of fiction before and after Auschwitz have identified resonances among them. All my texts have shown that perhaps the most urgent legacy of Auschwitz is the way it keeps before us our perpetual responsibility to make "impossible decisions," such as those Morrison's Sethe made or those Kertész's Gyuri made in a life he explicitly compares to moving forward at Auschwitz in the line leading toward the moment of *Selektion*. Kafka's heroes do their best to avoid such decisions, to postpone their ultimate fates, while Kafka's decision to try to ward off forebodings of Auschwitz in his writing by having those writings burned unread, in a catastrophic conflagration, was thwarted by Max Brod's decision to save and publish the manuscripts. Was that a good thing or a bad thing? That is a perhaps impossible decision each reader will have to make for herself or himself. I think it was a good thing, but a lot hangs on just how you read Kafka.

Notes

PREFACE

1. See Martin Heidegger, "Der Ursprung des Kunstwerkes," in *Holzwege* (Frankfurt am Main: Vittorio Klostermann, 1972), 7–68; Heidegger, "The Origin of the Work of Art," in *Poetry, Language, Thought*, trans. Albert Hofstadter (New York: Harper & Row, 1971), 17–87.

2. Stéphane Mallarmé, "Crise de vers," in *Oeuvres complètes*, ed. Henri Mondor and G. Jean-Aubry, Éd. de la Pléiade (Paris: Gallimard, 1945), 368.

3. Theodor W. Adorno, "Cultural Criticism and Society," in *Prisms*, trans. Samuel and Shierry Weber (Cambridge, Mass.: MIT Press, 1983), 33 (henceforth cited by page number).

4. Niemand
zeugt für den
Zeugen.

[Nobody
bears witness for the
witness.]

Paul Celan, "Aschenglorie," in *Breathturn*, bilingual ed., trans. Pierre Joris (Los Angeles: Sun & Moon Press, 1995), 179, 178.

5. Christopher R. Browning, *Nazi Policy, Jewish Workers, German Killers* (Cambridge: Cambridge University Press, 2000), 32. Cited in Robert Eaglestone, *The Holocaust and the Postmodern* (Oxford: Oxford University Press, 2004), 1.

6. See n. 5.

CHAPTER ONE

1. Jean-Luc Nancy, *La communauté désoeuvrée* (Paris: Christian Bourgois, 2004), 11 (henceforth cited as *CD*).

2. Jean-Luc Nancy, *The Inoperative Community*, trans. Peter Connor, Lisa Garbus, Michael Holland, and Simona Sawney (Minneapolis: University of Minnesota Press, 1991), 1 (henceforth cited as *IC*); trans. modified.

3. Wallace Stevens, *The Collected Poems* (New York: Vintage, 1990), 418–19 (henceforth cited as *CP*).

4. Translator's note in Jean-Luc Nancy, *Being Singular Plural*, trans. Robert D. Richardson and Anne E. O'Byrne (Stanford, Calif.: Stanford University Press, 2000) , 201 (henceforth cited as *BSP*). The OED defines the word as (1) "to appear, make one's appearance, show one's face, esp. at a formal assembly," and as (2) "to appear in a court, as a party to a cause, either in person or by counsel."

5. Here are some of these: Benedict Anderson, *Imagined Communities: Reflections on the Origin and Spread of Nationalism* (New York: Random House, 1983); Jean-Luc Nancy, *Être singulier pluriel* (Paris: Galilée, 1996) (henceforth cited as *ESP*); *BSP*; Georges Bataille, *L'Apprenti Sorcier du cercle communiste démocratique à Acéphale: Textes, lettres et documents (1932–39)*, ed. Marina Galletti, notes trans. from Italian by Natália Vital (Paris: Éditions de la Différence, 1999); Maurice Blanchot, *La communauté inavouable* (Paris: Minuit, 1983); Blanchot, *The Unavowable Community*, trans. Pierre Joris (Barrytown, N.Y.: Station Hill Press, 1988); Giorgio Agamben, *La comunità che viene* (Turin: Einaudi, 1990); Agamben, *The Coming Community*, trans. Michael Hardt (Minneapolis: University of Minnesota Press, 1993); Alphonso Lingis, *The Community of Those Who Have Nothing in Common* (Bloomington: Indiana University Press, 1994).

6. For English translations of these essays see Martin Heidegger, "Building Dwelling Thinking," in *Poetry, Language, Thought*, trans. Albert Hofstadter (New York: Harper & Row, 1971), 143–61; and Heidegger, *Elucidations of Hölderlin's Poetry*, trans. Keith Hoeller (New York: Humanity Books, 2000). For the German originals see Martin Heidegger, "Bauen Wohenen Denken," in *Vorträge und Aufsätze* (Pfullingen: Neske, 1967), 2:19–36; and Heidegger, *Erläuterungen zu Hölderlins Dichtung*, 2nd ed. (Frankfurt am Main: Vittorio Klostermann, 1951).

7. Jennifer Bajorek, "The Offices of Homeland Security; or, Hölderlin's Terrorism," *Critical Inquiry* 31, no. 4 (2005): 874–902.

8. See W. B. Yeats, "A Prayer for My Daughter," in *The Variorum Edition of the Poems of W. B. Yeats*, 7th printing, ed. Peter Allt and Russell K. Alspach (New York: Macmillan, 1977), 405.

9. Jennifer Bajorek, "The Offices of Homeland Security; or, Hölderlin's Terrorism," online file of *Critical Inquiry* essay, accessed January 2010, http://www.journals.uchicago.edu/doi/full/10.1086/44518.

10. I have discussed Nancy's concept of community briefly from the perspective of its contrast with Derrida's idea of (non)community in "Derrida Enisled," chap. 6 of my *For Derrida* (New York: Fordham University Press, 2009), 119–20.

11. Jacques Derrida and Maurizio Ferraris, *A Taste for the Secret*, trans. Giacomo Donis, ed. Giacomo Donis and David Webb (Cambridge: Polity, 2001), 25.

12. Jean-Luc Nancy, *Le partage des voix* (Paris: Galilée, 1982).

13. Yet a third book on community by Nancy, *La communauté affrontée* (Paris: Galilée, 2001), extends but does not contradict what he says in the two much longer books.

14. Matthew Arnold, *The Poems*, ed. Kenneth Allott (London: Longmans, 1965), 242.

15. Charles Baudelaire, "Au lecteur," in *Fleurs du mal*, in *Oeuvres complètes*, ed. Y.-G. le Dantec, Éd. de la Pléiade (Paris: Gallimard, 1954), 82.

16. Blanchot, *The Unavowable Community*, 42–43. A longer passage on the previous page can serve as a gloss or preparation for the paragraph about Tristan and Isolde. Blanchot is speaking about the relation between the two lovers in Marguerite Duras's *La maladie de la mort* (*The Malady of Death*):

> In the homogeneity—the affirmation of the Same—understanding demands that the heterogeneous appear suddenly, i.e., the absolute Other in terms of which any relationship signifies: no relationship, the impossibility that willing and perhaps even desire ever cross the uncrossable, in the sudden and clandestine meeting (outside of time) that annuls itself with the devastating feeling that is never certain to be experienced by the one whom this movement consigns to the other perhaps by depriving him of his "self." A devastating feeling that is, in truth, beyond all feeling, ignoring pathos, overflowing consciousness, breaking with self-involvement and demanding—without rights—that which removes itself from all demands, because in my request there is not only the beyond of what could satisfy it, but the beyond of what is requested. An overbidding, an outrage of life that cannot be contained within life and which thus, interrupting the pretension of always persevering in being, opens to the strangeness of an interminable dying or of an endless "error." (41)

17. Jacques Derrida, *Rogues: Two Essays on Reason*, trans. Pascale-Anne Brault and Michael Naas (Stanford, Calif.: Stanford University Press, 2005), 60; Derrida, *Voyous: Deux essays sur la raison* (Paris: Galilée, 2003), 90.

18. Jacques Derrida, *Séminaire: La bête et le souverain*, vol. 2, *2002–2003*, ed. Michel Lisse, Marie-Louise Mallet, and Ginette Michaud (Paris: Galilée, 2010), 31. From 1st seminar, my trans.

19. See Wang Fengzhen and Shaobo Xie, "Introductory Notes: Dialogues on Globalization and Indigenous Cultures," in "Globalization and Indigenous Cultures," special issue, *Ariel* 34, no. 1 (January 1903), 1–13. See also my essay in that issue, "The Indigene and the Cybersurfer," 31–52. This present chapter adapts a good bit of material from that essay.

20. Wang Fengzhen and Shaobo Zie, "*Globalization and Indigenous Cultures*: Proposal for *Ariel* Special Issue 2003" (computer file circulated to participants), 1.

21. J. Hillis Miller, *The Medium Is the Maker: Browning, Freud, Derrida and the New Telepathic Technologies* (Brighton: Sussex Academic Press, 2009).

22. Mark Warschauer, "Demystifying the Digital Divide," *Scientific American*, August 2003, 29–32, 42–47 (last accessed online November 2009).

23. Katherine Hayles's abundant and widely influential work goes from *How We Became Posthuman: Virtual Bodies in Cybernetics, Literature, and Informatics* (Chicago: University of Chicago Press, 1999) to *My Mother Was a Computer* (Chicago: University of Chicago Press, 2005) and *Electronic Literature: New Horizons for the Literary* (Notre Dame, Ind.: University of Notre Dame Press, 2008). For Donna Haraway, see *Simians, Cyborgs, and Women: The Reinvention of Nature*) (New York: Routledge, 1991). For Derrida, see *Papier Machine* (Paris: Galilée, 2001); and Derrida, *Paper Machine*, trans. Rachel Bowlby (Stanford, Calif.: Stanford University Press, 2005). For a collection of essays about the intermediations of print technologies, film technologies, and digital technologies, see Kiene Brillenburg Wurth, ed., *Remediated Literature* (tentative title) (New York: Fordham University Press, forthcoming in fall 2011). This book contains abundant references to the immense literature that already exists on these topics. One somewhat disquieting sign of globalization is that the essays in this book are all in English, though many of the authors appear to have English as a second language.

24. See *Wikipedia*, s.v. "Buchenwald Concentration Camp," accessed November 14, 2010, http://en.wikipedia.org/wiki/Buchenwald_concentration_camp.

25. Cited from Foucault's *Power/Knowledge* by Giorgio Agamben in an essay on Foucault, "What Is an Apparatus," in *What Is an Apparatus? and Other Essays*, trans. David Kishik and Stefan Pedatella (Stanford, Calif.: Stanford University Press, 2009), 2. This paragraph and the next appropriate, modify, and extend sentences from an as-yet-unpublished essay of mine, "Anachronistic Reading."

26. Franz Kafka, *The Office Writings*, ed. Stanley Corngold, Jack Greenberg, and Benno Wagner, trans. Eric Patton with Ruth Hein (Princeton, N.J.: Princeton University Press, 2009). Both Wallace Stevens and Franz Kafka, by a strange happenstance, were high-level lawyers in accident insurance companies. Stevens worked as a vice president for the Hartford Accident and Indemnity Company. On the one hand, Kafka's office writings are fascinating, as are the commentaries and factual data the editors provide. Here are documents the great creative writer Franz Kafka wrote as a busy lawyer in a huge government bureaucracy. The editors are right to seek and to find parallels with Kafka's fictional writings, diaries, and letters. On the other hand, these writings with their endless nitpicking legal detail are bewildering and, it must be said, boring, like most bureaucratic documents, just as are, in their own way, the lengthy statements to Joseph K. made by the lawyer, Huld, and by the artist, Titorelli, in *The Trial*, though Joseph K.'s life depends on listening carefully, and to K. by Bürgel in *The Castle*. Bürgel's virtually endless and overscrupulous account of the responsibilities and evasions of responsibility by Castle officials puts K. to sleep, though if he had listened, he might have found a way to the Castle after all. All these scenes have their grimly comic side.

27. Louis Althusser, "Ideology and Ideological State Apparatuses (Notes towards an Investigation)," in *Lenin and Philosophy and Other Essays*, trans. Ben Brewster (New York: Monthly Review Press, 1972).

28. Stanley Fish, *Is There a Text in This Class? The Authority of Interpretive Communities* (Cambridge, Mass.: Harvard University Press, 1980).

29. Jacques Derrida, *L'université sans condition* (Paris: Galilée, 2001); Derrida, "The University without Condition," trans. Peggy Kamuf, in *Without Alibi*, ed. and trans. Peggy Kamuf (Stanford, Calif.: Stanford University Press, 2002), 202–37.

30. Miller, *For Derrida*; see esp. 130–31.

31. Derrida and Ferraris, *A Taste for the Secret*, 27. I have discussed this passage at some length in *For Derrida* (New York: Fordham University Press, 2009), 187–90. Derrida here claims he is not gregarious. *Gregge* is of course related to the English word "gregarious." It means "happy to be with others," to herd with them. Arnold Davidson tells me that *gregge* not only means "herd" in the sense of "a herd of sheep," but also has a special modern meaning as the name for the team of cyclists who help the star rider win a given segment of the race.

32. Gilles Deleuze and Félix Guattari, *A Thousand Plateaus: Capitalism and Schizophrenia*, trans. Brian Massumi (Minneapolis: University of Minnesota Press, 1987) (henceforth cited as *TP*).

33. U. Weinreich, W. Labov, and M. Herzog, "Empirical Foundations for a Theory of Language," in *Directions for Historical Linguistics*, ed. W. Lehmann and Y. Malkeiel (Austin: University of Texas Press, 1968), 125.

34. Gilles Deleuze and Félix Guattari, *Kafka: Toward a Minor Literature*, trans. Dana Polan (Minneapolis: University of Minnesota Press, 1986) (henceforth cited as *K*).

CHAPTER TWO

1. Cited by Walter Benjamin, *The Arcades Project*, trans. Howard Eiland and Kevin McLaughlin (Cambridge, Mass.: Belknap Press of Harvard University Press, 1999), 4, from Jules Michelet, "Avenir! Avenir!" *Europe* 19, no. 73 (January 15, 1929): 6.

2. Russell Samolsky, *Apocalyptic Futures: Marked Bodies and the Violence of the Text in Kafka, Conrad, and Coetzee* (New York: Fordham University Press, forthcoming in fall 2011). The first section of his chap. 1 is "Kafka and Shoah."

3. Gustave Janouch, *Conversations with Kafka*, trans. Goronwy Rees (New York: New Directions, 1971), 150.

4. Franz Kafka, *The Diaries, 1910–1923*, ed. Max Brod, trans. Joseph Kresh and Martin Greenberg, with the cooperation of Hannah Arendt (New York: Schocken Books, 1976), 399.

5. Walter Benjamin, *Illuminations: Essays and Reflections*, ed. Hannah Arendt (New York: Schocken Books, 1969), 143.

6. Janouch, *Conversations with Kafka*, 139.

7. Werner Hamacher, "The Gesture in the Name: On Benjamin and Kafka," in *Premises: Essays on Philosophy and Literature from Kant to Celan*, trans. Peter Fenves (Cambridge, Mass.: Harvard University Press, 1996), 299 (henceforth cited as Hamacher). For Deleuze and Guattari, see their *Kafka: Toward a*

Minor Literature, trans. Dana Polan (Minneapolis: University of Minnesota Press, 1986).

8. I have cited the standard English translation rather than the one made for the translation into English of Hamacher's essay: Walter Benjamin, "Franz Kafka: On the Tenth Anniversary of His Death," in *Selected Writings*, vol. 2, *1927–1934*, trans. Rodney Livingstone and others (Cambridge, Mass.: Belknap Press of Harvard University Press, 1999), 808 (henceforth cited as Benjamin). The translation of Benjamin's Kafka essay is by Harry Zohn.

9. For two moving photographs of Kafka with his sister Ottla, as well as many other photographs of Kafka, his family, and his friends, see http://www.kafka-franz.com/kafka-Biography.htm (last accessed May 14, 2010).

10. Imre Kertész, *Fatelessness*, trans. Tim Wilkinson (New York: Vintage International, 2004), 111 (henceforth cited as Kertész).

11. See Frank Rich, "The Real-Life '24' of Summer 2008," *New York Times*, July 13, 2008, http://www.nytimes.com/2008/07/13/opinion/13rich.html?th&emc=th (last accessed May 14, 2010), for a chilling account of the Kafkaesque or Orwellian situation in the executive branch of our government during George W. Bush's time as president. Rich's account is a review of Janet Meyer's book *The Dark Side*. "Antonio Taguba, the retired major general who investigated detainee abuse for the Army," writes Rich, "concluded that 'there is no longer any doubt' that 'war crimes were committed.' Ms. Mayer uncovered another damning verdict: Red Cross investigators flatly told the C.I.A. last year that America was practicing torture and vulnerable to war-crimes charges." So active was the fear that former officials high in the Bush administration, including the former attorney general, would be arrested and tried for war crimes in international courts that they were advised not to travel outside the United States except to two "safe" countries: "So hot is the speculation that war-crimes trials will eventually follow in foreign or international courts that Lawrence Wilkerson, Colin Powell's former chief of staff, has publicly advised Mr. Feith, Mr. Addington and Alberto Gonzales, among others, to 'never travel outside the U.S., except perhaps to Saudi Arabia and Israel.'" Of course, the real guilty ones are President Bush and, especially, Vice President Cheney. One of the links in Rich's story contains the following circumstantial account of one Iraqi's experience:

> Of the 11 men evaluated in the Physicians for Human Rights report, four were detained in Afghanistan between late 2001 and early 2003, and later sent to Guantanamo. The remaining seven were detained in Iraq in 2003.
>
> One of the Iraqis, identified by the pseudonym Laith, was arrested with his family at his Baghdad home in the early morning of Oct. 19, 2003. He was taken to a location where he was beaten, stripped to his underwear and threatened with execution, the report says.
>
> "Laith" told the examiners he was then taken to a second site, where he was photographed in humiliating positions and given electric shocks to his genitals.

Finally, he was taken to Abu Ghraib, where he spent the first 35 to 40 days in isolation in a small cage, enduring being suspended in the cage and other "stress positions."

He was released on June 24, 2004, without charge. (Warren P. Strobel, "General Who Probed Abu Ghraib Says Bush Officials Committed War Crimes," *McClatchy*, June 18, 2008, http://www.mcclatchydc.com/251/story/41514.html [last accessed November 29, 2010])

12. Or *The Man Who Disappeared*, or *Missing*: the novel has all these titles in different English translations. Kafka sometimes called it *Der Verschollene*, which means "the disappeared one." "Disappeared," you will remember, is the name given to those under totalitarian regimes who just vanish one day, after police or soldiers come to their doors, like that Iraqi named "Laith" whom United States soldiers or intelligence men arrested, though he was lucky enough to "reappear," what was left of him. *Desaparecido* was the term used in Argentina and Uruguay during the bad times there for those who were arrested and then just vanished for good. The term is still used in Chile for those who vanished in the 1970s after the coup. The United States has "disappeared" quite a number of people during the so-called War on Terror.

13. Franz Kafka, *Amerika (The Man Who Disappeared)*, trans. Michael Hofmann (New York: New Directions, 2002), 177 (citations from this translation will henceforth be identified by page number followed by "e"); Kafka, *Der Verschollene*, ed. Jost Schillemeit (Frankfurt am Main: Fischer Taschenbuch Verlag, 1994), 264 (citations from this edition will henceforth be identified by page number followed by "g").

14. For a photograph of this gateway see *Wikipedia*, s.v. "Buchenwald Concentration Camp," accessed November 29, 2010, http://en.wikipedia.org/wiki/Buchenwald_concentration_camp. I have seen this gateway with my own eyes. It is disarmingly small and decorative, though thousands and thousands entered through it to death or to abusive imprisonment. In this chapter and others I have dared to make several references to *Wikipedia*. The online encyclopedia *Wikipedia*, even more than any other encyclopedia, must be used with care and with suspicion, since the entries are anonymous and may be changed by anyone. The entries I have used, however, are supported by links to published material and are apparently trustworthy. I can testify from my own experience, for example, that the photograph of the Buchenwald gate is authentic. The entries I have used have also remained the same over years. This means both that they have most likely been vetted and that they have not been maliciously changed.

15. Franz Kafka, *The Trial*, trans. Breon Mitchell (New York: Schocken, 1998), 216 (henceforth cited as *T*); Kafka, *Der Proceß*, ed. Malcolm Pasley (Frankfurt am Main: S. Fischer Verlag, 1990), 293, 294 (henceforth cited as *P*).

16. Franz Kafka, *The Great Wall of China: Stories and Reflections*, trans. Willa and Edwin Muir (New York: Schocken, 1946), 287, trans. modified. For the German see Franz Kafka, "Betrachtungen über Sünde, Leid, Hoffnung und

der wahren Weg," accessed November 29, 2010, http://gutenberg.spiegel.de/?id=5&xid=1348&kapitel=3&cHash=663344485asuende#gb_found.

17. Ibid., 283.

18. Jean-Luc Nancy, in an essay called "Forbidden Representation," proposes the most cogent explanation I have encountered for how the Shoah came to happen and for why it is so difficult to "represent." (See Jean-Luc Nancy, *The Ground of the Image*, trans. Jeff Fort [New York: Fordham University Press, 2005], 27–50 [henceforth cited as "FR"]. The French original is in Jean-Luc Nancy, *Au fond des images* [Paris: Galilée, 2003].) I shall discuss Nancy's essay in my chapter on Kertész, chap. 6.

19. See *Wikipedia*, s.v. "Zyklon B," accessed May 15, 2010, http://en.wikipedia.org/wiki/Zyklon_B.

20. See the extremely disturbing photographic sequence, with explanatory captions, Holocaust Survivors Remembrance Project: "Forget You Not": Oliver Lustig, Text Presentation of Historic Holocaust Photographs from *The Auschwitz Album: The Story of a Transport*, accessed November 29, 2010, http://isurvived.org/Survivors_Folder/Lustig_Oliver/Commentary-PhotoAlbum-2.html#Up.

21. Jean-Luc Nancy, *The Inoperative Community*, trans. Peter Connor, Lisa Garbus, Michael Holland, and Simona Sawney (Minneapolis: University of Minnesota Press, 1991), 1; Nancy, *La communauté désoeuvrée* (Paris: Christian Bourgois, 2004), 11.

22. On this mode of "failure" in Kafka's writings, see Hamacher, 294–98.

23. Cited by Maurice Blanchot in "Kafka and Literature," in *The Work of Fire*, trans. Charlotte Mandell (Stanford, Calif.: Stanford University Press, 1995), 12. All Blanchot's Kafka essays, which are surely among the best readings of Kafka, have been conveniently collected, in the original French, in a single volume, *De Kafka à Kafka* (Paris: Gallimard, 1981). The English translations of these essays are dispersed among the various volumes of Blanchot's essays that have been recently published, primarily by Stanford University Press. An enormous and distinguished secondary literature on Kafka exists. Other notable essays on Kafka are the ones by Walter Benjamin and Werner Hamacher, cited above, and Jacques Derrida's "Before the Law," trans. Avital Ronell and Christine Roulston, in *Acts of Literature*, ed. Derek Attridge (New York: Routledge, 1992), 181–220.

24. *T*, 3, trans. slightly altered; "etwas Böses" means "anything bad or wrong," not "anything truly wrong," as Breon Mitchell's translation puts it; *P*, 7.

25. All these except "The Metamorphosis" may be found in a new authoritative translation, *Kafka's Selected Stories*, trans. and ed. Stanley Corngold, Norton Critical Edition (New York: W. W. Norton, 2007) (henceforth cited as *Selected Stories*).

26. See Hamacher, 309–18, for a brilliant investigation of this feature of Kafka's work.

27. Werner Hamacher's essay on Kafka, cited in n. 7, contains brilliant and definitive discussions of these two related aspects of Kafka's work, human-animal-thing-machines and multilingual puns. Hamacher is particularly perceptive in his discussion of "Odradek," the word and the thing, in what his translator,

Peter Fenves, translates as "The Cares of a Family Man" (Hamacher, 318–29). I have written about this text in "Ecotechnics: Ecotechnological Odradek," forthcoming.

28. See the second epigraph for chap. 1.

29. For such a photograph, one among dozens and dozens, of a postemancipation lynching, see no. 5 of James Allen, *Without Sanctuary: Photographs and Postcards of Lynching in America*, accessed November 29, 2010, http://www.withoutsanctuary.org/main.html (last accessed May 15, 2010). This photo records a double lynching of 1900 in Kansas, not Oklahoma. Many of these photographs were circulated on postcards, as, apparently, was this one, large as it is. The caption reads: "The corpses of George and Ed Silsbee. January 20, 1900. Fort Scott, Kansas. A large group of spectators holding kerosene lamps, downed fence in foreground. Gelatin silver print. Cabinet card. 7 × 10 in. Etched in negative, 'George and Ed SILSBEE HANGED by a MOB of CITIZENS IN FRONT OF JAIL. Jan. 20, 1900. Fort Scott Kan. Flash Light by Dabbs.'" These photographs are available in James Allen, et al., *Without Sanctuary: Lynching Photography in America* (Santa Fe, N.M.: Twin Palms, 2000).

30. Franz Kafka, *The Diaries: 1910–1923*, ed. Max Brod, trans. Joseph Kresh and Martin Greenberg, with the cooperation of Hannah Arendt (New York: Schocken, 2000), 252 (henceforth cited as *Diaries*).

31. Mauro Nervi, *The Kafka Project*, accessed November 29, 2010, http://www.kafka.org/index.php?id=111,101,0,0,1,0.

32. Franz Kafka, "Reflections on Sin, Pain, Hope, and the True Way," in Kafka, *The Great Wall of China*, 290.

33. "The Worry of the Father of the Family" (Corngold's translation of "Die Sorge des Hausvaters") in *Selected Stories*, 73. I have cited the German original from Nervi, *The Kafka Project*: *Ein Landarzt: Kleine Erzählungen*, accessed November 29, 2010, http://www.kafka.org/index.php?landarzt. The German does not have page numbers. I have discussed Kafka's short text at length in "Ecotechnics: Ecotechnological Odradek," in *Telemorphosis: Theory in the Era of Climate Change*, vol. 1, ed. Tom Cohen (Ann Arbor: Open Humanities Press in Conjunction with the University of Michigan Library's Scholarly Publishing Office, forthcoming in 2011).

For whatever it is worth, which is probably not much, Kafka himself had no permanent residence. Guides to those who visit Prague, as I know from experience, point out apartment after apartment where Kafka is said to have lived, mostly with his family, if what he did can be called living, which Kafka himself doubted. Most of these apartments are around the famous Old Town Square or on adjacent side streets, but at least one is in a quite different part of the city, across the river and near Prague Castle. Like Joyce in Zurich, Kafka moved a lot. Joyce moved from flat to flat because he could not pay his rent and was evicted. Kafka moved because his father was rising up in the world and wanted to live in more and more pretentious apartments.

34. George Poulet, *Études sur le temps humain* (Paris: Plon, 1950); Poulet, *Studies in Human Time*, trans. Elliott Coleman (Baltimore: Johns Hopkins Press, 1956).

35. Hartmut Binder, *Kafka-Commentar* (Munich: Winkler, 1976).

36. Franz Kafka, *Amerika*, trans. Edwin Muir, afterword by Max Brod (New York: New Directions, 1946), back cover (henceforth cited as *Amerika*, Muir trans.).

37. Franz Kafka, *The Castle*, trans. Edwin and Willa Muir, introduction by Thomas Mann (New York: Knopf, 1951), 329–30 (henceforth cited as *The Castle*, Muir trans.).

38. Franz Kafka, *The Castle: A New Translation Based on the Restored Text*, trans. Mark Harman (New York: Schocken, 1998), 316.

39. This is the sequence as presented in the new editions in both German and English. They seem to belong in this order because of the implicit chronology of the story, and because of indications in the manuscripts and in Kafka's letters, but they exist as free-floating fragmentary narrative segments that Kafka never got around to completing and inserting in a finished manuscript. See the "Nachbemerkung" by Jost Schillemeit in the new authoritative German edition (323–27g) for an account of the composition and the state of the manuscripts.

40. Nancy refers to the frequent use of the term "dramaturgy" in Wolfgang Sofsky, *The Order of Terror: The Concentration Camp*, trans. William Templer (Princeton, N.J.: Princeton University Press, 1997).

41. This is also available online, along with the rest of the German text of *Der Veschollene*, in Nervi, *The Kafka Project*: "Sie fuhren zwei Tage . . . ," accessed November 29, 2010, http://www.kafka.org/index.php?siefuhren. It would be a long business to explore with requisite specificity the effect on the reader's sense of Kafka's writings' meanings that so much of it is now available in searchable form online, in German, in English, and in many other languages. A short answer would be that digital Kafka encourages the reader to think of Kafka's writings as already, in their manuscript and print forms, an enormous simultaneous fragmentary hypertextual database, with almost innumerable possible cross-references and echoes. Something somewhat similar can be said of this present book, which not only has used digital resources and searching capabilities, but also has itself been written on the computer over a number of years, with virtually countless revisions, excisions, and additions, such as this footnote, which was added November 26, 2009. A footnote is a species of lateral hypertextual set of words or pictures, reached by a "link" in the form of the superscript number in the main text. Any text written on the computer is never really finished, only arbitrarily cut off. In the old days, I used to write essays and books in longhand, make many insertions and alternations, and then read the text into a handheld micro–tape recorder, from which an assistant made a typescript. It was extremely difficult to make any but minor handwritten changes at that point. Those were the days!

42. For Freud and Derrida on telepathy, see my *The Medium Is the Maker: Browning, Freud, Derrida and the New Telepathic Technologies* (Brighton: Sussex Academic Press, 2009).

43. For a different version, see the translation by Jeff Nowak in Nervi, *The Kafka Project*: "The Stoker," accessed November 29, 2010, http://www.kafka.org/index.php?missing1: "He caught sight of the Statue of Liberty in a sudden, strong advance of sunlight. Her arm with the sword rose upwards now, and

over her figure the free air blew." The difference between the two translations is not reassuring. Here is the German original: "Erblickte er die schon längst beobachtete Statue der Freiheitsgöttin wie in einem plötzlich stärker gewordenen Sonnenlicht. Ihr Arm mit dem Schwert ragte wie neuerdings empor und um ihre Gestalt wehten die freien Lüfte" (9g; also available at Nervi, *The Kafka Project*: "Der Heizer," accessed November 29, 2010, http://www.kafka.org/index.php?heizer).

44. The footnote by Brod to this entry says, "Rossmann and K. are the heroes of *Amerika* and *The Trial* respectively" (*Diaries* [1976], 498). The execution with a sword of K. by the twin executioners at the end of *The Trial* hardly seems like a "pushing aside," nor is it clear to me why Kafka referred to Josef K. as "guilty." Guilty of what? His "crime" seems to be negligence of his urgent case of unwarranted arrest, just as K., in *The Castle*, is guilty of impatience, of wanting to get to the goal without making his way through any intermediaries. Perhaps Kafka meant that Karl Rossmann was the guilty one, since he had, after all, allowed himself to be seduced by a servant girl, who then bore his illegitimate child. In any case, "K." might even be a proleptic reference to the hero of the not-yet-written *The Castle*, the ending of which was never written.

CHAPTER THREE

1. Franz Kafka, *Der Proceß*, ed. Malcolm Pasley (Frankfurt am Main: S. Fischer Verlag, 1990), 143 (henceforth cited by page number followed by "g"). I break convention and give footnote references for these initial citations, since they are not exactly epigraphs, but rather texts for commentary and elucidation in the chapter.

2. Franz Kafka, *The Trial*, trans. Breon Mitchell (New York: Schocken, 1998), 106 (henceforth cited by page number followed by "e"). In my citations from this novel I have inserted a few German words here and there where the nuances of the original German seem important.

3. In Franz Kafka, *The Great Wall of China: Stories and Reflections,* trans. Willa and Edwin Muir (New York: Schocken, 1946), 283 (henceforth cited as *GW*).

4. An earlier version of this chapter's last third, on speech acts in *The Trial,* was published in a German translation as "Geglückte und mißlungene Sprechakte in Kafkas *Der Proceß*," in *Franz Kafka: Zur ethischen und ästhetischen Rechtfertigung*, ed. Beatrice Sandberg and Jakob Lothe (Freiburg im Breisgau: Bombach, 2002), 233–46. I thank Professors Sandberg and Lothe for inviting me to the conference in Bergen that led to their book, and for doing me the honor of translating my essay into German for inclusion in it.

5. Shoshana Felman, "From 'The Return of the Voice: Claude Lanzmann's *Shoah*,'" in *The Claims of Literature: A Shoshana Felman Reader*, ed. Emily Sun, Eyal Peretz, and Ulrich Baer (New York: Fordham University Press, 2007), 313.

6. Dan Levin, "China Jails Environmentalist Wanted in U.S.," accessed November 30, 2010, http://www.nytimes.com/2009/11/28/world/asia/28china.html?th&emc=th.

7. Alissa J. Rubin, "Afghans Detail Detention in 'Black Jail' at U.S. Base," accessed November 30, 2010, http://www.nytimes.com/2009/11/29/world/asia/29bagram.html?_r=2&pagewanted=1&th&emc=th.

8. Bob Herbert, "How Long Is Long Enough?" *New York Times*, June 30, 2009, http://www.nytimes.com/2009/06/30/opinion/30herbert.html?_r=1&th&emc=th (accessed November 30, 2010). See also "Mohammed Jawad," on ACLU website, accessed November 30, 2010, http://www.aclu.org/search/Mohammed%20Jawad?show_aff=1.

9. Imre Kertész, *Fatelessness*, trans. Tim Wilkinson (New York: Vintage International, 2004), 40.

10. See "The Holocaust and Hungarian Jewry," accessed November 30, 2010, http://www.claremontmckenna.edu/hist/jpetropoulos/arrow/holocaust/holocaust.htm.

11. Joseph Conrad, *Lord Jim: A Tale* (London: Dent, 1926), 30. Also available as a Project Guttenberg eBook at http://publicliterature.org/pdf/5658.pdf (last accessed May 17, 2010).

12. See Sigmund Freud, "The Uncanny" (1919), in *An Infantile Neurosis and Other Works*, vol. 17 of *The Standard Edition of the Complete Psychological Works of Sigmund Freud*, trans. James Strachey et al. (London: Vintage, Hogarth Press, and Institute of Psycho-Analysis, 2001), 217–56.

13. Franz Kafka, "The Metamorphosis," trans. Willa and Edwin Muir, in *The Sons* (New York: Schocken Books, 1989), 53; Kafka, "Die Verwandlung," in *Erzählungen* (Köln: Könemann, 1995), 87. *Ungeheures* means "monstrous, atrocious, frightful," not just "gigantic," as the Muir translation has it. *Ungeziefer* is an odd word too. My Casell's German-English dictionary says it means "vermin," while *Geziefer* also means "vermin, insects." *Un-* is of course a negative prefix, so *Ungeziefer* is an antithetical word, like *unheimlich*, "uncanny," which means both "familiar" and "strange." What is the difference between a *Geziefer* and an *Ungeziefer*? Is it like the difference between a *Kraut* and an *Unkraut*, or between *heimlich* and *unheimlich*? A *Kraut* is a useful plant, for example, a cabbage, whereas *Unkraut* is the admirable German word for "weed." A weed is a noncabbage. An *Ungeziefer* must be a noninsect, a really noxious or monstrous insect, verminous. *Ungeheurlich* is another word in *un-*. According to my dictionary, *geheuer* exists only with *nicht*. *Nicht geheuer* means "uncanny," "eerie," "fishy," "haunted." *Geheuer*, if there were such a word by itself, would then, so it seems, mean the opposite of *nicht geheuer*, that is, common, everyday, accustomed, ordinary. *Ungeheurlich Ungeziefer* combines two words in *Un-* to say "extraordinary noninsect." Oh, the wonders of the German language!

14. Jane Austen, *Pride and Prejudice*, ed. Mark Schorer, Riverside Edition (Boston: Houghton Mifflin, 1956), 1.

15. *Wikipedia*, s.v. "Kafka," accessed May 17, 2010, http://en.wikipedia.org/wiki/Franz_Kafka. See my comment in n. 14 of chap. 2 about my use of *Wikipedia*.

16. "Karl Hoecker's Album," Slide Show, *New Yorker*, online only, accessed November 30, 2010, http://www.newyorker.com/online/2008/03/17/slideshow_080317_wilkinson/?slide=1#.

17. See, for example, *Wikipedia*, s.v. "Abu Ghraib Torture and Prisoner Abuse," accessed May 17, 2010, http://en.wikipedia.org/wiki/Abu_Ghraib_torture_and_prisoner_abuse.

18. Franz Kafka, *Parables and Paradoxes*, bilingual ed. (New York: Schocken, 1961), 25, 24 (henceforth cited as *PP* followed by the page numbers, first of the English translation and then of the German).

19. The chief texts about autoimmunity by Derrida are "Foi et savoir: Les deux sources de la 'religion' aux limites de la simple raison," in *La religion*, by Jacques Derrida and Gianni Vattimo, ed. Thierry Marchaisse (Paris: Seuil, 1996), 9–86; Derrida, "Faith and Knowledge: The Two Sources of 'Religion' at the Limits of Reason Alone," trans. Samuel Weber, in *Acts of Religion*, ed. Gil Anidjar (New York: Routledge, 2002), 42–101; Derrida, "Auto-immunités, suicides réel et symbolique," a dialogue with Giovanna Borradori, in *Le "concept" du 11 septembre: Dialogues à New York (octobre–décembre 2001),* coauthors Jürgen Habermas and Giovanna Borradori (Paris: Galilée, 2004), 133–96; and Derrida, "Autoimmunity: Real and Symbolic Suicides," a dialogue with Giovanna Borradori, trans. Pascale-Anne Brault and Michael Naas, in *Philosophy in a Time of Terror: Dialogues with Jürgen Habermas and Jacques Derrida* (Chicago: University of Chicago Press, 2003), 85–172. See my discussions of these essays in *For Derrida* (New York: Fordham University Press, 2009), 123–30, 222–44.

20. Robert Walser (1878–1956) was a Swiss writer whose works Kafka much admired.

21. As the reader of Revelation, the last book of the Christian Bible, is enjoined to do in a dire warning in its last verses, "For I testify unto every man that heareth the words of the prophecy of this book. If any man shall add unto these things, God shall add unto him the plagues that are written in this book: And if any man shall take away from the words of the book of this prophecy, God shall take away his part out of the book of life, and out of the holy city, and from the things which are written in this book" (Rev. 22:18–19). The punishments for adding or taking away, that is, for not reading absolutely *à la lettre*, are just about as bad as they could be, but how can any commentary avoid doing one or the other?

22. Sigmund Freud, *Jokes and Their Relation to the Unconscious* (1905), trans. James Strachey, vol. 8 of *Standard Edition*, 62 (henceforth cited in the text by page number).

23. The story of the kettle is referred to again on p. 205, where it is explicitly related to the "unconscious mode of thought," in which "either-or" is replaced by "and": "In dreams, in which the modes of thought of the unconscious are actually manifest, there is accordingly no such thing as an 'either-or,' only a simultaneous juxtaposition." The story of the kettle is also referred to in *The Interpretation of Dreams*, trans. James Strachey, vol. 4 of *Standard Edition*, 119–20, in connection with Freud's interpretation of his dream about Irma. It would be easy enough to argue that *Der Proceß* obeys the logic of dreams and the unconscious as worked out by Freud, but I think it would be a mistake to push this analogy with dreams and the unconscious too far as a full accounting for what is strange about *Der Proceß*. "Real life," it may be, all too often also obeys the kettle logic of dreams, as many people from Kafka's time to the present have experienced.

24. In another reflection Kafka asserts that "all human error is impatience, a premature renunciation of method, a delusive pinning down of a delusion" (*GW*, 278). "Method": it means, etymologically, "according to the way." What method can be appropriate or other than an impatient renunciation of method in a situation in which the road is endless or in which there is a goal but no way? It could only be an infinitely patient method, one that would attempt with unremitting care to account for every detail and element of *The Trial*, every letter of its law, though at the end the interpreter would not be one fraction of an inch closer to the goal. Her or his attention to each detail would be no more than the application of the interpreter's own childish yardstick. Josef K. thinks of defending himself from being tried for a crime he cannot identify by writing down every detail of his life from its beginning, an impossible task, but if he could do it he might hit by accident on a means of exoneration.

25. Franz Kafka, "The Judgment," in *The Sons*, 15; Kafka, "Das Urteil," in *Erzählungen*, 47.

26. Here is a more or less complete list: J. L. Austin, *How to Do Things with Words*, 2nd ed., ed. J. O. Urmson and Marina Sbisà (Oxford: Oxford University Press, 1980), 4, 7, 13, 19, 22, 24, 31, 33, 35, 36, 40, 41, 42, 57, 59, 65, 85, 88–89, 98–99, 122, 128, 130, 141, 153, 154, 155, 157 (henceforth cited as *HT*).

27. In J. L. Austin, *Philosophical Papers*, 3rd ed., ed. J. O. Urmson and G. J. Warnock (Oxford: Oxford University Press, 1979), 175–204 (henceforth cited as *PP*, 3rd ed.).

28. Dennis Kurzon, *It Is Hereby Performed . . . : Explorations in Legal Speech Acts* (Amsterdam: John Benjamins Publishing Company, 1986).

29. Judith Butler, *Excitable Speech: A Politics of the Performative* (New York: Routledge, 1997).

30. See Mark Spilka, *Dickens and Kafka* (Bloomington: Indiana University Press, 1963), esp. 199–210; and Murray Krieger, "*Bleak House* and *The Trial*," in *The Tragic Vision* (New York: Holt, Rinehart & Winston, 1966), 138–40.

31. Charles Dickens, *Bleak House*, ed. Nicola Bradbury (London: Penguin Books, 1996), 118.

32. Franz Kafka, *The Office Writings*, ed. Stanley Corngold, Jack Greenberg, and Benno Wagner, trans. Eric Patton with Ruth Hein (Princeton, N.J.: Princeton University Press, 2009).

33. Lida Kirchberger, *Franz Kafka's Use of Law in Fiction* (New York: Peter Lang, 1986).

34. Derrida, "Faith and Knowledge," 80.

35. Jacques Derrida, "Signature Event Context," in *Limited Inc*, trans. Jeffrey Mehlman and Samuel Weber (Evanston, Ill.: Northwestern University Press, 1988), 12.

36. Jacques Derrida, "'Le Parjure,' Perhaps: Storytelling and Lying ('Abrupt Breaches of Syntax')," in *Without Alibi*, ed. and trans. Peggy Kamuf (Stanford, Calif.: Stanford University Press, 2002), 181–84.

37. See Franz Kafka, *Letter to His Father/Brief an den Vater*, blingual ed., trans. Ernst Kaiser and Eithne Wilkins (New York: Schocken, 1966), 72, 73: "Er fürchtet, die Scham werde ihn noch überleben" (He is afraid the shame will even outlive him).

CHAPTER FOUR

1. I have argued these presuppositions in detail in chap. 6, "Derrida Enisled," of my book on Derrida, *For Derrida* (New York: Fordham University Press, 2009), 101–32, by way of discussions of Benjamin, Heidegger, Raymond Williams, Nancy, Blanchot, Husserl, Bataille, Agamben, Alphonso Lingis, Jacques Lacan, Levinas, and Derrida. An earlier version of this argument can be found in my "Derrida Enisled," in "The Late Derrida," ed. W. J. T. Mitchell and Arnold I. Davidson, special issue, *Critical Inquiry* 33, no. 2 (Winter 2007): 248–76.

2. I have noted one case in which these rules are abrogated, a passage in which the narrator appears to know what the landlady is thinking: "The landlady considered it unseemly [*ungebührlich*] that K. wanted to barge in at this point with his own affairs, and gave him an irritated side-glance" (*The Castle*, trans. Mark Harman [New York: Schocken Books, 1996], 79 [henceforth cited by page numbers followed by "e"]; Kafka, *Das Schloß*, ed. Malcolm Paisley [Frankfurt am Main: Fischer Taschenbuch Verlag, 1997], 100 [henceforth cited by page numbers followed by "g"]). Possibly other such passages exist that I have not noticed, but they are exceedingly rare.

3. This inflection was to some degree brought about because the chapter was originally written, in a much shorter and considerably different form, as my contribution to a conference (eventually a book, now out from the Ohio State University Press; see acknowledgments) on narratological approaches to Kafka. This conference took place in Oslo as part of the work of a research group on narratology led over a two-year period by Jakob Lothe at the Norwegian Academy of Sciences in Oslo. See my dedication of this book to Lothe and comments in the last paragraph of my preface.

4. See Wayne C. Booth, *The Rhetoric of Fiction* (Chicago: University of Chicago Press, 1961).

5. See Nicholas Royle, "The 'Telepathy Effect': Notes toward a Reconsideration of Narrative Fiction," in *The Uncanny* (Manchester: Manchester University Press, 2003), 256–76.

6. Franz Kafka, *The Castle*, trans. Edwin and Willa Muir (New York: Alfred A. Knopf, 1951), 329–30.

7. See the second and third aphorisms of Kafka's "Reflections on Sin, Pain, Hope, and the True Way" for Kafka's concepts of impatience and laziness. I have already cited these in chap. 3 but cite them again as memory aids relevant to the argument I am making now about *The Castle*. The second aphorism says, "All human error is impatience [*Ungeduld*], a premature renunciation of method [*Abbrechen des Methodischen*], a delusive pinning down of an illusion," while the third aphorism, after having distinguished between impatience and laziness ("Because of impatience we were driven out of Paradise, because of laziness [*Lässigkeit*] we cannot return"), ends by saying there is only one cardinal sin, impatience: "Because of impatience we were driven out, because of impatience we cannot return" (*The Great Wall of China: Stories and Reflections*, trans. Willa and Edwin Muir [New York: Schocken, 1946], 278; for the German original see *Aphorismen (II, 4)*, aphorisms 2 and 3, in Mauro Nervi, *The Kafka Project*, accessed December 3, 2010, http://www.kafka.org/index.php?aphorismen). "Method," as I said in n. 24 of chap. 3, derives from a Greek word meaning "according

to the path" or "the way." To give up method is to abandon through impatience the slow, methodical pursuit of the true way. The way, however, for Kafka is endless. No method will reach the goal. K. in *The Castle* is impatient. He wants to go directly to the goal.

8. Franz Kafka, *The Diaries, 1910–1923*, ed. Max Brod, trans. Joseph Kresh and Martin Greenberg, with the cooperation of Hannah Arendt (New York: Schocken Books, 1976), 280–87.

9. *The Castle*, Muir trans., 45.

10. Joseph Conrad, *Heart of Darkness*, ed. Ross C. Murfin, 2nd ed. (Boston: Bedford Books of St. Martin's Press, 1996), 36–37.

11. J. Hillis Miller, "Franz Kafka and the Metaphysics of Alienation," in *The Tragic Vision and the Christian Faith*, ed. N. A. Scott, Jr. (New York: Association Press, 1957), 281–305.

12. See Jacques Derrida, "Foi et savoir: Les deux sources de la 'religion' aux limites de la simple raison," in *La religion*, by Jacques Derrida and Gianni Vattimo, ed. Thierry Marchaisse (Paris: Seuil, 1996), 68–69; Derrida, "Faith and Knowledge: The Two Sources of 'Religion' at the Limits of Reason Alone," trans. Samuel Weber, in *Acts of Religion*, ed. Gil Anidjar (New York: Routledge, 2002), 87. I have discussed Derrida's concept of auto-co-immunity in chap. 3 of this book, as well as in my *For Derrida*, 123–30, 222–44.

13. Franz Kafka, *The Trial*, trans. Breon Mitchell (New York: Schocken, 1998), 3; trans. altered.

14. I have changed Mark Harman's translation of *Rauschen* from "murmuring" to "rustling," which is given as a primary meaning in my Casell's German-English dictionary. *Rauschen* also means the "background noise" of a radio (or, I suppose, telephone). Kafka was always sensitive to the sound of words. *Rauschen* sounds more like rustling than murmuring to me. The word used early in *The Castle* that Harman also translates as "murmuring" is *Summen*, which does sound like murmuring. A word related to *Rauschen* is *Rascheln*, at least in sound. *Rascheln* is used in "The Worry of the Father of the Family" (Die Sorge des Hausvaters) to name the rustle in fallen leaves ("das Rascheln in gefallenen Blättern"). This rustling figures the sound of Odradek's voice. "Odradek" is the name of the strange little animal-person-machine that so much worries the father of the family. See "The Worry of the Father of the Family," trans. Stanley Corngold, in *Kafka's Selected Stories*, trans. and ed. Stanley Corngold, Norton Critical Edition (New York: W. W. Norton, 2007), 72–73; and "Die Sorge des Hausvaters," in Nervi, *The Kafka Project: Ein Landarzt: Kleine Erzählungen*, accessed December 3, 2010, http://www.kafka.org/index.php?landarzt.

15. Laurence Rickels, "Kafka and Freud on the Telephone," *Modern Austrian Literature: Journal of the International Arthur Schnitzler Association* 22, nos. 3/4 (1989): 211–25; and Rickels, *Aberrations of Mourning* (Detroit: Wayne State University Press, 1988), esp. chaps. 7 and 8.

16. Marcel Proust, *À la recherche du temps perdu*, ed. Jean-Yves Tadié, Éd. de la Pléiade (Paris: Gallimard, 1989), 2:431–33; Proust, *Remembrance of Things Past*, trans. C. K. Scott Moncrieff (New York: Vintage, 1982), 2:133–36. I have discussed this passage in some detail in the section entitled "Granny! Granny!" of chap. 5, "Proust," in my *Speech Acts in Literature* (Stanford, Calif.:

Stanford University Press, 2001), 185–98. Patience Moll has written brilliantly in graduate seminar papers for me about this episode in Proust. See her "Community, Communication and Multiplicity in Proust," in *Philosophia: Philosophical Quarterly of Israel* 36, no. 1 (2007): 55–65.

17. For a collection of essays exploring this topic through diverse examples and from diverse perspectives see my *Topographies* (Stanford, Calif.: Stanford University Press, 1995).

18. Lewis Carroll, *Alice in Wonderland*, ed. Donald J. Gray, Norton Critical Edition (New York: W. W. Norton & Company, 1971), 120–23.

19. Maurice Blanchot, "Kafka and Literature," in *The Work of Fire*, trans. Charlotte Mandell (Stanford, Calif.: Stanford University Press, 1995), 21; Blanchot, "Kafka et la littérature," in *De Kafka à Kafka* (Paris: Gallimard, 1981), 86. "Kafka et la literature" was originally published in *La part du feu* (Paris: Gallimard, 1949), 20–34; the passage in question is on 28–29 of the latter.

20. For opposing analyses of irony see Wayne Booth, *A Rhetoric of Irony* (Chicago: University of Chicago Press, 1974); Søren Kierkegaard, *The Concept of Irony, with Constant Reference to Socrates*, trans. Lee M. Capel (London: Collins, 1966); Paul de Man, "The Concept of Irony," in *Aesthetic Ideology*, ed. Andrzej Warminski (Minneapolis: University of Minnesota Press, 1996), 163–84; J. Hillis Miller, "Friedrich Schlegel: Catachreses for Chaos," in *Others* (Princeton, N.J.: Princeton University Press, 2001), 5–42. An enormous secondary literature on irony, much of it recent, exists. Many scholars have wanted to have a shot at mastering irony, in defiance of Friedrich Schlegel's claim that it is unmasterable.

21. Kafka, *Diaries, 1910–1923*, 224.

22. Edmund Husserl, in the fifth of the *Cartesian Meditations*, called this indirect access to the mind of another person "analogical apperception." See Edmund Husserl, "Fifth Meditation: Uncovering the Sphere of Transcendental Being as Monadological Intersubjectivity," in *Cartesian Meditations: An Introduction to Phenomenology*, trans. Dorion Cairns (The Hague: Martinus Nijhoff, 1960), 89–151, esp. paragraph 50, "The mediate intentionality of experiencing someone else, as 'appresentation' (analogical apperception)" (108–11).

23. For an analysis of Derrida and Husserl on this topic, see chap. 6, "Derrida Enisled," in my *For Derrida* (n. 1 above), 101–32.

24. Henry Sussman, *Idylls of the Wanderer: Outside in Literature and Theory* (New York: Fordham University Press. 2007).

25. Franz Kafka, "The Coming of the Messiah," in *Parables and Paradoxes, in German and English* (New York: Schocken, 1969), 81e; 80g.

26. Kafka, *The Trial*, 217, 220; Kafka, *Der Proceß*, ed. Malcolm Pasley (Frankfurt am Main: S. Fischer Verlag, 1990), 295, 298. The contradictory readings of "Before the Law" by the priest and Josef K. anticipate a similar give-and-take of conflicting interpretations in discussions K. has with one or another interlocutor in *The Castle*. One statement by the priest, in *The Trial*, formulates by anticipation the law of such formulations in *The Castle*: "The commentators tell us: the correct understanding [*richtiges Auffassen*] of a matter and misunderstanding [*Mißverstehn*] of the matter are not mutually exclusive" (*The Trial*, 219; *Der Proceß*, 297).

27. Kafka, *Diaries, 1910–1923*, 495.

28. Ibid., 122; trans. altered; Mauro Nervi, *The Kafka Project: Tagebücher*, Heft 3, accessed December 3, 2010, http://www.kafka.org/index.php?h3, no page numbers.

29. Kafka's knowledge of Kabbalah and his comparison of his writings to a "new Kabbalah" have been discussed by Russell Samolsky in the Kafka chapter of his *Apocalyptic Futures: Marked Bodies and the Violence of the Text in Kafka, Conrad, and Coetzee* (New York: Fordham University Press, forthcoming in fall 2011).

30. Maurice Blanchot, "The Wooden Bridge (Repetition, the Neutral)" in *The Infinite Conversation*, trans. Susan Hanson (Minneapolis: University of Minnesota Press, 1993), 388–96, esp. 392–94; Blanchot, "Le pont de bois (la répétition, le neutre)," in Blanchot, *De Kafka à Kafka*, 185–201, esp. 192–95. "Le pont de bois" was originally published in book form in *L'entretien infini* (Paris: Gallimard, 1989), 568–82, esp. 574–77.

31. Kevin Kelley, "We Are the Web," *Wired*, August 2005.

32. See my discussion of this in chap. 2.

33. Jacques Derrida, *Séminaire: La bête et le souverain*, vol. 2, *2002-2003*, ed. Michel Lisse, Marie-Louise Mallet, and Ginette Michaud (Paris: Galilée, 2010), 31. From 1st seminar, my trans.

34. Kafka, *The Great Wall of China*, 283.

35. *Aphorismen (II, 4)*, aphorism 26, , in Mauro Nervi, *The Kafka Project*, accessed December 3, 2010, http://www.kafka.org/index.php?aphorismen.

36. Augustine, *Confessions*, 3.6.11, accessed December 3, 2010, http://www.stoa.org/hippo/text3.html; *Confessions*, trans. Albert C. Outler, accessed December 3, 2010, http://www.ccel.org/ccel/augustine/confessions.vi.html.

37. Raymond Williams, *The Country and the City* (London: Chatto & Windus, 1973).

38. Jacques Derrida, "Le Facteur de la vérité": "A letter does *not always* arrive at its destination, and from the moment that this possibility belongs to its structure one can say that it never truly arrives" (in English in *The Post Card: From Socrates to Freud and Beyond*, trans. Alan Bass [Chicago: University of Chicago Press, 1987], 489; in French in *La carte postale: De Socrate à Freud et au-delà* [Paris: Flammarion, 1980], 517).

39. Kafka, *Diaries, 1910–1923* (n. 8 above), 302.

40. Henry James, *The Portrait of a Lady*, in *The Novels and Tales of Henry James*, vols. 3–4 (Fairfield, N.J.: Augustus M. Kelley, 1976–77; this is a reprint of the New York edition of 1907–9), 4:192.

PROLOGUE TO PART III

1. "No one / bears witness for the / witness" (Paul Celan, "Aschenglorie," in *Breathturn*, bilingual ed., trans. Pierre Joris (Los Angeles: Sun & Moon Press, 1995), 179, 178.

2. For example, the collection of thirty-six authoritative essays in *Teaching the Representation of the Holocaust*, ed. Marianne Hirsch and Irene Kacandes (New York: Modern Language Association of America, 2004). See also Arne

Johan Vetlesen, *Evil and Human Agency: Understanding Collective Evildoing* (Cambridge: Cambridge University Press, 2005); Michael Rothberg, *Traumatic Realism: The Demands of Holocaust Representation* (Minneapolis: University of Minnesota Press, 2000); Efraim Sicher, *The Holocaust Novel* (New York: Routledge, 2005). See also Naomi Mandel's review of Rothberg's book in *Cultural Critique* 51 (Spring 2002): 241–45. Further examples of recent Holocaust literature are listed in n. 11 in chap. 6 of this book.

3. David Denby, "Look Again: 'Shoah' and a New View of History," *New Yorker*, January 10, 2011, 80–81.

4. Timothy Snyder, *Bloodlands: Europe between Hitler and Stalin* (New York: Basic Books, 2010).

5. Cited by Deborah R. Geis in her "Introduction" to *Considering "Maus": Approaches to Art Spiegelman's "Survivor's Tale" of the Holocaust*, ed. Deborah R. Geis (Tuscaloosa: University of Alabama Press, 2003), 5, from James Young, *Writing and Rewriting the Holocaust: Narrative and the Consequences of Interpretation* (Bloomington: Indiana University Press, 1990), 91.

6. See Jacques Derrida, *Chaque fois unique, la fin du monde*, ed. Pascale-Anne Brault and Michael Naas (Paris: Galilée, 2003).

7. Toni Morrison, *Beloved* (New York: Vintage International, 2004), 235.

8. Naomi Mandel has made this analogy the basis of her fine book *Against the Unspeakable: Complicity, the Holocaust, and Slavery in America* (Charlottesville: University of Virginia Press, 2006). Mandel discusses Morrison's *Beloved*, my topic in chap. 7 of this book, as well as the Steven Spielberg film of *Schindler's List*, discussed briefly in chap. 5 of this book. Mandel's persuasive argument is that the notion that such atrocities as the Holocaust or American slavery are "unspeakable" can be used as a cop-out to avoid confronting these horrors, to evade trying to come to terms with them and bearing witness to them. See *Against the Unspeakable,* 168-71, for a fuller discussion of "Sixty Million and more."

9. See C. Vann Woodward, *The Burden of Southern History* (New York: Vintage, 1960).

CHAPTER FIVE

1. Thomas Keneally, *Schindler's List* (New York: Scribner Paperback Fiction, 2000), 9 (henceforth cited by page numbers).

2. For an astute discussion of the Steven Spielberg film of *Schindler's List,* as well as of the large secondary literature on the film, see Naomi Mandel, *Against the Unspeakable: Complicity, the Holocaust, and Slavery in America* (Charlottesville: University of Virginia Press, 2006), 71–98. Mandel focuses critically on the claims by commentators on the film that it too much claims to represent what is essentially unrepresentable, that is, the Holocaust.

3. Ian McEwan, *Black Dogs* (New York: Anchor Books, 1999), vi (henceforth cited by page numbers).

4. Nor does commentary I have seen relate the novel to McEwan's life—for example, the chapter summarizing the secondary literature on *Black Dogs* in *The Fiction of Ian McEwan: A Reader's Guide to Essential Criticism*, ed. Peter Childs (Houndmills: Palgrave Macmillan, 2006), 90–103.

5. Majdanek is the best preserved of the camps, since it was liberated by the Red Army before the Nazis had time to destroy more than part of the crematoria. See *Wikipedia*, s.v. "Majdanek Concentration Camp," accessed May 30, 2010, http://en.wikipedia.org/wiki/Majdanek_concentration_camp. Google also leads to a number of other Majdanek websites, many with photographs. Cyberspace is one of the places where much documentary evidence of the Shoah is easily available to anyone with a computer and a connection to the Internet (as are denials that it ever happened). Of course, you must be willing to open the websites. I find much of the evidence almost unbearable, especially the photographs, as I do the photographs of Abu Ghraib available online.

6. See, for example, the essays collected in *Considering "Maus": Approaches to Art Spiegelman's "Survivor's Tale" of the Holocaust*, ed. Deborah R. Geis (Tuscaloosa: University of Alabama Press, 2003).

7. Lewis Carroll, *Alice in Wonderland*, ed. Donald J. Gray, Norton Critical Edition (New York: W. W. Norton & Company, 1971), 25.

CHAPTER SIX

1. Maurice Blanchot (1907–2003) was one of the most important French critics and fiction writers of the twentieth century. One of his characteristic locutions, as many of his critics have noted, takes the form of "X without X." In the case of my epigraph, Blanchot affirms that we have knowledge-without-knowledge of Auschwitz. My citation is taken from a section about the Shoah in a late aphoristic work by Blanchot, *The Writing of the Disaster* (Maurice Blanchot, *L'écriture du désastre* [Paris: Gallimard, 1980], 131; Blanchot, *The Writing of the Disaster*, new ed., trans. Ann Smock [Lincoln: University of Nebraska Press, 1995], 82). Here is the French original: "Nous lisons les livres sur Auschwitz. Le vœu de tous, là-bas, le dernier vœu: sachez ce qui s'est passé, n'oubliez pas, et en même temps jamais vous ne saurez."

2. I accessed an online edition of *Sorstalanság* in 2007. For the printed original, see Kertész Imre, *Sorstalanság* (Budapest: Szépirodalmi Kőnyvkiadó, 1975), also published in Budapest by Magvető in 1975 and in more recent editions by Magvető. For a Kertész bibliography, see Steven Tötösy de Zepetnek, *Bibliography of Works by and about Imre Kertész, Nobel Laureate in Literature 2002*, CLCWeb: Comparative Literature and Culture (Library) (2008), accessed January 11, 2011, http://docs.lib.purdue.edu/clcweblibrary/imrekerteszbibliography. For a collection of essays about Kertész's work see Louise O. Vasvári and Steven Tötösy de Zepetnek, eds., *Imre Kertész and Holocaust Literature* (West Lafayette, Ind.: Purdue University Press, 2005). Further essays about Kertész and a text by Kertész are included in *Comparative Central European Holocaust Studies*, ed. Louise O. Vasvári and Steven Tötösy de Zepetnek (West Lafayette, Ind.: Purdue University Press, 2009).

3. Imre Kertész, *Fatelessness*, trans. Tim. Wilkinson (New York: Vintage, 2004) (hereafter cited by page numbers in the text).

4. *Fateless*, directed by Lajos Koltai (2005; ThinkFilm, 2006), DVD.

5. Imre Kertész, *Kaddish for an Unborn Child*, trans. Tim Wilkinson (New York: Vintage International, 2004).

6. I am extremely grateful to Susan Suleiman, Jakob Lothe, and James Phelan for their careful reading of the first, much shorter, version of this essay and for the helpful suggestions and corrections they made. I am grateful also to the suggestions for revision of the initial shorter version of this chapter made by the two anonymous readers of the manuscript of *After Testimony: The Ethics and Aesthetics of Holocaust Narrative*, ed. Jakob Lothe, Susan R. Suleiman, and James Phelan (Columbus: Ohio State University Press, forthcoming in 2012). I have incorporated some of the readers' suggestions in this longer, differently organized, and differently oriented chapter.

7. *Fatelessness*'s protagonist's formal name is György Köves, but his family calls him Gyuri. I shall refer to him as Gyuri (pronounced something like "Jury"), since that probably corresponds best to what we are to imagine was his most commonly used name, perhaps even the name by which he referred to himself. The English subtitles in the film transcribe his familiar name as Gyurka, but I shall use the name as it is given in Tim Wilkinson's translation.

8. Franz Kafka, *Der Proceß*, ed. Malcolm Pasley (Frankfurt am Main: S. Fischer Verlag, 1990), 7; Kafka, *The Trial*, trans. Breon Mitchell (New York: Schocken, 1998), 3; trans. altered.

9. Albert Camus, *The Stranger* (New York: Vintage, 1961), 1 (henceforth cited by page numbers in the text). For the French original, see Albert Camus (1913–1960), *L'étranger*, accessed December 15, 2010, http://www.bibliopax.com/pagelitt30.html.

10. My trans. The French is " Quand j'aurai inspiré le dégoût et l'horreur universels, j'aurai conquis la solitude," in Charles Baudelaire, "Fusées," in *Oeuvres complètes*, ed. Y.-G. le Dantec, Éd. de la Pléiade (Paris: Gallimard, 1954), 1199.

11. Some important work in the abundant and growing secondary literature in Holocaust studies has focused on this question. Examples are Sidra DeKoven Ezrahi, *By Words Alone: The Holocaust in Literature* (Chicago: University of Chicago Press, 1980); Ezrahi, "Representing Auschwitz," *History and Memory* 7, no. 2 (Winter 1996): 121–54; Thomas Trezise, "Unspeakable," *Yale Journal of Criticism* 14, no. 1 (Spring 2001): 39–66; Erin McGlothlin, "Narrative Transgression in Edgar Hilsenrath's *Der Nazi und der Friseur* and the Rhetoric of the Sacred in Holocaust Discourse," *German Quarterly* 80, no. 2 (Spring 2007): 220–39. I am grateful for the last three of these references to the anonymous reviewer of my essay on Kertész's *Fatelessness* for *After Testimony*, forthcoming from Ohio State University Press. These essays and Naomi Mandel's *Against the Unspeakable: Complicity, the Holocaust, and Slavery in America* (Charlottesville: University of Virginia Press, 2006) have helped me get some sense of current thinking on questions of the "unspeakable" and on consequent challenges to representing the Holocaust. Mandel, for example, argues persuasively that claiming the Holocaust is "unspeakable" may be a way to avoid talking, writing, or thinking about it at all. Mandel discusses critically and at length, from the perspective of the Holocaust's alleged "unspeakability," many examples from the voluminous secondary literature on representing or understanding the Holocaust. (See esp. 1–70.) If consideration of representation were defined more broadly, it would include the immense secondary literature on problems of representation in fiction generally, for example, Alexander Welsh's wide-ranging,

learned, and astute study of circumstantial evidence in English law, science, and "natural religion," as a context for readings of English fiction from Fielding to Henry James: *Strong Representations: Narrative and Circumstantial Evidence in England* (Baltimore: Johns Hopkins University Press, 1992).

12. Primo Levi cites a version of this argument from Simon Wiesenthal's *The Murderers Are among Us* in *The Drowned and the Saved*, trans. Raymond Rosenthal (New York: Vintage, 1989), 11–12.

13. Jean-Luc Nancy, "Forbidden Representation," in *The Ground of the Image*, trans. Jeff Fort (New York: Fordham University Press, 2005), 27–50 (henceforth cited as "FR"). The French original is in Jean-Luc Nancy, *Au fond des images* (Paris: Galilée, 2003). Nancy's essay, especially the footnotes, refers to many of the most important books and essays out of the multitude that have dealt with the question of representing Auschwitz.

14. Art Spiegelmann, *Maus: A Survivor's Tale* (New York: Pantheon, 1997), 10.

15. Paul de Man, "Autobiography as De-Facement," in *The Rhetoric of Romanticism* (New York: Columbia University Press, 1984), 81.

16. Jean-François Lyotard, *The Differend: Phrases in Dispute*, trans. Georges Van Den Abbeele (Minneapolis: University of Minnesota Press, 1988), 3; cited by Giorgio Agamben in *Remants of Auschwitz: The Witness and the Archive*, trans. Daniel Heller-Roazen (New York: Zone Books, 2002), 35.

17. Jacques Derrida, *Paper Machine*, trans. Rachel Bowlby (Stanford, Calif.: Stanford University Press, 2005), 161 (henceforth cited as *PMe*); Derrida, *Papier Machine* (Paris: Galilée, 2001), 396 (henceforth cited as *PMf*).

18. He said this quite emphatically in the generous conversation he held in Berlin on June 29, 2007, with members of the Oslo research group on narratology that sponsored an earlier and shorter version of this chapter.

19. Blanchot, *The Writing of the Disaster*, 80; Blanchot, *L'écriture du désastre*, 128.

20. Paul Celan, *Breathturn*, trans. Pierre Joris (Los Angeles: Sun & Moon Press, 1995), 178, 179.

21. Primo Levi, *Survival in Auschwitz: The Nazi Assault on Humanity* (New York: Simon & Schuster /Touchstone, 1996); Elie Wiesel, *Night*, in *The Night Trilogy: Night; Dawn; Day*, trans. Marion Wiesel et. al. (New York: Hill & Wang, 2008).

22. See Friedrich Schlegel, fragment 108 of the "Critical Fragments," in *Philosophical Fragments*, trans. Peter Firchow (Minneapolis: University of Minnesota Press, 1991), 13; Schlegel, *Kritische Schriften* (Munich: Carl Hanser, 1963), 20–21. For a discussion of Schlegel's theory of irony, see my "Friedrich Schlegel: Catachreses for Chaos," in *Others* (Princeton, N.J.: Princeton University Press, 2001), 5–42.

23. James Joyce, *Finnegans Wake*, 2nd ed. (London: Faber, 1950), pt. 1, episode 6, p. 188, line 14; also at *Finnegan's Wake Concordex*, accessed December 15, 2010, http://www.lycaeum.org/mv/Finnegan/finnegan.cgi?mode=new&simple=boolean&kwor=twosome+twiminded&kwnot=.

24. James Phelan, *Living to Tell about It: A Rhetoric and Ethics of Character Narration* (Ithaca, N.Y.: Cornell University Press, 2005).

25. *English to Hungarian Dictionary; Hungarian to English Dictionary*, s.v. "naturally," accessed December 15, 2010, http://www.freedict.com/onldict/hun .html.

26. *[origo] sztaki szótár; English-Hungarian*, s.v. "naturally," accessed December 15, 2010, http://dict.sztaki.hu/english-hungarian.

27. For an English translation, see Sigmund Freud, "The Uncanny" (1919), in *An Infantile Neurosis and Other Works*, vol. 17 of *The Standard Edition of the Complete Psychological Works of Sigmund Freud*, trans. James Strachey et al. (London: Vintage, Hogarth Press, and Institute of Psycho-Analysis, 2001), 217–56.

28. Agamben, *Remnants of Auschwitz*, 166–71 (henceforth cited by page numbers).

29. Levi, *The Drowned and the Saved*, 83–84.

30. Ibid., 84.

31. Efraim Sicher, *The Holocaust Novel* (New York: Routledge, 2005), 48.

32. Art Spiegelman, *The Complete Maus* (New York: Pantheon, 1997), 189.

33. Sicher, *The Holocaust Novel*, 51.

34. Henry James, *The Wings of the Dove*, vol. 1, in *The Novels and Tales of Henry James*, vol. 19 (Fairfield, N.J.: Augustus M. Kelley, 1976), vi.

35. De Man, "Autobiography as De-Facement" (n. 15 above), 81.

36. Jacques Derrida, *Memoirs of the Blind*, trans. Pascale-Anne Brault and Michael Naas (Chicago: University of Chicago Press, 1993), 30; Derrida, *Mémoires d'aveugle: L'autoportrait et autre ruines (*Paris: Éditions de la Réunion des musées nationaux, 1990), 36.

37. Spiegelman, *The Complete Maus*, 6.

38. An e-mail message of January 18, 2010, from Orion Anderson, titled "Warfare as Collective Suicide," sent me the latest *Ideologies of War, Genocide and Terror Newsletter*. Richard Koenigsberg, "Warfare as Collective Suicide," in *Ideologies of War, Genocide and Terror Newsletter*, ed. Orion Anderson, for January 18, 2010. This is an e-mail newsletter, subscription available at *Ideologies of War, Genocide and Terror: A Website Sponsored by Library of Social Science*, ed. Orion Anderson, accessed December 15, 2010, http://www.ideologiesofwar .com/. This brief essay cites a pamphlet of September 26, 1943, by Joseph Goebbels that said the bombing raids by the Allies were putting the Germans on the "verge of becoming a real *Volksgemeinschaft*"—a folk community bound together by the threat of of imminent death. The same brief essay cites Hitler's assertion that the German people had to be thrown into "the great melting pot, the nation," in order to be "purified and welded one to another." As Koenigsberg observes, the German folk were indeed horribly melted together in the firebombed German cities, e.g., Dresden, in a reflex mirror image of the Holocaust. For a good essay on the history of Dresden from before and after the firebombing of February 13, 1945, to the complex and problematic rebuilding down to the present day, see George Packer, "Letter from Dresden: Embers," *New Yorker*, February 1, 2010, 32–39. As Packer observes, the firebombing, which killed between twenty-five and forty thousand people, may have been "immoral—Churchill himself later expressed qualms—but it was not

irrational, or even unusual" (33), since it was one of many saturation bombings of German cities by the Allies that helped them defeat Germany. Dresden did have eight small concentration camps and some slave labor military factories. In modern war, it is not "irrational" to kill tens of thousands of civilians in a single night! Nevertheless, Dresden was a center of anti-Semitism and Nazi sympathizing and still today has a vocal population of neo-Nazis. Its synagogue was burned down on *Kristallnacht*, in 1938. At the time of the firebombing only one hundred and ninety-eight Jews remained in Dresden of a prewar Jewish population of six thousand, and the remnant were being sent one by one to Auschwitz or Theresienstadt (33).

39. Jacques Derrida and Maurizio Ferraris, *A Taste for the Secret*, trans. Giacomo Donis, ed. Giacomo Donis and David Webb (Cambridge: Polity, 2001), 25; first published as *Il Gusto del Segreto* (Rome: Gius. Laterza and Figli Spa, 1997).

40. Jacques Derrida, "Abraham, the Other," trans. Gil Anidjar, in *Judeities: Questions for Jacques Derrida*, trans. Bettina Bergo and Michael B. Smith, ed. Bettina Bergo, Joseph Cohen, and Raphael Zagury-Orly (New York: Fordham University Press, 2007), 15; Derrida, "Abraham, l'autre," in *Judéités: Questions pour Jacques Derrida*, ed. Joseph Cohen and Raphael Zagury-Orly (Paris: Galilée, 2003), 23–24.

CHAPTER SEVEN

1. See note 6 of the prologue to part 3 of this book for a reference to Naomi Mandel's working-out of this analogy in her admirable book, *Against the Unspeakable: Complicity, the Holocaust, and Slavery in America* (Charlottesville: University of Virginia Press, 2006). I read her fine chapter on *Beloved* after writing the early drafts of this chapter, but her reading has inflected the final revision of my own reading. Mandel's discussion of the distinction between "calling" and "naming" is particularly perceptive. Sethe's murdered baby daughter is called "Beloved," but that is not her name. The novel never utters or reveals her given name. Mandel also includes thoughtful responses to the abundant secondary literature on *Beloved*. She attends particularly to their problematic assumption that the sufferings of American slaves are "unspeakable" and therefore, it is implied, something we do not even need to try to speak about. This, Mandel persuasively argues, would be a form of silencing. Silencing is elaborately thematized in *Beloved* itself.

2. Toni Morrison, *Beloved* (New York: Vintage International, 2004), xviii–xix (henceforth cited by page numbers).

3. Fredric Jameson, "Postmodernism; or, The Cultural Logic of Late Capitalism," *New Left Review*, no. 146 (July–August, 1984), 59–62. This essay, under the title "The Cultural Logic of Late Capitalism," now forms the first chapter of Jameson's *Postmodernism; or, The Cultural Logic of Late Capitalism* (Durham, N.C.: Duke University Press, 1991), 1–54. Jameson observes in the introduction to this book that the essay of 1984 is reprinted "without significant modifications, since the attention it received at the time (1984) lends it the additional interest of a historical document" (xv).

4. See my "*El Colloquio de los Perros* como Narrativa Posmoderna," trans. María Jesús López Sánchez-Vizcaíno, in *La tropelía: Hacia el coloquio de los perros*, ed., with a prologue, by Julián Jiménez Heffernan (Tenerife: Artemisa Ediciones, 2008), 33–98. My essay was developed from a lecture given at Córdoba to celebrate the four hundredth anniversary of *Don Quixote*'s publication. I thank Professor Heffernan for giving me an opportunity to think about these issues. My essay juxtaposes Cervantes's wonderful "exemplary story," *The Dogs' Colloquy* (the topic of the conference), with Thomas Pynchon's early short story "The Secret Integration" (1964), from his book of stories *The Slow Learner: Early Stories* (Boston: Little, Brown, 1984 [the year of Jameson's essay on the postmodern]). My essay makes a number of references to Morrison's *Beloved* as also exemplifying so-called postmodern narrative style. My argument in the essay is that if Pynchon's story is an example of postmodern narrative, which it surely is, if there is such a thing, then Cervantes's *The Dogs' Colloquy* must be postmodern too, since it has all the formal features and themes identified by Jameson as "postmodern" and exemplified by Pynchon's story. Cervantes's greatness lies partly in his putting in question, before the fact, of attempts at periodization such as Jameson's. Cervantes's fictions preprogrammed in the early 1600s all the repertoire of stylistic devices and themes in the fiction that has come after him.

5. This list is drawn from my essay on Cervantes identified in n. 4.

6. W. B. Yeats, *The Variorum Edition of the Poems of W. B. Yeats*, ed. Peter Allt and Russell K. Alspach (New York: Macmillan, 1977), 581; Yeats, *Collected Plays* (London: Macmillan, 1953), 595–617; 679–89.

7. Christoph Peters, "Obama at the Gates," *The New York Times*, July 17, 2008, http://www.nytimes.com/2008/07/17/opinion/17peters.html?th&emc=th (accessed December 16, 2010).

8. Jonathan Dee, "Right-Wing Flame War!," *New York Times Magazine*, January 24, 2010, http://www.nytimes.com/2010/01/24/magazine/24Footballs-t.html?th&emc=th (last accessed June 10, 2010).

9. Jacques Lacan, "Le stade du miroir comme formateur de la fonction du Je telle qu'elle nous est révélée dans l'expérience psychanalytique," in *Écrits* (Paris: Seuil, 1966), 93–100; Lacan, "The Mirror Stage as Formative of the Function of the *I* as Revealed in Psychoanalytic Experience," trans. Alan Sheridan, in *Écrits: A Selection*, ed. Alan Sheridan (New York: Norton, 1982), 1–7.

10. Other scholars have made the same comparison. See, for example, Walter Benn Michaels, "Plots against America: Neoliberalism and Antiracism," *American Literary History* 18, no. 2 (2006), 288–302. Extrapolating from the position of "the notorious black racist Khalid Muhammid," Michaels asks: "Why should what the Germans did to the Jews be treated as a crucial event in American history, especially when, given the absence of any commemoration of American racism on the Mall, what Americans did to Black people is not?" (290). Michaels's essay makes some problematic assertions, e.g., "Anti-Semitism was never a very significant factor in American life—the fact that Jews were white was almost always more important than the fact that they were Jewish, and Jewish success in America today is less an effect of the triumph over racism than it is an effect of the triumph of racism" (291). Michaels deploys, as I do in this book, though to a

somewhat different end, the distinction between performative (testimonial) and constative (representational) language. See his "'You Who Never Was There': Slavery and the New Historicism—Deconstruction and the Holocaust," in *The Americanization of the Holocaust*, ed. Hilene Flanzbaum (Baltimore: Johns Hopkins University Press, 1999), 161–97. For me, implicit performatives are a feature of representation, not wholly opposed to it, even in representations of the Holocaust or of American slavery. The latter always imply a speech act: "I swear to you that I saw with my own eyes what I am describing," or "I swear to you that I believe what I am describing really happened. I affirm this on the basis of what seems to me irrefutable testimonial evidence." I am uneasily aware, once more, in proferring these formulations, of Paul Celan's assertion that no one bears witness for the witness. Naomi Mandel, in *Against the Unspeakable*, cites a number of other scholars who have compared American slavery to the Holocaust.

11. *Conversations with Toni Morrison*, ed. Danille Taylor-Guthrie (Jackson: University Press of Mississippi, 1994), 272.

12. Jacques Derrida, *"The Gift of Death," Second Edition, and "Literature in Secret,"* trans. David Wills (Chicago: University of Chicago Press, 2008), 76; Derrida, *Donner la mort* (Paris: Galilée, 1999), 107.

13. See John D. Caputo, "The Story of Sarah," in *Against Ethics: Contributions to a Poetics of Obligation with Constant Reference to Deconstruction* (Bloomington: Indiana University Press, 1993), 139–46; cited and commented on by Derek Attridge in his *Reading and Responsibility: Deconstruction's Traces* (Edinburgh: Edinburgh University Press, 2010).

14. Stamp Paid's slave name was Joshua. The biblical Joshua led the Jewish people across the river Jordan into the Promised Land. In abandoning his slave name so his wife Vashti can return to him after being his master's son's mistress for months, Stamp Paid revises the biblical narrative into a story of debts paid off: "Born Joshua, he renamed himself when he handed over his wife to his master's son. Handed her over in the sense that he did not kill anybody, thereby himself, because his wife demanded he stay alive. Otherwise, she reasoned, where and to whom could she return when the boy was through? With that gift, he decided that he didn't owe anybody anything" (218). Stamp Paid goes on to echo his biblical namesake by helping slaves cross the Ohio from Kentucky into Ohio and freedom: "So he extended this debtlessness to other people by helping them pay out and off whatever they owed in misery. Beaten runaways? He ferried them [as he ferried Sethe and the newborn Denver] and rendered them paid for; gave them their own bill of sale, so to speak. 'You paid it; now life owes you'" (218). The biblical Vashti was King Ahasuerus's wife, who refused to come when he ordered her to show herself to his guests. The king then divorced Vashti and promulgated a universal law of wifely obedience (Esther 1). This counts as another complex and ironic biblical echo in *Beloved*. I refer the reader to Naomi Mandel's *Against the Unspeakable* (200) for the best account I know of the complex implications of *Beloved*'s epigraph from Romans 9:25: "I will call them my people, / which were not my people; / and her beloved, / which was not beloved."

15. Joseph Mallord William Turner, *Slavers Throwing Overboard the Dead and Dying—Typhoon Coming On ("The Slave Ship")*, The Artchive, accessed

December 15, 2010, http://www.artchive.com/artchive/T/turner/slave_ship.jpg.html.

16. Katrina Harack, "The Heterological Writer and the Gift of Art: Writers on Writing, Performativity, and Ethics in Twentieth-Century America" (PhD dissertation, University of California, Irvine, 2008).

17. In an interview with Robert Stepto of 1976, well before *Beloved* was written, Morrison discusses both her childhood experience of a segregated black community in Lorain, Ohio, and her representation of community in her two earliest novels, *The Bluest Eye* (1970) and *Sula* (1973). See Robert Stepto, "Intimate Things in Place: A Conversation with Toni Morrison, 1976," in Taylor-Guthrie, *Conversations with Toni Morrison*, 10–29, esp. 10–12. The interview was initially published in the *Massachusetts Review* 18 (1977): 473–89.

18. See Nicolas Abraham and Maria Torok, *The Wolf Man's Magic Word: A Cryptonomy*, trans. Nicholas Rand (Minneapolis: University of Minnesota Press, 1986); Abraham and Torok, *Cryptonymie: Le verbier de l'Homme aux Loups* (Paris: Aubier Flammarion, 1976).

19. See Jacques Derrida and Bernard Stiegler, *Echographies of Television: Filmed Interviews*, trans. Jennifer Bajorek (Cambridge: Polity Press, 2002), 57; Derrida and Stiegler, *Échographies: De la télévision: Entretiens filmés* (Paris: Galilée/Institut national de l'audiovisuel, 1996), 68.

20. Jacques Derrida, "Faith and Knowledge: The Two Sources of 'Religion' at the Limits of Reason Alone," trans. Samuel Weber, in *Acts of Religion*, ed. Gil Anidjar (New York: Routledge, 2002), 42–101, esp. 79–89; Derrida, "Foi et savoir: Les deux sources de la 'religion' aux limites de la simple raison," in *La religion*, by Jacques Derrida and Gianni Vattimo, ed. Thierry Marchaisse (Paris: Seuil, 1996), 9–86, esp. 58–71. I have elsewhere analyzed in detail Derrida's development of the figure of autoimmunity. See chaps. 6 and 10 of my *For Derrida* (New York: Fordham University Press, 2009), 123–32; 238–40. I have adopted a few sentences from chap. 6 of my *For Derrida* in this present chapter. An earlier version of *For Derrida*'s chap. 6 is also available in my "Derrida Enisled," in "The Late Derrida," ed. W. J. T. Mitchell and Arnold I. Davidson, special issue, *Critical Inquiry* 33, no. 2 (Winter 2007): 248–76, esp. 268–76.

21. See W. J. T. Mitchell's brilliant essay, "Picturing Terror: Derrida's Autoimmunity," in Mitchell and Davidson, "The Late Derrida," 277–90, esp. 282.

22. Derrida, "Faith and Knowledge," 80; trans. modified; Derrida, "Foi et savoir," 59.

23. For a good translation, see *Kafka's Selected Stories*, trans. and ed. Stanley Corngold, Norton Critical Edition (New York: W. W. Norton, 2007), 35–59.

24. Derrida, "Faith and Knowledge," 87; Derrida, "Foi et savoir," 69.

25. J. Hillis Miller, "Boundaries in *Beloved*," in "Cinema without Borders," edited by Jeffrey R. Di Leo and Allyson Nadia Field, special issue, *Symplokē: A Journal for the Intermingling of Literary, Cultural and Theoretical Scholarship* 15, nos. 1–2 (2007): 24–39.

26. The reference is to Henri Bergson's *The Two Sources of Morality and Religion* (*Les deux sources de la morale et de la religion*) (1932), often alluded to in Derrida's "Faith and Knowledge."

27. Note that word "beloved." It is more than just a word Sethe hears at the burial ceremony for the daughter she has slain. It is a key word in *Beloved*, as well as a key word in the Abraham and Isaac story and in what God says about Jesus in the New Testament. God speaks as a voice out of a bright cloud: "This is my beloved Son, in whom I am well pleased" (Matt. 17:5). The word "beloved" also appears in the epigraph for the novel (see n. 14 above). I agree that Saint Paul here defines Christianity as the conversion from "unbeloved" to "beloved" of Jew and Gentile alike.

28. Derrida, *"The Gift of Death," Second Edition, and "Literature in Secret,"* 68–69; trans. modified; Derrida, *Donner la mort*, 98.

29. Jacques Derrida, Jürgen Habermas, and Giovanna Borradori, *Philosophy in a Time of Terror: Dialogues with Jürgen Habermas and Jacques Derrida* (Chicago: University of Chicago Press, 2003), esp. 99; Derrida, Habermas, and Borradori, *Le "concept" du 11 septembre: Dialogues à New York (octobre–décembre 2001)*, trans. Christian Bouchindhomme and Sylvette Gleize (Paris: Galilée, 2004), esp. 152.

Index of Names, Titles of Works, and Characters